HISTORY

OF

NEWTON COUNTY,

MISSISSIPPI,

FROM 1834 TO 1894.

BY A. J. BROWN,
OF NEWTON COUNTY.

A FIREBIRD PRESS BOOK

PELICAN PUBLISHING COMPANY
Gretna 1998

Manufactured in the United States of America
Published by Pelican Publishing Company, Inc.
1000 Burmaster Street, Gretna, Louisiana 70053

JUDGE JOHN WATTS.

PREFACE.

The writer of this History entertains the hope that his labors will be appreciated not only by resident citizens of Newton county, and those who formerly lived there, but that they will be found of some interest and value to the general reader. He has endeavored not only to give a full and faithful chronicle of local events and personages, but in discussing the war and reconstruction periods, necessarily referred to matters of State and national interest. And what has thus been accomplished in the case of Newton county may be done in many other counties of the State. It will require much patience and perseverance, but the people will respond generously to any earnest effort in that direction. In this way many facts and incidents will be preserved from oblivion, and the names of men and women who have served well their day and generation will be cherished in perpetual remembrance.

It is the purpose of the writer to speak of some things but partially understood by the older cittizens, and of many transactions entirely unknown to the younger people of the county, for forty years, and to place before the public the most important persons of that period, will be a part of this work. To give the early appearance of the county; earliest settlers; first public buildings; as well as private enterprises, will engage the attention of the writer. All this important information will be derived from men and women who have lived in the county from fifty-five to sixty years.

The information necessary to "write up" the war period

will also be obtained from active participants, as it is only from those sources that reliable data can be had. The child of the future will be as anxious to know what part his ancestors took in the late war between the States as the young man of the present.

The old people now in the county who can give information of the early settlement will soon be gone. The old soldiers that enlisted from 1861 to the close of the war will soon be numbered with the great majority who have passed over the river; but placed upon the pages of history, they will be handed down to future generations.

In this work a period of sixty years will be embraced, from 1834 to 1894. The best efforts have been made to have statements correct. Federal, State, county and railroad records have been used in gaining the data needed. The loss of the public records of the county by fire has greatly increased the difficulties of preparing this volume, and should any inaccuracies or omissions appear, this fact is suggested in extenuation.

To those who have so generously assisted in giving this information, and others who have so ably contributed to this work, the thanks of the writer are most gratefully acknowledged, with a hope that a perusal of its contents may both benefit and instruct.

Resspectfully submitted by

THE AUTHOR.

ILLUSTRATIONS.

JUDGE JOHN WATTS	Frontispiece
COURT HOUSE	Page 103
R. H. HENRY	Page 197
DR. J. B. BAILEY	Page 225
BAPTIST CHURCH AT DECATUR	Page 263
NEW METHODIST CHURCH AT NEWTON	Page 335
MALE AND FEMALE COLLEGE AT NEWTON	Page 349
HICKORY INSTITUTE	Page 359
ELDER N. L. CLARKE	Page 397
A. B. AMIS, ESQ	Page 463
A. W. WHATLEY, ESQ	Page 467

CONTENTS.

CHAPTER I.

Organization of County—Commissioners—for whom County named—pages 1 to 3.

CHAPTER II.

The Indians, first Settlers—Their Removal—Legendary Accounts of the Tribes—Present Number and Condition—Missionaries—pages 3 to 13.

CHAPTER III.

Indian Ball Play—Visit to Indian Church—Old and New Customs—pages 14 to 27.

CHAPTER IV.

Number of White Settlers when first organized—Face of the Country—Game—Style of Society—Ardent Spirits—Morals af the People—pages 28 to 35.

CHAPTER V.

First Officers—First Representatives—First White Settlers—Grasses and Stock Range—Wild Fruits—pages 36 to 44,

CHAPTER VI.

Settlement of Decatur, the County Seat—Number of Men Killed there from First Settlement to 1861—Decatur Bank, its Failure—Churches—pages 45 to 52.

CONTENTS.

CHAPTER VII.

Character of Lands—Market for Stock and Cattle—What was Made on the Farm—Home-Made Clothing—Population first Ten Years—pages 53 to 57.

CHAPTER VIII.

Attempts to Move Court House from Decatur—Re-building Court Houses—Influx of Population—Old-Time Teachers—Number of Schools now in County—Annual Cost—Enrollment and Attendance—pages 58 to 67.

CHAPTER IX.

First Railroad Through County—Railroad Lands—Advantages of Railroads—Railroad Tax now Paid County—pages 68 to 74.

CHAPTER X.

The Civil War Period—Secession of the State—The First Company to leave for the War—Scenes at its Departure—Total Enlistments in the County—pages 75 to 82.

CHAPTER XI.

Military Companies that went from the County—Their Officers, Numbers, Battles, Casualties—pages 83 to 99.

CHAPTER XII.

The Problem of Feeding and Clothing the Army—The Blockade—High Price of Cotton—Scarcity of Salt—Planting of Cereals—Our Patriotic Women—Their Labors and Sacrifices—100 to 107—Tribute to the Women of the South, by Capt. J. J. Hood—pages 107 to 114.

CHAPTER XIII.

Grierson's Raid—Sherman's March from Vicksburg to Meridian—Both Pay their Respects to the Farmers of Newton County—pages 115 to 120.

CONTENTS.   XI

CHAPTER XIV.

Condition of Country After Sherman's March—Depreciated Currency and High Price of Goods—Confederate "Tax in Kind"—Value of Slave Property Freed by the War—Confidence in President Davis—The Collapse and Consequent Confusion—The People Take Courage and Enter on a New Experience—pages 121 to 127.

CHAPTER XV.

The New Order of Things—Labor Contract with Freedmen—The Deed of Trust Law—Reconstruction—Removal of Gov. Humphreys—Constitution of 1868—Jas. L. Alcorn Elected Governor—Ames and Revels Elected U. S. Senators—R. C. Powers Elected Governor—Heavy Taxation—Emancipation from Alien Rule—Administrations of Governors John M. Stone and Robert Lowry—The Convention and Constitution of 1892—The Cotton Crops from 1866 to 1894—pages 128 to 140.

CHAPTER XVI.

Introduction and Use of Commercial Fertilizers—Great Benefit to the County—Official Analysis of the Principal Brands—pages 140 to 156.

CHAPTER XVII.

Reconstruction Period—Removal of Gov. Humphreys and Attorney-General Hooker—Political Excitement—The Reign of Carpet-Baggers, Scalawags and Negro Teachers—The Election of 1869—Alcorn Chosen Governor—Brilliant Canvass by Gen. Robert Lowry—pages 157 to 161.

CHAPTER XVIII.

Freedmen's Bureaus—Race Troubles—The Dennis Brothers—Arrests—pages 162 to 172.

CHAPTER XIX.

Secret Political Organizations—Arrest of Prominent Citizens, Notably, T. M. Scanlan—The "Black and Tan Convention"—Extravagance and Corruption—Proscription Clauses of Constitution of 1868 Rejected by the People—A Solid South—pages 173 to 181.

CONTENTS.

CHAPTER XX.

The Year of Jubilee, 1875—Tax-Payers' Convention—Enormous Increase of Taxation, amounting to Confiscation—Democratic State Convention of 1875—Presided Over by Ex-Governor Clarke; Addressed by Col. Lamar; Gen. George Elected Chairman State Executive Committee—Riots at Vicksburg and Clinton—Citizens interview Gov. Ames—Radical Ranks Broken—A. K. Davis Impeached—Cardoza and Ames allowed to Resign—John M. Stone Becomes Governor—Home Rule Inaugurated—pages 182 to 185.

CHAPTER XXI.

Prominent Men of all Classes—Lawyers, Physicians, Preachers, Politicians, Merchants and Other Citizens in all the Walks of Life—pages 186 to 193.

CHAPTER XXII.

Newspapers of the County and their Editors—The Newton Ledger, and Portrait of R. H. Henry; New Democrat, Newton Bulletin, The Report, The Free Press, The Dispatch, The Mississippi Baptist, Conehatta Index, Newton County Progress—Commercial—Duty to Patronize the County Paper—pages 194 to 206.

CHAPTER XXIII.

Introduction of the Grange—The Alliance—Their Influence in Politics and Effect on Society—Good Results of the Grange—Officers of County Grange and Local Granges—The State Grange—pages 206 to 223.

CHAPTER XXIV.

Patrons' Union—Its Benefits as an Educator—Organization, Location, Value of Property—How Exercises Conducted—Officers—Camp Meetings and Normal Institutes—Portrait of Dr. J. B. Bailey, President—pages 224 to 236.

CHAPTER XXV.

Benevolent and Secret Orders: Masons, Knights of Honor, Knights of Pythias—Large Sums Paid to Beneficiaries—pages 237 to 239.

CONTENTS. XIII

CHAPTER XXVI.

Free Schools in County—How Attended—Number of Educable Children in County—State Colleges—Schools in County, Teachers and Cost—Indian Schools—Text-Books—Should be a Uniform Series for State—pages 240 to 260.

CHAPTER XXVII.

Religious Denominations in the County—Churches and Membership—Picture of Church at Decatur—pages 261 to 273.

CHAPTER XXVIII.

Sabbath Schools — Number in County—Teachers and Scholars — The County Sunday School Convention—The Sunday School a Special Attraction to the Colored People—pages 274 to 279.

CHAPTER XXIX.

A Law-Abiding, Orderly People — Sobriety and Good Morals the Rule—Harmonious Relations of the Races—The Negro knows his Place and keeps it—The White Caps—pages 280 to 283.

CHAPTER XXX.

Land Acreage and Value—Railroad Grant—Timbers and Grasses—Creeks and other Streams—Agricultural Productions—pages 284 to 293.

CHAPTER XXXI.

Products Shipped by Rail—The Lumber Interest—Cotton Gins, Planing Mills—Profitable Timber—pages 294 to 297.

CHAPTER XXXII.

Stock-Raising—Number of Horses and Mules in County—No Large Buyers, but Sellers—Poultry Raising—the Egg Industry—pages 298 to 305.

CONTENTS.

CHAPTER XXXIII.

County Taxation—Value of Land and Live Stock—Advice to the Young Farmers of Newton—pages 306 to 308.

CHAPTER XXXIV.

Spirit of Improvement—Quality of Dwelling Houses now being Built—Improved Fencing—The Stock Law—pages 309 to 313.

CHAPTER XXXV.

Advantages of Co-operation—Emigration vs. Immigration—Health of the County—Young People Disposed to Marry at Home—Abundant and Good Water and Rich Soil—Good Society—Some Suggestions to all Classes—Elements of Prosperity—Population—Rate of Taxation—pages 314 to 320.

CHAPTER XXXVI.

Professional Men of the County: Lawyers, Physicians, Teachers—Some of the Good Old Doctors—pages 321 to 327.

CHAPTER XXXVII.

Various Towns of the County—First Settlement of Each—Professional and Business Men and other Citizens—The Court-Houses Built and Burned—Pictures of the New Methodist Church at Newton and Hickory Institute—pages 238 to 265.

CHAPTER XXXVIII.

County Officers Since Organization of County—Senators and Representatives from 1837 to 1894—pages 366 to 370.

CHAPTER XXXIX.

Circuit Judges: Thos. S. Sterling, Henry Mounger, A. B. Dawson, John Watts, Jonathan Tarbell, R. E. Leachman, A. G. Mayers. Chancellors: Thos. Christian, — Dennis, Thos. B. Graham, Sylvanus Evans, Wm. T. Houston. District Attorneys: George Wood, Richard Cooper, Thomas H. Woods, Simon Jones, A. Y. Harper, S. H. Terral, Green B. Huddleston, R. S. McLaurin—pages 371 to 395.

CHAPTER I.

ORGANIZATION OF THE COUNTY—ACT OF THE LEGISLATURE OF MISSISSIPPI AUTHORIZING SAME—NAMES OF COMMISSIONERS WHO ORGANIZED THE COUNTY—SIZE AND FORM OF THE COUNTY—NUMBER OF SQUARE MILES IN THE COUNTY—NUMBER OF ACRES OF LAND IN THE COUNTY—WHAT THE COUNTY DERIVED ITS NAME FROM—WHAT COUNTY WAS DIVIDED TO MAKE NEWTON COUNTY—WHAT PART OF THE CHOCTAW PURCHASE NEWTON COUNTY WAS TAKEN FROM.

BY an act of the Legislature of the State of Mississippi, approved 26th of February, 1836, a certain territory, comprising the southern half of Neshoba county, was set apart as the county of Newton.

The names of three citizens of this new territory were mentioned and commissioned by the Legislature of the State to organize the county of Newton, namely, William Donalson, Michael Thomas and Francis Jones. These men had power to meet and go through whatever form was necessary to organize a county, and also to buy, or receive by gift, not more than eight acres of land on which to build or locate a county site for the court-house, as near as was practical in the center of the county.

The form of Newton county is a square, there being no other county in the State, unless it is Leake county, of the same form. It is twenty-four miles square, which will give it 576 square miles and 368,640 acres of land.

The county derived its name from Sir Isaac Newton, the great scientist and philosopher. Newton county, or that part of the territory now forming the new county, was the southern part of Neshoba county, which was nearly as large as any two of the new Choctaw counties coming in through the last Indian purchase. The people in the lower part of the large county of Neshoba wanted a county of their own, and although the population was very small, the Legislature heard their petition through the Representative, James Ellis, who was afterwards Newton county's first representative.

The court-house for the county of Neshoba, previous to the division of the county, was near where the town of Union, in Newton county, is now situated. An old settler, who is now living, says it was a black-jack oak cabin with dirt floor; that Judge Wm. Sterling as judge, and Hon. Jno. Watts as district attorney, held the first court for the new county of Neshoba. After the division of the county, the county site for Neshoba was removed to Philadelphia.

The town of Decatur, the present site for the court-house, was chosen by the commission as a suitable place for the court-house, and there it has remained although repeated efforts have been made to remove it.

Newton county is a part of the purchase made by the United States Government through its commissioners, John H. Eaton and John Coffee, of the one part, and the Choctaw Indians, through their Chiefs and Mingoes, on the other. This treaty is called Dancing Rabbit Creek; in Choctaw, "Chookfa Hitla Bogue." This treaty was concluded and signed the 28th day of September, 1830.

Dancing Rabbit Creek is in Noxubee county, near one of the original trading points where the Choctaws were in large numbers. There had been seven treaties with the Choctaw Indians previous to the one last named. The treaty of Hopewell, concluded January 3d, 1786; Fort Adams, December 17th, 1801; Hoe Buck-in-too-pa, August 31st, 1803; Mount Dexter, November 16th, 1805; Trading House, October 24th, 1816; Doak's Stand, October 18th, 1830; Washington, January 20th, 1825; and the last named, Dancing Rabbit Creek, 28th September, 1830. This treaty stipulated the immigration of the Choctaw Indians as fast as they could get off with safety to themselves in removing. They were to have the lands occupied by them in 1831, '32 and '33, which they complied with. The removal in 1833 took place in Newton and Jasper counties. The rendezvous was at Garlandsville, and they were taken largely from these two counties.

That part of the State known as the Choctaw Purchase, embraces the counties of Noxubee, Neshoba, Leake, Newton, Scott, Smith, Jasper, Clarke and Lauderdale, and six others in more remote parts of the State. These were all admitted as counties December, 1833. This did not include the admission of Newton only as a part of Neshoba county. After the division it was separately admitted, as has been stated, February, 1836. This county is situated near the center of this group, having Lauderdale east, Neshoba north, Noxubee northeast, Scott west, Jasper south.

This county being centrally located in this purchase, may also be said to be central in point of convenience for settlement and for passage of railroads, being traversed the full length by one road, and the first survey of the Gulf & Ship Island road ran nearly centrally through the county from north to south.

CHAPTER II.

THE INDIANS WHO OCCUPIED THIS COUNTY BEFORE THE WHITE MAN CAME—THEIR PROBABLE NUMBER—THE DIFFICULTY IN FINDING ANY SATISFACTORY EVIDENCE OF HOW MANY WERE REMOVED—INFORMATION FROM THE TREATIES, AND ALSO FROM THE FEDERAL RECORDS FROM WASHINGTON—STIPULATIONS OF THE TREATY, AND THEIR REMOVAL FROM THE STATE—LEGENDARY ACCOUNTS OF THE INDIAN TRIBES—THEIR REMOVAL FROM 1831 TO 1856—THOSE THAT REMAIN AMONG US—THEIR CONDITION, PHYSICALLY AND RELIGIOUSLY—INDIAN MISSIONARIES THAT HAVE BEEN SENT TO THIS COUNTY.

THE Indians were in large numbers in the part of the country ceded by them to the State of Mississippi. From the best information obtainable, there were from 20,000 to 25,000, and it is supposed that Newton county had rather over an average number of Indians in comparison to the other parts of this acquired territory.

This county was a fine range, well watered, and an excellent hunting ground, and the supposition is that large numbers came here for an easy living, and to amuse and interest themselves. Much open land and wide-spreading prairies in the southwestern part of the county offered large scope for recreation and engagement in their national ball play.

These people, however, offered a very interesting

topic for thought and speculation, as to where they came from, and the length of time that they had occupied the country before the white man came among them. There is nothing that has ever been obtained from the Indians themselves as to where they came from, or how long they have lived in the country. Some of the older ones of the Choctaw tribe claim that they came out of a great mound on the head-waters of Pearl river in Winston county, near the central portion of the State. Some historians claim that they overran the country very rapidly after their appearance, and that they are from the province of Kamtschatka. They, in all probability, came from the west at some very remote period of time, as one tribe, and as they increased their numbers, and it was necessary to provide a better hunting ground, that they divided and came east. After being separated for centuries, they, from certain circumstances, changed their languages, and many of their customs and habits of life were different from their ancestors. Difference in climate and a change of food made them, to some extent, differ in appearance and size; also changed their dialects, and thus out of the same original tribe that came from the west, all the various tribes have sprung.

The length of time that has elapsed since the first Indian came on American soil is one of those things that no human being can tell. In estimating their numbers various sources of information have been sought, and even then it is all uncertain as to the numbers that were emigrated, to say nothing of what it was when the white man came among them.

The Hon. Charles Gayarre has the following in reference to the original proprietors of the magnificent territory to which attention has just been called:

"The Choctaws occupied a very large territory between the Mississippi and Tombigbee from the frontiers of the Colapesas and the Biloxi's, on the shores of lake Ponchartrain and Borgne, up to the frontiers of the Natchez, of the Yazoos, and of the Chickasaws.

"They owned more than fifty important villages, and it was said at one time they could have brought into the field twenty-five thousand warriors."

The portion of the State above described, a large part of its territory and the numbers expected in the small portion of country as is embraced in the treaty of "Dancing Rabbit Creek," of course will be very small in comparison. From information received from the Congressional Library at Washington, it is found that the original number of Choctaw Indians, which were to be received under the treaty of "Dancing Rabbit Creek," was 18,500. From a report of the Commissioner of Indian Affairs, of 1838, it is found that out of the total 18,500 there had emigrated at that time 15,177. In the report of 1844 and '45 the same figures are given, showing that no more had emigrated up to that time. It is well known that a large emigration took place, and the Choctaw Indians from Newton and Jasper counties, were in rendezvous at Garlandsville, Jasper county, in the year 1845, and yet no mention of it can be found in the Congressional Library at Washington. A further report of the Commissioner of Indian Affairs, states under date of October 31, 1849, that "Within the last twelve months 547 Choctaws have been emigrated" from the old Choctaw country east of the Mississippi to the Choctaw Nation west of the Mississippi.

The Choctaw Agent, in his report of September 6, 1852, says that about 300 Choctaws have been removed from the States of Mississippi and Louisiana, within the present year, mostly from the latter State. In the year

1856, the United States government closed its relations with the Indians in this part of the State. There was still a number left in different parts of the State, and the Indian agents came to the various counties and paid the Indians off what was supposed to be due to them, in gold, and many white men profited by trading with the Indians, and in some instances, no doubt got largely the advantage of them, and sold to credulous, unsuspecting Indians property at fabulous prices. It is now estimated by our last census, and by good private authority, that there are about 2,000 Indians in the State of Mississippi of the Choctaw tribe. This, with the number reported to be emigrated from time to time, would bring pretty nearly, counting for loss by death, the close approximation of 25,000, as stated in the preceding pages.

The Indians thus paid off were now citizens, assum- the responsibilities of such, being amenable to the laws of the State and made to conform to them in most instances, yet they were not allowed to vote. Some of them went west and afterwards returned to this country, having a greater love for their old homes, than for a new and better hunting ground.

A very interesting legendary account is given by Lowry and McCardle of the origin of the Choctaw Indians in this State, which is taken from Col. Claiborne's volume, and furnishes the following tradition given in his own words: "The Choctaws believed that their ancestors came from the west. They were led by two brothers, Chacta and Chicsa—at the head of their respective Iksas or Clans. On their journey they followed a pole, which, guided by an invisible hand, moved before them. Shortly after crossing the Mississippi the pole stood still, firmly planted in the ground, and they construed this as an augury that there they must halt and make their homes. What connection this may have with, and how far it has been derived from the exodus of the Israelites, and the 'cloud by day and pillar of fire by night,' is left for the curious to determine. But the pole moving in the march before them is the oldest and best established tradition of the Choctaws and Chickasaws. The two leaders concluded to reconnoiter the country. Chicsa moved first, and ten days after Chacta followed, but a tremendous snow-storm had obliterated his brother's trail, and they were separated. He went southerly to Nanawayya, on the headwaters of Pearl river, about the geographical center of the State, and the other brother, it was afterwards ascertained, settled near where Pontotoc now stands.

"At the first meeting of the brothers it was determined that the two clans should constitute separate tribes, each occupying their respective territory, and that the hunters of neither band should encroach on the territory of the other. The present Oktibbeha and Nusicheah are indicated as the lines of demarkation."

The Chickasaws are said to have been a very warlike tribe, while the Choctaws were, on the contrary, powerful but not a very warlike people. They assisted the American people from first to last against all foreigners who made war against us, and also against all unfriendly Indians whom the nation had difficulty in subduing.

From all the information on the subject it is not safe to say that Newton county, though a favored spot for the Indians' home, had more than from 3000 to 5000 Indians subsequent to the treaty. These people, in their primeval state, were the most honest, virtuous people of which we have any account. It is true that some things were tolerated among them not allowed in civilized nations, such as a plurality of wives, and some customs which were revolting to the refined notions of the white men —such as scaffolding their dead until the flesh would come off the bones, and with human hands remove the flesh and bury the bones ; and yet they had great reverence for their dead, and buried their bones near their dwellings ; were very loth to leave them and go to another country, evidently believing that the spirits of their dead were present but invisible. When they came into very close relations with the white man, and became addicted to the vice of intemperance, to which most of them fell victims, they became badly demoralized and lost much of that purity of character which originally distinguished them. As a race, children of nature, deriving much of their support from the spontaneous production of the soil, and game that were abundant around them, they knew but little about hard work ; yet they by nature are economical, lived on little, and wonderfully enjoyed their social relations, engaged with zeal in their national game, and attended closely to their time-honored customs of crying, dancing and feasting over their dead. They were by nature endowed with good minds, capable of being greatly improved by education—being as apt to learn as the white race. They also display much ingenuity in the construction of anything in mechanics as well as fine arts, and often good taste in anything that they propose to construct. They have gone from our midst. A peculiar people has passed away. Only a remnant of a once powerful tribe is left among us, and they are to-day as free from an amalgamation of their race with the white and black man as they were when they first mingled together. This remnant is fast declining. There are about three hundred now in Newton county. Many of this small number appear to be in a decline—

not the robust, hardy people as of years ago. The probabilities are that there is too much consanguinity of blood. Various diseases, not originally known to them, particularly of a pulmonary character, seem to attack them. If this remnant would go West and mingle and marry with their race in the Indian Territory, it is probable that they would be much bettered.

Many of them in this county have embraced Christianity. About fifteen years ago a missionary from the Choctaw tribe in the Territory came to Newton county. He was quite an old man, probably seventy years old. He said that he was born in Scott county; was the son of a white man who came from Virginia and married his mother. He, with his parents, went to Gainesville, Ala., where there was a trading post kept by George S. Gaines and Allen Glover. There the attention of some persons who were engaged in immigrating the Indians was first called to the young half-breed, Peter Fulsom. He was taken and to some extent was educated and became a Baptist preacher. He early went west, as the tribe was emigrated. The Mount Pisga Association, embracing this county, asked that a missionary be sent to these Indians in this part of the country. Peter Fulsom came, was a good and pious man, but too old to do much service. He went back to the Nation after the first year and was succeeded by Jesse Baker, a young Choctaw Baptist preacher, who had received a tolerably good education at Upper Alton in the State of Illinois. He was a consecrated man and did wonderful work among his people. He mingled freely with them, learned them to sing religious songs, preached to them, taught them to read and write, which they readily learned to do, and reclaimed most of them with whom he came in contact, from strong drink, and made a general reform among them in the county.

In this county they have mostly abandoned their ball plays, which were very demoralizing and wicked places when dominated by drunken white men and negroes. They have two or more preachers in the county, with fifty to sixty members. These preachers are remarkable for the way in which they preach, and their understanding of the scripture, and for the correct and orderly way in which they conduct divine service. They have one public school taught at different places in the county. This school is provided for in the same way as other public schools of the county. Mr. Halbert, a white man, teaches these schools. He appears to be devoting himself studiously to the improvement of all the Choctaws in his reach.

The Indian preacher, Jesse Baker, labored for a part of two years, going to college after the first year and returning to his work. Soon after his return the second year, he took fever and died, at the house of Mr. Frank Russell, at Hickory, who treated him very kindly. In a short time another Choctaw preacher came, and he also died very soon after coming. Since that time the native Indian, with the help of the white preachers of the county, have been able to carry on the work.

Much has been said and written about the treatment that the "poor Indian" has received at the hands of the white man—that is, the government of the United States. It is said that their lands and country were taken away from them, and they were forced away from the homes they reverenced and loved, which was their's by inalienable right of inheritance and possession, for ages past.

It is all true, that the Government took or exchanged countries with Indians of various tribes of the United States. The Choctaws are the ones which have been most particularly under discussion, and for the information it may impart it is shown from good authority that the Choctaws ceded in all to the U. S. Government 19,000,000 acres of land, and received in return 20,000,000 and $2,225,000 in money and goods. These people, after they were removed, had schools that were free, school-houses and books furnished. They had the gospel preached to them; they had thrown around them the protecting care of a strong government that would not allow a white man to buy or own land among them. They were not allowed to sell their lands, had no tax to pay upon them, and could remain on and rent out the land as long as they lived and their children after them. The Indian Territory in which they live, is one of the most fertile, well-watered and beautifully situated States in the Union. It has abundance of game, a diversity of soil, besides being rich in coal and mineral production. It has 74,125 square miles, nearly twice as large as Mississippi. Its population in 1860 consisted of Cherokees, Creeks, Seminoles, Choctaws, Chickasaws and remnants of smaller tribes, amounting in all to 66,680. Since that time other remnants have been moved to the Nation and the population is now much larger. In some instances the government has apparently been severe with some tribes of Indians. This sometimes became necessary, the Indians often committing crimes which deserved severe punishment.

Taking everything into consideration, the Indians have received from their civilized conquerors good treatment. It is often stated that their numbers are much smaller than when the white man came among them. This may be granted, to a small extent; while others claim that there are as many now, or nearly so, as there were when the country was first discovered.

Various are the conclusions as to what will become of the Indian. The prevailing opinion is that of the "survival of the fittest," and that they will be obliterated from the face of the earth by the superiority of the white race, with whom they come in sharp contact. The conclusion most reasonable to the writer is, that at no remote period of the world's history they will be amalgated by the white race. Although no white man is allowed to own land among them, nor to live except as a tenant, they can become a citizen by marrying an Indian woman, and the offspring of this union will be as much the beneficiaries of the provisions of the Territory as if they were full-blood. These half-breeds will become educated, and are good looking and intelligent. The white race, by amalgamation, always predominates, and as those who are mixed-blooded will take precedence, and encouragement to this end will be established, so that at no great distance in the vista of coming years will these people not be destroyed, but their race so interchangeably connected with the white race as not to be known.

CHAPTER III.

INDIAN BALL PLAY—VISIT TO INDIAN CHURCH—CONTRAST BETWEEN THE OLD AND NEW CUSTOMS OF THE INDIANS.

To ONE who, like the writer, was born among the Choctaw Indians, when there were thousands of them in the counties of the Purchase, even after the first large emigrations, a ball play, or description of one, might interest to revive the old and long since passed national game of these wild savages, who probably for a thousand years had celebrated these gay and festive occasions, displaying great feats of manhood, great dexterity in the use of their very peculiar "ball sticks" and their fleetness unequaled by any people, probably, in the world. But to the youthful readers, who may become, or who are now, interested in these once wild and untutored savages, it may be of interest. The impression made by the Indians in the long ago, and the recollections were those connected with his dissipation and wickedness, in all his social and convivial relations in the time-honored ball play. In these games they yearly participated, and were in constant practice.

The Indians speaking the same language usually divided into different clans, and were governed by a chief or captain, who was spokesman and to whom a becoming reverence of superiority was acknowledged. Jasper county had the Sixtowns and Beaver Creeks.

HISTORY OF NEWTON COUNTY.   15

Newton county had the Turkey Creeks and Bogue Chittos, etc. The Sixtowns and Beaver Creeks would challenge the Turkey Creeks, and probably some of the Bogue Chittos, or all, at a grand play, would come.

The place of meeting would be on mutual grounds between the homes of the different tribes. These games were not played for sport or recreation, but for the profit that was in them. There was not much money bet. They put up clothing, ponies, household goods; almost anything they had would be freely staked on the contest. Not only the men, but their women felt great pride and a consciousness of success of their own clan. Before the game commenced they would meet, and parties who bet would place things which they proposed to wager with each other on a common scaffold constructed for the purpose, each pair of betters having the things proposed to bet bound together and thrown on the scaffold. If it were their ponies, they would be secured together at some convenient place, to be taken by the winning party. This betting and depositing on a common scaffold is never done until just before the play commenced. On the evening before the play the two tribes or clans who have made the arrangements to play, meet on chosen ground. The males dressed in primitive style, their bodies as near nude as could be allowed, all the upper portion of the body having no clothing, hair long; some have on deer-skin leggins with a number of small bells attached; a deer tail well adjusted to the belt or waistband of the trowsers, face painted white, yellow and black in spots, so as to give the most hideous appearance possible. They appeared to assume on these occasions their wild animal natures, being perfectly oblivious to everything around them except the matter now in hand.

On each side they numbered twenty, thirty, forty,

fifty or more. They arrayed themselves together on the previous evening before they play—on each side at their respective headquarters, on the ball-ground, boasting, dancing, daring with the greatest assurance and self-satisfied air that they would be victorious over their opponents on the morrow. With their ball-sticks in their hands they make a charge at each other, both converging to a common center of the ground between the poles, like two contending armies. Their war-whoops that rent the air were deafening. They come to close contact but do not meet' in conflict. They do not salute each other, but appear angry. In this way they sally back and forth boasting of their prowess, of what they expect to do to-morrow, and in that way pass the balance of the afternoon.

The ball-sticks they use are something peculiar in their way. They are made of tough pieces of hickory, about thirty inches long, three quarters of an inch square; the wood at one end of the stick is made thin so as it can be made into a bow; after it is bent and bowed it is tied with strings. This bow is threaded with a string of deer skin, so with the pair a player can catch, hold and throw with great precision and force. As the night comes on they go through many of the forms and ceremonies previous to the play; now they shout the war-whoops, now they surround the supposed condemned victim; now they fill the air with shrieks and boast of anticipated victory over their opponents on to-morrow; now they, with confident emotion, declare their enemies' defeat; now they declare their manhood and great ability to vanquish.

These proceedings go on by both opposing parties, but on different parts of the play-ground most of the night before the day appointed for the contest. Profoundly superstitious in all these performances, they had what they called a "witch killer" who was all the time chasing the evil spirits from their midst by the most peculiar and unbecoming gesticulations and gyrations of the head, hands and lower limbs, that could be thought of or imagined. Yet this "witch killer" was essential to them; they would not play without him. The women well performed this part.

The old women, the children and the dogs, surrounded the camp-fires. These old crones looked grum, talked in low, incoherent and gutteral tones, attended to the cooking and took care of the children, scolded the dogs and enjoyed silently the prospect of to-morrow's. victory It must be remembered that all the Indians belonging to these different clans, male, female, old and young, from the youngest infant to the oldest man and woman, came to the ball-play.

It was a great social reunion when they met their friends and witnessed a great fete. The young women went to dance. It was no old-fashioned reel; no cotillion, where time, order and grace prevail, nor no "modern waltz" or German. The men were not allowed to take part in this gay and festive sport. These dusky maids, six or eight on each side, with locked arms, stood facing each other. Between these two rows of facing maidens sat an old man with a drum made of a pot with a piece of raw-hide stretched over the top. This was all the musical instrument used. He sat down upon his feet, and in a low, melancholy voice sang: "Hummy hoga! Hummy hoga!" repeating it five or six times. The Indian girls would then sing in loud voice and high key the same "hummy hoga" a dozen times, and just as they would commence to sing they would commence to dance. The dancing was with locked arms of six or eight, facing a like number, jumping up and down with right and left movement, with feet and body all at the same time, raising themselves three or four inches and coming down flat on the ground. Then they would rest a few moments and commence again. In this way they danced most of the night without changing partners.

The next day the warriors meet, painted and stripped of most of their clothing. They continue to boast and dare until about the middle of the day. After that the poles, two large pieces of timber, made of a tree cut down and split open, or two smaller trees hewn on two sides, about fifteen feet high, placed perpendicularly in the ground with small space between, so that the ball could pass through. Each contending party had their poles, and they were about two hundred and fifty yards apart. The ball was to be thrown up at an equal distance from each end, or on neutral ground, and was to be thrown with the ball sticks, so as to strike one of the poles or go between them. After the men on each side had been placed on the grounds to the best advantage the signal was given. The best runners were placed in the field; the ablest, strongest men were placed at the poles of their opponents. The men on each side were placed to the best advantage, adapting each to a position where speed or strength or ability to throw or catch the ball best suited him.

No game ever witnessed was more closely contested than an Indian ball play. The spirit with which they entered the contest was enough to win the admiration of all beholders. The perfect manner in which each one performed his part was sufficient to demand the pride of all. The dexterity with which they handle the sticks and throw the ball is a surprise to every one. Their powers of endurance under the scorching sun, for they choose the warm weather for such a contest, would satisfy the most incredulous that they were brought up to, and able to bear, the greatest hardships. The Olympic games were not more closely contested nor often more dearly won. Dreadful falls, terrible blows, bleeding and broken limbs, were the results of their efforts to win. Their property was staked, their manhood was matched. Their ambition to vanquish a rival, or reclaim a former defeat, all urged them to their best efforts. Their women ran with water, cheering by their presence and applause and with words of encouragement to deeds of valor, and if need be, to desperation. They not only played ball, but they fought; they worked, used every effort of mind and body, every cunning scheme and every deceptive ruse. And after the hard contested fight was nearly over; after one or the other side had eleven balls, unless each had eleven, the twelfth ball was to be thrown up at the poles of the ones having eleven. Sometimes those behind would make a desperate effort and win, and continue to do so until each had reached eleven. Then the last ball was played, and thrown up on a common center of the grounds. This last one would probably be the severest contest of any, as they claim to be so nearly matched. When the final result was reached, amidst the greatest excitement of spectators and participants, the vanquished, without a word, gave up their property, and the victorious rushed to the scaffold containing the goods, appropriating what they had won, receiving the compliments of their admirers, and rejoicing in the victory over their rivals.

After these plays, if the Indians were in reach of whisky, the whites would commence to treat by buying enough to make many of them drunk. They would then commence to fight; not with knives, but with small sticks, and to pull each other's hair, not doing much damage. The women always acted as peacemakers and usually staid sober, while their lords drank; when a fight took place, as soon as they could separate them they did it. Sometimes they would have to tie them in order to control them. In this way nearly a week would pass in this general debauch. After all their money was spent for liquor, and their provision had given out, they slowly plodded their way home to repair their losses and allow their broken and bleeding limbs to heal.

Having been accustomed to see these people only in their wild state, and their abandoned condition; to hear their wild revelry, and drunken orgies, listen to their weird songs, and endless dissipations, presenting at these times, haggard faces, wounded and bleeding forms, imagine the change in seeing them under religious and civilizing influences. After the death of the two Indian missionaries sent out from the Territory to preach to those in this and adjoining counties, they were left without any help except their own native Indians, and what the white preachers could do for them. This writer was invited by Charley Jackson—Lo-man-ta-kub by is his Chootaw name—to attend their regular monthly meeting, which was cheerfully accepted. This church is situated about fourteen miles from the railroad, near Connehatta. It is a small frame building, very well suited, and comfortable and commodious enough for those who worship there. Arrived in very good time, about 10 o'clock, just as the early services were over. Their treatment was very kind—and they appeared pleased that white people would go to their meetings. This was the Sabbath of a three day's meeting, and there were gathered about one hundred Indians at the little church for public worship. The Indians had come, as they usually do, bringing their children, large and small, also their dogs. Some had walked and brought their baggage and provision, in their large baskets; others had ridden on horseback, while a number came with oxen and wagons, much as they had done when they attended the ball-plays, and at their cries, to mourn for their dead, and to have a homely and frugal feast. They were dressed in their best attire, more like the white citizen's dress, than is usual, for in all these years of association with the white race they have preserved some of their peculiar and primitive fashions. Some of the women wore bonnets made of cloth, not a fashionable one.

They were generally dressed in the style well known and practiced by themselves. In the decorations about their heads high colors prevailed—with variegated trimmings, gaudy handkerchiefs, strands of cheap beads around their necks, band-combs carrying the hair all back. Some of the women wore mourning, a very unusual thing. Most of the women wore shoes, yet some of them were barefoot. The men had on their best suits, most of them had on coats and cravats. All of them had on shoes. Some of them wore vests, and no coats. The very black hair of the men was cut short, resembling the style of the white citizen. The men originally wore their hair very long, and cut it only on certain portions of the head very short. Some of them were old but their hair was not much gray; none with very white hair, like some of our old white men. There was not a bald head among them; that seldom occurs among the Indians.

This church has a regular organization, with between twenty and thirty members. This is a Baptist church, and it is claimed that four hundred have been immersed in various portions of the county.

The Catholics claim about three hundred nominal members. The Methodist church has had a missionary among them for the last two years and claim to be doing a good work. This work is in this county, and several adjoining counties having Indians in them.

The Methodist Conference which convened at Natchez, in December, 1892, licensed Simson J. Tubby to preach. He got up before that large body of learned men and in a plain way gave his experience and what he considered his conversion. A sufficient amount was subscribed to send him for a time to Millsaps College, at Jackson, and while the young man is now preaching to a church in Neshoba county, it is contemplated to send him to school and further prepare him to preach to his people.

Most of the younger men read and write their own language. Very few of their women have learned to read or write. Jesse Baker, the Choctaw preacher, who came from the Nation, learned these young Indian men in a part of two years to read and write and sing religious songs. He did a good work for his people. Baker was a consecrated man, who had the work of the ministry and the salvation of souls as the ruling thoughts of his mind. His labors were not in vain. He died at his post, and it is fondly hoped went to enjoy a rich inheritance.

At 11 o'clock we were called to the regular preaching of the day. Having good seats near the speaker, could easily hear what he said. It was a funeral and also a sacramental occasion.

The preacher was Ben Williamson, Ne-nac-intu-Cubby, a man looking to be about thirty-five years old, having preached three years. He had a fine appearance, dignified, cheerful, intelligent. He was tolerably well dressed, though his suit looked rather worn. He wore cuffs and cuff buttons, shirt collar, collar buttons, without cravat. He was assisted by Thompson Baker, who said he had no Indian name, which is very uncommon. He is a fine looking man, younger than Ne-nac-intu-Cubby, though not so intelligent. He came from one of the adjoining counties. The speaker was born in Newton county. Baker wore good clothes, which fit him well, wore a watch, one of those "gold watches" "warranted" and cost about five dollars. He took it out of his pocket to learn the hour, then he put it to his ear to learn if it were still alive. He wore a nice cravat and Derby hat.

Old Jack was the third preacher; he appeared to be about 60 years old. Jack has a young wife. He looks sad and dejected; has a poor voice and looks to have very poor health. Jack has seen the Choctaw Indian in all his wild, untutored state. He grew up as a devotee to all their wild ideas and shrank from all civilization. He engaged in all their time-honored customs, games and dances, believed in all their superstitions and participated in everything the Indian called pleasure and dissipation. In his more than mature manhood he became a convert to the Christian religion and a preacher of righteousness to his fallen race. He was the first preacher among them, and no doubt he has done good and is trying to live a Christian life and persuade others to do so. Yet his speech is slow, his frame is bowing, his noble manhood is gone and he now looks forward to the reward of hereafter. He is reverenced and respected by his people and will be missed when he is gone.

The text on this funeral occasion was from 1st Corinthians, 15th chapter, verses 51-52: " Behold, I shew you a mystery: we shall not all sleep but we shall be changed in a moment, in the twinkling of an eye at the last trump, for the trumpet shall sound and the dead shall be raised incorruptible and we shall be changed." In a very feeling way did he allude to the death of the child whose funeral he preached. He then presented his subject to his hearers; at first he appeared slow, making no gestures, and in rather conversational style; but after a short time he warmed up with his subject. He became more fluent; commenced to use his hands and arms, first in one way and then in another; now at full length, now brought close to his body. Then his head and his whole frame became in constant motion. His voice expanded and at no time lacked for expression of apparently the most appropriate phrases. He tenderly wept while he warned and persuaded his audience. He brought many of his hearers to tears. He came down from the platform from which he preached, talking all the while, walked to the middle of the house, addressing himself in the most earnest and emphatic language to his hearers. He preached about three quarters of an hour, his audience giving marked attention. White persons who heard him were favorably disappointed. Something was said that no white man in the county ever expected to hear—a Christian Indian preaching in his own language, and one brought up in a wild and unlettered state until he was twenty-five years old.

After the sermon Thompson Baker exhorted the people and presented to them Christ and baptism by immersion. He asked those desiring the prayers of the church to give their hands, and many of them, the older men and women, signified their desire to be prayed for. The elements of the Lord's Supper being present, the two younger ministers proceeded to the work of administering it. Thompson Baker read a portion of the eleventh chapter of 1st Corinthians, commencing, "That the Lord Jesus in the same night in which he was betrayed," etc., and proceeded to talk on the subject. Then the element representing the body of Christ was distributed. Ne-nac-intu-Cubby read another portion of the same chapter and proceeded to talk upon it; the deacons then handed the wine. The preacher impressed upon his hearers that long ago the Indian was much given to strong drink, but this was very different, representing as this did the blood of Christ, and that they must drink a very small portion of it. They offered an opportunity for membership, and one weeping woman came forward, was examined by the elder and admitted into the church. This was all done with as much order and decorum as it is in any of our white churches in the county.

One is amazed and encouraged at the progress these people have made in Christianity, contrasting the situation of the Indians now and when they were first discovered in America, the progress being made by them and the wise and munificent provisions by the Government for them. They are becoming civilized, educated, and in many instances Christianized. One is reminded of the speech made by a New England orator, probably seventy-five years ago, that believed that the white man would drive away the Indian and probably annihilate him from the face of the earth. Mr. Sprague said:

"Not many generations ago, where you now sit, surrounded by all that elevates and embellishes civilized life, there lived and loved another race of beings. Beneath the same sun that rolls over your head the Indian hunter pursued the panting deer; gazing on the same moon that shines for you the Indian lover woed his dusky mate. Now they paddled their light canoe along your rocky shores; now they dip their noble limbs in your sedgy lakes; here they warred and here they fought, and when the tiger strife was over, here curled the smoke of peace.

"Slowly and sadly they climb the distant mountains and read their doom in the setting sun. They shall soon hear the roar of the last wave that shall settle over them forever."

That language sounds like the cruel pale-face would exterminate the red man from the face of the earth. The prediction of this eloquent orator, though no doubt sincere in his ideas of the true condition of the Indians, is very far from being realized. On the contrary, the Government has assumed a fatherly care and guardianship over the Indians, and has furnished them with millions of dollars and substantial support and protection. The result is, they live upon their lands, holding lifetime rights, with no power to spend or waste them. They have splendid schools in the Nation, and elegant training schools in the States. They have good church privileges. Some of the tribes have an annual income from the Government. Some have fine fortunes, and some have princely sums in the hands of the Government. In several instances the United States Government has had to punish some of these restless and warlike tribes. Yet they find the "Great Father" and his people are their best friends—that "the hand of justice has been tempered with mercy," and if they will obey they will be rewarded and blessed.

The singing at the Indian church was also a surprise. The Indian songs that had been most popular among them were not as many as the whites have, but they had a song of rejoicing, a song of victory, and a song of sadness. They had no hymns or poetical songs. They would announce in their songs the loss by death of a child thus: Pus-cus Conneya Sally Hoga! The loss of a gun: Ta-napo Conneya, Sally Hoga! If they should leave their blanket as security for a quart of whisky, after they had drunk it they would sing: Shuckabo boly Sally Hoga! They would express their grief or sorrow with the same chorus as their rejoicing. They had a song to be used at their cries, and one at their dances. These songs were familiar to every one who had listened to them, and it was strange they had no new songs. The one used on various occasions appeared to be as old as the race. The first song sung by the congregation the day they were visited was, "How tedious and tasteless the hours," etc. They sang in Choctaw, but the old tune, so familiar to these words, as is sung by the whites. The beautiful words of this hymn, "Christian Experience," by Dr. Newton, could not well be sung to any other tune than the one used by us. The next was a plain, old, common measure tune, suggesting the familiar and sublime words by Samuel Stinnet, "Majestic sweetness sits enthroned," etc. When they administered the sacrament they used, "Pass me not, Oh, Gentle Savior." They were deficient in vocal music, but not more so than some white congregations. They need teaching in vocal music by competent instructors, yet they do well even in this part of their worship.

CHAPTER IV.

Number of White Settlers in Newton County When it was Organized—Face of the Country at the Time of Settlement—Amount and Kind of Game in the County at this Time—Style of Society—Use of Ardent Spirits—Morals of the People, etc.

The number of white citizens at the time of the organization of the county was necessarily small. An old citizen remarked that less than one hundred votes elected the sheriff. Say that it took one hundred votes to elect an officer at that time, it may be inferred that his opponent received nearly as many but was slightly in the minority. It may have been that there were nearly two hundred votes; probably quite that number, as it is not usual that all go to the elections. To multiply that number by four would give eight hundred white population, and it must be remembered that there were quite a number of negroes, probably one-third as many as whites. This would have given about one thousand persons, exclusive of the Indians, who were then more numerous than the whites.

The first census ever made in the county, in 1840, gave the population of Newton 2,527. This included the negroes as well as white people. It will be seen from this statement that Newton county had more than doubled the population from 1838 to 1840. If the first figures be correct, that there was 1,000 or a little over when the first officers were elected, this would be a very rapid increase in population in four years, and we must either admit that it is true or claim that the county had more inhabitants at its settlement than 1,000.

It will be recollected Newton county offered very flattering prospects to the new settler. The county had been a portion of Neshoba, and for three years, or nearly so, there had been officers of the county with a representation in the Legislature, so it was not as if the county had no organization before 1836.

As early as 1834 quite a number of persons had moved and made permanent settlements in this county. A few came even before the county of Neshoba was admitted in 1833. The lands were surveyed in 1832, and with that came a few adventurers and traders, who settled among and traded with the Indians. They could not enter lands, but they could for a time live in the Purchase. In the year 1833 there was a very large emigration of the Indians from this part of the country, which gave room for settlers and their families and immediately following it was that many came from the counties of Wayne, Simpson, Hinds and Copiah. In connection with these early settlements, from 1834 to 1837, came settlers from most of the States east of Mississippi. Quite a number of land speculators, merchants and general tradesmen came to the new county hoping to make favorable investments, and many for permanent settlement. The county continued to grow in wealth and importance, and when the second census of 1850 was taken, the population amounted to 4,467, nearly doubling itself in this decade.

FACE OF THE COUNTRY.

What the face of the country was when the white

man came to Newton county, can only be learned from the few old men who are left in the county, who came as early settlers. This number is very small—will probably not reach more than a dozen. All agree that the county was a beautiful one, very inviting to the new comer. The Indians were in considerable numbers, but they did not wantonly destroy the country or kill the game in waste. They used what they needed and allowed the balance to remain for the future. They only cultivated small patches of ground and had only paths to go through the country. There were no large trees that had ever been cut. The large timbers were confined to the swamp and the long leaf pine forests. The swamp at that time had no undergrowth except cane, which grew in great abundance, not so large as on the rivers and creeks in the western part of the State, but sufficiently thick and high as to completely cover the swamps in many places—making secure hiding place for wild animals, and affording a wonderful winter pasture for cattle and hogs. The latter used the acorns that fell from the massive oaks that in many places grew thick in the swamp.

In these swamps not only grew the oak, but gum, ash, poplar, beech, magnolia, bay, elm, hickory, and in some places a few walnuts, and occasionally a few cypress, frequently very large, short strawed pine. The long leaf pine forests were covered as an undergrowth, only, with grass, that grew up in some instances as high as a horse's back. This grass was killed to some extent every winter, and in the spring it came out fresh and looked beautiful.

Occasionally the forests were burned off. Sometimes these fires were very dangerous and very hard to stop. That part of the country known as the "flat woods," and ridges and hill lands of the county not growing the long leaf pine, were very open, only occasionally showing a few trees. This part of the county was beautiful to observe, and offered a place of great sport for the hunter. The same kind of grass did not grow in all respects on the flat lands as in the pine woods. A most luxuriant growth of ferns, wild roses, small flowering vines, besides the grass, all mingled in solid mass so as to almost obstruct a passage through it; also a wild pea grew in the pine and flat woods that served as fine food for stock, especially the deer.

A gentleman relating his recollections of the beauty of the "flat woods" section in the north-western part of his county, says the ferns grew in a mass two feet high; that a small flowering vine climbed upon and showed its blossoms in profusion over the ferns. The wild roses entwined themselves among the foliage, and all together, vines, ferns and roses presented a solid body, looking like one grand bouquet covering the ground. When the hunter came with gun and dogs and the deer are "jumped," the race commences. The yielding mass of ferns and flowers are so interwoven that when it is disturbed by deer, dogs and hunters it resembles the waves of the sea.

In the southwestern part of the county were open prairies, covered with a growth of very rich grass and a very parterre of flowers. These bald places were occasionally relieved by a clump of trees, forming an oasis as in a desert, and sometimes a stream of water was there which served to allay the thirst of man and beast.

These open spaces were called the "shell lands," and in many instances, had large accumulations of small shells in the soil, and a great number of oyster shells of large size. The oyster shells were largely used in the early settlement of the county in making lime. These shell lands were only productive of corn and other grain. They would not make cotton—it would "rust." The woodland prairie made fine cotton and corn. When the growth was post-oak it produced cotton better. These lands required good plows to break and to bed up the ground. Long ago the plow known as the Carey plow, was used. It had a long point with wooden mould-board. This plow was drawn by two horses, or oxen, and was considered an excellent plow for the work; and when this land was well broken, and particularly in winter, the crop was almost assured and with but little more work. In late years the steel plow, without the wooden mould-board, is used, and does good work.

Newton county had quite a number of "Reed-brakes." These were not considered desirable at first, but after trial, became the most fruitful sources of corn of any lands in the county. They were very boggy places, covered with reed. This species of cane differs from that growing in the swamps. These brakes were well ditched, which to a great extent dried them. The places occupied by the brakes are usually in valleys, in the long leaf pine woods. These valleys at one time had pure streams of water flowing through them, from one large or several small springs. At a remote period the grass began to grow along the margin of these flowing streams, and then the reed came also on the edges of its banks. This invited the black birds to roost, and after the lapse of centuries, perhaps, this stream is filled up by these bird deposits, and becomes a sluggish, dangerous quagmire, until after it is ditched; then it becomes a thing of beauty and profit. There is a considerable amount of these lands in Newton county, but in small bodies. The depth of the soil is sometimes several feet. The cane of these reed-brakes is not of the same character of that grown in the swamps. The leaf of the reed-brake cane is larger and greener; the reeds are much thinner and more easily broken. These brakes are evergreen and particularly attractive are they in the cold season; they all grow up very even and near the same height, and when everything around is nipped by the frost their symmetrical forms, waving gracefully in the breeze, presents an appearance both attractive and beautiful.

In these deep swamp jungles, high grass and reed-brakes, there must have been great quantities of game and snakes. It seems that the county was not infested to any great extent with snakes, yet in all new wooded and swampy country they abound more or less. The rattle-snake was rather numerous, and the moccasin and ground rattle-snake abounded to some extent. There were quite a number of less poisonous snakes, but most of the rattle-snakes are gone.

The amount of game in the county at the time it was settled was almost incredulous. From the statements of all the old settlers it existed in great abundance—deer, turkey, squirrels, coons, wild cats, some bear, panthers, and many wolves. These last named animals were so plentiful and destructive that by an act of the Legislature of 1837, a reward of five dollars was offered for every wolf killed in the county. Deer were so plentiful that a hunter could go out and find a herd and easily take choice as to the one he would shoot.

A very truthful man who came to the county in 1835 or '36, says that he could go out in sight of his dwelling house and see as many as twenty deer feeding. He states that he and his brother, besides doing the plowing for several hands, usually went out hunting in the afternoon, and the two killed one hundred deer from the first of January to the first of July. The Indians did not kill the game of the country as the white men; they killed it as they needed it. The white man kills for use first, then for sport and for the hides, and in this way very soon destroys the game in the country. Quite a number carried the hams of venison to distant markets after they were dried whole, which they did vary nicely, and brought good prices. Not many years elapsed before the game became much wilder and scarcer, and much harder to secure, and for more than twenty years it is rarely the case that deer are found. There was a large number of turkeys, abundance of squirrels, considerable amount of fish, great numbers of birds, some ducks, a large number of rabbits. A variety that has almost become extinct was the large swamp rabbit—nearly as large as the jack rabbit of Texas—he is now rarely seen.

STYLE OF SOCIETY.

The style of society was rough at this time and of the most primitive character; so were also the houses in which some persons lived. There was no building material except what was gotten out by hand; the great haste to get a shelter for the present caused the houses to be rough and small log cabins, with dirt or puncheon floor, put up almost, if not entirely without nails, using what was called the weight poles to fasten on the boards on the roofs, not having rafters but ridge poles forming the place to lay the boards.

Sometimes a man would make a neat cabin by chinking the cracks and filling with mud, so as to keep out the wind. For a floor he would take a small pine tree or sapling, hew it to a straight edge on two sides, then he would face it six inches wide and chop in on the opposite side to fit his sleepers, and by this means he would make what resembled a six-inch plank after it was laid on the sleepers. This method, if the puncheons were dressed after they were laid down, formed an excellent floor. Sometimes a whip-saw was used. This was a large rip-saw resempling a long cross-cut saw, by which two men sawed logs into plank--one standing on top of the log, the other in a pit in the ground under the log. It was hard work, but these pioneers were accustomed to it and enjoyed it. A good "stick and dirt" chimney was then put up, sufficiently large to warm the family and for the wife to do the cooking. Those fireplaces would sometimes be from five to six feet wide. A degree of comfort, with much hospitality and welcome to a visitor, made these rude houses of the pioneers something to be remembered. The style of society was as rough, or more so, than the houses in which the early settlers lived. These rough people would entertain a stranger, were glad to have his company and would not charge a cent for entertainment.

The use of ardent spirits was very free among the early settlers, most of them using it without stint. It was not uncommon to find it in the houses of most of the people, and all who visited them were welcome to it and expected to use it. It was openly sold in any part of the county when a man wished to do so. The morals of the people in those times were necessarily bad, with some notable exceptions. Profanity, gambling, horse-racing and fighting, and numerous immorralities were indulged in, and the people felt free and easy to violate the Sabbath in any way that suited them, and no one questioned these violations.

There was a great scarcity of schools and churches at this time, and want of them was keenly felt. This state of society continued for a term of years, until the population, by its increase in numbers and improvement in morality, demanded a change.

CHAPTER V.

NAMES OF THE MEN WHO FIRST HELD OFFICE IN THE COUNTY—FIRST REPRESENTATIVE—NAMES OF THE MEN WHO FIRST SETTLED IN DIFFERENT PARTS OF THE COUNTY—KIND OF GRASSES THAT GREW AND THE RANGE FOR STOCK—KIND OF FRUITS THAT GREW SPONTANEOUSLY IN THE COUNTY.

THE most important county officer in a new county is expected to be the sheriff. It is said that Myer Bright was the first sheriff elected for Newton county; that he and W. S. Thompson, a citizen for years after the war of the town of Newton, and father of Ben Thompson, of Brandon, ran for the office, and that Bright beat Thompson three votes. It is further stated that Bright would not qualify or give bond, and by that means forfeited his place as sheriff of the county. After that Hullum Redwine was elected sheriff and served two terms. As the records of Newton county are burned for about forty years, and it was impossible to get the State record showing the election of officers in the county, the information here recorded is from old settlers, and in some instances errors may come in as to who among the very first were the men to hold office in the county. The sheriff is very probably correct.

The probate judges whose names were given as those who early held office are Hudson, Furgerson and Shelton. It is not known with certainty which one held the office first, but probabilities are that it is in the order in which their names appear, with Judge Hudson as the first probate judge.

George Armstrong, well known in the county for years, was one of the first clerks of the probate court. James Armstrong, not the brother of George Armstrong, but a man who was conspicuous in the Decatur bank, was the first circuit clerk.

It is not definitely known who was the first assessor. Thames, Graham and Armstrong are mentioned. J. O. Kelly is mentioned as the first treasurer; Booker as first surveyor.

The first representative was James Ellis, who was the father of Mrs. Joe and Zach Gibbs, of this county. Ellis was the representative of Neshoba county before the counties were divided; was run in the interest of a division of the county, and continued to represent Newton county until the end of 1841.

Oliver C. Dease, of Jasper county, was the first Senator, Newton and Jasper being in the same senatorial district.

The above gives only the names of the first officers elected in the county. In another part of this volume will appear the names of all the officers of the county in the order in which they were elected and the term they served, given as far as can be stated from the information attainable.

The early settlers of Newton county did not by any means converge all at one point as if for mutual protection. There was no fear of the Indians. They were peaceable and very social and friendly, and very honest in regard to the taking of stock on the range. The early settlers, therefore, selected the portion of the county which they fancied, or that part which they came to first on approaching it.

38 HISTORY OF NEWTON COUNTY.

Mr. Alexander Graham came to Newton county in 1834. This is the father of Judge Wm. Graham, and quite a number of his descendents are still in the county. His wife is still living, probably the oldest lady in the county. These people live in the northeastern part of the county where the father settled sixty years ago.

In that same neighborhood lived the Reynolds, McMullens, Clearman's, Mathesis, Castles, Gilberts, Lairds, Harrises, Jones', Thames', and near Union lived Breland, Hubbard, the Smiths, Boyds, Lewis', Gordons, Isham Daniel, an old North Carolina merchant and postmaster at Union; Claiborne Mann, a large land and slave owner, who married as his second wife the mother of Hon. A. G. Mayers, now judge of this district; and the Hunters.

Towards the southeast were Jno. Blakely, John, Joshua and Kit Dyess, John and Edward Ward, Joel and James Carstarphen, two brothers who were Methodist preachers; the Sims', Williamsons, Joshua Tatum, Daniel Sandall, York and Edward Bryant, Henry, Fountain, George C. Hamlet, Elisha West, Wade Holland, a famous Baptist preacher, the Biggs', Williams' and Williamsons'.

In the southern part of the county were Roland Williams, the Walkers, Gibsons, Hamilton Davis, Fatheree, William and Isaac Gary, William and Thomas Mallard, Thos. Caldwell, Thos. Laird, Abel E. and E. E. Chapman, and Henry Evans.

In the western and southwestern part, Watson Evans, John McRae, Judge Duncan Thompson, the McFarlands, McCraney, Archy Black, John Murry, Bird Saffold, William and Elias Price, J. M. Kelly, Thos. Davis, Elezear Harris, Lewis and Hardy Nichols and A. B. Woodham, who is the only one of the old

HISTORY OF NEWTON COUNTY.

settlers now living, also Ralph Simmons, (who had eight sons in the late war), and the McDaniels.

In the northwestern part were the Ames, Bright Ammonds, (probably the first white settler in that part of the county), the Paces, Ben Bright, Coot and Sid Sellars, Volentines, Wm. Spradley, Absalom Loper, the Wares, Dempsey Smith, Cornelius Boyd and James Anderson.

Those just west of Decatur, Hamilton Cooper, E. S. and Joel Loper, Hollingsworths.

Those south of Decatur and centrally in the county : James Dunagin, David Riser, Stephen and John Williams, Samuel Stephens, Mint Blelack, Thos. J. Wash and sons. Mr. Thos. Wash was probably the oldest white man that ever died in the county, except Thos. Caldwell, who lived to be 99 years old. Mr. Wash was a native Georgian, came to this county from near Tuscaloosa, Ala., settled northwest from Newton in 1836, and was one of the wealthy men of the county when the war of 1861 commenced. He lived nearly one hundred years.

Also, south of Decatur, lived Willis, Jesse and Wm. Norman and the Wells brothers, Archilaus and Charley. The former is referred to in Col. Claiborne's History, as a captain in some of the Indian wars. He had a large family and quite a number of his descendents are in the county now. R. W. Doolittle, who lived on the site where the town of Newton now stands, was a man having a large family, and many of them still survive him and are citizens of the county. Judge Abner Harralson, one of the early probate judges of Newton county, lived south of the town of Newton; also his son-in-law, Lewis Shotts.

Decatur was early settled, and there were quite a number of citizens making up what was then known as one of the principal towns in east Mississippi. The most prominent men were the McAlpins, Armstrongs, Monroes, Hurd, the Teas brothers, T. S. Swift, Redwines, Dr. Bailey Johnson, R. P. Johnson, Myer Bright, E. E. Scanlan, A. Russell, Rev. N. L. Clarke, W. S. Thompson, Heidleberg, Turner, Lynch, Fred Evans, Russell B. Hide, Elisha Boykin, James Ellis, and Dr. Walker. Those compose most of the early settlers. There may be some inadvertently left out, of whom honorable mention should be made, yet it is impossible to get all from memory.

Quite a large number of the descendents of these old families are still in the county. The most numerous from the old settlers appear to be from the Hollingsworths, Wauls, Chapmans and Paces. These have probably the largest connection of any families in the county, all coming from some of the very early settlers.

Whenever there is a court held in the county, or any public business requiring good citizens to attend to it, the names of some, probably all, these prominent names are in it. Whenever there is a neighborhood matter to be settled by arbitration, it is usual to find the names of some of these families to do it. There has not been a great emigration of these families from their native county.

STOCK RAISING.

As a stock raising county there could be none better than Newton. Being well watered with creeks and small streams, abundant grass in the pine woods, and level, open upland, and in the southwestern part of the county, fine prairie.

This upland grass was good, but nothing like that on the prairies. There was almost the same difference in the strength of the grass for milk and to produce fat on animals, as there was in the strength of the land. These afforded splendid pasturage in the summer, and in the winter the grass on the hills that was not killed entirely by the frost, and the swamps of cane, offered a fine winter retreat and good grazing. Cattle were in excellent order all the winter. Horses as well as cattle did well on the range and could be as easily raised as they are in Texas.

This was also a very fine range for hogs. The swamps rarely failed to produce a splendid crop of acorns, beech nuts and scaly bark, thin hulled hickory nuts, which were fine for hogs — also excellent for persons to eat. The flavor of the nut was equal to the English walnut. These nuts were in great abundance and were used by the Indians as food. The nut possesses quite an amount of oil, and by boiling with food requiring a seasoning, it answered a good purpose. In preparing them for cooking the Indians took one at a time and crushed them between two small stones until the hull was broken very fine; they then threw the whole mass —including the hull with the kernel—into a pot containing ingredients of peas, corn, dry venison, beans, etc. These nuts furnished the grease, and all combined made what the Indian called sof-ky. Some of the other tribes, by the aid of their white friends, have Anglicized the word and call this mixture of food "Tom-fuller." When done it appears of a consistency something like thick soup and was served from a spoon made of a cow's horn. Four or five Indians would sit down around a pot of sof-ky and use only one spoon. The first would help himself and pass to the next, and so the spoon went round like the pipe which a crowd would smoke from by passing it in the same way. Besides this mast of acorns, nuts, etc., from trees, a fine amount of food for the hog was obtained from the ground, of succulent roots, worms, herbs, etc., which added much to their stock of provisions, and the summer wild fruits of plums, haws, grapes and all kinds of berries which grew in great abundance, caused the hogs to thrive like the cattle at all seasons of the year. The sheep, which are always able to subsist on less than cattle or hogs, had pasture all the year. This grass that grew so luxuriantly in the pine woods, and that gave such pasture for cattle in summer, and also to some extent resisted the winter, when it came up it resembled the common sedge of the old fields, but did not make as much straw in the woods as it did in the open field. Then there was what is called beggar lice, and which in the fall afforded fine feed for cattle; also a vine bearing a wild pea which was good. The flat woods had also a native grass which served well for cattle and horses. The prairie grass was a mixture of grass and herbs indigenous to the soil, and different from the upland grass, of which cattle were very fond and which was a great milk and fat producer. Most of these grasses have become extinct, or so dwarfed by constant grazing and tramping by stock, as not to be observed as an original grass.

The wild fruits of the county were very abundant; strawberries early in the spring on prairie soil; also on the same soil the early plum; next came the early swamp huckleberry, the best variety of huckleberry, but is usually killed by the spring frost; then the summer huckleberry, growing in the pine woods, the gooseberry and the fall huckleberry; summer grapes and muscadines were abundant. Black haws, parsley haws and the hog haws were in great abundance, the latter only good for hogs. There was a summer plum something resembling the wildgoose plum of this county at this time, only had better taste and an odor equal to the most fragrant of apples; it was considered the finest wild fruit that grew; it was confined mostly to prairie or lime land. Some of them still remain, but the best production of this kind is stamped out. The winter grapes and persimmons were also among the fruits. The persimmon is now more plentiful, like the second growth short leaf pine, than in the earlier settlement. It appears that these two growths prefer and use older and more worn soil. Most of the earlier fruits still exist in the county, but as a general rule, like grasses, they appear to be stunted by "civilization," and are giving way to cultivated fruits and grasses. When the ground has been cultivated and the original grasses and trees have been exterminated, if this land is left uncultivated a new growth of trees, different from the original, will come up. On most of the oak and hickory lands that were cleared up in the early settlement of the county and that were worn down and turned out as not being worth anything, there has come a growth of short-strawed pine which covers the ground with shade and straw, and to some extent have reclaimed these lands..

After a long-strawed pine forest is denuded of its large timber for mill purposes, there usually comes up a very different growth, generally oak and hickory on this pine land and at once the soil is improved. This undergrowth gives more shade and the heavy draft to support these pine trees is taken off and the land is relieved of a great burden. A long-leaf pine forest never renews itself on the same land. When once taken off it never returns. This is very much the case with the grasses that originally covered the ground. Their places have been taken by some grasses of different character. In some instances these grasses are an improvement upon the original crop and serve a better purpose than the growth originally found on the ground.

CHAPTER VI.

SETTLING OF DECATUR, THE COUNTY SEAT—NUMBER OF MEN KILLED AT DECATUR FROM EARLY SETTLEMENT TO 1861—BANK AT DECATUR—ITS OFFICERS AND FAILURE.

It will be remembered that the town of Decatur was settled early in the year 1836. The act of the Legislature allowing the commissioners of the county who organized it to proceed to select a site not farther than five miles from the center of the county and to buy or accept by gift not more than eight acres of land as a situation for court-house and jail.

The selection was made and it is said that Isaac Hollingsworth gave the land on which to build. The lots are said to have been sold in the fall of 1836, and the work of building court-house and jail was commenced.

The first court-house is said to have been a small log house situated where the post.office is now being kept. That would be directly south of where the court-house now stands and east of Gaines', blacksmith shop. The first jail is said to have been built by Sam'l Hurd. This new county site in a new county where there were quite a number of citizens of wealth in the way of slaves, stock and real estate, is soon to become a business center for trading as well as the business of the county. There is quite an amount of work to be done by the first board of police and it is to be regretted that their names cannot here be reproduced. These were then, as well as now, important officers of the county. There were many new roads to be cut and some new bridges to be built, though the number as compared with the roads and bridges of to-day, is very small. Yet it was a large work for the population. All the necessary work incident to a new town and new county devolved upon those worthy citizens now composing this board of police.

After the sale of the lots new houses sprang up ; they were of rude character, the material being taken from the woods, and the best houses that could be constructed were in this way put up. Store houses were built, and as a matter of course, the liquor shop, then called a "grocery," was considered as one of the essentials for forming a new town. Decatur being the county site for, and the trading point of most of the citizens of the new county. The goods that were sold here had to be brought from a long distance, usually from Mobile, as Jackson was a place not doing much business at that time. Some goods were hauled from Tuscahoma, on the Bigbee river, though not much of that was done at that time. Some hauling was done from Vicksburg, and probably some from Yazoo City.

BANK ESTABLISHED.

Probably as early as the years 1837, Decatur was visited by men of some enterprise and of speculative tendency, who saw an opening to make money selling goods and doing a general banking business. The Decatur Bank was established. The exact date is not given. It does not appear in any of the Legislative acts when the bank was chartered. It appears to have been a chartered institutiou. They had regular officers, and issued a currency of paper money, which was good for the time and place as far as the appearance of the bill was concerned.

As to the origin of the bank, or its capital stock or basis of credit, but little can be found out. It was suggested by one gentleman that the bank was formed in connection with the Enterprise Navigation Company, which meant that the Chickasahay river would be navigable to Enterprise, then a turnpike would be built to connect it with Decatur, and extend through the county. There was at one time a turnpike road constructed which reached a portion of the western part of this county, but it had no connection with the Decatur bank, nor did the Enterprise Navigation Company (as far as known).

It is learned from a gentleman, W. H. Strebeck, now living at Lone Oak, Texas, a very old man, who was employed in the Decatur bank in a clerical capacity, that the bank was organized by a board of directors, a president, cashier and teller. He states further that the president was J. C. McAlpin; cashier, T. S. Swift; teller, James Armstrong. Some of the directors were Jourdan and Albert Teas, Russell B. Hyde, Jno. C. Heidleburg, —— Lynch, —— Turner, and probably Fred Evans. He says the basis of the money was in landed security, and the bank officers being mostly composed of lawyers, they secured lands by deeds to the bank, and issued the money on the faith of the real estate. A bank note of the denomination of fifty dollars, now in the hands of Mr. Harris Bonds, of Decatur, will in some way corroborate Mr. Strebeck's statement, but does not verify the whole. By taking both, a very good idea can be had as to the basis of credit on which the bank operated.

This note bears on its face the following:

$50
              Ninety days after date

The Mississippi and Alabama Real Estate Banking Co.
  Stock secured by real estate and payable in Cotton.
Decatur, Miss., February 5th, 1839.
                      Fifty Dollars to Bearer.
T. S. SWIFT, Cashier.   J. A. McALPIN, Pres't.

The above is a copy of the bill, an actual issue of the bank. Shortly after this the bank was burned. Let Mr. Strebeck, who was an eye witness, state the manner of its burning. He says that the burning of bank took place early one morning while the president and cashier were out of the county:

"The safe was recovered by Jourdan and Albert Teas and James Armstrong. Almost every one in the place flocked to the burning. The safe, although nearly red hot, was drawn from the fire and water thrown on it and before entirely cool burst open with a crow bar and water thrown on the inside. The books were saved with little damage, and also a small amount of fifty-dollar bills, which were on the inside with the books."

With this the bank was a failure. No doubt it was broken before the fire, yet this served as a good pretext; so there were no more issues of money. There was quite an amount of this money in the hands of the citizens of the county, and no doubt large losses were sustained on account of the failure. Yet it was in keeping with the banking institutions of those times. It is said that the soldiers during the war were enabled to pass quite an amount of the Decatur money in the Army of Virginia. It was said anything with a picture on it would pass then. There were some small issues of "shinplasters," as they were then called, in different parts of the county, probably at old Pinkney, where there was a store.

The State of Mississippi was, after 1837, practically without banks and was dependent on other States until after the war for her circulating medium, except silver and gold. This was on account of the Repudiated Bank bonds, and after that the State could get no credit to establish banks.

Not only did Decatur have a bank by which the people had an easy and convenient circulation of paper money, but land speculators, or as they might now be termed, real estate agents and brokers. They had a regular race-course, quite a number of race-horses, kept at the place; among them was the famous Bullit Neck, a horse of great reputation at that time, trained for the turf, and was carried to other parts of the State, and large amounts of money staked on him. It is stated by an old resident at that time, that the new town exhibited quite an amount of sociability and general amusements, such as a dancing school, writing school, and of course other social parties. The same party being interrogated as to the preaching of those days, says, sermons mostly were preached from the texts of "ace, duce and jack high, low, jack and the game." He further states that court would be held in the court-house during the day and at night be used for faro bank.

These were free and easy times, and the state of society brought about by drinking and gambling, and horse racing caused many difficulties, which resulted in the killing of a number of men at Decatur. As the records of the trials of these men are burned, it is only from the recollections of the old citizens of the county that the names of parties to these tragedies can be obtained. If all the fights that had occurred in the old county site could be reported they would fill a volume. For it must be recollected that in those days of boasted strength and manhood most of the difficulties were settled by fair ring fights, and the one who was the best man came out victorious. An old settler, living in this county at the present time, says he saw a fifty dollar bill of Decatur money bet on a dog fight, probably in 1838. Dog fights are always prolific of fights between men. The old settler says that the fight between the dogs caused forty fights between men. This statement must be taken with some degree of allowance. The probabilities are that one or more fights were the result of the dog fight. In those days of fist-fights, when a man wanted to fight or was insulted, he pulled off his coat the first thing. One man doing so would cause another to do so, and the mutual friends of the beligerents all over the ground divested themselves of their coats, and the young man, as he was then, saw the number that were fighting and those who were willing to fight, and taking it all together it appeared to him as if forty couples were willing to take a hand on the result of the dog fight.

Long ago the town of Decatur was noted for the number of men killed in it. It was reported that sixteen or eighteen men had lost their lives in the town. From careful inquiry and comparison with the old men and women of the county, only nine persons lost their lives in deadly combat. There were several persons who were accidently killed, and one who suicided, and they may be included in the number above stated.

The following are the men who were killed and the parties committing the deed and are given in the order of their committing as correctly as can be ascertained :

HISTORY OF NEWTON COUNTY. 51

Joshua Tatum killed Hezekiah Hargrove; Thos. Redwine killed George McAlpin; Dr. Bailey Johnson killed Adams; James Ellis killed Neighbors; William Spradley killed Absalom Loper, Jr.; Buckhannan killed Leslie; Cornelius Mann killed Cordaway; Martin killed Vance.

There were none of these men punished except William Spradley, who was sent to the penitentiary. Most of these acts of violence were committed while the parties were under the influence of liquor; yet it appears that several of them were justifiable or had able criminal lawyers to defend them. These murders were all before the war; not one since. The last one was not earlier than 1856 to 1858.

BUILDING OF CHURCHES.

There was very little disposition among the earlier settlers of Decatur to establish churches. If the people of the new town had any inclination to go to church they went to the country. This was in keeping with the early settled towns of the State. Notably is the town of Winchester, in Wayne county, which was established in 1809; was one of the original counties sending delegates to the State Convention in the year 1817, asking the State to be admitted. Winchester was the county site of Wayne county from the time it was organized until after the war. There was no church in the town for forty years after it was settled. After it lost its trade and importance as a town; after other towns were established in the county; after the railroad came through the county in 1854, then the people paid some attention to the building of a church. It appears that the morals of the people who lived in the town were averse to churches. That liquor was sold openly on the Sabbath and much drunkenness on that day; so it was found more profitable for the preachers of those days to have the preaching out of the small towns. In another part of this volume the various towns of the county are spoken of, and the town of Decatur will again come in after great reformation and improvements have taken place.

CHAPTER VII.

The Character of the Lands in Newton County—Kinds of Lands that were First Cultivated—How the Fresh Lands Produced—How People Disposed of their Stock and Cotton Increase of Population for the First Ten Years After Settlement.

The lands of Newton county are divided into what is termed the ridge and branch lands. Some loamy, sandy upland, some level with good clay foundation, some red clay sub-soil. Quite an amount of bottom and creek lands, and the prairie in the southwestern portion of the county.

Though Newton county is not one of the rich counties of the State, there are a great many bodies of fine land in the county. They are very much diversified, there being many kinds on a small area. The character of the lands first cultivated in the county were usually the level table lands. On these there was very little undergrowth, and after the turf was broken the virgin soil was rich and produced remarkably well, with very little cultivation.

Very frequently the new comer settled on an Indian's place and they appeared to be very good judges, and in many instances had selected such places for their homes, as were very attractive to the white settler. The prairies of the county were very open; thousands of acres of this kind of land were entirely unobstructed by timber or undergrowth, and were very easily brought into a state of cultivation. The level, sandy and uplands were much more in demand, as the people much preferred the level uplands to the ridges or prairies.

There was no disposition to, or knowledge of terracing or circling land in those days. Farmers had great pride in having the fields laid off in very straight rows. No fertilizing to any extent was practiced at that time; very little attention paid to rotation of crops, and the consequence was that these level lands were soon worn down; more fresh lands were cleared up, and the old fields allowed to lie out and grow up in short-leafed pine trees, and in this way most of the choice places were brought in at an early day and put under cultivation, and many of them allowed to go to ruin. These same grounds when they lie level and were allowed to lie out and take a second growth of timber, are among the most valuable of the county.

They have been reclaimed, and in many instances nature has done wonders in recuperating them. Having an abundance of vegetable mold, the intelligent application of commercial fertilizers has brought them up to a production equal if not greater than when they were first cleared. These lands, though level, are terraced so as to retain the greatest amount of moisture, and crops can be made with less rain than when they were fresh.

Great improvement in the proper kind of plows to work the crops have much improved the yield and greatly protects them from washing and wearing out. Newton county, as has been stated, was eminently a stock raising county as well as an agricultural one. A man had very little labor to perform to make corn or cotton; had only to keep his stock gentle to secure heir increase and growth.

MARKET FOR STOCK AND CATTLE.

The market for stock and cattle was far from home; much of the cotton was taken to Mobile, a distance of 135 miles; some to Vicksburg and some to Jackson; and after the railroad reached Brandon, Newton county took there a large amount of the cotton raised. Cattle were driven to Mobile and sometimes shipped to New Orleans from there. Sometimes they were sold at Baton Rouge and from there sent to New Orleans. Cotton was lower in the forties than it has been since; the people made it then and hauled it to the markets referred to, and many times sold for five cents per pound. The price of cotton gradually increased, fluctuating much, and in the year 1851 it reached a point of from $12\frac{1}{2}$ to 14 cents per pound. The average price of cotton in the Mobile market, which was the market for this county for ten years before the war, was from 1850 to 1860, eight cents per pound.

WHAT WAS MADE ON THE FARM.

Corn, peas, potatoes, pumpkins, and everything necessary to live upon were made at home; there was always corn enough made in the county to do the citizens; some few were non-producers, and accordingly a few would fail; in this event they could be supplied by their neighbors. The same was true as to bacon and other provisions, which could be raised in the county. Sugar, coffee, molasses and some flour, were bought. There was a good deal of wheat made in the county; the fresh lands, and particularly the red lands in the northern portion of the county, brought good wheat. No sugar or molasses were made; it was not known then that this county could grow the Louisiana cane. Considerable rice and some tobacco were made.

CLOTHING MADE AT HOME.

Large amounts of clothing were made by the women of the county, both cotton and woollen goods. These goods were of the most lasting character. Large amounts of the coarse shoes were made at home; many farmers tanned their own leather, while others carried their leather to the tan-yards of the county and exchanged hides for leather, getting half the weight of the hides in leather, if it were sole, and proportionately according to size and finish if it were upper leather. Farmers made their plow-lines, plow-stocks, hames and backbands at home. The county and town blacksmiths did new plow work and repaired old work so as to keep them busy most of the year. When they were not working on plows they were repairing and ironing wagons, whose wood-work was made at some neighboring shop in the county. People lived close at home and made more of the implements with which to work the farm than they now do. Quite an amount of money was derived from the sale of beef cattle, sheep and hogs, driven from this county to market. In some instances prices ran very low; at others they were very high, and as the stock grew up on the range and became very fat, much profit was gained from the raising of them. Thousands of cattle and other stock were driven to market from this county in the first twenty years after its settlement.

POPULATION AGAIN CONSIDERED.

The population of Newton county, when settled, is supposed to be from ten to twelve hundred, not counting the Indians. The first census after the organization of the county in the year 1836, was taken in the year 1840, which showed Newton county to have

HISTORY OF NEWTON COUNTY.

2,528 of all classes, not including the Indians. This was quite an increase on the population of 1836. In the year 1850 the census gives 4,465, not to include the Indians. This showed that Newton county was still increasing very fast, and much of the good lands were being taken up, and all the advantages which this new county could give were being appreciated.

By this time much more interest was taken in schools and churches, and the general civilizing of the country. Better houses were being put up; quite an amount of negro property brought to the county, and many things done to give the county respectability and importance in the State. A new court-house had taken the place of the old log house built in early days, and a new jail, and the Baptist church, had by this time, or a little after, been built, all showing a tendency towards improvement.

This new court-house, or the second one to be built in the county, was a two-story frame building on the site occupied by the present brick structure. It was built by Willis Norman, but the price paid for it cannot be learned, nor the date it was built, possibly, as early as 1840 to 1841.

CHAPTER VIII.

Three Attempts to Move Court House from Decatur—Building of two Court-Houses—Rebuilding of Court-Houses—Steady Increase of Immigration up to 1855 and 1860—Improvement of the County at this Time—Advancement in Civilization.

It appears that after the building of the second court-house the people became restless in some parts of the county, and proposed to move it to the geographical center. This central location in the county would be a half mile south of the Isham Hollingsworth place on the road from Decatur to Newton, about three hundred yards east of the road. This is a very broken, hilly place, and apparently a very unsuitable place for a town, yet it is said that there was some town lots sold on the location designated. A great gathering of people collected at the place, an old-fashioned barbecue was given, (the old barbecue pit is still there). This was no doubt a great meeting of the people; probably some speeches made favorable to the location and removal. Doubtless there was a large amount of liquor drank, many fights, and much that was exciting and amusing, but all to no avail; when the vote was taken the court-house still remained at Decatur. It is not known at precisely what date this occurred, but the supposition is that it was between 1842 and 1845.

HISTORY OF NEWTON COUNTY. 59

In February, 1864, Gen. Sherman's army marched through the county on its way to Meridian. It stopped at Decatur, and besides many other things that the soldiers did, they burned the court-house. This house was not a valuable one, but it answered the purpose at the time, and supplied the wants of the people. The records were saved and the court-house business done in a private house, northeast present site of business, where Mrs. Hinton now lives.

Thus matters went on until after the close of the war in the year 1865. Soon after this time an agitation of the same question was had, and at the first meeting of the Legislature after the war, the question of removing the county site at Decatur to Newton was submitted to this body at Jackson, and again it was put before the people. When the vote was taken it was shown that Decatur was again chosen by the voters. At once steps were taken to build a new court-house on the old site. The board of police at once met and passed an order for the building of the new court house, and the contract was awarded to Montgomery Carleton, the amount said to be $3000. This house was about the size of the one that Sherman's army burned, and was a very peculiarly constructed building. The court was held on the ground floor, and the rooms for the officers were on the second floor. The house was not as convenient as if the court had been held on the second floor and the rooms for the officers on the first. It, however, served a very good purpose and was a great loss to the county when it was destroyed. The jail was built by Thomas Wells for $1500. Much business was done in this court-house. There were stirring times in the county; great political events were happening; much was done to excite the people. In this court-house officiated the radical appointees and the scalawags elected to office. Here speeches were made by patriotic Democrats urging the people to strive to get from under the yoke of political oppression. Here it was that the Radical speakers, from various parts of the State, came and used this court-house as a place to proclaim to the few people who would follow them then, the doctrines of the Radical party. Here, too, in this court-house, was the Radical party overthrown and the Democrats returned to power.

In the month of September, probably the second day of the term of circuit court in 1876, this court house was burned. It was at first supposed to be the work of an incendiary, and a man by the name of Spencer, a lawyer attending the court, was suspected. So strong was the suspicion in the minds of the grand jury that a true bill was found against Mr. Spencer. He, feeling that this was all wrong, demanded a speedy trial, which was given him, and he was honorably acquitted. It is now supposed that the fire was accidental, occuring from the leaving of some candles that burned down and ignited the wood on which they were placed, and that fired the building.

This entailed a great loss to our county, as the court-house had to be rebuilt, and a greater loss in the records of the county, which for forty years were gone. A minute book and docket and a few papers were all that were saved. The records of the county, including all important matters that had been there from the commencement of the county, with the record of all the land deeds, and all other important transactions, were gone, and without power to reclaim many of them. Judge Mayers was holding the court, and the day after the burning the court repaired to the Baptist church, where the term was finished, and probably one or two subsequent courts were held there.

As soon as the news of the burning of the court-house was well understood in the county, the people began to agitate again as to the removal, and at the next meeting of the Legislature, which took place during the year 1877, a petition was presented by the representative of the county, Hon. Isaac L. Pennington, and a bill was passed allowing the court-house site to be removed from Decatur. Now comes an exciting time in the county of Newton.

The town of Newton claims the right to have the court-house. The town of Decatur claims the right to have the court-house remain, and the town of Hickory claims the right to have the court-house go there. Decatur is about three and one-half miles from the center of the county; Newton about six and one-half, and Hickory a little greater distance probably than Newton. The excitement ran high and quite a feeling was evinced by the citizens of the county against Newton particularly. Hickory being a business rival of Newton, her people preferred that Decatur, rather than Newton, should have the court-house, though the latter would be more convenient for them. Newton made a proposition to donate the building lot and to build the court-house. The election came off and resulted in the court house remaining at Decatur.

The people of Hickory were not to blame for the part they took against Newton. The people north of Decatur felt that the county site ought to remain at Decatur and they acted right. It is said, however, that enough voters remained away from the polls in the beat that the town of Newton is situated to have carried the court-house to Newton. They felt it their privilege to defeat Newton; they had that right and yet it appears strange, if these statements are facts, that they should have acted so. It was a severe blow to Newton's business interests. The people in the northern part of the county were for years estranged to the town and gave their trade to Hickory. It is but of recent years that this animosity has passed off.

As soon as the result of the election was known, and at the first meeting of the board of supervisors, steps were taken to rebuild the court-house at Decatur. The board was not sparing of the county's money in its appropriations, and their actions appeared to be sustained. They passed an order in the spring of 1877, that the county of Newton was to have a brick court-house, to be built on the old site. Proposals were received and the contract was let to Mr. Scully, of Meridian, for $7,000, who went immediately to work and in a few months had the house ready for occupation.

This house is a two-story, 60x40 feet, with four rooms on first floor for offices and grand jury; has splendid court-room above, with two rooms in the rear of the judge's seat for consultation of lawyers and their clients, and other purposes of convenience to the court. This house has flat roof covered with tin; has blinds to the windows; has two good fireplaces; and taking it altogether, is in every way convenient and suitable for holding the courts of the county.

After the building of the new brick court-house, the old jail was found to be inadequate and unsafe. A good frame jail house was constructed immediately after the court house; and after the jail was built it was found expedient to have iron cages placed in the jail for a more safe-keeping of prisoners. These were placed in the jail by a St. Louis company at the cost of about three thousand dollars for jail and cages. It was thought by the board of supervisors in the year

HISTORY OF NEWTON COUNTY. 63

1893 that the safe in the court-house then, which cost $550.00, was not sufficient to protect the records and important papers of the county. They passed an order to have a brick vault outside at one of the east windows of the chancery clerk's office, immediately connected with and adjoining the chancery clerk's office. This vault to be 8x12 feet. The contract was taken by W. H. Wilson, of Meridian, who burned the brick and with the assistance of C. H. Dabbs, placed the brick vault as an annex to the chancery clerk's office, at the cost of $849.00.

It will be seen that the county of Newton is now well provided with all the necessary houses for county business; a safe jail out of which no prisoner has ever escaped except at the door; good safes and brick vault to protect the interests of its courts, and records and those of its citizens who have an interest there. This is as it should be, and the boards of supervisors are to be complimented for the manner in which they have provided for the county and with no very great outlay of the people's money.

INFLUX OF POPULATION.

It has been shown that the increase of population from the decade from 1840 to 1850 nearly doubled, and from 1855 to 1860 was a period in which was a greater increase proportionately than at any other period of the county's history. About this time and a little previous, came many Alabama and Georgia people. J. F. N. Huddleston, a prominent lawyer and Congregational Methodist preacher, with large family, came to the county from Georgia; also the McCune family, the Todds, McMullens, Stampers, Quattlebaums, Edmunds, Hoye, Hunters, Abneys, McElhaneys, Freemans, Watsons, Masseys, Flints, Portiss', Barrets, Carletons,

Keiths, Nimmocks, Gardners, Daniels', Cleavlands, and others whose names are not recollected.

As mention has been made of an influx of Georgia and Alabama immigration to the county, it would here be proper to mention as a large and valuable contingent in the way of citizenship, the Irish settlement in Newton county. Some of them came at a date much anterior to 1855 and 1860—probably as early as 1845 to 1850—and so distinct and separate were they as an Irish community, that it was called New Ireland, in honor of the " old Emerald Isle." The names of these Irishmen were: Vances, of which there is a large family; Blackburns, Frenches, Dowdles, Gaults, Willises, Hogans, Mercers and Davidsons.

With this addition of population from Georgia and Alabama, and the foreign element, new life seemed to be infused into the county. These people had come from older States, where different methods of living prevailed; hence it was better farming, better stock, and much new land opened, better state of society, more schools, more churches, more preaching. There was more enterprise, more disposition to make better improvements in the county. Especially was this very noticeable in Decatur, the county site. Up to that time only one church was in the town. A new Methodist church was built, and good schools provided. Up to, say 1855, there was probably not over $1000 paid out in the county for schooling by private citizens.

Very soon after the period referred to, Decatur had a high school, and paid a principal as much as $800 a year for teaching. In the year 1890 Newton county had nearly ninety schools, and paid out nearly $14,000. At the laying of the corner-stone of Hickory Institute, November 8, 1889, Col. J. L. Power, who officiated on that occasion, made this statement: "There are few counties in the State that make a better showing in the matter of attendance compared with total enrollment. Of the 5935 educable children enrolled, 4359 were in school during the year, leaving only 576 (white and colored) who were not in school any time during the year."

OLD TIME SCHOOL TEACHERS.

There was a school teacher in the year 1860-61 in the county engaged in teaching, and who had been employed in this profession at a much earlier period, both in Newton and Jasper counties. He was a man of superior education, of strong convictions, and whose political tenets came very near causing him to lose his life. The man referred to was John Bissett. He was an Englishman, and said he had been educated for the ministry. His intemperate habits had caused his ruin. He came to Jasper county as early as 1833, and in that county and Newton taught school alternately until 1861. He usually taught in the neighborhood of the Loper families in Jasper county, and in the Blakely families, in Newton county. He was a man wonderfully gifted in conversational power; discussed any topic that agitated the public mind, or that interested any private individual. His manners were good, his address was gracious and attractive, and his language such as to have no defects, no slang, no common, rough phrases, but rich, fluent and instructive, with a brogue that was attractive, but not objectionable. These were his characteristics when sober, but when drunk, "none so poor as to do him reverence." He then became an object of scorn and reproach. To his intimate friends it had long been known that he was opposed to slavery. Upon a memorable occasion in the town of Decatur, in the spring of 1861, he gave utterance to opinions so much in opposition to the spirit of "those times" and so opposed to the politics of the South, that his life was endangered. It is said a rope was brought with which to hang him. But his old friends and the old people that had known him since he came into the county, and to whom he had been so kind, and many of them his pupils in school, rescued him from the infuriated people, made up money and sent him away to another State.

Jeremiah Hennessey was another old landmark among the early teachers of this county. Hennessey was an Irishman, a very competent teacher, a faithful worker in the discharge of his duty. He did not teach in Newton county as much as Bissett. Hennessey will be remembered by the older citizens of the county who went to his school. He had his peculiar ways of teaching, which were considered good at that time, and probably one peculiarity of his school government may be more impressed upon his old pupils, and that is the punishment he inflicted. He may well have been called a "threshing machine." But he was one who loved the children he taught, and who gave largely of his salary to the children in presents, and particularly to those who excelled in their studies. He was a very austere man, and yet had much kindness in his nature. His loved his school, his profession, and greatly respected his patrons. He was another victim of intemperance. He lived to a great age and died about the period referred to—1860 or 1861.

There were some other old-time teachers in the county, of less note. Thomas Car, Beale, Young, Wilson, Waterman, Stroud and Welch were among the early teachers recollected by the old settlers.

Speaking again of the Irish settlement, these people are Protestants, and usually belong to--when they are attached to any church--the Cumberland Presbyterian. They are usually men who make good livings at home, and are very independent characters. They are very little given to an undue use of liquor, but most of them will take a drink and care not who sees them. Upon the whole they are a valuable addition to our population, and Newton county would be proud of a thousand more of such immigrants fom the "ould country." There are very few Catholic families in the county; Dr. F. G. Semmes and family at Hickory, and John Kirby and wife, and his son and son-in-law and family, are all that are recollected.

If the reader should wish a hearty welcome, a good joke, a warm shake of the hand, a plain but plentiful meal, let him go and spend the day with John Kirby and his " old lady." John and his good wife are both old, but they are jolly and well fixed at home by hard work. There are very few foreign-born citizens in the county except those named. One Chinaman at Newton; one Englishman, Uncle Dick Trathan, at Hickory. The Indian population, according to the census of 1890, is 349 in this county.

CHAPTER IX.

INTRODUCTION OF THE RAILROAD INTO THE COUNTY—BUILDING RAILROADS IN THE COUNTY—WHEN THE RAILROAD ENTERED THE COUNTY — ITS COMPLETION THROUGH THE COUNTY—NUMBER OF MILES OF RAILROAD IN THE COUNTY — NUMBER ACRES OF LAND DONATED BY THE GENERAL GOVERNMENT TO RAILROAD LOCATED IN NEWTON COUNTY— NUMBER OF ACRES OF RAILROAD LAND NOW IN THE COUNTY —THE ADVANTAGES OF THE RAILROAD TO THE COUNTY—TAX IT NOW PAYS THE COUNTY.

Between the years 1850 and 1855 work was begun on the railroad running from Vicksburg in an eastern direction from Brandon. This road was called the Southern Railroad; was started out from Vicksburg probably in the year 1839, and progressed very slowly, and finally reached Clinton, in Hinds county, and was there for a time, but was completed to Jackson about 1845. It remained at Jackson for a period of years, and probably about 1848 was built to Brandon, in Rankin county. About that time the directors went to work more seriously to put the road through. Persons connected with the road were sent to Virginia to buy negroes to work on it. While the road remained at Brandon it proved a fine market, and much of the cotton raised in Newton county was taken to Brandon and sold, and supplies bought for plantation use. During the year 1858 the road was finished to Morton, in Scott county, and that town remained the terminus for about two years.

The work on the road now went on more rapidly. Outside contractors took the work, and it soon reached completion. E. Gresham and James P. Clark and Warren Clark, of Scott county, took contracts, and W. N. Raines, of Newton county, living near Hickory, did a large amount of work for the road. Col. Raines was a large slave owner and employed his own negroes and hired other negroes in the county and did good service. Col. Raines was a Virginian by birth, but had lived in Georgia and had seen much railroad work, and had good experience and was a very suitable man to intrust with the building of the road. It was some time in the year 1859 that the railroad reached Lake. It was on the 20th day of September, 1860, that the first train reached the town of Newton.

The arrival of the cars at Newton was welcomed by a large crowd of ladies and gentlemen, mostly from Garlandsville, in Jasper county, who came to Newton and gave the railroad officials who were there, quite an ovation. A fine dinner was spread for the officers' benefit. Mr. Vossburg, the very accomodating railroad official, welcomed them, and gave all the crowd a free ride to the tank below Forest and return. Newton county came near losing the passing of the road through its territory. The crossing of the many streams east of the town of Newton, and the Chunkey Hills, offered a barrier that the builders of the road would gladly have missed. One of the directors lived at Garlandsville, in Jasper county, who appreciated the value of a railroad, proposed to carry it through the entire length of Jasper county. The direction indicated was to turn south, west of Lake, and go to Garlandsville, then go down the valley of Souinlouvy to

Enterprise. In that event Enterprise would have been the city that Meridian is, probably larger. Jasper county would have had a railroad running through its entire length from east to west, and Newton county would have been left without a probability of a road for all time. But the voters of the counties of Jasper and Clarke could not see it to their advantage, and refused to be taxed a very small sum, and thus they lost the prize of a great railroad. This opportunity lost to them is never in all probability to offer again. They are behind the counties who have railroads.

This is a great railroad age, and yet there are some who complain that the roads were allowed to come into the country, saying that they did better in the good old days of long time ago, before they were introduced. This is an erroneous impression entertained by persons usually denominated "constitutional grumblers." There cannot be too many railroads for the convenience and benefit of the people. There can be too many for the benefit of the companies operating them.

If the people will do their duty and make something to send to market, the great thoroughfares of the country will carry them cheaper than the same things will reach the same market by the old conveyance. If the Legislatures of our State would guard the granting of too many charters to companies for the building of roads, and the State Railroad Commissioners would see that the people are not imposed on with exhorbitant rates of freight, but so as a fair profit may be made on the investment and great responsibility and loss many times attending the operation of roads, it would be an exercise of the law-making powers in the right direction.

All property near a railroad is enhanced by being

in close proximity to it. More people move to a county where they are in operation. With such a state of things, where population is larger and property more valuable and greater quantities of it, taxes are reduced. The road after a time becomes a large taxpayer. All classes of society are improved, if the people who live on the road will take the advantage of the situation and use the benefits offered, to their profit. It is all in the hands of the people who live on the road, to make the country good or bad, prosperous or insolvent—all owing to the thrift, management and economy.

The advent of steam into the United States, as applied to machinery, which was in the years of 1807 and 1808, may be considered as the commencement of great prosperity for our country. After a period of about thirty-six years the electric telegraph was brought in; at a still later date the telephone and electric lights, and other uses to which electricity has been applied as a motive power. The use of steam as applied to machinery as a great motor has probably reached near the height of its ability and usefulness. But the use of electricity is as yet in its infancy, and wonderful events may be looked for, and to follow in rapid succession those already in operation. Electricity is now produced at comparatively large cost when the means considered in its production is the consumption of coal to move the dynamos; yet this is considered cheaper to be used for all purposes now practiced than steam or gas.

In the near future the production of electricity by great water powers of our country will be utilized and the great falls of water in various portions of the United States will be brought into requisition to save the consumption of coal and produce cheaper and in greater quantities the coming motive power.

Our railroad, first called the Southern, and chartered among the first roads of the United States, was operated by that name, until after the war; when it was again changed to suit the times and occasion to the Vicksburg and Meridian road, and after that to the Alabama and Vicksburg road. These changes have come very appropriately, as the road has extended its connections, and enlarged its sphere of operations.

This road has had many changes, has been diverted long since from the original owners, and twice placed in the hands of receivers. It is a very useful road, running as it does from east to west, almost centrally across the State from Meridian to Vicksburg, one hundred and forty miles. It carries probably the largest passenger traffic in the State, and a heavy local freight. It carries heavy through freights to other States, and enjoys an immense transfer of coal from the coal fields of Alabama, which product is finding its way to all the adjoining States needing it.

The road running east from Vicksburg, enters Newton county at the town of Lake, a portion of which is in this county, the other in Scott, runs almost due east a distance of twenty-six miles, through the southern portion of the county—the south line of the county being about eight miles from the railroad.

After the Southern railroad concluded to extend the line through the State, Congress made a grant of land in 1855, giving the road along the line the alternate even sections of public land for a certain distance, probably five miles on each side of the road. It was found that there were not a sufficient number of vacant section as near as five miles, and the grant was extended to fifteen miles on each side of the road until a sufficient amount could be obtained. The original number of acres of land granted by Congress in New-

HISTORY OF NEWTON COUNTY. 73

ton county, was 34,240. Of this amount 12,880 acres still remain unsold.

When this grant was made by Congress it was stipulated that all government troops should be transported free. The road was not completed before the Confederate States government was using this as a very important line for the transportation of troops, and continued to do so for the whole time of the war. Doubtless the value of the grant to the railroads of all the lands in the State was nearly met in the four years war between the States.

This road commenced to pay taxes on the land in Newton county in 1876—a little over twenty years after the grant was made. After this the State imposed a privilege tax for the running of the road through the State, and also an advalorem tax on other railroad property in the State. It is now understood that this road pays one hundred dollars per mile. This would include the eighty dollars advalorem tax, and twenty dollars per mile privilege tax. The amount collected by the sheriff of Newton county is $2,500. This proves the road to be one of the largest tax payers in the county, as well as being the great convenience and civilizer spoken of in preceding pages.

The railroads of the country and the people should be on the best of terms. They exist, or should do so, as a mutual benefit. The road should charge such tariff rates of freight as will be compensating to the owner. The managers should be frugal and careful in the operation of the road so as not to pay too much for the operation of its line and not be forced to charge its patrons what would be considered excessive rates of transportation. By such mutual intercourse and concession, one to the other, there will be a harmony and general good feeling that will redound to the welfare of all. The people want the road. The road wants the people. We cannot do without each other. Counties without the road would be pleased to have it transferred to them.

In connection with the railroad the county has two lines of telegraph; one running parallel with and on the line of railroad. This is the Western Union, a powerful and wealthy corporation, having lines all over the Union, and cable connections with Europe. The other is the Postal Telegraph, a line running about the same distance through our county as the Western Union, and on the public roads of the county. This corporation is also very wealthy and influential, having two cable connections and all the necessary facilities for doing a large business. These telegraph companies also pay a tax to the county and towns of the county, amounting to a considerable sum. With all these conveniences, few inland counties in the State are better equipped for doing business than Newton county.

This road through the county was completed and made the connection on the east side of Chunkey in June, 1861. The stage ran from Enterprise to Newton from September or October of 1860, until June of 1861. Newton was for a time the terminus and a great number of passengers came through on this route.

CHAPTER X.

1860—War Spirit—Great Excitement on the Subject of Secession—Newton County Patriotic and to the Front—Volunteer Companies—Patriotic Men and Women of the County—First Military Company to Leave the County—Military Display when it Left the Town of Newton—Supposed Number of Men Enlisted for the Service During the War.

Mention has been made of the rapid strides in the way of wealth and population, made in the county from 1855 to 1860. New ideas, new improvements, new citizens with their patronage of schools and churches, have diffused life and vigor into the masses. Many things done in this way to further prompt other and greater improvements. In point of wealth and political influence and the intelligence of its people, the county by this time has fully gained recognition for a place of prominence in the State and can no more be called "one of the cow counties of east Mississippi."

In the year 1860, the people in this county, as in every county of the State, had fully realized their political situation. After the November election of that year in which Mr. Lincoln was elected President of the United States, the excitement ran to fever heat. There were quite a number of the voters of the county, as in every other county in the State, that were "Union men." Most of them belonged to the old Whig party, and were very conservative in their views on the subject of secession. They were disposed to try the Republican administration and wait for an "overt act," or to demand the rights which the South claimed and remain in the Union. There were some Democrats who were for the Union. But the prevailing sentiment was for secession; some for secession *per se ;* some would qualify somewhat like the Whigs by asking further guarantees from Congress. But the majority in the county believed that the election of Mr. Lincoln to the office of President was a sufficient cause for Mississippi to withdraw from the Union; that the election of a Freesoiler meant danger to the property of the Southern slave owner, and that it was not only expedient, but the duty of the State to withdraw from the the Union.

Very great excitement on these political topics and public questions now prevailed. There was much public discussion at public places and at the courthouse in the fall of 1860 and the spring of 1861 by men who believed strongly in the doctrine of secession. The people were aroused, and a majority of them were convinced of the necessity of an immediate withdrawal of the State from the Union.

At the election held in the county to send delegates to the State secession convention—which was held in Jackson on the 7th day of January, 1861, and the ordinance of secession of the State of Mississippi from the Federal Union was adopted on the 9th day of the same month and year—Dr. M. M. Keith and G. T. Flint, afterwards Captain of the Pinckney Guards, and Colonel of the Eighth Mississippi Regiment, were candidates. Dr. Keith was elected by a handsome majority. Immediately after the withdrawal of the State, every county—and Newton was not behind—made preparations to resist the enemy.

Everything now pointed to war. The people were very much divided as to the supposed length of the war—some claiming that as soon as the South showed resistance, she would be allowed to go in peace; others claiming that it was necessary to secede to get our rights, and then go back into the Union; while others "swore eternal vengeance" against the whole yankee nation, and wanted the Union divided in fifteen minutes, with no possibility of its ever being again united. The war policy to the bitter end found many advocates and willing participants. The slogan of war was sounded. The spirit of resentment was fully aroused. Old men and young men were willing to leave home and sacrifice their interests and their lives in defense of the great question now at issue between the North and South.

When a free people, who are the immediate offspring of Revolutionary sires whose blood and valor had secured the liberty of a people oppressed and wronged—when they thought that their rights were taken away from them; when they felt that every pledge heretofore made had been violated which secured the rights and inherent possession to their property; when they felt that what they had acquired by honest toil and by inheritance was being taken; when they contemplated an invader's foot upon Southern soil; when they realized Northern armies besieging Southern States, every feeling of resentment in the Southern patriot's breast asserted its rights. Every duty to defend the home, the fireside, the Southland, was fully impressed upon the people of the seceding States, and to demand a speedy redress of all grievances—supposed or real—which had been imposed on a minority holding the same rights, and being and feeling equally free with the other and more populous parts of the Government. It was with these feelings of repeated wrongs being thrust upon the South, and with a confidence that these wrongs could be and would be redressed, that the Southern soldier went to battle against great odds.

It is not intended in this brief history of our county, to argue the great questions which then divided the people of the two sections, and which culminated in one of the greatest fratricidal wars of modern times. It is not our purpose to pronounce upon the wisdom or unwisdom of such a course. It is not our wish to tear open wounds that should be allowed to heal, nor to widen the breach between the sections which are now at peace, and should remain so. Yet it is right to let the youth of the county know what part their fathers took in this great struggle, and to commend them for what they then thought was their right and their duty. Southern valor, heroism and sacrifice can not be too highly spoken of. What was true of the South was true of Mississippi soldiers, was true of her counties; our own county of Newton was not an exception, and was early to the front.

Great anxiety was felt in reference to going into the army. Many thought unless they applied early the number required would be filled, and that there would be no chance for them to participate. The call for sixty days troops was soon answered. The whole county was in great excitement and the question was who would be allowed the first honor of being Confederate soldiers. Aside from the demonstrations of the men of the county, the women were equally patriotic and went heartily to work with their own hands in preparing uniforms for the soldiers. Volunteer companies were now in order in the county, and the call for them was answered as fast as requisitions were made. There was nothing so attractive as the young volunteer donning his Confederate uniform, meeting his comrades in arms assembling on the parade ground, going through the various evolutions and manual of arms. These instructions were usually from an inexperienced drill-officer, a young captain or lieutenant, who had been chosen and was trying to impress the company with the imperfect knowledge he had of military tactics. It was all done with such a unanimity of feeling, and with such cheerful acceptance, that no one complained or offered a criticism.

These companies constantly received the congratulations and encouragement of their friends and especially the ladies. Every honor that a patriotic people could bestow upon the young soldiers of Newton county was done cheerfully and lavishly. The restless war spirit of all classes had found congenial employment in taking up arms and preparing the soldiers for the approaching bloody conflict.

The call of Mr. Lincoln for 75,000 troops with which to subdue the South had cemented all political parties. The Whig and Democrat, the union and disunion men, all now agreed that the "overt act" had been committed—that time for resistance was at hand. Those who were opposed to secession were now forward among those to offer their services to go to the army. All, all now agreed that the time had come to throw off the yoke of Northern oppression and become a free and independent people in a Southern Confederacy— which were the slave-holding States. There was no trouble to make up a company then, and more men offered their services than could be accepted.

THE FIRST MILITARY COMPANY TO LEAVE THE COUNTY.

The first military company to leave the county was known as the Newton Rifles, commanded by Montgomery Carleton. Every preparation was made for its organization and equipment. It was made up from various parts of the county, though organized at Decatur, where Capt. Carleton lived. The people all over the county were interested in the movement. A spirit of patriotism never known before was rife among the people; the old and young, male and female, vied with other as to who should show the greatest solicitude in accomplishing their successful equipment, and give encouragement to the movement. Some of the best men of the county were in this company. Capt. Carleton was the oldest man in the company, by far, being at the time about fifty-five years old. He then looked a "veteran," and to behold him now, heading and commanding the first company from his county, the flower and manhood of his section, to lead to battle this invincible body of young men, was the pride of his maturer life, the desire of this brave and ambitious man. Dr. M. H. Watkins was first lieutenant, John A. Keith was second lieutenant, and A. J. Smith was third lieutenant.

On the 13th day of May, 1861, the company came to the town of Newton to take the cars to their new field of active operations. This was not immediately to the "front," but were put in camp of instruction at Union City, Tenn., (after spending a short time at Corinth, Miss.) After becoming accustomed to the manual of arms, they were attached to the 13th Mississippi regiment, that was commanded by the brave and lamented Col. Wm. Barksdale, and were sent immediately to Virginia and were favored with the great privilege of participating in the wonderful victory of the first Manassas battle, on the 21st of July, 1861.

It was a bright May day that the Newton Rifles left the town of Newton. The gay uniforms of the young soldiers and officers; the excitement incident thereto, being the first military company to leave the county; everybody was pleased, cheered and admired the scene. Ladies gathered from the surrounding country, not only from Newton but Jasper county, to do honor to the gallant Newton County Rifles.

The soul-inspiring strains of martial music from fife and drum were heard while the new company marched in line, obeying the quick commands of their officers. The fife on that day was played by Uncle Steve McMullen, an old colored Georgian. He was old then. He is still living and must be almost a centenarian. Music is a wonderful contingent in battle. Military men well know its value. It has its effect— to soothe, to inspire, and to provoke to deeds of daring. Many have been the soldiers who, under these same inspiring strains of martial music, have charged the enemy's breastworks, caring not for the missles of death flying thick and fast about them; who, with intrepid feet, fearless heart, strong hand, steady aim, have charged with fixed bayonets, the thundering cannon and apparently impregnable earthworks, have secured a victory amidst carnage and death, that would not have been done in the absence of this stimulant.

The time approached for them to take the train. Judge Watts addressed the company with great feeling, encouraging them and speaking good words to these young men, many of them leaving home for the first time. Other speakers addressed them, and upon the whole it was one of the most imposing scenes that has ever been witnessed in the county. Finally the train came, and then followed a general hand-shaking and bidding good-bye, with fathers and mothers, sisters and sweethearts. All bade a final farewell, and then departed the first military company from Newton county.

Then followed in rapid succession the raising of other companies until thirteen companies, including several companies of State militia, went from this county. The number of men usually ran up to about 100 to the company. Yet there were some having over that number and they were recruited from time to time, and it is computed that each company had from first to last, 120 men, which would make 1560 men furnished by the county. It is presumed that some of these men came from other counties, but Newton county furnished a sufficient number of soldiers for other counties to make up for as many as were furnished her companies from other counties. The 1560 men taken from a population of 9560, and about one-third of these were negroes, shows that this county made as good an appropriation of men as any county in the State.

CHAPTER XI.

VARIOUS MILITARY COMPANIES TO LEAVE THE COUNTY—NAMES OF THE DIFFERENT OFFICERS COMMANDING EACH COMPANY—NUMBER OF SOLDIERS SUPPOSED TO HAVE LOST THEIR LIVES FROM THESE DIFFERENT COMPANIES.

It is intended in this chapter to give as far as possible some information as to who were engaged in the late war between the States. In doing this it is impossible to get all the information wanted, as the rosters of the various companies are not to be had ; except from the first company, which left the county there is no written record. After the fall of Vicksburg, Col. J. L. Pówer, now one of the editors of the *Clarion-Ledger*, was commissioned Superintendent of Army Records for Mississippi, under Acts of Congress and of the State, his duty being to compile the best records possible, of the troops from this State, as well as to assist in the collection of amounts due deceased soldiers. The records that he succeeded in completing, shows the entire enrollment of each company, the original officers, and changes by promotion, casualties, etc., the battles in which each company partipated and the casualties occurring therein.

There was only one company from Newton county seen by Col. Power. That was the Newton Rifles, called in the Regiment, Co. E., (in the first of the war, Co. D.,) 13th Mississippi Regiment. This statement made out by Col. Power, with the assistance of Thos. Keith, Thos. Shockley and M. R. Watkins, all belonging to that company, and going through the war, and all now living, will be of interest to those who belonged to that command, and also to their friends.

CAPT. CARLETON'S COMPANY.

This company, the first in Newton county, was organized at Decatur, and called the Newton Rifles. The organization was completed as early as the first of March, 1861, Montgomery Carleton being the Captain; was mustered into service on the 9th of March, same year, by Capt. Yerger. On the 13th May following it left the town of Newton for Corinth, Miss., and entered the 13th Mississippi regiment of infantry, commanded by Col. William Barksdale. From there they were ordered into camp of instruction at Union City, Tenn., and there remained six weeks; from there to Jackson, Tenn., where they remained but one day, and were ordered to Virginia, where they participated in the first Manassas battle, on the 21st of July, 1861. The officers were: Montgomery Carleton, Captain; 1st Lieutenant, Dr. M. H. Watkins; 2d Lieutenant, John A. Keith; 3d Lieutenant, A. J. Smith; 1st Sergeant, Robert M. Patterson; 2d Sergeant, Jacob Dansby; 3d Sergeant, A. F. Clarke; 4th Sergeant, John A. Clarke; 5th Sergeant, James M. Stephens; 1st Corporal, John Allen; 2d Corporal, Job Taylor; 3d Corporal, B. F. Quattlebaum; 4th Corporal, Jourdan Oakley. When the 13th Mississippi Regiment was re-organized, 26th April, 1862, Captain Carleton was left out, and came home and organized another company, and Thomas W. Thurman, a lawyer from Decatur, was chosen captain. George W. Williams succeeded as first lieutenant, and Wm. C. Goodwin as second lientenant; A. F. Clarke, as third lieutenant. Wm. C. Goodwin resigned as second lieutenant, August, 1863, and A. F. Clarke took his place. George W. Williams resigned the place of first lieutenant, and A. F. Clarke, by promotion, took his place, and M. R. Watkins took the position of second lieutenant. Captain Thurman lost a leg at Fredericksburg, and was for a time retired, but was nomin.ally the captain of the company. In the absence of the captain, the first lieutenant, Clarke, commanded the company, and after his capture, the command devolved upon lieutenant M. R. Watkins. This company was in many engagements, and probably lost as many men as any company from Newton county.

The number of engagements are as follows: First Manassas, July 21st, 1861; Leesburg, Garrett's Farm, Savage Station, Malvern Hill, Maryland Heights, Sharpsburg, second Fredricksburg, second day at Gettysburg, third day at Gettysburg, Chickamauga, Knoxville, November 16th, 1864; Knoxville, November 29th, 1864; Wilderness, Spottsylvania, Horse-shoe, May 12th, 1864; Hanover Junction, Cold Harbor, June 3, 1864; Cold Harbor, June 5th, 1864; Petersburg, June 21st; Petersburg, June 22d; Charlestown, Berryville, Va., Rock Fish Gap, Cedar Run. These battles were up to the first of March, 1865. From that time up to a few days before the surrender of General Lee at Appomattox on the 9th of April of same year, was a continuous series of battles and skirmishes with the enemy in defense of the Confederate Capital. A few days before the surrender of General Lee, this company was captured and taken to Washington City, and from thence the officers were taken to Rock Island.

The casualties of this company were seventeen killed and died of wounds, twenty-two died of disease, thirty-five discharged from disability, six discharged from wounds. The total enrollment, from first muster to the surrender, was 139 men.

Mr. M. R. Watkins, who made out the roster from which this information is taken, added the following interesting statement, which indicates the spirit that prompted these self-sacrificing soldiers, and how uncomplainingly they bore the hardships and dangers of the battle-field:

"The Newton Rifles, the first company formed in Newton county, was organized at Decatur March 1st, 1861; Montgomery Carleton, captain, being elected on March 9th, 1861. The company was mustered into State service by Captain Yerger. On the 13th of May following, it left Newton county for Corinth, at which place it entered the organization of the Thirteenth Regiment on the 15th of May, William Barksdale, colonel. From there we were ordered to Union City, Tenn., and remained six weeks; from there to Jackson, Tenn., where we remained but one day, and received orders to go to the scene of action at Manassas plains, where we arrived just in time to participate in the first of the many bloody battles in which the veterans of Lee's Army of Northern Virginia distinguished themselves and shed lustre on the cause. This company was composed of young men, who responded with alacrity to the first call of their beloved country to meet and repel the invaders of their homes and liberties. Many of our boys, noble heroes, have fallen a willing sacrifice to their country's cause, while others wear the wooden leg or the empty sleeve; but others yet remain, a small remnant of as brave and patriotic an army as ever trod the earth, to avenge the loss of our comrades by emulating their devotion and heroism in a cause that deserves, if it may not achieve, success.

'*Dulce et decorum est pro patria mori*,' is our motto. (It is sweet and glorious to die for one's country.)

M. R. WATKINS,
2d Lieutenant Commanding.

RICHMOND, VA., March 1, 1865."

THE HARPER RESERVES.

The next company reported is Harper Reserves, afterwards Company C., 36th Mississippi Regiment. This report is made by Mr. George P. Clarke, a member of the company. The company went out with ninety men. Captain Partin (who was the doctor who died in 1893 at Decatur), was the first commanding officer. He was succeeded by G. M. Gallaspy, who died at Hickory, March, 1894; 1st Lieutenant, John Watts; 2d Lieutenant, John Dyess. This company was recruited until it had in all 110 men.

The engagements in which this company participated are as follows: Farmington, May 9th, 1862; Iuka, September 19th, 1862; Corinth, October 3d and 4th, 1862; Seige at Vicksburg from May 18th to July 4th, 1863; skirmish at Adairsville, Ga., May 17th, 1864; skirmish at Cass Station, May, 1864; New Hope church, 1864; Latimer House, June, 1864; Kennesaw Mountain, June 27th, 1864; Smyrna church, July 9th, 1865; Atlanta, Ga., July and August, 1864; Lovejoy, Ga., September, 1864; Altoona, Ga., October 7th, 1864; Tilton, Ga., October 9th, 1864; Franklin, November 30th, 1864; Murfreesboro, December, 1864; Nashville, December 15th and 16th, 1864; Spanish Fort, March, 1865.

It will be seen that this company was in nineteen battles and skirmishes, including the seige of Vicksburg; that it lost fourteen killed, fifteen wounded and two missing. These engagements comprise some of the most important battles of the war south of Virginia.

CAPT. REYNOLDS' COMPANY.

Mr. Thos. J. Reynolds, superintendent of education of Newton county, furnishes a report of his company. This company was made up from the eastern and southeastern portions of the county. First Captain, Wiley B. Johnson, of company D, 3d regiment Mississippi volunteer infantry; entered Confederate service in the summer of 1861. W. J. Johnson, captain; W. E. Thomas, 1st Lieutenant; T. J. Reynolds, 2d Lieutenant; A. Gressett, 3d Lieutenant. Capt. Johnson resigned and Lieut. Gressett died during the second year of the war. Then the roster stood: W. E. Thomas, Captain; T. J. Reynolds, 1st Lieutenant; G. W. Johnson, 2d Lieutenant; J. P. Gressett, 3d Lieutenant.

First light engagements of this company were: Pass Christian, Chickasaw Bayou, Baker's Creek and Jackson; then came Resaca, Cartersville, Good Hope Church, Peach Tree Creek, battles around Atlanta, Lovejoy Station — all in Georgia — Decatur, Ala.; Columbia, Tenn.; Franklin and Nashville, Tenn., making a total of fourteen battles. Total enrollment, 145 rank and file; killed in battle, 20; wounded and not killed, 18; died of disease, 29. He closes by saying there are probably not exceeding twenty members of the company now living.

Wm. M. Lewis, the present treasurer of the county of Newton, has kindly furnished the necessary information of three companies from Newton county. Mr. Lewis was too young at the time to be a soldier, but has succeeded in getting up good information in regard to the part taken by these three companies and which is cheerfully transferred to these pages. The companies referred to are the Pinkney Guards, Tatum's Infantry, of 36th Mississippi, and Rayborn's Cavalry company. Mr. Lewis writes:

THE PINKNEY GUARDS, CO. B.,

"Was a volunteer infantry company, and was organized in May, 1861; composed of citizens of Stamper and Union, with Capt. G. F. Flint as commanding officer. They were mustered into service by Capt. J. M. Jayne, of Brandon, at Union, on the 21st day of August, 1861; ordered to Enterprise under Gen. John W. O'Farral. In forming the 8th Mississippi Regiment Capt. Flint was elected Colonel. They were drilled in this camp of instruction a month or more as State troops, then mustered into Confederate service and ordered to Pensacola, where the term of enlistment expired (twelve months).

The first roster stood after the regiment was formed: P. P. Austin, Captain; B. B. Martin, 1st Lieutenant; J. P. Maxey, 2d Lieutenant; A. Red, 3d Lieutenant; J. F. Kennedy, Orderly Sergeant; R. W. Berton, 2d Sergeant; R. G. Cleavland, 3d Sergeant; G. W. Smith, 4th Sergeant, and T. J. Red, 5th Sergeant; W. G. Peteet, 1st Corporal; M. W. Stamper, 2d Corporal; Tobe Smith, 3d Corporal; A. H. Corley, 4th Corporal; W. J. Robuck, Ensign.

The regiment was then enlisted for the war and the following changes were made: Lieutenants Martin and Red came home, and corporals Stamper and Smith were elected as lieutenants. After the evacuation of Pensacola the regiment went into the Army of Tennessee and participated in all of its successes and reverses until the close of the war, surrendering in North Carolina, losing about twenty per cent. in killed and about twenty-five per cent. missing and by deaths from sickness. The company numbered at first 120, and was recruited from time to time with 30, making a total of 150."

CAPT. TATUM'S COMPANY.

He writes of Tatum's company of volunteer infantry:

"The company was organized at Union in March, 1863; numbered 113 men; composed of citizens from Newton and Neshoba counties, about one-half from each. Tatum brought 25 to 30 men from Beech Springs neighborhood, and joining Dr. Lewis and J. B. Fulton, at Union, making a good company of 113. In the organization Tatum was elected Captain; Lit Thornton, 1st Lieutenant; W. M. Walton, 2d Lieutenant, and John Rayburn, 3d Lieutenant; Charles Holland, Orderly Sergeant. The company went to Meridian and was organized into a regiment about the 12th of March, 1862, with E. Brown, as Colonel. He was from Copiah county. This regiment was accepted as twelve months troops and was ordered to Corinth before the Shiloh fight, at which place the regiment enlisted for the war.

The engagements of the company were at Iuka, Corinth, Abbeville and Coffeeville, under General Price, of Missouri; Snyder's Bluff, under General Hebert; Vicksburg seige under General Pemberton; all the Georgia campaign from Adairsville to Atlanta, under General J. E. Johnson; all around Atlanta and at Franklin and Nashville, under General Hood, and at Blakeley under General Maury. After the death of several officers in command, F. L. Thompson, of Union, Adjutant of the 36th Regiment, was petitioned for by the company to General Hebert to have him appointed as captain of the company. Capt. Thompson, a very gallant and efficient officer, was killed at Nashville, and Lieut. Smith succeeded to the command of the company.

This company was surrendered at Blakely, Ala., 9th April, 1865, during one of the hottest contests that it had met in any engagement during the war. About one-third of the company were killed and about the same number died of disease. This was considered a hard fighting company. The regiment was known as "The Bloody Thirty Sixth." Dr. William Lewis, now living at Union, went out, first as company doctor, and surrendered at Blakely as assistant surgeon.

The same writer says of

RAYBORN'S CAVALRY COMPANY:

"Capt. John Rayborn, a brave and dashing man, was a member of Company D., 36th Mississippi Regiment. It will be recollected in the mention made of Rayborn as a member of Capt. Tatum's company, that he was wounded early in the Corinth fight. He was at home recovering from his wounds, and to meet an emergency for defense of the State, he raised a company of cavalry, composed of the men whose term of enlistment for twelve months had expired and of the young men who were as yet too young to enter military service. Of this material he made up his company, and the first engagement that they were in was at Jackson, Miss.

"When Gen. Sherman's army came through Newton county, Capt. Rayborn's little band of thirty or forty men and boys, with inferior arms, did excellent service as scouts, preventing straggling and foraging parties from covering too large a space from the main army.

From Decatur to Union was nearly all a battle

ground, and near Union, late in the afternoon, Capt. Rayborn, by too reckless exposure of himself, was killed. None braver went down. Lieutenant Martin succeeded him in command of the company, which was subsequently increased to 100 men, and at Columbus, Miss., an organization was made and the company passed into regular service, again meeting and surrendering to their old combatant, Gen. Sherman, at Greensboro, North Carolina. Officers: John Rayborn, Captain; B. B. Martin, 1st Lieutenant; Thos. Gardner, 2d Lieutenant.

COMPANY I., 36TH REGIMENT.

Was formed near Hickory, in Newton county, and information is furnished by Mr. J. A. Waul, who was a lieutenant in the company. He says the number of men was 113. R. D. Ogletree was the Captain; Dr. G. E. Longmire, 1st Lieutenant; A. W. Whitman, 2d Lieutenant; J. A. Wade, 3d Lieutenant. This company was in the memorable "Bloody Thirty-Sixth" and saw the same severe service and hard fighting that was participated in by the other companies of the regiment.

The engagements of this company were: The battles of Iuka, Corinth, Abbeville and Coffeeville, under General Price of Missouri; Snyder's Bluff, under General Hebert; Vicksburg seige, under General Pemberton; all the Georgia campaign, from Adairsville to Atlanta, under General Johnston; all around Atlanta and at Franklin and Nashville, under General Hood; at Blakely, in April of 1865, one of the severest battles of the war to them, under General Maury. The number of men killed, 14; died from sickness, 20. Nearly the whole company received wounds of more or less severity.

HISTORY OF NEWTON COUNTY.

THE NEWTON HORNETS.

Mr. Eugene Carleton, of Decatur, who has fine memory, and was well in position to know, sends the following information of his company, which is very thankfully received. He writes:

"The Newton Hornets, Company D, 39th Mississippi Regiment, Colonel W. B. Shelby, was raised at Decatur, Miss., but was composed of citizens from all parts of the county; was mustered into service about the first of May, 1862. They went out 113 strong; about thirty joined afterwards. The company went out with Dr. J. C. McElroy as captain; James A. Ware, D. M. Bradham, M. J. L. Hoye, lieutenants. McElroy and Ware resigned. Bradham was then captain. Robert Wells and Charley Chaney were elected to fill their places. Bradham died and Wells resigned. James W. Hardy and Wm. J. Johnson were then elected lieutenants. James T. Thorne was elected in Hardy's place, but was never commissioned. Eugene Carleton was then made brevet-lieutenant, and commanded the company until it reached Atlanta; then he was appointed assistant adjutant of regiment, and Lieut. Jenney, a Missourian, appointed to command. George Wise was elected a lieutenant, and served until after the battle of Nashville. Before the 36th Regiment was ordered to Georgia under General Johnston, it had gone through the seige at Port Hudson of seven weeks. All the officers of Company D. were sent to Johnson's Island, and the men paroled and sent to camps at Enterprise, and on being exchanged were sent to Georgia."

The engagements of this company were: Skirmish at Abbeville; Corinth, October, 1862; the seige at Port Hudson of seven weeks; were in all the skirmishes and battles from Adairsville to Lovejoy Station (except the two heavy charges made by Hood before Atlanta) ; Good Hope Church ; Kennesaw Mountain ; the battles of Atlanta ; those before Tilton and Decatur ; battles of Franklin ; second battle of Murfreesboro, Tenn ; battle at Nashville, when Lieutenant Wise was in some way lost, never to be heard from again. The regiment was then captured at Blakely, Ala., April 16, 1865. There were 13 killed and died of wounds ; 32 died of disease during the war, and 27 since. The latest information shows 57 now living.

COMPANY A., FIFTH REGIMENT STATE TROOPS.

Judge Bolton kindly furnishes the information of Company A, 5th Regiment of State troops, which was was brought into service in August, 1862. This company belonged to what was called the State troops, and no man under the age of thirty-five years was admitted. Montgomery Carleton was again chosen captain; John Graham, 1st Lieutenant; Andrew Gordon, 2d Lieutenant; Joel Loper, 3d Lieutenant. Gordon was soon discharged and J. L. Bolton was elected 2d Lieutenant. The company was assigned to the 5th Regiment, State troops, of which H. C. Robinson, of Kemper county, was Colonel; Metts, of Winston, Lieutenant-Colonel; Randall, of Lauderdale, Major. Our General was Harris, of Columbus, Miss. The company was originally composed 70 men, but by process of discharge and recruit, 120 men were connected with it. In May, 1863, we were ordered to Vicksburg, and entered that town on the last train that went in before its investment. Captain Carleton and Lieutenant Graham, on account of sickness, did not go to Vicksburg, and the command devolved upon Lieutenant Bolton while there. We were in no regular engagement. I remember only four men dying

HISTORY OF NEWTON COUNTY.   95

while in service—Halford, Fountain, Simmons and Yager. We were in service eleven months, all told."

COMPANY D., FIRST MISSISSIPPI CAVALRY.

Wm. M. Lewis again furnishes the information of Company D., 1st Mississippi Cavalry:

The company was organized at Union, one hundred strong. The officers were A. B. Hunter, captain; — Williams, first lieutenant; James Moore, second lieutenant; James Cooksey, third lieutenant; Henry Chaney, orderly sergeant. First Brigadier-General, Brandon. General engagements were at Harrisburg and Oxford; about twenty-five per cent. loss from all sources; general services, scouting; surrendered at Columbus to Gen. Canby.

COMPANY B., SECOND MISSISSIPPI CAVALRY.

Mr. C. H. Doolittle, who was a member of this company, and for a time the color-bearer, of the regiment, and Mr. I. W. Walker, now a citizen of Newton, and also a member of the company, furnish some valuable information.

Mr. Doolitle writes:

"The company was known as Perry's company; was company B. of the fourth, but afterwards, the second Mississippi cavalry. J. J. Perry was captain from the organization, April, 1862, until December, 1863, when he was promoted to major. M. E. Blelack, who was first lieutenant, became captain of the company. The roster now stood: M. E. Blelack, captain; Dan'l Johnson, H. W. Todd, A. J. Smith, lieutenants. Johnson resigned and Joseph Jackson was elected as one of the lieutenants. This company, when it went out, had one hundred and eight men, and was recruited from time to time; also, some discharged. The second Mississippi cavalry served under Van Dorn, Forrest, and S. D. Lee. It was a part of Gen. Frank Armstrong's brigade, and was in eight or ten regular engagements, besides numerous skirmishes. Company B. did the greater part of the skirmishing for the regiment, as it had what was considered the best officers. Mr. Walker says: "The first engagement of this company was at Duck Hill; then at Rome, Georgia; then all through the Georgia campaign; then to Franklin and Nashville, and Columbia, Tenn.; and thence back to Alabama; surrendered at Selma. The company lost six killed, twelve or fifteen wounded."

This company stands very prominent among those who went to the army from Newton county. Capt. M. E. Blelack, who was a very large and fleshy man, looked to be unable for active service, but be it said to his honor that he was one of the bravest and most efficient officers that ever went from the county. He could have staid at home, but he preferred to go and risk his life for the good of the Southern cause.

FIRST MISSISSIPPI CHOCTAW BATTALION.

This battalion of Choctaw Indians, was made up from the surrounding counties of Neshoba, Jasper, Scott, and probably some others having Indians in them, Newton furnishing her quota, about one-third, or one company. This battalion had three companies of about sixty men each; contained one hundred and eighty men. They were camped at Newton and drilled for service. J. W. Price was major of the battalion; B. F. Duckworth was captain of the Newton company; C. H. Doolittle was first lieutenant; Wm. Robinson, second lieutenant. This battalion was sent to Camp Moore, near Tangipaho, La., where they were being instructed. They were in close proximity with the enemy, and they were suddenly surrounded and taken prisoners before they had ever seen any service. Most of the officers, who were white men, escaped. They were taken to New Orleans and Mr. Wm. Robinson, who was in command of the Newton company, captured with the Indians, says the men were separated from the officers, and nothing is known of what became of the Indians. Some suppose they were sent to the Choctaw Nation and have never returned.

Mr. C. H. Doolittle, who was the 1st Lieutenant of this company, was first a member of the Newton Rifles, the first company to leave Newton county, was detailed from the 13th Mississippi Regiment, then in Virginia, to come and join the Choctaw Battalion. He states that the day of the capture he and some others had gone to search for some of the Indians who had left the battalion with the intention of permanently leaving it and consequently escaped capture. There was not enough of the Choctaws left to be of any service, and Mr. Doolittle reported to Gen. Johnston at Morton, Miss., who advised him to join some other company, and then he joined the 2d Mississippi Cavalry, becoming a member of Capt. Blelack's company. Thus he was a member of three companies during the war.

COMPANY I, 46TH MISSISSIPPI REGIMENT OF INFANTRY.

Dr. Jubal Watts, of Harpersville, Miss., kindly furnishes the information in connection with the above company. Says it was organized about the last of April, 1862, at Union, Newton county, though there were a few from Neshoba and Scott counties in the company. Some few joined at Meridian, belonging to Lauderdale county. The commanding officers were: Dr. W. J. Hoye, Captain; B. F. Tingle, 1st Lieutenant;

J. M. R. Adams, 2d Lieutenant; T. R. Gardner, Jr., 3d Lieutenant. The company joined the 6th Mississippi Battalion, making the 9th company in the battalion—Lieut.-Col. J. W. Balfour commanding. July 4, 1862, was ordered to Vicksburg to garrison the town. After the fall of Fort Donelson the 6th Mississippi Battalion was organized into a regiment by the addition of Capt. Durham's company, of Kemper county. This regiment was the 46th Mississippi, commanded by captain—afterwards General—C. W. Sears. This regiment was in the seige of Vicksburg. Sergeant Smith was killed at Port Gibson; several others wounded. During the seige of Vicksburg three were killed by cannon balls, and several by smaller shot. The greater part of company I died of camp fever and pneumonia in camp and hospital.

This company had originally 80 men, the greater part from Newton county. Capt Hoye resigned in June, 1862; Lieutenant Tingle was promoted to his place; Lieutenant Adams died at his home of fever contracted in camp; Lieutenant Gardner resigned and joined a cavalry company; Captain Tingle resigned in spring of 1863, and J. Watts was promoted to captain; T. Burgess, 1st Lieutenant; S. R. Martin, 2d Lieutenant; T. H. Creel, 3d Lieutenant. J. Watts resigned after the fall of Vicksburg.

SIXTY-DAY TROOPS.

T. B. McCune, Esq., furnishes very good information of Capt. Samuel Hollingsworth's sixty-day troops. He writes, that directly after the Belmont fight, in 1861, there was a call by the Governor of this State for sixty-days troops to go to defend Columbus, Ky.

The company was organized at Decatur, and Samuel Hollingsworth elected Captain; Archey Chaney, 1st

HISTORY OF NEWTON COUNTY.   99

Lieutenant; Thos. B. McCune, 2d Lieutenant; D. W. Johnson, 3d Lieutenant. The company went to Grenada, Miss., and was organized into 2d regiment. Roselle was elected colonel. There were three regiments under General J. L. Alcorn, and repaired at once to Columbus, Ky. The weather was intensely cold, and persons not accustomed to camp life, from a mild climate like Mississippi, were very much distressed with the great change. The troops took measles, and many died. Our captain was more thoughtful of his company, and shipped them to Jackson, Tenn., as there was no fighting to be done, and we stayed there until our time was out; so ended the sixty-days troops from Newton county, as we came home.

This company was composed of many men who went into other companies from Newton county, and all who did of course are numbered in other companies. This company makes fourteen that went into service from Newton county. The Indian company did no service and was a loss to the county, as they were captured before doing any service and did not return to the county.

There are twelve companies that were organized and served from the time of their organization until they surrendered to the enemy, or until the close of the war. The twelve companies would easily make 1,500 men that were taken from the county, and considering the population of the county in 1860—of less than 10,000, and one third of them negroes—makes an excellent showing for the county. There were quite a number of men in Newton county companies from other counties, but it may also be said that there was quite a number of men from Newton county in companies from other counties, making it very nearly equal. Newton county, in this like all other things for the good of the State and nation, did her best.

CHAPTER XII.

PATRIOTIC WOMEN DURING THE WAR—THEIR WORK AT HOME—TO HELP SUPPORT THE ARMY AND MAKE THE CROPS—ASSISTING TO CLOTHE THE SOLDIERS—THEIR ATTENTION TO SICK AND WOUNDED—TRIBUTE BY MAJ. J. J. HOOD TO THE WOMEN OF THE SOUTH.

THE volunteering of the soldiers was now nearly over. By the end of the year 1862 most of the companies had been formed and had gone into regular service. The people saw, after the fall of Fort Donelson and other places, that the war in all its severity and alarming proportions was upon us. No one could tell about the length of time it would last, though everything pointed to a prolonged struggle. A very grave problem now confronted the people, and that was the support of the army in the field. It now devolved upon the few, comparatively speaking, left at home to make the supplies to feed the soldiers, and means must also be devised to clothe and shoe them. Every man and woman left at home now went to work to make something to live upon and support the army.

After the first battle at Manassas, on the 21st of July, 1861, which was a victory for the South, the people became intensely interested, and it was no trouble to get recruits for the army. Meanwhile the North, seeing they had a greater and more warlike adversary to combat than they expected, made additional calls for troops, and by the last of the year 1862, most of the volunteer companies had gone from this county.

The work of making something to feed the Southern army was now a matter of the greatest concern. Cut off by a strong blockade by the United States Government, it was impossible to obtain all the supplies that had heretofore been brought to Southern ports by foreign vessels. Many vessels ran this blockade from the Confederate side, and the munitions of war, medicine, not manufactured in the South, also many articles of food and clothing, passed through the same channel, and were landed in our ports, and quite an amount of cotton and tobacco, of which the South had plenty, was sent out in return for these goods, and thus it was that a pretty lively and uncertain commerce was kept up between the Confederate States and the outside world. Cotton ran to fabulous prices, and is quoted by a cotton price-current giving the extreme prices paid from 1862 to 1865—from 38 cents to $1.90 per pound. The latter price was only spasmodic and may have had much to do with the depreciated currency. But it is safe to say that cotton averaged through the years designated above, from 50 to 60 cents. All other goods were correspondingly high In this crisis many risks were run and many losses sustained in running the gauntlet of the Northern gunboats stationed at every Southern harbor. The want of the luxuries of life which our people had so long enjoyed, sharpened their wits and doubled their energies to supply at home what they had usually purchased abroad.

The county had the negroes and the older men and boys left. At this time the conscript law was in force requiring all between certain ages to report to headquarters for military instruction.

It was soon found that the supply of salt was very

short in the country. As fast as possible the salt was brought from the cities having any, and then the people resorted to various places where salt was found by digging wells, some in this State probably near West Point, and also in Alabama, on the Bigbee river. In some instances the floors of the smoke-houses were dug up, the dirt leached and the water boiled down, thus obtaining some salt in this way for use in saving pork. By using great energy and economy, and by the benefits of running the blockade, the supply of salt was made sufficient.

The farmers of the county at once turned their attention to the raising of grain. In the early settlement of the county wheat had been grown successfully on the fresh lands, and by preparing well and properly fertilizing it was again produced. Lands that had heretofore been planted in cotton, were now put in corn, wheat, rye, oats, tobacco, potatoes, sorghum cane—anything that would serve to feed stock and supply bread-stuffs. From this generous planting of cereals came a large product of pork, beef and other stock, dependent on the use of grain. A country farm with this kind of management had more of the substantials of life upon it than it had before the war commenced.

Our women were not idle in the supply of clothing for the home-folks, and also made largely for the soldiers in the army. For two years before the war closed the Southern soldiers were largely clothed in excellent jeans suits made by the women of the South, from Southern wool and cotton. The younger women had not learned to make cloth; but many of the old mothers of the land had not forgotten how to use the old-time method. The familiar sound of the old wheel was heard; cotton and wool cards, though very hard to obtain, and only through the blockade, were brought

NEWTON COUNTY COURTHOUSE.

into active service. The old country loom, with its sley and thread harness; the old clock reel and old-time winding blades; the old warping bars—everything that had assisted to furnish the Revolutionary soldiers with clothing—was now brought into requisition. Dye-stuffs were extensively procured from the woods; bark of the walnut, chincapin and oak; the sumac berries and the walnut hulls, were all used with good results.

These materials were used in the manufacture and dyeing of the suits so much criticised by the Yankees as butter-nut suits, and black, home-made wool hats, which the Southern prisoners wore. A beautiful black jeans was made by using a dye of logwood and blue-stone; both of these ingredients were contrabands of war and were hard to obtain. There was a splendid gray jeans made, and that was a prevailing color. It could be made so as to dispense with dye-stuffs altogether, by using the black wool from the sheep's back and the white wool from same, and carding together, making a beautiful gray. This black wool could be deepened in color a few shades by using walnut bark or walnut hulls, and set with copperas, and would make a suit very attractive. Then by using material to dye the wool blue, a lighter gray would be obtained, which made good uniforms for officers. Good oak tanned leather, made by the farmers and the country tan-yards, supplied the shoes for the soldiers.

Thus it was that the old men and the women, and boys too young to go to the war made the crops, with the great help of the slaves, who, be it said to their credit, conducted themselves exceedingly well, and did a large work and stayed at home with their owners, with very few exceptions until after the close of the war. This was not all. Many have been the good women whose husbands were in the army, who had no slaves to assist them. The little boys were too small to plow and make a crop. They put their hands to the plow and hoe and made and gathered the stuff, supported the family and helped to sustain the army. Some of these good and industrious women sometimes failed to make support; in that event they were supported by generous farmers or appropriations made by the county to aid them. The Athenian women, it is said, in a great emergency used their beautiful long hair to make rigging for vessels.

"The women of Poland stripped the jewels from their delicate fingers and snowy necks and cast them into the famished treasury of their bleeding country. Our grandmothers—God bless them—having no jewels, stripped their beds of their covers, moulded their pewter spoons into bullets and sent their sons with Washington to fight the battles of the Revolution." A sublimer spectacle still do we see in the Confederate women. They plied their willing hands to the raw material of the country and made warm and comfortable clothing. They devoted themselves to continuous toil in the fields, to make something for themselves and little ones, besides sending their husbands and sons to fight the battles of the Southern cause. Not only were the women active and watchful at home; zealous in the cause of Southern freedom and Southern rights; but when occasion required they were those ever watchful guardians around the sick and dying in every form which presented itself in the great struggle. If it were hospital service, or if it were just after a great battle, these good women could always be seen wending their way to administer substantial aid to the living or Christian comfort to the dying.

In every age of the world, wherever great emergencies are to be met where great sacrifices are to be made, "woman, who was last at the Cross and first at the sepulcher," has been found bearing the burdens of those engaged in the great struggle. Sympathizing with her tears and affection, animating and inspiring with her ever sanguine temperament, encouraging when needed by her smiles of approval, and dying when occasion required it, on the altar of church or State.

TRIBUTE TO THE WOMEN OF THE SOUTH, BY MAJ. J. J. HOOD.

Major Hood, whose trenchant pen has wielded a potent influence in everything pertaining to patriotic impulses and true devotion to the Southern cause, and is particularly facile in his tribute to the women of the South, has kindly furnished the subjoined article which will be seen to be a fitting tribute to the noble qualities and sublime heroism of our women during the war period :

"It is not my purpose to recall the many thrilling scenes of camp and march, and battle, and to graphically portray in brilliant word-painting, the glorious deeds of the heroes of the lost cause—those who stood to the last undaunted amidst the many trying storms of shot and shell and the terrible carnage that shook the foundations of the Confederacy. I aim not to laud these heroic men whose valor is admired and applauded by all nations. But I write of those who cannot speak for themselves, those whose modesty and silence is and has ever been their crowning glory; these true, patriotic, noble, self-sacrificing heroines, who though they faced not the enemy, most keenly felt the shock of battle—for every ball that struck their defenders went crushing into their hearts!

" I desire to put on record a few feeble words in behalf of the glorious womanhood of the South, whose tenacity to the cause was a miracle of patriotic devotion, and whose terrible sacrifices in every way, have been the marvel and the admiration of the world. Shut out from the world, practically, at home without protection, subjected to want and privation, the loneliness and suffering of fearful suspense that was cruel in the extreme, they never murmured, never ceased in their devotion to the cause and never failed in duty. In many a country 'home women endured, day after day, 'crucifixion of the soul,' yet heroically, patiently toiled, hoped and prayed on. Startled by flying rumors, tortured by suspense, weary with unwonted labor, they never dreamed of leaving the post of duty or of neglecting the interests confided to their care. Many of them superintended all farm work—and aided materially in furnishing supplies to our army. They were the sentinels at our homes—and no human interest was more faithfully guarded; no comforter had they save their God, no resource but unwearied prayer and hope. Unyielding, thus they stood behind our glorious armies, and were their inspiration from Fort Sumter—with its brilliant flame of hope—to the cruel, humiliating end at Appomattox, where all was shadow and darkness."

> "Nay, tell it as you may,
> It never can be told,
> And sing it as you will
> It never can be sung.
>
> Nay; no singer yet has sung
> Song to tell how hearts had bled
> Where our soldier's home among
> Wept eyes waiting for the dead!"

Edward Everett, speaking of the Crimean war, asks pertinently, who carried off the acknowledged palm of that tremendous contest? Not emperors and kings, nor generals, nor admirals, nor engineers launching from impenetrable fortresses, and blazing entrenchments, the three-bottled-thunders of war. No, but an English girl, cultured, refined, appearing upon that dread stage of human action and suffering, in no higher character than that of nurse. Florence Nightingale's noble display of energetic benevolence, mingled with all the tenderness of woman's love, encircled her brow with the only enduring wreath of the Crimean war—a wreath that will preserve in perfect bloom, when all the laurels of the Alma and Inkerman, and the Malakoff have faded!

"And yet, with this glowing tribute to one who is a perpetual honor to her sex, I do not hesitate to assert, that there were thousands in the late war more heroic and self-sacrificing, more devoted and attentive, whose names are scarcely known—wives and daughters of heroes, worthy the cause. Noble, cultivated, great women, who made sacrifices, holy sacrifices, and performed trying duties which have eclipsed Florence Nightingale with all her deserved and justly won laurels!

"The women of the South, under the watchful care and tender training, and through the stimulus of the chivalrous sentiment peculiar to the warm, generous Southern heart, were fair, delicate, cultivated and refined—yet in times of great mental and soul-strain these women had strength in self-abnegation, deprivation and the numberless terrible sacrifices incident to civil war. Their patriotism was more enthusiastic than that of the men; the sacrifices they made transcended theirs, because they were sacrifices of the heart, whilst the immolation they made on the altars of Southland of husbands, brothers and sons, were more trying than facing the destructive fire of the enemy. This patriotism was not simply the outcome of sentiment only, but a pure, steady flame, which from the beginning to the end of the war, burned brightly upon the altars of sacrifice which they set up all over the land.

"'The power behind the throne' never ceased to be felt. Its spirit pervaded every breast of the living barricades which opposed the invaders, nerved every arm to battle for the right, inspired to valorous deeds which dazzled the world and glorified our cause.

"I heard a prominent gentleman say that a distinguished officer read a letter from a lady friend of his to his men before going into battle, and that it was more inspiring than any words of his. Its eloquent, thrilling, patriotic words moved his men to most heroic action. Lord Nelson, sailing into Trafalgar bay with his ringing words, 'England expects every man to do his duty;' Napoleon among the pyramids, with their forty centuries of glorious achievements looking down upon him, could not have thrilled and electrified their armies more than the burning, inspiring words of this heroic Southern woman!

"It thrills me now, when I contemplate, through retrospection, what I have seen of the matchless women of the South, making sacrifices, enduring hardships and performing holy duties, to which facing the fiery thunderbolts of the enemy were a blessed mercy. Nothing but their superior moral worth, their exalted spiritual power and strength of patriotic womanhood, could have sustained them in those trying, crushing emergencies. To the noble and heroic who were sick and wounded during the war, and who had the care and ceaseless attention of these messengers of mercy in hospital, camp, and on the terrible field of carnage; who had their pity, tears, prayers in their last expiring moment, it were a benediction of devotion and love only a little less than the constancy and love of woman at the cross when the great Pan was dying and dead.

"I have seen these cultivated Christian women under all the cruel trials of war, subjected to the blasting, fiery wrath of internecine strife ; I have seen her with watchful, unflagging attention by the side of the sick and wounded, performing trying and unpleasant duties, and often risking her life ; I have seen her by the hard cot of the dying soldier, in the soft and wonderful tenderness of touch, of her sympathy, unceasing attention and love ; I have known of her burying the dead—of her standing over the graves of our fallen comrades, 'where no soldier discharged his farewell shot' during the last sad funeral rites.

"In our own city here you have one of the noble women of Virginia, wife of a distinguished divine whom he first met over the grave of his brother. Surely if there was anything that would touch and command the admiration and love of man, it would be to behold a strange, beautiful and patriotic woman giving Christian sepulture to a brother.

" When Stuart made his celebrated raid around McClellan's army, he lost but one man killed—Captain Lataine, of Louisiana. The enemy refused him burial service. Mrs. Page (all honor to her name) with an old servant and some young ladies visiting her, read the service over his grave and gave him burial. The artist, Washington, of Virginia, made this scene the subject of a fine painting, representing an open grave, the heroic dead soldier upon his bier, and standing on one side the sad and attentive darkies ; on the other side the young ladies, with bowed heads, sad faces and tearful eyes, whilst at the head of the grave stands

Mrs. Page, with prayer-book in hand, and eyes raised heavenward, in the holy and touching act of performing the last sad rites. It is a scene so full of pathos, so full of eloquent impress, that we cannot look upon it and contemplate it in all its suggestiveness without being moved to tears.

"I have seen her grandly majestic, as she stood without murmuring by the precious, holy altars, where lay in glorious state the bodies of her priceless sons—later, weeping bitter, cruel tears of anguish and despair—and yet glorifying the sacrifice! I have seen her in the thralldom of intense suspense, when the flashing bolts of war shook the foundations of her hope, and she trembled in breathless agony under the blaze of the fiery conflict, fearful of the fate of her loved! I have seen this hope rise heavenward, hovering above the mad whirl of wild battle fury and havoc, and rest there like a star of benediction, serene in its heroic confidence! I have seen this glorious hope trailing, bleeding, broken and dead 'neath the battle-chariot wheels of the triumphant enemy and victor! 'And when the end came, when the bravest soldiers returned, wretched and despairing, even weeping bitter tears within the faithful arms that sheltered them, the faces which bent above them still bravely smiled. Beloved voices whispered of encouragement and hope; patient hearts assumed burdens under which men fainted and failed.'

"I have seen her since the final ruin and wreck, in the trying humility of defeat, with everything reversed, doing the work of menials, encouraging the crushed manhood of the land in building up the waste places, never complaining, never tiring, always true, always glorious, always divine! I have seen her at the graves of our fallen, another Rizpah over the bodies of slain, warding off the vultures of hate! I have seen her annually on our memorial occasions, at the tomb of valor, Confederate alone in her mourning and memories, with her tears and floral offerings doing womanly homage to knightly chivalry! I have seen her glorified in heroism and immortalized through devotion to cause and duty. I have seen her with proud head erect 'midst the ruins of her home, and the debris of wrecked prostrate States—still unflinching and unbending as she walked with almost 'unsandaled feet' the hot lava beds of sectional bitterness and oppression underlying these ruins! And yet, whether in the days when she wore 'midst the splendor of the South's prosperity and glory, her crown of diamonds, or now 'midst the broken columns and ruins of her dear Southland, her crown of thorns, she has towered always a proud, peerless, matchless queen. Well can it be said of her—

> 'Though thy heart was seared and wounded,
>   Though thy eyes were dimned with tears;
> Though in sack-cloth and in ashes
>   Thou grieved o'er thy children's biers,
> Like the captive queen Thusneida,
>   'Mid the scoffing of the rabble
> Thou wast proud and peerless still.'

"As I behold her erect form, tried in the hot and seething crucible of war, purified and illumitated with moral and heroic splendor, the only beautiful thing 'midst this Southern waste and ruin, reverently I thank God, that he spared us at least, as a glorious, sustaining compensation for our great sacrifices, our "divine gallery" of noble womanhood!

" With the millions of heroic women of the past confronting me, crowned and imposing, I can point the young womanhood of the land to examples no purer, no higher, no more heroic, than to the thousand heroines of our own loved Southland. Matchles women, women that would be brilliant gems in the heroic crown of any land and age. Women that are a revelation of human possibilities and perfection, and that are a nobleness of heroic grandeur! Women that are in every sense worthy to be the mothers, wives and daughters of that grand army of immortals who wreathed the four years of the Confederacy with imperishable lustre and glory.

No historian can faithfully recount the story of the war and leave untouched the glorious record made by Southern women. The work is so closely interwoven with the stirring incidents and actions of that eventful period, that it cannot be ignored, and it will prove the most brilliant page in that thrilling history.

"We are building monuments continuaily to the illustrious men who wrote history with their swords. We are doing all in our power to perpetuate their names and fame, but who has raised, or will raise a monument sometime, somewhere, to commemorate the virtues, the self-abnegation, the noble sacrifice, the sublime patriotism of the noblest women of the earth?

" 'If from every wreath that ever adorned the brow of a hero, the brightest laurels were plucked, all would not form one offering too resplendent to lay at the feet' of those in whose behalf I have written these weak and inadequate words.

" The Confederate Government was born in war, culminated in the fiery flames of war, and died in war. It was purely a government of of war, and of all the glorious results of its brief four years of brilliant achievement, sublime dramatic action and heroic splendor. the greatest legacy it has left us is the glorious lesson of heroic sacrifice, trying self-abnegation, and unyielding patriotism of its matchless, peerless womenhood!"

CHAPTER XIII.

Col. Grierson's Raid Through the State, Including Newton County—Gen. Sherman's March from Vicksburg to Meridian—His Return from Meridian.

While Grant's and Pemberton's forces were contending for Vicksburg, a raid was made through the State by Col. Grierson, commanding three regiments of cavalry, carrying a few small pieces of artillery. They entered on the northern border of the State and traveled nearly centrally through the State. The raid came into this county near Union, on the 24th day of April, 1863, came directly from Union to Decatur, and then to the town of Newton. They marched very rapidly. As a general thing they were well mounted. They took the farmers of the county greatly by surprise, and whatever property was exposed. they appropriated as far as they needed it. They mostly took horses and mules and whatever they needed as supplies, feeding themselves and their horses very bountifully. They would take the best horses on a plantation and usually leave nearly as many as they took off, of stock that was completely broken down and unfit for their use. They needed the best of stock to make the forced marches, anticipating an attack at any time. In some instances they were fired upon by citizens and a few were killed on the march. Mr. R. C. Payne, just across the Newton line north of Union, shot and killed one of the soldiers. This was done by Mr. Payne without a moment's reflection. As the enemy could not see the man who did the killing, they burned his house and probably a mill belonging to him. They did not burn anything at Decatur, only appropriated whatever they wished of the people's provisions and horses. The same thing prevailed all along the road until they reached the town of Newton. At that place they burned the depot and all that was in it. They burned one or two store houses and probably one hospital building. They found also some army stores loaded on a car at Newton which they destroyed. Then they went south to Jasper county. At the town of Garlandsville some resistance was made and one man shot and some other slight damage done. They fared remarkably well at that place; the people had plenty for them to eat and fine horses and good mules and they made a heavy impressment on whatever they wanted. They went southwest to Raleigh, in Smith county, thence to Westville, in Simpson county, crossed Pearl river at Georgetown; they struck the I. C. railroad at Hazlehurst, went south to Brookhaven; then they made the shortest route to Baton Rouge. This raid was confronted by Wirt Adams' Cavalry in the southwestern portion of the State, but no serious conflict came off between them. Grierson was not disposed to fight a force equal to his, but his purpose was to make the raid and he did it without much loss to his command and not greatly damaging the counties in the State through which he passed.

Gen. Sherman leaving Vicksburg with a large army, marched to Jackson and thence to Brandon, and thence to Hillsboro, in Scott county, and entered this county east of Conehatta about three miles. It is supposed his destination was Mobile, but for some cause he went no further east than Meridian and Enterprise. On his return west he did not follow the exact roads by which he came out, taking such as had not been so badly raided by his foraging party, so that provisions might be more easily obtained. He passed going east through Conehatta, to Decatur where he camped for the night and did great damage to the town and citizens. The court-house and Methodist church were burned, all the store houses, two hotels and a number of dwelling houses.

From Decatur he went directly east on the Meridian road and made his headquarters at Mr. Reynolds, and remained in that portion of the county two days; he passed out east, on same road, by Beulah church, and camped near where Mr. S. B. Gilbert now lives. After spending a few days in Meridian, and destroying most of the town, he returned on the Jackson and Montgomery stage road, going back through the same neighborhood, but not exactly the same roads. As has been said, it was in the month of February, 1864, and much of the road from Vicksburg to Meridian at that season of the year is almost impassable, especially that portion of prairie in Scott county east and west of Hillsboro.

Yet it proved to be that the month of February of that year was more like October or November—remarkably pleasant and dry. The sun shone and the smoke setled like Indian summer, and the army made as pleasant and easy trips as if it had been in the fall of the year. His army was large and well equipped with everything necessary to carry on the project he had in view. His men kept pretty close together and were able to resist any force sent against them. There was a slight skirmish at Decatur by small parties of Confederates, and probably one man killed on the enemy's side. There was considerable fighting between Decatur and Union by Capt. Rayborn, of Newton county, who was killed while bravely defending his home and people. As the army went west it entered the county by the Meridian and Union road, and camped at different parts of Newton county, always choosing some neighborhood where there was plenty for man and beast.

To attempt to give the estimated damage done to a county which such an invading army passed through would be impossible. No one can properly state the damage. It is not supposable that they got all they ate from the county through which they passed, as they had large supply trains, as well as wagon trains carrying their ammunition. They fed their teams and drew largely for their meat supply from the county through which they passed. The soldiers preferred to forage for what they ate, liking better what they got at the average farm house to army rations. Just at that time might be expected in the larders and pantries of the country homes fresh smoked pork, including fine hams; also smoked sausages, butter-milk, chickens, turkeys, geese, fat shoats—in fact, everything a hungry soldier wanted. This was far preferable to the " hardtack " and salt pork, which were the usual rations of the soldiers.

The night before General Sherman entered Newton county he stayed at the residence of L. P. Murrell, just over in Scott county, and it is interesting to hear his brave and patriotic wife tell of the the occurrences of that eventful period. The next night he stayed at Decatur; the next at Mr. William Reynolds'; so he made no hasty marches through our county. Doubtless he fared well and was pleased with our country.

It is a dreadful catastrophe, in connection with the war, to have a great army pass through a country, especially if it is a hostile one. Many losses and hardships were entailed upon our people even when our own soldiers marched through the country, and particularly if they were following an invading army. As General Ross' Texas cavalry brigade followed Sherman's army, they were forced to subsist on a people over which the enemy had twice passed, as he was not prepared to carry any army supplies.

It so occurred during the war that Newton county had Grierson's raid to pass centrally through the county from north to south, and General Sherman's great army marched from west to east and from east to west, clear through the northern part of the county, and then followed by Ross' Texas brigade—all of whom had, in a great measure, to be subsisted from the private stocks of provisions and provender for horses from the citizens, besides taking the very best of the stock that was not hid away beyond their reach.

When the Federal army approached a farm-house at which they proposed to stay all night, the work of destruction commenced at a terrible rate. The commanding general would take the dwelling-house for his headquarters, and he would usually place guards at the door and the family would feel protected. As a general thing no insult would be offered and whatever was on the inside of the house was safe. But it was impossible to restrain the soldiers, nor did their chief officers care much the property they destroyed. If they wished to feed their teams they did not go in at the door of the crib. These cribs were usually of logs. They would knock off the roof, then throw off the logs until they reached the corn; from that position the corn would be taken, and the waste was about as great as the use. All kinds of fowls were indiscriminately killed. All the hogs they could find that were fat enough, would be killed, and a most wanton use of hams and the joints of the smoked meat, only the choice part be used, the other thrown away. A farmer had but little left after the army had gone. They used for fuel the rails around the fields and the palings around the yards and premises, and after the army removed the place looked like a cyclone had struck it. Cotton, either in the seed or bale, was destroyed; any valuable houses--like churches, court-houses, hotels, etc., were burned.

With over fifteen hundred of the best men of the county in the field defending the Confederacy at other points than at home, with the invading armies of the enemy and the pursuing army of our own passing to harrass and punish as much as possible, Newton county felt the iron heel of war. It did so permeate the whole of our southern country that not a household, (like the Egyptian passover), nor an individual but felt the terrible plagues and destruction and horrors of war. Quite a number of negroes followed Sherman's army, though they did not wish many of them—a few, probably, to wait on the officers. They wanted good horses and plenty to feed them on, and the best provisions the country people had. So passed the great raid and army through the county, the recollection of which will be long in the minds of the people.

CHAPTER XIV.

CONDITION OF THE COUNTRY AFTER SHERMAN'S MARCH, DEMORALIZATION OF THE COUNTY AND THE SOLDIERS IN THE FIELD BY SUCH DESTRUCTION OF PROPERTY—SOLDIERS IN THE COUNTY ABSENT WITHOUT LEAVE FROM THE ARMY—GREAT FORTITUDE AND STEADFASTNESS OF SOME MEN AT HOME AND SOME SOLDIERS IN THE ARMY—GREAT CONFIDENCE IN MR. DAVIS AS THE EXECUTIVE HEAD OF THE CONFEDERATE STATES—THINGS AS THEY APPEARED JUST AFTER THE WAR—PRICE OF COTTON AND OTHER GOODS.

The year 1864 was one of serious reverses as well as some victories to the Southern cause. The great necessity of massing large bodies of Confederate troops at important points in the South to defend and keep back the enemy, left many portions of the State virtually without resistance. Under these circumstances many raids were made on this unprotected territory. Sherman's march was made through Mississippi in 1864, and through Georgia and the Carolinas in 1864 and 1865, which so devastated the country as scarcely to leave anything in the line of his march. These things had a very demoralizing effect on the people. The most patriotic and self-sacrificing men felt the uncertainty of final success of the South. The hope of further recruiting the numbers of Southern soldiers was of the most uncertain character. The soldiers in the field showed to some extent the same feelings of those at home. Their ranks were constantly lessened by absences without leave; some went off with no purpose to return under any circumstances.

The enemy, anticipating a speedy close of the war, pressed hard upon the Southern army. Well fed and clothed, with the best and greatest abundance of arms and recruits whenever they were needed, were now making terrible inroads upon the Confederacy, whose soldiers stood as a solid wall of defense against this great odds with death hourly staring them in the face, their ranks constantly being lessened by disease and the casualties of battle. It took the best stuff of which men are made to stay at these places under such circumstances. Confederate money was at such a discount as to make it nearly worthless. Ten, twenty, fifty, and probably a hundred dollars of Confederate money would have been refused for one in gold. All kinds of goods not made at home were scarce, and very hard to obtain with Confederate money. The prices of goods, where they were sold at all, were fabulously high. Calico ran to ten dollars per yard, while a pair of good boots, towards the close of the war, would have been considered cheap at five hundred dollars. Many patriotic and liberal men, who, at the beginning of the war had willingly parted with their gold and all kinds of valuable property, were reluctant to make any greater sacrifice. A "tax in kind" had long since been levied that brought in supplies for the army and hospital stores. A large money tax was also levied, and thousands and hundreds of thousands of dollars were now paid into the Confederate treasury by the citizens. Newton county at that time—say for two years—paid three hundred thousand dollars beside "one-tenth" of the farm products as a tax in kind. The

Confederate tax imposed by the Congress at Richmond, was probably one of the most searching that was ever presented to the tax-payers of any country. This included an income tax on all amounts of profit in any business of over $250.00. This tax was met, and as a usual thing paid cheerfully by the people, as they felt it was a common cause for which they were contending, and the contributions of money, like the blood of the South, was profusely poured out.

There were some who still felt confidence in the final success and complete separation of the South from the other States. Many there were, who, inspired by the undying patriotism of the executive head, Jefferson Davis, felt assured in his too sanguine belief that we would still be victorious, and to some the end was a great surprise. But it came with blighting and destructive force, severing the domestic relations of master and slave from the positions they had respectively occupied for centuries.

It is stated in Mr. Davis' "Rise and Fall of the Confederate Government," page 167, 2d volume, that the number of negroes freed was upward of six million, and would deprive the owners of the value of five thousand million dollars. This great loss fell with such force as to almost paralyze the energies of the stoutest heart. Crushing the hopes and blighting the prospects of our most wealthy citizens, not only was it a loss of most they had, but a mortification and humiliation of their pride, unexpected and unparalleled.

On the 9th of April, 1865, when General Lee surrendered at Appomatox Court-house, went down all the glory of the old South. General Johnston surrendered on the 11th of the same month. Then Generals Kirby Smith and Dick Taylor very speedily followed, and then came the close of the war which few looked for so precipitately. There was great confusion in the the country; the Confederate currency, which had poorly supplied a medium of exchange for a long time, was now entirely worthless; but very little gold and silver were left in the country. Everything was now, and for some time afterward, brought to a stand-still; paroled soldiers, from their distant commands, began to return to the counties of their homes. In one sense there was a great relief. The tension of suspense had been so great, and so many things suggested for relief and nothing yet tangible for cessation of hostilities, that when the end came, soldiers who had been spared to see the end of the war, though greatly disappointed at the result of its close, and patriotic men and women at home who had done all they could, and though like the veteran soldier regretted the terms of capitulation, rejoiced that the war closed.

Many soldiers came home that never expected to have that privilege. Many a noble, brave man fell defending the Southern cause, whose memory is cherished by his companions in arms and whose loss is mourned by his relatives at home. Yet there was great rejoicing in the return of the Southern soldiers. Some of them were in a Federal prison and others detained on account of transportation, and in many instances it was late in the year 1865 before they reached home. And with the surrender a new order of things appeared. Most of the farmers of the counties had made arrangements for the cultivation of the crops before the return of the soldiers. The negroes, now free, usually stayed with the former owner until the crop was gathered. The returning soldier went immediately to work to plant a corn crop or to assist his family to cultivate the crop planted. There was corn and other provisions enough to do the country and people lived at home, having very little communication with the outside world. Men who had been accustomed to great responsibility in business and who had, before this time, large credit and the confidence of the business world, were now without aid—all they had acquired for years swept away by the result of the war or by the torch of the enemy—were now powerless to do for the present. They looked around for a mooring. Many yet had youth and health, talent and energy. They yet had their landed estates and some of them had credit with the monied world. They take courage. A gleam of hope is seen. They commence to retrieve their fallen fortunes or try to make a support for those dependent upon them.

The saddest cases, perhaps, are the old men and women who early in the war gave their young sons, reared in the lap of luxury and wealth, to go and fight the battles for the South. They rushed gladly to the front to do battle for their country. They fell in the thickest of the fray. These old folks are without stay or comfort in their old age. Their money is spent, their servants are free, their untenanted lands are all they have. Their age precludes the possibility of their ever being able to do anything towards reestablishing their fallen fortunes. Under such pressure many an old man became despondent and prematurely died of grief and misfortune.

Confederate money, as has been said, served the best purpose possible as long as it could be used, now serves as an heir-loom of the war between the States or to paper the walls of the houses. All kinds of wearing apparel was "home-made" and was scarce. Most of the fine dressing of the good old days of plenty had been worn out. Very few of the luxuries of life were left. Most of the best stock of the country had been taken by the enemy or impressed by our government. Everything around the premises and plantation was in a dilapidated condition. Yet there was a reserved force left in the country and without that the people would have been desperately poor. It will be recollected that the year 1860 was one of the greatest cotton producing years that had been known up to that time. There were, 4,675,770 bales made, and some parts of the cotton making States, made cotton in 1861, the two years taken together left a large supply in the country. Much of this was disposed of in one way or another. Much was sold to the government and ran the blockade, and much of the government cotton was kept in the country in the hands of the farmers who held Confederate bonds for it. Many planters had a few bales of cotton left which had escaped the enemy's reach. This staple now commanded fabulous prices; fifty to sixty cents per pound was paid for cotton. The temptation of private individuals using government cotton was too great, and before the Federals could take possession in all parts of the country, much was used in an illicit way. This use of this cotton, with what was in the hands of merchants and farmers, put into circulation a large amount of money.

A soon as people began to dispose of their cotton there were a few goods brought into the county, and some business was done in the summer and fall of 1865. Goods for the money that was current, even for gold and silver, were very high. Calico was 40 cents; domestic, of coarse quality, was thirty to forty cents; cotton yarn was sold at six to seven dollars for five pounds even as late as 1866 and 1867; shoes, boots and clothing and all sorts of merchandise were at prices that would prevent the purchase and sale at all under ordinary circumstances, but the great scarcity and high price of cotton warranted it, and the people accepted the situation.

Among the many things that commanded large prices was wines and liquors. There was much of it placed on the market at prices never before known except in the depreciated currency of war times. The people had become so accustomed to paying these prices during the war, there was not much complaining about it. They had been "dry" so long that they did not hesitate to buy freely when there was any money.

Cotton, after 1866, commenced to go down, and most lines of goods followed; though the prices of cotton and all other goods remained comparatively high for several years.

CHAPTER XV.

SERIES OF YEARS FROM 1866 TO 1894—LARGE EXPECTATIONS ON THE PART OF THE FARMERS TO MAKE COTTON—COTTON STILL HIGH—NEW EXPERIMENTS IN THE WAY OF EMPLOYING THE LABOR OF THE COUNTRY—THIS YEAR (1866) A VERY BAD CROP YEAR AND GREAT FAILURE OF SOME TO REALIZE THEIR EXPECTATIONS FROM FREE LABOR—SAME THINGS REPEATED FOR SEVERAL YEARS WITH CONTINUED FAILURE TO MAKE GOOD CROPS.

THE years of 1866 and 1867 formed an epoch in the history of the country unparalleled and unthought of for the Southern States. By the freedom of the slaves a new order of things was brought upon the farming communities which affected all other occupations. A sudden parting of the relations between master and slave had brought about such an anomalous state of affairs as scarcely to be accepted by the former owners of negroes.

The year of 1865 passed off with but few changes in the domestic relations. The beginning of 1866 is a new era. The Indians, at certain periods of their history, after the lapse of so long a time, would allow all the fire in the country to go out, and after it was all supposed to be gone, they took two sticks, and by long and severe friction with these sticks, produced a new fire, which was distributed to all the inhabitants belonging to that tribe. So it was, the old fire of government was quenched by the result of the war. A new fire is now distributed. Many a time it may have been quenched by inability to maintain the standard intended to be introduced among the new freedmen, or many a time it was caused to burn too brightly, and consumed those who should be its beneficiaries. The Legislature of the State had made some laws governing the freedman and others regarding contracts to be entered into between the employer and the employe, and at the beginning of the year great numbers of these contracts were mutually signed, and the negroes went to work. In many instances the negroes preferred to leave their old masters and go to a stranger whom they might address as Mister and not master. There was great effort to make cotton. Seed were scarce; teams were poor, and in many instances, a resort to oxen, or very young stock, was made to plow the ground. The seasons for making a crop were very unpropitious, and a very small crop of cotton (2,154,476 bales), also short corn crop was made.

There was considerable business done on the railroads. Merchants who had some means and credit brought goods to the railroad towns and in some cases did some credit business at high prices, for goods were still up. The cotton that was made brought a good price, say average about 40 cents, which in some degree made up for short crop. Corn was scarce and high. As yet the Federal government had not removed the county and State officers and no political trouble had as yet ensued that would disturb the relations of the two races. There was an election held in the fall of 1866, and county officers were elected and were duly commissioned and served, without molestation. There were no conflicts between the whites and blacks. Order was maintained in the county; but little lawless-ness among the people. The people already poor and needy, and with small crops, the government saw proper to levy a tax of fifteen dollars per bale on all cotton made in the Southern States. This was for the years of 1866 and '67, and it was afterwards reduced to ten dollars per bale. This has been considered a very unjust tax and there have been various propositions to return it. It would entail great expense and much uncertainty to attempt to return this large amount of money to the various planters who paid it, but it might be given back to the States and the amount placed as a school fund in trust with the States and in that way be more benefit and less expense than to reach individual farmers.

The year of 1867 was very much a repetition of the preceding year. It will be remembered that after the retirement of Wm. L. Sharkey, as Provisional Governor, on the 16th of October, 1865, Gen. Ben. G. Humphreys was inducted into the office of Governor of the State of Mississippi, whose people elected him before the idea of reconstruction of the States had come up before Congress, and after the Convention of August, 1865, when the State, by the action of that Convention, resumed its place among the States of the Union. His administration was wise and patriotic, and there was little disturbance of any sort among the people, as all wished to be law-abiding and went heartily to work to that end. On the 27th of March, 1867, General E. O. C. Ord was made Military Commander of the district in which Mississippi was embraced and Governor Humphreys was removed by this "Reconstruction Act." He was removed by General McDowell June 5th, 1868.

In November, 1867, Gen. Ord ordered an election of delegates to a convention called for the purpose of revising the organic laws of the Commonwealth of Mississippi. In this election the most intelligent white men of the State were deprived the right to vote, being excluded by the test-oath, on account of participating to certain extent in the late war, while the colored people at this election cast their first votes. They followed the advice of the "carpet-baggers," who, as political adventurers, had come among us for the spoils, and succeeded in electing a majority of their own delegates to the convention. This was the first political experience that had been felt between the whites and the "newly enfranchised." Some disturbances and difficulties, as a matter of course, came up between the races, but nothing yet of very serious nature.

The crop of 1867 was 1,951,988 bales of cotton, with comparatively poor crop of corn. There was also much neglect in the raising of stock and the care of the farm, and all home industry in the way of making clothes, such as had gone on during the war, was to a great extent abandoned. The high price of cotton had turned all industries into that channel, and to the neglect of everything else. White men stood for the negro, and the high price of goods, the short crop of cotton, caused thousands of dollars to be lost to the planters and merchants, as in many instances the planter who stood for the freedman on his place was unable to meet his obligations with all the crop surrendered.

The year 1868 was very memorable in the history of the State and particularly of Newton county. General Ames was acting now as Military Governor after June of this year. None of the acts of the Legislature, or executive officers who were elected by the people, were considered binding, and hence followed a general removal of judicial and county officers. This was the year that a great conflict between the whites and blacks occurred in Newton county, of which more will be said in another place. Great excitement prevailed and there was much unrest in the county. Business was to a large extent paralyzed; labor was hard to control, as a Freedman's Bureau had been established both at Meridian and Jackson, and with the least provocation a white man would be reported, and probably arrested and caused much trouble. However, with all the trouble the cotton crop was a little better than previous years, and 1868 is put down as producing in the cotton States 2,430,893 bales—15½ cents.

The year 1869 was also a very memorable year in the history of the State. The Constitution submitted to the people in 1868 was again voted on, and the whole vote, white and black, defeated the objectionable features so much disliked by the white people of the State. James L. Alcorn was elected Governor. No very serious trouble had come between the races, and the white people, although preferring General Dent as Governor of the State, welcomed General Alcorn in place of Ames, whom they despised. The cotton crop was not as good as last year, footing up 2,260,557 bales, with the price reduced to 16 cents. The people still neglecting to plant largely of corn, became buyers of necessaries of life as well as the luxuries.

The Legislature of January, 1870, elected two Senators to fill unexpired terms, Adelbert Ames and Hiram G. Revels, the latter the first colored representative at Washington from the State of Mississippi, and the first colored Senator ever in that body. Governor Alcorn served something over one year, and was elected to take the place of Revels, November, 1871.

The year 1870 was probably a little more prosperous. A still larger crop was made than the year previous—

the crop of cotton amounting to 3,114,529 bales, with the price advanced to 25 cents. Large amounts of corn and bacon were advanced to farmers on credit.

The rising generation of young men, who will live in and govern and make the laws of the State, may enquire how so much credit was obtained by the poor planters to make these immense crops of cotton, to the neglect of corn and provisions which they might have made at home? The prostrate condition of the people just after the war induced our Legislature to devise some measure by which the planters of the country could get their supplies by giving a mortgage or deed in trust on their growing crops as well as on their personal and real estate. The time honored deed in trust on any property that was tangible, anything really in existence, is as old as the laws of credit and the provisions to secure the creditors. But to make a law by which something not in existence could be mortgaged was new as well as unique in the way of legislation. In the year — probably 1867—the law referred to was passed and went into active operation all over the State. The first law was afterwards changed, and it allowed the creditor to take deed in trust on crops fifteen months before it was to be grown and delivered. To this, as well as the general deed in trust law, many objections were offered, and many attempts maed to repeal the whole of the law, not allowing any money to be collected on such contracts. It has finally been compromised so as to allow the planter to give deed in trust on the crop after it is planted and growing.

This deed in trust law was intended to offer relief to the poor farmer who had no money or property by which he could get supplies, and if it had been prudently and wisely used would have proved a great blessing to them. Yet this law, like many made for the benefit of the country, has been greatly abused, and men, both debtor and creditor, have suffered. Many men making this arrangement to give lien on crop and stock and homestead, have indulged too much in extravagance and have been forced to give up all they had to pay debts. The merchants being the purchasers have in many instances burdened themselves with unsaleable stock and real estate, and in the end both parties have been injured. Many men have used their credit prudently and have benefitted themselves and their merchants. In many instances much that is not correct between honest men is the outcome of the mortgage law. Very often contracts are not carried out and the property that should be forthcoming when due is not delivered. With this state of affairs many complaints are made, and war on the deed in trust system has often been waged by grangers and others opposed to the system. The law may be good enough until it is abused. Farmers should not give trust deeds if they can avoid it. When they do give them they should stand square up to the conditions of the contract, and so should the merchant. If both will do right no harm but great good may result to the man needing credit. Upon enquiry it is found that there was recorded in the chancery clerk's office in the town of Decatur for Newton county, in the year 1894, eight hundred and fifty-one deeds in trust. If we will refer to years ago, we will find that in the year 1886 eight hundred and twenty-five were recorded in ths same court in Newton county.

The first of the year 1871 was much as the preceding years, and in November of this year, Lieut.-Gov. R. C. Powers succeeded Gov. Alcorn. The balance of the year was more marked with Radical rule than under the leadership of Gov. Alcorn, who had interests in the State and felt that he was a Mississippian. Gov. Powers seemed disposed to act with the tax-paying citizens, but was powerless from the fact that he was shackled by the Radical Legislature. The county of Newton succeeded above many counties in the State in throwing out the Radical element. Most of the State was yet under heavy taxation and no representation. The respective cotton crops for 1871 and 1872 were 4,347,000, and with a price of eighteen cents ; that of 1872 was 2,974,351 with a price of seventeen cents; 1872 was a large cotton crop, but showed a great falling off with prices just a little lower. The next year, 1873, was very much in the usual way—large amounts of goods sold on time, most of them secured by deeds in trust on crops and property. Planters largely in debt; great lack of corn and home supplies, with crop of cotton 3,930,508 bales, with a price of about twenty-two cents.

A general election was again held this year, in which Gen. Ames defeated Gov. Alcorn, and he was installed as the chief executive of the State the second time ; in January, 1874, he was installed into office.

The citizens who were the loyal tax-payers and natives of the South, were by this time very impatient to throw off this alien and oppressive yoke. Active measures were contemplated in 1874, and more active were promulgated in 1875, which year marks the epoch in the history of Mississippi in which her white citizenship, by the assistance of many good colored voters, broke the bonds of Radical thraldom, and were again free American citizens. When this was accomplished the people felt that they would no longer bear the insults of a man who had violated the constitution of the State, and had laid himself liable to impeachment, which important event culminated in January, 1876, two years after Gov. Ames had been installed into office the second time. So also, Lieut.-Gov. Davis, and Superintendent of Education, Cardozo. Davis was tried and thrown out of office. Cardozo was allowed to resign. Ames had twenty-one articles of impeachment preferred against him, and would have been also removed from the office of Governor, but he indicated his willingness to resign if the articles of impeachment were withdrawn, which was done, and he did resign. Hon. John M. Stone was President of the Senate, and succeeded Gov. Ames, and became Governor March 29, 1876.

Newton county elected, in the year 1875, Isaac L. Pennington as our representative, who was a respectable and strong-minded man, and who always voted the Democratic ticket.

The crop of cotton of 1874 was large, amounting to 4,185,534, at $17\frac{1}{2}$ cents. The crop of 1875 was 3,832,991, at $16\frac{1}{2}$ cents. The crop of 1876 was 4,699,288, at $15\frac{1}{2}$ cents. The latter showing by far the largest crop of cotton ever produced in the cotton States.

With the inauguration of John M. Stone as our Governor, began the good work of reform in our State, and our prostrate people, depleted treasury and depreciated State warrants, assumed creditable attitude again, and prosperity and peace reigned in our State. The administration of Governor Stone had been so satisfactory, at the end of the two years of Ames' unexpired term, that the people again returned him to that high position for four years, from 1878 to 1881.

These years were marked with quite a degree of prosperity in the State. Our taxes were reduced; law and order were maintained, and quite a good feeling

HISTORY OF NEWTON COUNTY. 137

prevailed among our people. The cotton crops, as shown, are as follows: 1877, 4,885,423, at 19½ cents; 1878, 4,773,865, at 12½ cents; 1879, 5,074,155, at 10½ cents; 1880, 5,761,262, at 13½ cents; 1881, 6,605,750, at 12½ cents. There seemed by this time to be an over-production of cotton, and the prices rated lower. But the people still bought largely of corn, bacon and flour, most of the necessaries and all of the luxuries of life.

January, 1882, General Robert Lowry was inaugurated as Governor of the State of Mississippi, and held the office eight years, being returned a second time. During his term of office great strides were taken for the education of the youth of the State. The Industrial Institute and College, for young ladies, at Columbus, Miss., suggested by Governor Lowry, was built and put into active operation during his administration. Railroad Commissioners were also appointed, and a greater number of miles of railroads were built than at any subsequent time in the history of the State. The agricultural interests of the State were very closely looked to during this period, as the following figures on the cotton crop will show: The crops for the years spoken of are respectively reported: The year 1882 is reported as having produced, 5,456,048 bales of cotton; 1883, 6,949,756; 1884, 5,713,200; the year 1885, 5,706,065; the year 1886, 6,575,691; the year 1887, 6,505,087; the year 1888, 7,046,833; the year 1889, 6,938,290; with prices ranging from 9¾ cents to 13 cents, the higher prices being confined to the earler years when the production was smaller.

These eight years were years of peace and comparative prosperity—the people feeling that they had a stable government; that the carpet-bagger had gone;

that the State affairs were in the hands of our own loyal citizens. They now had no fear of making monied investments or permanent and substantial improvements.

At the next general election, in the year 1889, Gov. John M. Stone was again chosen by the people, and installed into office January, 1890. This was a memorable year in the State. The United States census was taken, and a Constitutional Convention called to change the Constitution of the State that had been acted upon by the people in 1868, and was not adopted. It was discussed by the Radical committee appointed to press it through, until the election of General Grant, who they supposed would force the whole of the Constitution as coming from this body upon the white people of the State. In this they were mistaken, as the President recommended the holding of another election, and allow the people the privilege of voting for or against the disfranchising clauses separately, as well as for State officers, Representatives in Congress and in the Legislature. This provision, so submitted, embraced the xiv and xv amendments to the Constitution of the United States, which provided for the right without regard to race, color or previous condition of servitude.

"The election was held November, 1869, and the white people of the State accepted the Constitution as modified and recommended by the president."* This Constitutional Convention of 1890, was to change the one of 1869, and give the people of the State one wholly made by the loyal tax-payers of the State. The acts and deliberations of this noted body, composed as it was, of some of the leading men of the State, in session three months, and after great pains-

---

* Lowry's History, pp. 376 and 377.

taking and careful law making, many things were done, much affecting the condition of the political status of the State.

The most important feature of the Convention, was the regulation of the election franchise. In this provision an educational qualification is necessary, in which "every elector in the State, on and after the first day of January, A. D., 1892, shall be able to read any section of the Constitution of this State, or he shall be able to understand the same when read to him, or give a reasonable interpretation thereof." This clause, as a matter of course, disqualified many who had heretofore voted, both white and colored, from taking part in the election of officers in the State. The Convention also provided another very important law which prevents any State Treasurer or Auditor of Public Accounts, or any sheriff or county treasurer from immediately succeeding themselves or each other in office. An ordinance of the Convention extended the terms of State officers then serving. Those terms would have expired January, 1894, but are extended to January, 1896. It also provided that the Legislature of the State meet after January, 1894, every four years in place of every two years, as was the old law. Many other changes were made, but these were considered the most important. This Convention had some of the ablest men in the State as its members, some of its most experienced legislators and State and Federal officers, and upon the whole it is regarded as one of the best Constitutions in the United States.

If Gov. Stone lives his term out as elected by the people and extended by the Convention, he will have been the Chief Magistrate of the State for a period of twelve years, which is four years longer than any other man has ever held the office.

140   HISTORY OF NEWTON COUNTY.

The period from the year 1890 to include 1893, includes an interesting epoch in the history of our State and county. With good home rule and schools well established, with a large majority of the country having no public sale of liquor—and Newton county among the latter—with a larger amount of corn and cotton and other agricultural products grown upon our State soil; with more attention paid to the raising of stock; this, taken with the fact that Mr. Cleveland is elected for a second term, and that the country for the first time in over thirty years, is fully in the hands of the Democratic party; that manufacturies are being established, many new industries have been inaugurated in the State, shows a growing interest that our people are taking in their State, and should invite a good immigration to our soil and particularly Newton county.

The cotton crop for the years named are as follows: 1890, 7,311,322, with a price from $9\frac{1}{2}$ to 10 cents; 1891, 8,652,597, with $7\frac{1}{2}$ to 10 cents per pound; 1892, 9,055,379, with a price of 7 to 8 cents per pound; 1893, 7,500,000, with a price from 7 to 8 cents per pound. The year 1892 is unprecedented in the history of the world in the production of cotton.

CHAPTER XVI.

Introduction and Use of Commercial Fertilizers.

It will be remembered that the statistics shown in the preceding chapter, of the large and increased growth of cotton, was accomplished largely by the white population of the State. It is very true that the negroes did a large part of the work, and yet the white man does much of the labor and particularly in the poorer counties of the State. The white farmers have learned much since their first failures to make cotton and corn with free labor without giving it their attention. It is well understood that the negro is the best hired labor that the South has ever had or probably ever will get; yet if this labor is not given the assistance, advice and control of the white man, it is worthless. With the presence and help of the white man—with kind but firm enforcement of his discipline and practical direction—it is the best our country can get.

It must be borne in mind, as has heretofore been stated, that at a very early period of the cultivation of the lands of Newton county, many of the very best and most level portions were cleared up and put into a state of successful cultivation. Very great neglect in allowing the lands cultivated to wash away by careless ploughing and want of ditching, was practiced by early farmers. Also a continual use of the lands in one product—say corn, cotton and oats—was allowed and proved very injurious to the lands. This failure to rotate the new and fertilize the old lands, caused much that had been very valuable to be turned out and to grow up in a second growth of timber—mostly short-leafed pine. Young men, looking at the prospect of making a living and money from such a source, were discouraged and turned their eyes to a new country—to fresher and richer soils—and in that way our county lost, it may safely be stated, thousands of her citizens and some of our best farmers by their removing to Texas and other States.

In the year 1870 or '71, a commercial fertilizer was introduced into Newton county — it being the pioneer county in the State in the use of this commodity on the general field crop — Mr. I. I. Barber, of Hickory, being the man who first conceived the idea that it was necessary to the improvement of the crops and particularly the cotton crop, by its judicious use. It will be seen by a comparison in the production in Newton county, that from the introduction of this fertilizer commenced a brighter dawn for its farmers.

The virgin soil of this county, where it is rich, does not so much need this stimulant; and yet it is found that it pays' on rich, fresh lands, to cause the cotton to mature earlier, and in this way often prevents the worm from destroying a late crop. It also would need the same help to prevent any deterioration, and by this means would be kept in a normal, if not in an improved condition by its application. But soils that are naturally poor and worn out by use and want of rotation of crops, and have been allowed to wash and leach the soil from the clay, these are the lands that need to be fertilized, and if necessary subsoiled. S. M. Harris, New York State Chemist, says: "The food of plants consists of a number of elements, including nitrogen, phosphorous (in the form of phosphoric acid), lime, magnesia, iron, silica, potash, etc. A sufficient quantity of all these necessary elements, except nitrogen, phosphoric acid and potash, exists in nearly all agricultural soils. Nitrogen is nearly always deficient; phosphoric acid usually, and potash often. In some soils there may be enough of all the elements of plant food except one. Let us assume that this is nitrogen. In this case the growth and yield of the crop will be limited by the quantity of nitrogen it can obtain. There might be an abundant supply of the other elements, but the plant could not use them without nitrogen. This would be true of any other element that might be deficient. The plants must have these all at the same time to develop in perfection."

"What the farmer must do, therefore, is to furnish the plants with the elements of plant food that are lacking in the soil. Nitrogen is the one that is nearly always deficient. This is due to the fact that nitrogen in a soluble form is easily washed out of the soil, while phosphoric acid, potash and the other mineral elements will not wash out. The question that presents itself to the farmer, gardener and fruit-grower is, how can I supply my plants with nitrogen, phosphoric acid and potash in the best forms and at least expense? We will try to throw some light upon this question in the following. We first take phosphoric acid:

"There are two sources of phosphoric acid, namely: bones and rock phosphates. Of these the rock phosphates is the cheapest source. A prevailing impression exists that superphosphates made from rock phosphates are not as good as that made from bones. It has been shown by many experiments that this idea is entirely without foundation. What the plant wants is soluble phosphoric acid, and it makes little or no difference from what source it is derived. The largest deposits of rock phosphates exist in South Carolina and Florida. These beds of phosphates are supposed to be composed of petrified bones and excrements of extinct animals. When this substance is ground and mixed with a sufficient quantity of sulphuric acid, the larger part of the phosphoric acid which it contains becomes soluble in water. The knowledge of this fact was one of the greatest agricultural discoveries of the age.

"When the rock phosphate is thus treated with sulphuric acid, it becomes what is commonly known as superphosphate of lime. The same is true of ground bone treated in the same way. A good sample of superphosphate contains fourteen per cent. of soluble phosphoric acid.

"The cheapest sources of potash are German kanit or muriate potash (or, as is more perfectly called, chloride of potassium), and wood ashes. Wood ashes, if unbleached, contain from three to five per cent. of potash, in the form of carbonate of potash. They also contain from one to two and one-half per cent. of phosphoric acid (insoluble). They are worth as plant food from $7.00 to $12.00 per ton, according to the amount of potash and phosphoric acid they contain."

It is well known that all the uplands in Newton county need fertilizing, and it should be commenced as soon as the land is put under cultivation. If it is applied to the new grounds of the county planted for the first time, it will cause the cotton to mature early, and open before it would be injured by frost, or before the worms would destroy it in the month of August. It should also be applied to new ground corn, as it will more generally cause the corn to mature and make, which it would not do without it. A perfect fertilizer for cotton is ammonia or nitre, phosphoric acid and potash. The lands of Newton county have more potash than any other ingredient. In order to fertilize intelligently (and that is the only way that it can be used with safety), is to know the analysis of the lands to be enriched. Sometimes soils in the same county, like ours, differ very widely in the kind of fertilizer that they need, some requiring one essential ingredient and some another. When it is known what lands need it is a very easy matter to have the deficiency supplied, or to discover any element that may preponderate. This analysis of lands is a great expense and much trouble, yet it is the only reliable way to know what it actually and definitely needs. This is, to some extent, often overcome by experienced manufacturers who have studied the needs of our soils and know what plant foods the various sections need. The same fertilizer that would make a fine crop of cotton would also make a fine crop of corn on the same land, it being perfect for both; but certain fertilizers suitable for corn would not do so well for cotton. There are certain contingencies to be met in making the cotton fertilizer that are not observed for corn. It is due to the fact that it does not require the amount of phosphoric acid for corn that it does for cotton.

It is well known that cotton seed will make good corn on poor upland, if properly applied, with sufficient quantity to meet the demand. They will make also sweet or Irish potatoes, and many other things. But cotton seed alone will not do well for cotton, as a large stalk will be the result, without the good results of fruiting, which is the most necessary requisite in furnishing satisfactory crops. To combine the green seed with the acid phosphate, putting them in the ground together in the month of February, say 20 to

30 bushels of seed and 200 pounds of acid phosphate, will in almost every instance, insure a fine crop. The ground, which is nature's great "laboratory," will manipulate these two elements and form a perfect fertilizer. There are other formulas for the fertilizing of cotton and corn with which the farmers are more familiar than the writer, and which are alternated from year to year, as it is seen, which pays the best on different lands; as it is often the experience of the farmer teaches him what is best for one part of his farm is not so good for another. Hence, the use of compost heaps and the mixture of home made fertilizers with the commercial so as to obtain the best results. Much importance just now, and for a period long anterior to the present, is attached to the value of cotton seed, and the necessity of their return to the soil from which they were taken. A farmer by judicious management may return just the seed that came out of the cotton that an acre of land will produce, or its equivalent if rotated by another production and continue to do so from year to year, it will be seen that the land will become gradually more productive by only receiving a part of the product back to it that has each year been grown upon it, though it may be cultivated every year. Quite a number of farmers are now selling their cotton seed, owing to the large advance just now. This parting with the cotton seed from the plantation should be well considered and seriously canvassed before doing it; and under no circumstances should it be done unless the equivalent of the seed be returned in cotton seed meal and other fertilizers to supplement the loss of the seed grown upon the land. It is officially stated by State Chemist, that a bushel of cotton seed is worth 28 cents as a fertilizer on the farm on which they are raised. The cotton seed meal is a fertilizer of very

great importance, and its growing popularity is becoming widespread and will continue to do so. The chemist tells us, and we cannot doubt this wonderful science, that the meal in a ton of green cotton seed, after having the oil and hulls taken out, is better than the whole amount as a fertilizer. That the oil is not possessed of productive qualities, and by taking it away there are other properties in the mass that are freed and go to make one of our most useful fertilizers known to man, and by supplementing some of the necessary elements found in other sources, it becomes far more useful and less trouble to distribute than the seed. Tnere is no doubt that there is a growing interest now evinced in the use of cotton seed meal. It is evident to every corn grower who has used it, that the amount of meal taken from a ton will go farther and be more evenly distributed and do more good than the ton of green seed. In the same ratio it applies to the fertilizing of cotton by mixing it with acid phosphate, a less amount will answer and be easier applied.

The farmer should bear in mind that certain proportions of ammonia with phosphoric acid and potash, form a perfect fertilizer, and if he can get them in proper proportions, and will apply intelligently, and work well, he will be sure of a crop. Many are the sources of these essential elements; like electricity, they are found in much material of the world's construction. It does not matter where they come from so they are available plant-food and soluble in water. Sources of ammonia are castor bean, fish scraps, cotton-seed meal, blood and tankage from slaughter-pens. Potash is from German kanit wood, also cotton-seed hull ashes and other sources.

Phosphoric acid, raw bone, charcoal, South Carolina and Florida rock, and many other sources are known to the skilled manufacturer and chemist. It matters not, as has been said, where they come from so they are in quantity great enough and soluable in water. The rock has the advantage over the raw-bone, that it has been treated with sulphuric acid—while bone is probably as good, but wants a little longer for the natural action of the ground to appropriate these magical qualities of fertilization.

Mississippi has an excellent law as regards fertilizers. It requires each manufacturer, whether in the State or out of it, to submit samples of the manufactured goods to the State Chemist of this State, of such goods as he expects to sell in our State. The chemist makes an analysis of the goods, and each merchant handling these goods has to post this analysis in his office so that all customers wishing can see what they are using. If the purchaser wishes he can take out of any sack of goods which he has bought and have an analysis made by the State chemist, and if it is not a satisfactory comparison he has his recourse upon his merchant, and the merchant upon the manufacturer; or the farmer buying the goods can reserve a portion out of several sacks, and if the results on his farm products are not satisfactory, he can have the samples reserved and examined, if they have been well preserved, and if that analysis does not prove satisfactory the same recourse can be had as above stated. Under this law manufacturers in this State have prepared and are selling a very fine class of commercial fertilizers, and are meeting with good success. The factory at Meridian, and the two at Jackson, are both doing a fine business. When these fertilizers are honestly made and the essential elements are placed in a good base so that they may be equally distributed, there is no reason of there being a failure.

It is not expected that the use of home-made fertilizers will be given up under any circumstances, but to increase them rather, would be urged upon the farmer. Use every particle of waste matter, every pound of animal excrement, and vegetable mold, and all accumulations around the place, and carefully husband it and so protect as the best results may be had from it. There is very little value as a fertilizer in forest leaves and pine straw. They will serve as a mulching for fruit trees or beds where you do not expect the grass to grow. They are excellent to put in stables and stalls where they serve as a filter or sponge after they have been well tramped, and in a great measure moulded and well rotted, so as to absorb the properties of the compost, and keep it from evaporating and wasting. They also serve when placed in the ground as something that will open and keep the soil from becoming packed. Yet in the decomposition of leaves and straw the merit is so small as scarcely to be observed. In gathering them up from the woods, there is a top soil and some vegetable mould that proves beneficial. To secure an amount of forest leaves and pine straw and top earth to go over an acre of poor land would require more work and cost more than would buy commercial fertilizer to enrich two acres.

A comparative view of the use of fertilizers between the years 1880 and 1890, and the great increase of all agricultural productions, with not a corresponding increase of the population, may serve to convince any one that the large use of commercial fertilizers has had much to do with it. The subjoined reports are from the United States census of the products of Newton county for 1880 and 1890:

"The agricultural products of Newton county for the year 1880 were: bales of cotton, 6,341; bushels of corn,

261,207; estimated value of products sold and on hand in the county, $634,264. The product of the county for the year 1890 was 13,097 bales cotton; 392,619 bushels of corn; estimated value of products sold and on hand, $919,330. These are the crops of 1879 and 1889, as the census was taken in the summers of 1880 and 1890, and the crops of preceding years had to be taken. If the product of the county could be shown for 1892, it would probably amount to 15,000 bales of cotton and a corresponding amount of corn and other products, and the aggregate estimate of all the products of the county would go largely over one million dollars. The report of the census on the amount of fertilizers used in the year 1889 is not reported, but is largely in excess of the amount used in 1879. The census shows fertilizers used in the county in that year to be $8,905; the population in 1880 was 13,336; in 1890, 16,600.

It will be seen that the production in the county of everything available for the farmer to plant has largely increased; also the amount of money value, as the estimate of the crop of 1889 over that of 1879 shows.

The most reasonable conclusion for this improvement in crops is the increased use of fertilizers. There is no doubt but that every acre of upland, and much of the swamp land and reed brakes, where they have been long used, should have fertilizers applied to them. They are now cheap, more so than they have been. The sale of these goods commenced in 1871, at $50.00 per ton on time, with about ten per cent. less for cash or if paid for early in the season. This price continued for about ten years, and from that time continued to decline until in the beginning of the year 1894 a good fertilizer is sold for $20.00 cash, and from $25.00 to $26.00 on time. Cotton seed meal has maintained its position on first prices better than other commercial goods, owing, no doubt, to a larger demand for it. The ruling price is about $20.00 cash, and $22.00 and upwards on time. Taking the price of cotton and fertilizers, on an average, the latter may be purchased for as little money as it ever has been—in fact for less money, but with the same number of pounds of cotton.

Every farmer should use these helps to make his crops, not alone on cotton—for of all the products this should be the one most neglected — but on corn, oats, rye, barley, potatoes, and on gardens and fruit trees. This should be done intelligently and with economy. What is meant by economy is not to restrict ourselves to one, two, or even three hundred pounds to the acre. But prepare the ground well, lessen the number of acres in cultivation; use freely home-made and compost manures, thoroughly incorporate into the soil; feed the young plants early and not allow the grass to absorb anything given to the crop; but work less land, plant prudently, cultivate fast, allowing the plants to appropriate every pound of the various feeders given them. Rotate the crops, stop the stock from running all winter on the fields to be cultivated. Occasionally allow the land to rest and grow up in grass undisturbed by stock. With this kind of labor and economy, Newton county will stand higher in the scale as the banner county, than she has ever done before.

Subjoined will be found some information to the farmers and purchasers of fertilizers as to the manner of making the analysis—some facts taken from Bulletin No. 3 of W. L. Hutchinson, State Chemist, at the A. & M. College, at Starkville, for the years 1893 and 1894. He says:

"How far the samples sent by manufacturers may be relied on in the purchase of fertilizers, judging from the results of the inspector last season, the samples fairly indicate the character of the goods which are to be sold. There were one or two marked exceptions last year, but otherwise we found the goods very much of the same composition as the official samples. We note with pleasure the fact that this season a number of manufacturers have been at great pains to have these analyses to indicate the average composition of their goods."

The prices used in calculating the relative values of different brands of fertilizers: A unit is twenty pounds, or one per cent. of a ton; nitrogen, commercial value, is quoted at $3.00 per unit; potash at $1.00 per unit; water soluble phosphoric acid at $1.20 per unit; citrate, soluble, $1.00 per unit. The following prices, commercial value, show what a ton would be worth:

2.03 per cent. water soluble Phos. Acid, at $1.20.............$	2 44
5.34 per cent. citrate soluble Phos. Acid, at $1.................	5 34
3.55 per cent. Nitrogen, at $3......................................	10 65
5.26 per cent. Potash, at $1	5 26
Would make a ton worth..................................$	23 69

Commercial value, $23.69.

A list of values guaranteed by the manufacturers is appended to show what the cost of each is to the manufacturers at the price of the elements composing them:

MERIDIAN FERTILIZER CO., MERIDIAN, MISS.

	Phosphoric Acid.			Nitrogen, per cent.	Potash, K. O., 20 per cent.	Relative value per ton.
	Water Soluble.	Citrate Soluble.	In-Soluble.			
Home Mixture...............	6.00	3.00	2.00	1.65	2.06	$17 45
Southern Soluble............	6.00	3.00	2.00	1.75	2.00	17 45
B. B. B.....................	6.00	3.00	4.00	1.75	2.00	17 45
C. C. & C....................	6.00	3.00	2.00	1.75	2.00	17 45
Southern Acid Phosphate.....	11.50	2.00	2.00			15 80

STANDARD GUANO AND CHEMICAL MANUFACTURING COMPANY, OF NEW ORLEANS, LA.

	Phosphoric Acid.			Nitrogen, per cent.	Potash, K. O., 20 per cent.	Relative value per ton.
	Water Soluble.	Citrate Soluble.	Insoluble.			
Stern's Ammoniated Raw Bone Phosphate..................	4.00	4.00	1.00	1.65	1.50	$15 25
Champion Farmer's Choice....	4.00	4.00	1.00	1.65	1.50	15 25
Standard Soluble	.....	.....	.....	.....	.....	.....
Ammoniated Guano..........	4.00	4.00	1.00	1.65	1.50	15 25
Kanit.......................	.....	.....	.....	.....	12.00	12 00
Acid Phosphate..............	10.00	2.00	1.00	.....	.....	14 00

MOBILE PHOSPHATE AND CHEMICAL WORKS, MOBILE, ALA.

	Phosphoric Acid.			Nitrogen, per cent.	Potash, K. O., 20 per cent.	Relative value per ton.
	Water Soluble.	Citrate Soluble.	Insoluble.			
Mobile Standard.............	7.00	2.00	1.00	1.86	1.00	$16 98
Eclipse Soluble Guano........	4.00	5.00	1.00	1.65	1.00	15 75
K. K. K	8.00	1.00	1.00	.85	1.00	14 15
I. X. L. Acid................	10.00	2.00	1.00	.....	.....	14 00

JACKSON FERTILIZER COMPANY, JACKSON, MISS.

	Phosphoric Acid.			Nitrogen, per cent.	Potash, K. O., 20 per cent.	Relative value per ton.
	Water Soluble.	Citrate Soluble.	Insoluble.			
Royal G.....................	6.50	.50	1.00	1.25	1.50	$13 50
C. C. Brand	6.00	.50	1.00	1 00	1.50	12 20
Gulf States Guano	6.00	.50	1.00	1.25	1.50	12 95
Complete Vegetable..........	3.00	3.00	1.00	3.00	4.00	19 60
German Kanit................	.....	.....	.....	.....	12.00	12 00
Acid Phosphate..............	12.50	2.00	1.00	.....	.....	17 00

CAPITAL CITY FERTILIZER COMPANY, JACKSON, MIISS.

	Phosphoric Acid.			Nitrogen, per cent.	Potash, K.O., 20 per cent.	Relative value per ton.
	Water Soluble.	Citrate Soluble.	Insoluble.			
Nonpareil...	6.00	1.50	.50	1.50	1.50	$14 70
Red Star...	6.00	1.50	.50	1.50	1.50	14 70
Acid Phosphate	12.50	1.50	2.00	......	......	16 50
Kanit...	......	......	......	..	1.20	12 00

NATIONAL ACID PHOSPHATE, NEW ORLEANS, LA.

	Phosphoric Acid.			Nitrogen, per cent.	Potash, K. O., 20 per cent.	Relative value per ton.
	Water Soluble.	Citrate Soluble.	Insoluble.			
Acid Phosphate...	......	11.00	2.00	1.00	......	$15 20

G. W. SCOTT & CO., MANUFACTURING COMPANY, ATLANTA, GA.

	Phosphoric Acid.			Nitrogen, per cent.	Potash, K. O., 20 per cent.	Relative value per ton.
	Water Soluble.	Citrate Soluble.	Insoluble.			
Gossymer Phospho...	7.00	2.00	1.00	2.00	1.50	$14 70
Scott's Animal, Ammoniated..	7.00	2.90	1.00	1.50	1.00	14 70
Scott's High Grade Acid Phospho...	10.00	2.00	1.00	......	......	16 50
Scott's Potasso Phospho...	10.00	2.00	1.80	......	2.00	12 00

NORTHWESTERN FERTILIZING ᴏ., CHICAGO, ILL.

	Phosphoric Acid.			Nitrogen, per cent.	Potash, K. O., 20 per cent.	Relative value per ton.
	Water Soluble.	Citrate Soluble.	Insoluble.			
Pelican Cotton and Corn......	2.00	6.00	2.00	1.65	.54	$13 89
National Bone Dust..........	2.00	6.00	2.00	1.65	.54	13 89
A. D. Bone.................	2.00	6.00	2.00	1.65	.54	13 89

MISSISSIPPI COTTON OIL CO., COLUMBUS, MISS.

	Phosphoric Acid.			Nitrogen, per cent.	Potash, K. O., 20 per cent.	Relative value per ton.
	Water Soluble.	Citrate Soluble.	Insoluble.			
Standard..................	7.09	3.67	1.42	2.45	3.03	$22.56
Acid Phosphate	11.95	3.57	.83			17.91

Let farmers study these formulas of the most respectable of standard goods offered to the people of this county, but made at different parts of the South. Wherever we can find to our advantage we should patronize our home companies, but a healthy and honorable competition is always helpful to trade and also to the consumer. Let the farmer think of and practice the advanced modes of farming. Cultivate less land; do it more thoroughly; enrich to some extent every acre. Plant peas, clover and such things on the ground that have a natural element of improvement in them. Pay special attention to hill-side ditching and terracing the land; bring all the ground upon a level as far as possible. Sub-soil when it is necessary, not using plows that turn the sandy soil over too much. Constantly rotate and rest, and by all means use commercial fertilizers, and good results may be expected. There are thousands of acres of old land in the county of Newton that owe their redemption to the use of fertilizers. There is no doubt but for its use this county would be deprived of some of the best citizens and farmers, and but for its use the census of 1890, which showed a population largely in excess of the preceding decade, would in all probability have been one-third less. Let our people feel that they are settled for life in Newton county, where they have good society, schools, church privileges, good laws, and a civil, well-governed population; where they have good water, good health, good markets, a county abounding in fine timber for use and export. With all these advantages, and with cheap lands, why not stay at home in our own county?

CHAPTER XVII.

RECONSTRUCTION PERIOD—GREAT EXCITEMENT IN POLITICS—INTRODUCTION OF CARPET-BAGGERS, SCALAWAGS AND NEGRO SCHOOL TEACHERS.

THE years of 1866 and 1867 passed comparatively quiet with the people of the State; also a part of the year 1868. Gen. E. O. C. Ord was commanding the portion of the district to which Mississippi was assigned.

On the 4th of January, 1868, Gen. Ord was superseded by Gen. McDowell, who, on assuming command soon issued orders removing from office Gov. Humphreys and Attorney-General C. E. Hooker, and appointing Adelbert Ames, Military Governor of the State. With this removal of the Governor and Attorney-General, who were elected by the people, began much trouble and dissatisfaction in the State. In many instances appointments to the important and lucrative positions were given to carpet-baggers from other States, who were merely adventurers coming among us for the spoils of office; also the scalawags, usually men who were objectionable to the Southern people. They were living among us and had gone over to the Republicans, not from a sense of duty and conviction of right, but to be promoted by appointment, as there would be no chance to be elected by the people. There were also some negroes appointed to office, which at that early date was very distasteful to the Southern people. Newton county was rather more fortunate than most of the counties, as a majority of the appointments to fill vacancies made by removal were given to good citizens and Democrats. Notable exceptions were in the appointment of one Harvey, as Justice of the Peace, and C. S. Swann, as Chancery Clerk. These men did us great harm. Harvey was a foreigner—that is, from some Northern State—and one of the worst class of dangerous and pliant tools in the hands of any who wished to use him. He came to the county as a negro school teacher; married one of the Newton county colored women with whom he lived a short time and then deserted her. He did more to estrange the black man from the white citizen, than any man in the county. He came near precipitating a riot between the races, which if it had started, would have resulted in great loss of life to the negroes. He was finally arrested and guarded for several days in the town of Newton, and no doubt but all arrangements were made to have him lynched, but wise counsel prevailed and he was allowed to escape, no more to trouble Newton county.

C. S. Swann was a Northern man, but had lived in the South for years previous to the war and had married a Southern woman. But he saw his opportunity to get office. He was postmaster for a time after the war at Newton, and then appointed chancery clerk, which he held until the people of the county had an opportunity to vote in 1872, when they elected a Democrat to every office in the county. Swann left Newton and went to Jackson, where he engaged in counterfeiting money; was arrested, tried and sentenced to the penitentiary, but by some means escaped, and the people have not been troubled with him since.

There was a notable exception to Swann and Harvey, in the person of Miss Lynch, a mulatto woman, who came to Newton county early after the war as a teacher of the colored people. She was a relative of James Lynch, the famous colored orator who went over the State and attracted so much attention from the public. He was a candidate on the State ticket for Secretary of State, when Gov. Alcorn was elected. This woman behaved herself and reflected credit on her race, and likely did a good work among her people while she remained a teacher in Newton county.

The year 1869 was one memorable in the history of the State. The objectionable features of the Constitution were voted upon and defeated. Gen. James L. Alcorn, one of the most powerful debaters and fearless antagonist on the stump, in the State, was a candidate for Governor against Lewis Dent, a brother-in-law of General Grant. In this great canvass Gen. Robert Lowry, afterwards Governor for eight years of this State, canvassed the State with Gen. Alcorn, contesting every inch of ground; claiming the rights of the South and Southern people; standing up against great odds, of both State and Federal opposition, and although he did not succeed in carrying the State for Dent, a lasting debt of gratitude is, and always will be due this distinguished Mississippian for the fearless manner in which he defended their rights and sacrificed himself for their interests.

Gen. Alcorn was elected and the 10th day of the next March, he was inducted into the office of Governor, being the first man to hold the position under the Constitution of 1868, and the first since the admission of the State, and under his administration fairly commenced the reconstruction period.

During the reconstruction period of the State, while it was under military government, Freedmen's Bureaus had been established both at Jackson and Meridian, and the newly enfranchised had become the "wards of the nation." These bureaus became great sources of annoyance and much trouble ensued in this country from their patronage, of which more will be said in another chapter. The negroes of this county, in some parts, became very insolent and did much to exasperate the white men; were insulting in the extreme; backed as they were by the military, they knew no bound to their rage and hatred and sometimes abuse to the white man, who was intimidated by knowing that a word from one of them would cause him to fill a felon's cell.

It is a noticeable fact that in all the trouble with the Radical and Military party, the appointment of bad men to hold office over regular citizens and tax-payers, and with all the provocations to bloodshed, that no man has ever been killed for his political opinions or his influence in political matters, in Newton county. That the people of the county bore a great deal, and that they were provokingly imposed upon, and that it was a severe trial of their high metal and test of their true courage, which they had ever evinced, that they had listened to more dispassionate counsel and bore what, under ordinary circumstances, would have fiercely resented and condign punishment visited upon the offender. No doubt the people feel better now that they bore so much. No doubt it was better for all concerned, as a persistent and peaceful effort on the part of the Democrats of the county, even at an early day, to throw off this yoke of oppression and assume the reins of government of the county, which they did in 1852, and much sooner than did many other counties of the State.

During the Radical rule in the county, from 1868 to

1872, the taxes had become very high; a very large issue of warrants had been made to defray the expenses of the county; there was no money in the treasury. The consequence was that they were depreciated to an extremly low rate, and those who did work for the county and took warrants for pay, had, in most instances, to sacrifice them to those who had money and could wait until they would be good. A great many school teachers lost largely by the disposal of their warrants. The time came, however, after return to home rule, that these warrants were all paid in full, which brought a large profit to those who had invested in them.

CHAPTER XVIII.

Race Troubles — Conflicts between Whites and Blacks — Resulting in the Killing of Both Races—Secret and Political Organizations — Arrest and Imprisonment of our White Citizens.

In order to bring prominently before the reader the events discussed in this chapter, it will be necessary to take a retrospective view of some things already mentioned. The great change in the relations of master and servant, brought about by the sudden disastrous termination of the war, did not for a time bring any conflict between the races. The negroes in the years 1866 and 1867, generally were peaceable, and very good relations were maintained between the races. In the year 1868 Freedmen's Bureaus were well established in the State, and a military government thoroughly engrafted upon it. This new state of things begat an idleness among the negroes heretofore unknown. They also became more insolent to the white people and harder to govern, and thus began trouble that ended in very tragic events in the county of Newton. When a negro felt himself aggrieved or insulted, he had ready recourse to the military headquarters, and if it were thought proper the white man was brought up and tried by military court, especially if an altercation had occurred between the parties. Negroes, in this state of strife and unrest, would not work, and in many instances resorted to taking things that did not belong to them. This was sharply resented by the owners of the property, and hence the conflict it brought about.

The most lamentable occurrence took place in the south-eastern part of the county, in which two men were killed and another wounded, the particulars of which are about as follows: The two Denis brothers, living about six or eight miles south-east of Hickory, missed some hogs and went in search of them among negro neighbors living near them, whom they suspected of being the thieves, and made such close search that they found a portion of the pork buried in the yard of one of the negroes whom they suspected of being the guilty parties. After an unsuccessful attempt to settle the matter by compromise, one of the Denises went to Hickory and sued out a warrant to have the guilty parties arrested.

Subjoined is an extract from an article published in the Meridian Mercury, Febr'y 8, 1868, giving a graphic account of the tragic events and things that followed in rapid succession after the first blood was spilled. The Mercury says:

"The precise scene of the shocking deed is about midway between Hickory station, Newton county, and Garlandsville, Jasper county. Daniel A. Denis and Edw'd R. Denis, originally from the State of Georgia, but more recently from the State of Alabama, came to the place about ten years ago and settled on a plantation, and have since been working together. Industrious, honorable and attentive to business, they made themselves a good name among their neighbors. They both served in the late war, passing through battles unharmed. Their ages were fifty-four and fifty-one. The latter only was married.

"There is a family of negroes living near the Denis

plantation, formerly belonging to the Dyess family. They lived near by when they were slaves. There are four brothers, perhaps five, believed to have been concerned in the murderous assault. There names are Prince, Orange, John, Sunny and Joe; all are the Dyess negroes. These were squatted about near by, and with them the difficulty originated.

"The Messrs. Denis had missed hogs. They suspected the Dyess negroes having stolen them. E. R. Denis, with W. H. Tucker, went to Prince Dyess' to search. They found Princes' wife cooking fresh hog meat, asked her where she got it; said she got it from uncle Henry. They went to see "uncle Henry" about it, who said they did'nt. This was Friday; Prince was not at home. Went after dark and he was not at home yet. Went in the morning and still not at home. Told the woman she would have to go to Hickory; she showed them the meat buried in the ground, in a box. Started with her; met Prince, her husband, and Orange, his brother; both had double-barreled guns; a conversation ensued. Prince confessed that he killed the hog, and said as he did it he thought the woman need not be carried to Hickory to appear before the magistrate. Denis told him (Prince), that he must go, and that he was willing to compromise and make it as light as possible, provided he would leave the country. Prince said he would go to Hickory and start as soon as he got some breakfast. The negroes talked and acted boldly, and defiantly."

"Denis proceeded to Hickory, in company with Tucker. He waited until evening, and Prince not coming as he promised, he went before Justice Gray and sued out a warrant and returned. The warrant was placed in the hands of Mr. Gibson as a special deputy constable to execute.

"Officer Gibson with the Denises, Ben. Griffin, Jonas Nelson and Jack K. Horn and Sim. Perry, as a posse, after dark proceeded to Princes' house, not more than a quarter of a mile from Denis' place, to execute the warrant. They did not find Prince at home. Failing in their object and not suspecting a conspiracy, lighted a torch, called up some dogs and turned the hunt commenced for a hog-thief into a 'possum hunt. They had caught one possum and were returning home. They were in one hundred yards of the house crossing a branch, E. R. Denis bearing the torch next to D. A. Denis in advance, others following, when a volley was fired into the party at close range. D. A. Denis it is upposed fell dead ; Gibson, Griffin and Nelson were more or less severely wounded by the fire. The negroes rushed from their ambush. Old John, the father of the five sons, encountered E. R. Denis, who seemed to have stood his ground. The three wounded men retreated in the dark as best they could, as did the ones not wounded. E. R. Denis was heard to exclaim, "Prince, don't kill me !" The voice of little John was distinguished saying, "kill him!" When all was over the report reached the home of the Denis', and Mrs. Denis, in company with some one went to the scene of conflict and hunted up the dead and wounded. D. A. Denis lay dead—shot twice, front and rear ; his head beaten and crushed in. E. R. Denis lay dead near by, his head horribly crushed, and run through, apparently with a sword, but no sign of a gun-shot wound.

"The (Black) Prince wore a sword by virtue of his office as commander-in-chief of the force, and thus it was that the black devil, Prince, "fleshed his maiden sword." Old John, the old daddy of these young devils, made the onset. He was so near E. R. Denis that he caught his gun and raised it so as to miss a man near by. They grappled and an unequal contest went on between the younger Denis and the whole gang. It is inferred that he gave some deadly wounds before he fell. He lay on his pistol and three barrels were empty. Old John, subsequently arrested, had two bullet holes in his body, the wound supposed to have been given by Denis. They were of a deadly character; and as old John will probably never be at another killing of white men, we will repeat here what he said after his arrest, that "E. R. Denis was the hardest man to kill that he ever killed," from which it may be inferred that he had tried his hand before. It is supposed that there were about eight negroes in the fight Saturday night, the men above mentioned and some of their friends.

"Runners were sent out that night to spread the alarm. The next morning about twenty men from Garlandsville appeared upon the scene. The negroes, too, seemed to have improved the time to recruit their forces. Flushed with their victory and confident of their numbers, they sent a defiant message to the party to come and arrest them where they were, at old John's house. The party of whites from Garlandsville dashed right up to old John's house without dismounting. A volley was poured into them from the house, from the woods and from the fence. A Mr. Lyle, a young man from Garlandsville, was severely wounded by a shot from the woods; less severely wounded Messrs. McCall and Land, the latter but slightly. Their horses were shot by the volley. The fire was returned and it is believed two negroes were wounded. It is negro news that one was killed, but doubtful. The negro party after firing, retired. The whites found old John in the house wounded as above stated, badly. Questioned, he said he was sick; examined, it was seen he was sick of two bullet wounds. Old John was first arrested. He was "sent to Hickory," where we lose track of him and will not attempt to find him again; Daniel Johnson, in the Sunday morning fight has been arrested and committed to the Jasper county jail. Tobe Gentry, in the Saturday night's massacre has been caught and lodged in Newton county jail. Besides old John, Joe, his son, "Uncle Henry," John's brother, both in Saturday's fight, were caught and "sent to Hickory," which is all we could hear of them. It was said here on Wednesday that the negroes engaged in the war at Newton, had sent here for reinforcements. A certain restless negro who is well known, has on several occasions shown a disposition to incite his people to violence, was out early on Wednesday morning, the morning after the snow, with an army gun, on the streets, pretending that he was waiting for his crowd to go hunting in the snow. It was not known except to the black Loyal Leaguers that any of the Newton warriors had arrived here, and there was only a suspicion that the aforesaid negro was demonstrating to get recruits to go to the field of operation beyond the Chunkey. The brother of the massacred men, with some friends, got here Thursday evening, still searching for the murderers of the two brothers. He put himself in communication with a few discreet persons and waited until morning and yesterday, Friday, the city marshal Pelton and Policeman Duke, having gotten a description of the negroes supposed to be about here from certain information of negroes being there, proceeded to the headquarters of the Bureau. There they saw four negroes answering the description, lazily lounging about, sunning themselves on the wood-pile. They went and informed

Capt. Thomas that they had come to arrest these negroes.

"They had been here since Tuesday, and had taken sanctuary at the Bureau, and had actually been making complaints against the whites of Newton and were then waiting for the agent to take steps to redress their grievances. We suppose they thought the Bureau would restrain the white people from hunting and capturing them to bring them to justice, and that among their newly acquired rights was the right to kill the white man to suit their pastime and pleasure, and to go about safely with the overshadowing protection of the Bureau. Capt. Thomas concluded to give them up, and it was unnecessary to ask him about it at all if a proper warrant were issued. Some delay occurred, the unsuspecting negroes still hanging about while certain parties were at Justice Bramlett's office getting the warrant issued, as it is reported to us one of the four negroes who had taken sanctuary was sent off by Capt. Thomas to buy bread for the crowd. The arresting party was returning as the negro was going for the bread, and it is supposed that he recognized the brother of the murdered men and has slipped away. Such are Bureau ways. It is justice for us to mention that Mr. Denis expressed himself to us quite satisfied that Capt. Thomas was disposed to do the right thing. The remaining three were locked up in the guard-house and a guard detailed for last night. The gun of one of the murdered men was found in possession of one of these (D. A. Denis, shot down at the first fire, carried the gun). The stock had been broken in beating one of the victims over the head. When asked by one of the arresting party where he got it, he said he captured it.

"The sheriff of Newton county was expected to

arrive to-day to take charge of the prisoners, to remove them to Newton county. We do not hear of his arrival. All the negroes here had guns; one of them, as stated, the gun of one of the men killed. Captain Thomas, Bureau agent, before he would deliver them to Mr. Denis and party, required them to pay $13.00 which amount he said had been pawned for provisions advanced."

The young man Lyles, (brother of J. M. Lyles, of this county) died of the injuries received in the charge on the ambushed negroes. It will be seen, when the men found one of their number had been brutally murdered from ambush, that a third (Mr. Ben Griffin's leg being broken) had been badly crippled, were determined to punish the parties who did it regardless of consequences.

The brave charge made upon the fortified house of the Dyess negroes on Sunday morning was the style of a charge that some of the old soldiers were accustomed to. They did not think of the consequences, and when the word was given the old rebel yell rang out, and it was only the work of a moment, and the capture of those in the house was accomplished. Punishment was at once dealt out to those whom they found. The law was not troubled with any trials of those assassins that were caught and known to be in the conspiracy to murder the Denis'. The vengeance of the white people was speedy. But they did not long enjoy the rest of their quiet homes. As soon as the facts, doubtless greatly exaggerated against the whites and mitigated on the part of the blacks, were carried to military headquarters by negro runners, soldiers were dispatched to the locality of the murder and lynchings to arrest all who were engaged in the punishment of the negroes. Hundreds of white men had gathered, some from Jasper county, and many from Newton county, had joined in the search and capture of those engaged in the murder, and to arrest those who had resisted the officers in the service of the warrant.

The Federal authorities received their information in reference to the particulars of the difficulties from the negroes. These informers did not always confine themselves to statements of fact, and many, no doubt, made reports upon doubtful surmises. When the military came into the county, many who had taken an active part fled the country, while others, who had only taken the part that every man ought, to catch the guilty parties, were arrested and sent to jail. Doubtless some who had but little to do with the arrest and punishment of the negroes were among the punished.

The arrests that were at once made were Sim Perry, Dr. S. G. Loughridge, R. L. Sanders, Dr. W. D. Bragg, F. M. Lewis, David Richie and Mr. Heath. Of these there were only three tried, namely: Sim Perry, Dr. S. G. Loughridge and R. L. Sanders. These gentlemen were tried before a military commission, with General Adelbert Ames as president and Jasper Myers as judge advocate. This trial took place at Vicksburg. The parties were detained there for three months. They had Hon. Wm. Yerger, Hon. Fulton Anderson, Hon. H. F. Simrall and T. B. Manlove, Esq., to defend them. They paid their attorneys $1500, and after a patient hearing were acquitted. These men were kept in a military prison, and were very well treated by the commission trying them. The four last named, who were not tried, had their cases decided favorable to them after the trial of the first named.

While these citizens of Newton and Jasper counties were in prison the times were very trying. The protection now given to the negroes made them very insolent and much harder to manage on the farm. The white people were intimidated. Knowing what their neighbors had undergone, and did not know at what moment they would be immured in a Federal prison, on the mere report of some negro who might have a spite at them, and with no way to get proof of their innocence; and even if the military authorities knew the accused innocent, they might be detained indefinitely, in order that others might be restrained from doing what the negroes did not like. Many who had taken some part in arresting the assassins were fugitives from home, or on the scout, so as not to be caught by the ever watchful Federal soldiers, who were on the lookout for them. A greater part of the year, the citizens who had escaped arrest immediately after the sad occurrences in the county, were compelled to stay from their homes.

The negroes, encouraged by the presence of the military in the country, became more bold, insulting and unbearable to the white man. It was not uncommon for them to meet and drill, and so bold did they become as to appear openly in day time on the streets of Newton and form lines and go through awkward movements of military drill, more to provoke the whites than anything else. In one or two instances a loaded gun was presented to a white man while the negro abused him. A point of desperation had then been reached, but much to the calm forbearance of the white man, this insolent conduct was borne with for a time. They proposed at one time to meet at a given point west of Newton, and march through the town, armed and commanded by military officers of their own choosing. A memorable occasion presents itself in that connection. A large body of negroes were in

Newton to hear what the white people had to say about their marching through town. Judge Watts, a very conservative man, willing to meet any emergency for the good of his people, mounted a stand in the streets and told them the impropriety of such a thing—what it might bring about, and there was no necessity for it. His speech was well received. After he closed, G. W. Cheek, a plain farmer, not accustomed to making speeches, rose and in a few sentences told them not to come, dared them to come, told them the consequences—they did not come. All praise to both men, but they looked at it from different standpoints.

CHAPTER XIX.

SECRET POLITICAL ORGANIZATIONS IN THE COUNTY—ARREST OF PROMINENT CITIZENS OF THE STATE—ARREST AND IMPRISONMENT OF A PROMINENT CITIZEN OF NEWTON COUNTY—HIS FIRMNESS IN RESISTING THE FEDERAL INQUISITION—REVIEW OF THE POLITICAL PARTIES AND THE DOMINATION OF THE REPUBLICAN PARTY IN THE STATE—EXPENSES OF CONVENTION OF 1868.

IN the year 1870 there was a secret political organization in the State, well known to most of the prominent citizens. This organization had for its purpose nothing more than the good of the country and the advancement of the Democratic party. There was nothing disloyal in it to the United States Government, nothing that would have been detrimental to a party if it had had anything like a fair showing with its great adversary, the Republican party. That was in the ascendancy all over the country, controlling every branch of the government. This secret society of Democrats, who were white men, had for one of its main features the ruling of the country by the Anglo-Saxon race, and by well concentrated action, bid fair to do a good work, and had it not been that this political organization shrouded itself in secret meetings, thereby exciting suspicions and giving excuse to the military power to thwart the plans, much might have been accomplished. If they had not concealed their existence and purposes, but declared an open hostility to the Republican party, their actions would not have excited such suspicion, and no pretext for arresting its members. Yet the Radical party in the State wanted some excuse to punish any respectable person found opposed in any such way to them. Prominent men were arrested in different parts of the State on the supposition that there was something treasonable in the secret meetings of the order. Newton county had more than one of these organized societies and was not an exception in the arrest and punishment of its members.

Prominent among the number was Mr. T. M. Scanlan, a popular citizen and merchant of Newton. A file of soldiers arrested and conveyed him to Jackson, to be tried in the Federal court at that place. This court of inquiry required Mr. Scanlan to make a revelation of all the facts connected with this secret political order to which he belonged. He did not deny that he belonged to it himself, stating that there was nothing treasonable or disloyal in its teachings, but he would not tell the small number of pass-words, grips and signs of recognition, etc., connected with it, nor would he tell who else in his county were members of this order. Upon such refusal he was placed in jail and kept for three months. A part of the time he was in prison an epidemic of yellow fever prevailed in Jackson. Had it not been for that they may have continued his confinement indefinitely, or until another term of the court.

Under all this force of circumstances, and the heavy demands made by the Federal Court, Mr. Scanlan was very firm and would rather remain in jail, unpleasant as it was, than to divulge the names of his associates and the secrets of the order. He nor his friends considered it any disgrace to be put in jail for such a cause. His friends sympathized with him and had cause to congratulate themselves that such a man would not betray them. He bore his imprisonment with the heroism of a brave Confederate soldier.

After Mr. Scanlan was released and came home, he was never called upon to appear in the Federal Court any more; the case was so settled that it was thrown out of court. There were many other arrests of the members of the order from Newton, as the names of all the members were given by some one to the authorities at Jackson. The arrested parties would plead guilty and pay the fine. The writer, a member of the order, was never arrested, but anticipating such thing, plead guilty through attorneys and paid the fine. Thus ended the secret political order that was intended only for good. Though it was broken up, yet it paved the way for further resistance to radical rule and strengthened those who were oppressed to make a more vigorous fight in a way that could not be attacked nor its members arrested and imprisoned; and only a few years and a Democratic victory was gained all over the State.

After the war the old Whig and Union parties were broken up. There were two great national political parties; there was the Republican party North, and by the success of that party in the results of the war, it claimed a large share of the most prominent men in the Northern States. This party was made up of the old anti-slavery elements—the ultra abolition party and the freesoilers of every class. The Whig party had largely gone to the Republicans and also some Union Democrats had gone with this party, and warmly participated with them in the suppression of the "rebellion." The party in power having conquered a peace, had put an end to the secession idea, and thousands of no very stable politics went to that party and caused it to be able to control the whole country. Backed up by active military operations all over the South, what could not be made law by the party could be enforced by the bayonet. A large standing army was now kept that presented a continual menace to anything that would hinder the prospects of their cause. Another important factor, as a political contingent, now added to their numbers, was the negro, who by the passage of the XV amendment to the Constitution, allowed all the Southern and Northern negroes to vote, and, as a natural consequence, they voted the Republican ticket. This great party North, who held complete control of all the Federal Government and complete control of the army and navy, was confronted by the solid South as far as the white vote went. There was an influx of foreigners, that is, adventurers from other States to the South in search of "assignment" to places of profit, together with the few scalawag elements, usually men who had held no office in the State; they with the carpet-baggers and negroes, opposed the Southern white vote and while, the military were in possession of the State, everything went the way that the party then in power wished it to go.

All the elections just after the war were carried for the Republicans—many of the best citizens were disfranchised for the part taken by them in the rebellion—and in this condition the Convention of 1868 was called to make a new constitution for the State of Mississippi.

This convention met on the 7th day of January, 1868, and is called the "Black and Tan Convention," composed largely of negroes and carpet-baggers. There were some very honorable exceptions of distinguished and patriotic Southern men who were in the convention, but they were powerless to do anything for the State of Mississippi. For reckless extravagance and waste of the people's money, this convention has no parallel in our State.

An extract, giving some of the main features, some important facts, with the expenses and time occupied, and other interesting matter connected with this convention, is taken from Lowry and McCardle's History. This extract thus states the particulars of the convention:

"These servile tools and trucklers to military power basely surrendered the right of all deliberative assemblies in America to judge of the election and qualifications to membership of their own body. The convention declared that it was not within its own province to determine, in cases of contest, who were the delegates to the convention, and that such contests could only be rightfully decided by the major-general commanding the fourth military district. In the case of Benjamin H. Orr, who claimed to be elected from Harrison county, a committee reported that Orr became a candidate for delegate to the convention with the *express consent of the military commander of this district*, contained in '*special orders 196*,' and the convention awarded the seat to Orr. So shameless an abandonment of all right and power, so disgraceful a travesty of deliberative proceedings, was never before or since exhibited to the admiring gaze of the world.

"The corrupt carpet-baggers, the ignorant negroes and baser renegades, who had tried their 'prentice hands' on the work of constitution making, for the few citizens of intelligence and decency had but little part in the construction of that instrument, completed their labors on May 15th, 1868, after having been in session four months and nine days. Each member of this multi-colored aggregation of ignorance, insolence and imbecility, including negroes, renegades and carpet-baggers, drew twelve hundred and ninety dollars ($1290) pay for his individual services, to which may be added the pay of 'Buzzard Eggleston,' the president of the convention, of twenty-five hundred and eighty dollars ($2580). The entire pay of the members alone aggregated the immense sum of one hundred and twenty-eight thousand, seven hundred and ten dollars ($128,710).

"This vast amount was greatly augmented by the pay of reporters, secretaries, sergeant-at-arms, chaplain, postmaster, door-keeper, pages, and all other places that the ingenuity of the reckless brigands could devise, to say nothing of the enormous amount expended for public printing. The aggregate cost of the convention may safely be estimated at no less than a quarter of a million of dollars. After these corrupt, unprincipled and vindictive buccaneers had expended their venom and adjourned, their handiwork of malice was submitted to the people for ratification or rejection. The white people of the State, incensed as they were beyond expression, avowed their determination to reject the mis-begotten and scoundrely constitution, maintain their free-born manhood, and let the consequences take care of themselves, and nobly did they accomplish their purpose.

"It will be remembered that the election at which the constitution was rejected was held under the direction and supervision of the miltary commander of the district, who according to his own report, took precaution to station troops at as many as sixty places in different parts of the State; and yet, notwithstanding the presence of the soldiers in nearly every county in the

State; in spite of the fact that the entire election machinery was in the hands of and controlled by the military, in spite of the fact that the gleam of the bayonet could be seen at many polling places, yet notwithstanding the odious and undeniable fact that a large number of the most intelligent and capable white citizens of the State were denied the right to vote, and were interfered with when they attempted to engage in the discussion of the wrongs and outrages sought to be perpetrated, the knavish instrument was voted down by an overwhelming majority. In this good work the white people of the State owe a large debt of gratitude to the negro voters for their voluntary and enthusiastic support in that great contest.

"In submitting the constitution for ratification or rejection there was a committee of five appointed by the convention, charged with the duty of making proclamation of the result of the election. In the hour of defeat, this committee, in its desperation, issued and caused to be published a statement that the counties of DeSoto, Rankin, Lafayette, Yalobusha, Carroll, Copiah, and Chickasaw had been carried against the adoption of the constitution by fraud, intimidation and violence, and recommended that the people of those counties should be denied representation in the Legislature, and that these people should be deprived of the right to vote for Representatives in Congress or for State officers.

"The suggestions of the committee of five were, however, not adopted. The members of the convention and committee of five continued to discuss the constitution they had made until the election and inauguration of President Grant, whom they fondly hoped would assist them in fastening manacles upon the people of Mississippi. In this, however, they were doomed to disappointment. That great soldier had as much contempt for them and their miserable work, as the people of Mississippi had recently manifested. With the manly frankness of the true soldier he recommended to Congress to provide for the holding of another election and allow the people the privilege of voting for or against the disfranchising clauses separately as well as for State officers, Representatives in Congress and the Legislature.

"This provision, so submitted, embraced the xivth and xvth amendments to the Constitution of the United States, which provided for the right of suffrage without regard to race or color, or previous condition of servitude.

"The election was held in November, 1869, when the white people of the State accepted the constitution as modified and recommended by the President. At the first election thereafter, by an odious and discriminating apportionment, the carpet-baggers, negroes, and renegades, were enabled to secure a large majority in the Legislature and the Senate and all the State officers, and Representatives in Congress. The Legislature when assembled elected two United States Senators."

Under these circumstances, it was no wonder that the original elements of the Democratic party South now cordially supported it as the only safety against the oppression of the Republican party. Old line Whigs and Union men who had opposed the precipitate action of the Democratic party in 1861, and had witnessed the opposition to that party bury the secession movement probably forever, were not, under any circumstances, disposed to affiliate with the Republican party.

There were too many that it so vitally affected their

social relations; there was so much oppression of the Southern people; they felt so near to each other that all old party differences were obliterated. The Whig and Democratic soldiers who for four years had battled for what they thought was their right, and home and property, were indissolubly cemented by ties of mutual protection stronger than hooks of steel. This soldier brotherhood in the tented field, in thick battle where death and carnage broke the ranks, and others with mutilated body and shattered limbs were captured and left in enemy's hands and carried to vile prisons. With victory or defeat the Southern man could not do anything but vote solid; a "solid South" it was; a "solid South" it will remain. Nothing can more securely cement the ties of affection and sympathy than to be thrown together in seasons of great peril to life and country; to home and wife and children. In great trials, when deeds of self-sacrifice, exposure to danger and death; and when men become banded together for a common cause, they appear to vie with each other, claiming that the "post of danger is the post of honor," when they are ready to sacrifice everything dear and life itself for their country. Then it is that these acts become a sublime spectacle. Under these circumstances, when men have escaped and return home, and it is expected by united political efforts they are to protect each other, men who have heretofore felt political estrangement are no longer opposed to that element, but now feel a congenial equality and a willingness to all vote the Democratic ticket.

CHAPTER XX.

Return of Home Rule in 1875.

The year 1875 is considered the Year of Jubilee for the State of Mississippi. The white people had borne the insults and reckless extravagance of the party in power until it became a load too heavy to be carried. The taxes had amounted to such proportions in the State and counties as to almost amount to confiscation. The citizens all over the State were terribly aroused at the idea of such conduct on the part of those controlling the affairs of the State government. As early as the 4th day of January of that year, some of the best, wisest, and most patriotic citizens met at Jackson in what was then called the Convention of the Tax-payers of Mississippi, in the hall of Representatives. Lowry & McCardle's History says:

"The Convention was called to order by Hon. W. L. Nugent, upon whose motion Gen. W. S. Featherston, of Marshall, was elected chairman. The Convention presented a petition to the Legislature showing the true condition of the State; they said that the general poverty of the people and depressed value of all property, and rate of taxation, made it an intolerable burden and much beyond their ability to pay. They insisted that the exorbitant expenditures must cease, or the means of the people would be exhausted; as an evidence of the extraordinary increase in taxation they cited the following:

"In 1869 the State levy was 10 mills on the dollar of assessed value of lands. For the year 1871 it was four times as great; for 1872 it was eight and a half times as much; for 1874 it was fourteen times as great as it was in 1869. They asserted that the tax of 1874 was the largest State tax ever levied in Mississippi, and the people were poorer than ever before. They stated that in many cases the increase in county levies for the same period was still greater. The petition was lengthy and gave the true state of affairs in an able and respectful manner, but they were called by Gov. Ames 'howlers.'

"The tax-payers' convention, held at the capital of the State, resulted in the organization of tax-payers' leagues, which were intended to be consolidated into a State organization, to check the process of confiscation inaugurated by the Radical party.

The Democratic State Convention assembled on the 3d of August, 1875. Nearly every county was represented. It was an assemblage of delegates of more than usual intelligence. General and Ex-Governor Clarke was made chairman, and Col. J. L. Power, Hon. J. L. McCaskill and Paul Botto were secretaries.

"Hon. L. Q. C. Lamar addressed the convention and was listened to with the greatest interest. Hon. J. Z. George was elected chairman of the State Executive Committee, and Marion Smith secretary."

On the 7th of December there was a riot, incited by Peter Crosby (a negro), at Vicksburg, in which there were many citizens wounded and slain. On the 4th of September, 1875, there was another riot, at Clinton, resulting in loss of life to both white and black. About the same time another riot, called the Yazoo riot, occurred, in which a few persons were killed. Says Lowry and McCardle:

"The canvass of 1875 was inaugurated with a fixed determination to no longer submit to the disgrace of being ruled by aliens, negroes and wreckers. Old men left their homes, and were found in the thickest of the fight, and not infrequently upon the hustings, encouraging young men to battle for constitutional liberty. Clubs were formed, and almost daily reinforced. Ames made frequent application to the President of the United States for troops to suppress the alleged violence in various parts of the commonwealth.

"Gen. George, the chairman of the Democratic Committee, wired the Attorney-General of the United States that there were no disturbances in Mississippi and no obstruction to the execution of the laws. Ames' continued applications for troops to assist him in his warfare induced Judge Pierrepont, the Attorney-General of the United States, to send C. K. Chase, Esq., a gentleman of intelligence and good address, to Mississippi to learn and report to him the true status of affairs.

"During Mr. Chase's stay at the capital a meeting was arranged for the 20th of October, between a committee of citizens and the Governor, in the interest of peace and order. The committee consisted of J. Z. George, W. L. Nugent, T. J. Wharton, John W. Robinson, H. Hilzheim, E. Richardson, R. L. Saunders, J. C. Rietti, David Shelton and Robert Lowry. The meeting was held in the parlor of the Governor's mansion. Terms were reached and mutual pledges given. The result of the conference with the Governor was made known, which was, that the militia was to be disbanded and the arms in their possession placed in the custody of the United States troops. The committee pledged that peace and order should be maintained. From that date the Radical ranks were broken, the leaders on the run, and a Democratic victory almost achieved. Barbecues, basket dinners, etc., were the order of the day.

"Hundreds and thousands of negroes were united with the army of whites. On the day of election the Democrats presented an impregnable column of determined men, aad won a victory, the importance of which was incalculable. After the smoke of battle had cleared away, the better opinion prevailed that Lieutenant-Governor A. K. Davis and T. W. Cardoza, State Superintendent of Education, both colored men, should be impeached." It resulted that Davis was impeached and turned out. Cardoza was allowed to resign.

Twenty-one articles of impeachment were preferred against Governor Ames, who, after seeing the certainty of being thrown out of office, was allowed to resign, the articles of impeachment being withdrawn.

Thus ended the Radical regime in the State. John M. Stone, president of the Senate, then became eligible to the office of Governor, and was inducted into that office March 29th, 1876.

In Newton county the struggle was not so great. The yoke of Radicalism had been thrown off in 1872, and although the people of Newton county did what was necessary in the last struggle, yet the forces to be met at home were not such as were in many of the other counties of the State. The people felt once more that they were free, with more liberty and enjoyment, more peace and good-will to both white and black, than had been enjoyed at any time since 1860.

CHAPTER XXI.

PROMINENT MEN OF THE COUNTY OF ALL CLASSES SINCE THE FORMATION OF THE COUNTY—PROFESSIONAL MEN OF THE COUNTY SINCE ITS FORMATION—PROMINENT MEN IN BUSINESS SINCE THE WAR.

It is expected that in the history of a county, there is more prominence to be given to professional men than any other. These men are expected to be better educated and to have more influence in a community than the average citizen. It is also expected that men who have been successful in the accumulation of wealth are more prominent than those who have not acquired it. Men to acquire wealth, when other men fail, are expected to have greater ability than those who, with the same advantages, have acquired none; and without disparaging the worth and merits of a man not having wealth and influence, it is well known that the men having wealth and influence, are usually men of talent and energy and will necessarily occupy higher positions in society. It is not a man's wealth that makes him a good citizen unless he uses it right; nor is it a a man's influence that should entitle him to place and power, unless that influence is for good, and yet both wealth and a bad influence are often used for unholy and improper purposes and will cause men to have a pre-eminence among their associates in communities; and without passing upon the merits of all who are mentioned, it is nothing more than right and proper in giving the history of a community to place prominently those who have in any way distinguished themselves.

Lawyers are usually among the most prominent men in a community. Newton county, before the war, had but few lawyers, and since has not a large number.

LAWYERS AT DECATUR.

J. J. Monroe, J. McAlpin, John W. Man, Judge Campbell, Wm. Saffold, J. F. N. Huddleston, T. B. McCune and Thos. W. Thurman, were the lawyers before the war. Thos. Keith and G. B. Huddleston have been added since the war. Keith and McCune are the only ones left as the others have removed or died.

LAWYERS AT NEWTON.

Hon. John Watts, W. T. Powe, Russell McInnis, Judge John Robb, Charles Murphey, J. F. Moore, Robt. Barrier, Ed. Watkins, W. H. Andrews, S. B. Ross, J. R. Byrd. Of these only Ross and Byrd remain, the others having died or removed.

LAWYERS AT HICKORY.

Gage and Boulton, the latter having removed.

John H. Regan was a lawyer of Newton county, living in the northern part of the county, is now dead. McCord, Benson and Bullard, lawyers of Connehatta. The latter having removed.

PHYSICIANS.

The physicians who have heretofore lived in various parts of the county, though now removed or dead, are: Drs. Bailey Johnson, Josiah and M. H. Watkins, S. G. Loughridge, Buckhannan, Evans, Frey, Jubal Watts,

M. M. Keith, Thos. B. McCord, L. M. Loper, Wesley W. Hall, N. L. Clarke, Jr., A. J. Pennington, S. B. Speed, G. W. Gilmore, E. Brown, W. J. Osburn, C. P. Partin, J. S. Parker, A. G. Bates, W. C. Lehr, J. A. Stephens, P. N. Wells, L. M. Clarke, J. V. Hamilton.

Those now practicing in the county are: Drs. J. B. Bailey, J. M. Cleavland, A. U. Gressett, W. A. L. Lewis, C. W. Carraway, F. B. Nimocks, G. G. Everett, J. C. McElroy, F. G. Semmes, A. H. Pucket, E. B. Partin, E. B. Pool, W. N. Davis, G. H. McNeill, J. J. Harralson, F. O. Horn, H. B. Ross, S. B. Hinton, O. L. Bailey, Wm. S. Norris, Clarence Gilmore, D. H. Leverett, and Dr. Spivey.

Dr. John H. Ferrell and J. P. Harris are resident dentists.

CHURCHES AND PREACHERS.

Newton county has eleven Missionary Baptist preachers as follows: J. W. Arnold, James E. Chapman, H. O. White, B. W. Dearing, T. I. Wells, N. L. Clarke, A. J. Freeman, W. P. Vaughn, E. W. Sumrall, Wm. Yarbrough, H. Bruce. The Primitive Baptist church has six ministers: W. J. McGee, W. S. Furguson, T. F. Gardner, A. Hollingsworth, E. S. Pennington, T. J. Stamper.

The Methodist Episcopal Church South, has four traveling ministers: J. M. Morse, Rev. Mr. Williams, L. P. Meadow and Rev. Mr. Witt, and three local ministers: R. W. Burton, J. H. Henry, and W. S. Partin.

The Old School Presbyterian church has one minister in the county—D. L. Barr.

The Cumberland Presbyterian church has

The Congregational-Methodist church has four (4) ministers—T. H. Rivers, J. M. Belew, J. C. Portis and Mr. Gilbert.

The Protestant-Methodist church has no ministers, though may have some members.

PROMINENT MEN IN POLITICS BEFORE AND SINCE THE WAR.

The men most actively engaged in politics before the war were usually those who held the legislative and county offices: Ullum Redwine, Armstrong, Jones, Johnston, Cooper, Graham, Thomas, Wells, Ware, Dansby, Keith, McElroy, Loper, Huddleston, McCune, Campbell, McAlpin, Williamson. These were representative men, and those who held office from among the first elected to the commencement of the war. Some of these names that were living were still in politics, and representing the county, and holding county office after the close of the war.

The year 1866, was the first election held after hostilities were over, and that year J. J. Perry, Thomas Keith, Jas. A. Ware, Wm. Thames, M. J. L. Hoye, Wm. Graham, were candidates to fill the county offices, and most of the men named were elected.

Those old office-holders continued active in politics, using whatever influence and zeal they possessed to carry the county for the Democratic party. After that, when politics became more excited and there were some opposed to Democracy in the county, others enlisted strongly in public matters. Eugene Carleton has been one of the most active men in politics in the county. He was largely instrumental in reclaiming the county from Radical rule, and has probably been more vitally interested than any other citizen of Newton county. The people were not unmindful of the work done by him, as in 1872 he was elected to the office of chancery clerk, and was continued in that place for sixteen years, and after that he was elected

Superintendent of Education. Marine Watkins took a large and active part in politics without asking an office, so did T. B. McCune. Added to these were J. B. McAlpin, Thos. M. Scanlan, J. C. Portis, J. F. Huddleston, A. E. Gray, W. N. Rains, G. M. Gallaspy, J. P. Dansby, Hamilton Cooper, Dr. J. B. Bailey, Dr. J. S. Parker, Thos. J. Bounds, Cornelius Boyd, I. I. Barber, G. B. Huddleston, W. C. Thornton, G. L. Doolittle, Jesse Pace, J. H. Regan, J. J. Armistead, J. L. Hardy, Dr. J. E. Longmire, J. F. Moore, Thomas B. Shockley, I. L. Pennington, C. S. Swann, J. R. Pace, J. K. Horn, R. K. Jayne, James A. Keith, G. M. Spencer, D. T. Chapman, I. L. Bolton, M. W. Stamper, G. B. Harper, F. B. Loper, Thos. Keith, A. M. Monroe, John F. Dearing, J. M. Lyles, Sim. Easterling, A. J. Freeman, F. N. McMullen, E. D. Beattie and S. M. Adams.

MERCHANTS OF NEWTON COUNTY.

At Decatur, R. J. Johnson, R. M. Johnston, Wm. McAlpin, W. W. Drinkwater, Steinhart, Sam'l Hurd, Nimocks & Loper, Montgomery Carleton, Scanlan & Huddleston, up to 1860; and Barrett, Russell & Hoye, Samuel Hurd, W. H. Gallaspy, Harris Barnes, James Hunter, F. N. McMullen—up to 1894. J. L. Shofner, and John H. Gray did a country business before the war in this county.

In 1860 there was some business done in the town of Newton by W. A. Payne, J. N. Shofner, J. R. Johnson, J. W. McGrath, and since by J. R. Johnson, R. M. Johnson, J. N. Shofner, E. & A. J. Brown, M. Watkins, Watts & Nimock, J. G. Moore & Co., Watkins & Williams, Richardson & Co., Williams & Gibbs, Scanlan & Scott, Clark, Dansby & Co., M. J. L. Hoye & Co., Jno. T. O'Ferrall, Clark & Russell, Manders & Dreyfus, R. K. Batte, Rue & McClinton, Schwab & Presser, W. T.

Dunagan & Co., Baucum & Leverett, E. P. Armistead, Sim Perry & Co., Bingham & Parker, G. H. McNeil, J. S. Davidson, S. NcElroy, M. Williams, I. I. Barber & Co., T. C. Viverett & Co., Mercantile Company and Racket Store.

The town of Lawrence was established after the war, E. D. Battie, J. Z. Jones, W. H. Sisson and J. A. McCain were the principal business men; up to the present a part remain.

Merchants at Hickory before the war were: Gray, Hidle, Edwards, and James Bell. Since the war: Barber & Thompson, W. N. Rains, Gray & Ward, Lem Nelson, Harper Bros., Ogletree & Brown, Penington & Bro., Norman & Co., Cook & Johnson, Osburn & Grissett, J. A. E. Dowling, D. H. Leverett, Wm. Hyde, I. I. Barber & Bros., Frank Russell, Rob. Barnett, Nelson Hopkins & Co., J. H. Wills, Wells & Hailey, Walton Gallaspy & Russell, McDonald Bros., Frank Pierce, Buckley Bros., and Davis G. Rayner.

Other prominent men in the county—some for wealth, some for influence, good character, citizenship, etc., energetic and otherwise—among whom are Mint Blelack and his sons, Samuel, M. E. and J. C. Blelack — the former, Mint Blelack, was one of the wealthiest men ever in the county; W. R. Norman and sons, James and Wm. Thames, Wm. Price, Bird Saffold and sons, E. S. Loper and sons, Samuel Hurd, J. M. Trussell, T. J. McMullen and sons, Wm. Reynolds and sons Hugh, Lock and Daniel; McFarland, Absalom and Joel Loper, Duncan Thompson, Watson and Henry Evans, A. E. and E. E. Chapman and sons, Hiram and Ben Walker, Ezekiel Arrington, Hardy Nichols, Abner Harralson, Archy and Chas. Wells, R. W. Doolittle and sons, John Blakeley and his sons, John and Thomas Dyess, John and Ed Waul, E. Scanlan, W. N. Raines, James Dunagen, Joseph A. Ware, and sons, Dr. Josiah Watkins and sons, William Graham and sons, Hamilton Cooper and sons, Alec Russel and sons, Vances, Amis's, Gordons, Hunter, Walton, Jesse Richmond, Dempsy, and Thos. Pace and their sons, N. L. Clarke and sons, M. P. and Stephen Williams and sons, Isaac and Isham Hollingsworth and sons, W. J. and Arthur Blackburn, Wm. Willis, Ben Bright, Bright Ammons, Samuel Stephens and sons, Wm. and James Cooksey and sons, Thos. Wash and sons, Thos. Caldwell, George and Thomas Laird, Archey Laird and sons, Samuel and Jackson Everett and sons, A. B. Woodham and sons, Richard McGhee and sons, Samuel Furgerson and sons, James Caraway and sons, Hamilton Davis and sons, Sim Castly and sons, Gilbert and sons. These names appear in the county history at an early day, and many of these names are still prominent in the county.

In a later period appear the names of Todd, Hoye, Huddleston, McCune, Adams, Cleavland, Flint, Stamper, Porter, Maxey, Thornton, Robuck Daniel, Lewis, J. G. and Wm. Moore, Allen and Williamson Glover, J. M. Kelly, the McDaniels, Wm. and Henry Walker, M. and M. R. and M. M. Watkins, W. L. McIntosh and sons, Jehu Pannel and sons, George Neil, and David Thomson, Sim Easterling, Jerry Barber, the Welch brothers, T. C. Viverett, Sim Perry, J. T. Watts, T. F. Pettus, Thos. Watts, John T. O'Ferrall, C. H. Rew, E. P. Armistead, E. P. Blelack, F. L. Loper, T. H. Selby, J. M. Hoye, J. W. Jones and sons, E. Dean and sons, Robert Jones and sons, H. W. Williams and sons, Henry and James Robinson and sons, Daniel Fore, John Everett, E. H. Woodham, John M. Nicholson and sons, H. C. Simmons and sons, G. W. Cheek and sons, W. W., J. L. and J. D. Hardy and Dr.

Longmire, R. H. Henry, J. E. Carteledge and sons, M. J. Chandler and sons, Dr. C. W. Carraway, Benton H. Rayner and brothers, McDonald Brothers, Barnetts, Harpers, Gilmores, Dowlings, Johnsons, Hannahs, Frank and Joe Russell, Bartlett, Hughes, Jones, McGees and Furgerson.

CHAPTER XXII.

VARIOUS NEWSPAPERS OF THE COUNTY, AND SOME MENTION OF THEIR EDITORS.

The publication of a newspaper is a great work, and the people owe much of their education and knowledge of the great and small things of the world by the publication of papers. A good paper, and that in its broadest sense, is a great benefit to any State and community. There is no doubt but the public prints of the country do more to shape legislation and the laws of the land than any other power that may be put into action. The free discussion of all topics connected with the country, the many good suggestions coming from such a great number of learned men, as the editors usually are, formulate opinions and make and crush great men and parties. This aggregation of knowledge, coming from so many sources, arguing the same subject from a different standpoint, bring out all the good and bad connected with any great measure; using a criticism sometimes very sharp, sometimes very timely, and at others very untrue, cause a much discussed political tenet, or party dogma, to take shape and crystalize into law and general adoption in a way much different from what it was originally intended.

The useful State and national paper stands as a sentinel to warn of danger and commend the good, reprove the bad which public men are trying to enact for the people. The useful county paper also acts as a faithful watchman, to do all the good possible for the constituency whom it represents, advocating the good and condemning the bad in party or people.

The religious paper is a power in the circulation of that kind of literature so much needed in christianizing the country. It also acts as a censor upon the conduct and lives of professed christians and others with whom it may come in contact; and is often the source from whence the most wholesome advice, as well as the promulgation and defense of the particular doctrines which it advocates. And then it is a great and good literary and christian journal. Aside from the advocacy of the great political and religious tenets and principles of the various parties and sects to which these papers belong, it is the duty of the great and small journals of the country to give the very best reading matter, of history and current news; to educate up to a higher plane of civilization and rightdoing; to wield the pen, "mightier than the sword," for the good of all concerned.

There is another class of newspapers—and their name is legion—which appear only to pander to a vitiated taste; to write and print only those things that cater to the gratification of depraved, licentious, perverted appetites; to publish only that which would excite; to gratify only that which is sensational, and by their adroit and spicy publications manage to capture a large number of readers, and reap rich rewards for their labor.

NEWSPAPERS OF THE COUNTY.

There were very few newspapers in the Sta'e before the year 1860, probably not more than 40. Now there are probably 162. There was no newspaper in Newton county until after the war. An attempt had been made to establish one at Decatur in 1861, but there was probably not a copy issued. The paper that had the circulation in this county for about twenty years before the war, was the *Eastern Clarion* published at Paulding, in Jasper county, about twenty miles from the railroad. This paper was owned and edited by Simeon R. Adams, who was a man of marked ability as a journalist. The *Clarion* was the largest paper in the State, had the largest circulation of any other journal in the State and an advertising patronage worth much more than any other State paper. It employed a steam power press and was said to have a net income of $10,000 per annum. The price was $2.50 cash, $3.00 at the end of the year. This paper was established in the year 1837, by Need & Duncan, who, during the next year, sold it to Jno. J. McRae, afterwards Gov. McRae. It is now published at Jackson as the *Clarion-Ledger*, and has never suspended since its first appearance.

In the year 1871, R. H. Henry, now editor of the *Clarion-Ledger*, came to the town of Newton, a very young man, not having reached his majority. With him he brought a newspaper outfit and commenced the publication of the *Newton Ledger*. This was the first paper ever printed in the county.

It is a little remarkable that the first paper ever published in Jasper county, established in 1837, and the first one ever published in Newton county in 1871, both adjoining counties in East Mississippi, should be blended as the *Clarion-Ledger*, and form one of the strongest newspaper firms in the South, and published at the capital, yet it is so.

The *Newton Ledger* was a paper of good size, fine print, and in every way a good county and family

paper. Mr. Henry was a practical printer, of good morals and sober, and well understood everything in connection with the printing business, having mastered all details during an apprenticeship of four years.

The tone of the paper was high; the politics Democratic; its news fresh and reliable; it had a good circulation and was well patronized as an advertising medium in the towns and county, to say nothing of its foreign business, which was large.

Mr. Henry moved the *Ledger* to Brookhaven in 1875, where it remained several years, absorbing the *Citizen* during the time, and in the year 1883, the paper was removed to Jackson, and published as the *State Ledger* till 1888, when it was merged with the *Clarion*, and has since been published as the *Clarion-Ledger*, and with J. L. Power and R. H. Henry as its owners, making it one of the most prosperous and useful papers in the South, its patronage and circulation is larger than ever before.

It is a pleasure to refer to R. H. Henry, who, as a poor but energetic, sober and industrious youth, came to Newton county and commenced the publication of the *Ledger*, his first paper. How well he has succeeded in life, is well known to the people of Mississippi. His portrait and sketch from the *Times-Democrat*, shows the appreciation of such men by those who have a right to known.

The *Ledger* was succeeded by the *Newton Democrat*, edited by Judge J. W. Robb, who had come to the town of Newton from Hinds county, to practice law. Judge Robb was an educated, talented gentleman, and was assisted in the *Democrat* office by his son, J. W. Robb, Jr., who was one of the sprightly young writers and poets of this State. The paper did not succeed, was removed to Morton and was there suspended.

Both father and son are dead. J. W. Robb, Jr., was engaged in newspaper business in the Delta country, and has been dead for a number of years. Judge Robb also removed to that part of the country, and has recently died.

In the year 1876, B. C. Carroll commenced the publication of the *Bulletin*, at Newton. Mr. Carroll was a very worthy man, an excellent citizen and brother-in-law to A. J. Frantz, of *Brandon Republican* notoriety. The *Bulletin* was a sprightly paper, but did not get the patronage to justify a longer stay than about one year. Mr. Carroll left Newton and has since died.

The *Bulletin* was succeeded by the *Report*, edited and published by Mr. R. K. Jayne, commencing in the fall of 1877. Mr. Jayne was teaching the school at Newton with marked success, and concluded that to to add the *Report*, as an advertising medium, would prove a success. The paper also took part in the county and State affairs, and proved a very readable and agreeable journal. It was continued until the year 1880, and was moved to Jackson and continued as an educational journal under another name. Mr. Jayne was an educated man, a good teacher and strong writer, and during his stay at Newton gathered around him some warm friends who have not forgotten him. He is living at Jackson, engaged in the building and loan association.

After the removal of the *Report* from Newton, W. H. Seitzler established the *Free Press*. This paper was continued for about one year, but did not succeed in making it pay, and it was sold to J. F. Moore, Esq., who was a lawyer at Newton. W. H. Seitzler now edits the Hickory *Progress*. There is no doubt that he gets up one of the best county papers in the State; that he has rare facilities for pleasing his readers, and should feel encouraged at the progress he has made in the management and editing of his paper. J. F. Moore edited and owned the *Free Press* for about two years, and probably made a little more of a financial success of the paper than his predecessor, though having many other things, connected with his legal profession and business matters, to call off his attention, he did not give it the care that he otherwise would. It appears that after the removal of the *Ledger* it was quite difficult to keep up a paper in the town, and if money was not lost in the investments there was none made. Mr. Moore died at his home in Newton.

In 1889 W. H. Andrews, a young lawyer, bought the *Free Press* and was its editor for a short time. There was very little circulation to the paper during the time Mr. Andrews had charge of it, and probably no money made; more likely some was lost. Mr. Andrews removed to Texas as a practicing attorney, and is now in California and supposed to be doing well. After the removal of Andrews, S. B. Ross, a lawyer and printer, took editorial charge of the paper at Newton, then called the *Dispatch*, in 1886, and continued to edit until sometime during the year 1887, when it was sold to J. J. Armistead, and the name was continued. Mr. Ross probably made some money in publishing the *Dispatch*, and was also engaged in the practice of his profession. He is still one of the prominent men of the town of Newton, engaged in the practice of law, also a correspondent of literary journals, and agent, in connection with his partner, J. R. Byrd, for Shattuck & Hoffman, a large monied syndicate, who loan money on real estate in this and adjoining counties. They have loaned about $40,000 about one-half in Newton county. These debts are usually met promptly, very little property having been sold.

J. J. Armistead commenced the publication of the *Dispatch* at Newton in the year 1887, and continued for nearly three years, and then sold the whole outfit to a corporation at Hickory, in this county, and was called the Newton County *Progress*. Mr. Armistead had no experience in editing a paper and commenced the business after he was well advanced in life. He was a man of strong convictions and very fearless in his utterances. Yet the *Dispatch* was conducted with a very good degree of prudence, and was very well liked by its patrons. It espoused the cause of temperance and reform as probably no other paper had ever done in the county. Usually took a decided stand in politics, and was a very independent paper. It was probably not a monied success.

Mr. Armistead is still at his home in New Orleans. After the removal of the *Dispatch* office to Hickory, in the year 1890, there was no paper at Newton until September of that year the *Mississippi Baptist* was established under the direction of the Mount Pisga Association, with Rev. N. L. Clarke as as editor; S. B. Ross assisted as secular editor of the *Baptist*, but did not long remain in that position. The paper was intended to be an incorporated journal under the management of a certain number of directors. It never fully complied with the requirements of the charter, and did not assume the position of an incorporated paper, but was conducted under the management of directors and editor until May, 1893, when the whole outfit was destroyed by fire. The loss was not total; there was a small insurance, which helped to establish it again; another outfit was purchased by Viverett & Ross, with the same editor, with L. S. Tilgham as publisher. In the month of August, 1893, the first issue after the fire was published.

HISTORY OF NEWTON COUNTY. 203

The editor of the *Mississippi Baptist* is one of the oldest and best known men in the county. He has been preaching in the county for about fifty-two years, and is considered one of the most zealous and active workers the church has ever had. Mr. Clarke is a man of good acquirements, of liberal education, extensive reading, a close student, and is thus fitted to fill well his place. The *Baptist* has probably not made any money, to include the loss sustained by the fire, yet it is a paper desired by the Baptist people of this Association, and it is pretty well patronized. The publisher is L. S. Tilgham, a young man of sober habits, well qualified as a practical printer, and the paper is always on time.

The *Conehatta Index*, a paper published at an interior town, eleven miles north of the railroad, was established about the 1st of March, 1889, formed by a stock company of the citizens of the town and surrounding neighborhood. The paper was published by J. W. Brooks, Dr. Bailey, Prof. Scott and T. P. Williams conducting the editorial department. Brooks published the paper for about two and a half years, when Prof. McBryde and J. S. Scott assumed the management, Scott as editor, assisted by Dr. Bailey. Under this management the paper was published about one year. In February, 1892, the stockholders placed the editing and business management in the hands of Victor Hamilton. He conducted the paper until August, 1892. The paper since that time has been conducted and edited by T. P. Williams. The *Index*, since its first issue, had a Grange department, edited and controlled by Mrs. Dr. Bailey, but has never been a Grange paper. The *Index* is a substantial Democratic paper, with something from Mrs. Bailey to encourage the Grangers and to do good for the country. It is a moral, good family paper. Its editor is a sprightly, well educated man of good moral habits, and should be patronized by his community. The *Index* has not been a large monied success, but has done good work for the Patrons' Union and Conehatta.

The Newton County *Progress* was commenced in 1890 with J. M. Gage as the editor. This paper was established by a co-operative association of merchants and others, who made a stock company, and operated the paper for a time in this way, with Mr. Gage as editor. It then was edited by Mr. Hickey, who for about two years conducted the editorial and other management of the paper. After Mr. Hickey left the paper, the present management, with W. H. Seitzler as editor, has continued. The *Progress*, as has been said, is one of the best county newspapers in the State, and deserves the patronage of the public, and is well sustained by home advertisements.

On the 1st of June, 1894, the *Commercial*, a newspaper, was started at Newton. This is the fourth paper now in the county. This paper is edited by S. B. Ross, Esq., who has had considerable experience in the newspaper business. He established the *Dispatch* at this place, and also assisted in the secular editorial department of the *Baptist*. Mr. Ross is a young man of talent and will strive to make the *Commercial* a readable and useful paper. The *Commercial* is thoroughly Democratic in its tone, and doubtless will take active part in the politics of the county. Mr. Ross has associated with him Mr. Colson, who is local editor and publisher of the *Commercial*. Mr. Colson is a steady and sober man, and a creditable publisher. In connection with this office is a thoroughly equipped job office that does good work in its line.

The newspaper business in this county has never

proved very profitable. Several reasons may be assigned for this failure. One is that there is not usually enough capital; that necessarily prevents the employment of an agent to travel and secure advertisements, and subscribers. There are a number of first-class city papers who employ large corps of trained newsgathers in all the surrounding States, and have correspondents in most of the inland towns, who furnish all the important items of the various States, and it is these great dailies that are brought through the county, morning and evening, by the railroad, that supply the people with most of the reading matter in the way of newspapers. The mail facilities are also excellent, conveying to the county from the railroad, mail matter from all the large cities in the country, thereby making it a very easy and cheap method of supplying the people and educating them up to the latest and best of the news, both from our own State, the adjoining States, and our Federal Capital. More enterprise and greater displays of energy and ability to circulate the first-class journals is now seen than at any other age of the world. Yet the people of the county want a paper published in their own county. There are many advertisements that should only appear in such a paper, and there is county news that should only be published in such a paper; and thus it is that this want is only supplied by a paper published in some of our towns. The people of the county should patronize the county paper, should feel a laudable pride in its support. Our merchants and others wishing their business known should advertise in these papers, as they form a good medium for letting their business be known to the people who come to market.

Every editor should use his best efforts to present to his readers an interesting paper every week. To fill it with matter largely connected with the county and places in which the paper circulates. The subscriber should promptly pay in advance the small price asked for the county paper, and in this way publishers and subscribers may be mutually benefitted.

CHAPTER XXIII.

INTRODUCTION OF THE GRANGE INTO THE COUNTY—ALLIANCE MOVEMENT—THEIR INFLUENCE IN POLITICS—THEIR EFFECT ON SOCIETY—WHAT HAS BEEN THE GENERAL GOOD RESULTS ON THE FARMING POPULATION FROM THESE ORDERS.

THE Grange movement in this county occurred very early after the order was introduced into the Nation and State. The first Council, as they were first called, met at Decatur, January, 1873. The first County Grange was held at Decatur, January 2d, 1875. The order at once attracted great attention, and for years there was much said and published with regard to its movement. It was supposed by many that the Grange was an order which only had an interest in the farm and the productions of the country. By others that it only required a man to be a member to be the recipient of some special benefit and that large provisions would be made for the poor man.

The order being a secret organization and a nominal fee charged for admission, also made it attractive to many who were curious to know its hidden mysteries. It also allowed the female portion of the community to join, and that was attractive and profitable to both male and female members.

The Grange was not long in operation before much was said of it as a political factor in the elections in the country. Very soon were found newspapers which advocated the Grange and also urged that the organization should take a place in the political world. Very many have been the tilts that the order has taken in politics. Many have been the men who professed to like well the order, only to have ridden into office on that hobby.

The Grange, as a great organized body of industrious farmers, has claimed as its peculiar prerogative to attack any law of the land not conforming, in its judgment, to the advancement of the interest of the masses. It is bold in its denunciations of trusts, combines, plutocracy, improper accumulations of wealth; undue use of monied power; improper usurpation of executive and judicial authority; unfair discrimination against any section, or favored individuals, or the enactment of any laws that would in any way make an invidious distinction against the farming interests of the nation.

It has been free to attack any law governing the financial system of the country, criticise any action of the State or national government supposed to be class legislation, or anything infringing upon the rights of the farmer. Its demands also have been strong for the passage of certain laws which would be of great advantage to the people at large. Their representatives have had large audiences at the national capital in suggesting and originating the laws of the land. It has had great weight, no doubt, with the representatives of the nation in the framing of those laws looking to the sale of the products of the farmer; to the introduction into foreign markets with as little delay and duty as possible, the articles that are for sale by the farmers of the United States.

The Grange insists on laws to prevent the manufacture of any article for home consumption that is impure or injurious, or that does not come up to standard grade. Every form of legislation and commerce having for its end the good of the people of the country has been more or less inquired into by the Grangers. What are the rights of this organization? is a question which has been answered, sometimes satisfactorily, and at others the very reverse, to most of the members of this order. Some would relegate them to the rear as a class of citizens that knew little and that had no place in State and national affairs. Others claim that it was not at any time considered as competent that they should engage in politics, nor should they dictate or suggest anything to the State or national Legislature; that from their position in life they would not be expected to know what were the wants of the country, and that their suggestions would more clog the wheels of government than assist in the great machinery, which was only the work of statesmen; that the Grange should not be a political machine, but one to make the products of the country, to place them upon the market, and then their responsibility ceased. Those who hold to these opinions are very much mistaken. There are nearly half of the people of the world engaged in agriculture; about nine-tenths in the agricultural counties of this State. This, as a matter of course, if all combine, always places a majority of their number in office, when such majorities obtain. As a natural consequence, one of the first and great principles of the Granger or farmer should be to look to the very best development of the business in which he is engaged, and to study well what would be his best interest; what he should plant that would yield the best results; how to cultivate the land to make it more subservient to him; everything, both scientific and practical, every method should be studied that will conduce to his benefit. Let the Grange not be named a political party, but have a right to elect any man to office that is worthy and competent and that will act in conformity to the principles of justice and equality to all men. A man who would carry out the precepts of the order consistent with the rights of all, and for the good of all, would be a proper man to elevate, whether he be a Granger or not.

The Grangers should recognize that the law-makers should not all be of their order, but power should be vested in the hands of those who are willing to work for the best interests of the country, and to give to those who are the largest constituency, an equal right in all things connected with the government of the country. No spirit of agrarianism should be allowed to take root in this organization. If any may succeed in life by any legitimate and honorable pursuit, he should be allowed to enjoy it free from insidious attacks or envious molestation. No communistic or anarchistic spirit should invade this body. Let a principle be encouraged that every one should work and provide for himself.

The farmers have rights in the country. They should maintain that high position which is and ought ever to be accorded to them from their superior numbers, and they should always exercise their rights, prerogatives and liberty, in a way that will be for the best interests of the masses in the great agricultural country in which we live.

The first Grange in Newton county was organized at Oakland in 1874. The first County Grange, then called Councils, was organized at Decatur, January 2d, 1873, with the following delegates from various Granges, but mostly from Newton county:

HISTORY OF NEWTON COUNTY. 211

Bethel Grange, No. 243, sent Jas. E. Chapman and C. J. Johnson, as delegates; Dixon, No. 400, represented by W. F. Kirkland; Pinkney, No. 223, sent J. C. Edwards and A. Gardner; Mt. Hebron, No. 391, sent W. A. Taylor and A. Laird; Centreville, No. 250, sent J. R. Pace; New Ireland, No. 243, sent J. J. Vance; Beaver Creek, No. 484, sent A. T. Nicholson and H. B. Haddon; Oakland, No. 175, sent T. J. Reynolds and H. C. McMullen; Garlandsville, No. 296, sent W. H. Bonner and R. H. Weir; Spring Hill, No. 234, sent Sim Perry and I. L. Bolton; New Hope, No. 249, sent H. Cooper and D. M. Carr; Pine Forest, No. 188, sent J. S. Parker and Isaac Bufkin; Golden Grove, No. 418, sent A. W. W. Grafton and P. Nicholson.

This information is taken from the official records at Decatur and kindly furnished by Mr. A. M. Monroe, who has also given other valuable information which will be appended in connection with statistics of Newton county Granges. The above are the accredited delegates at this meeting. M. W. Stamper was Worthy Master and D. M. Carr, Secretary of the Council. On July 10th, 1874. delegates were, according to call of S. B. Gilbert, Special Deputy, and the County Grange was organized with the following officers: S. B. Gilbert, Worthy Master; M. W. Stamper, Overseer; Wm. McCraney, Lecturer; T. C. McMullen, Steward; J. P. Partin, Assistant Steward; Wm. Graham. Chaplain; G. M. Gallaspy, Treasurer; T. J. Reynolds, Secretary; C. H. Doolittle, Gate-keeper; Mrs. M. E. Hardy, Ceres; Mrs. R. R. McMullen, Pomona; Rachael Reynolds, Flora; C. C. Stamper, Lady Assistant Steward.

January, 1875, the County Grange convened, and the following officers were elected: M. W. Stamper, Worthy Master; S. B. Gilbert, Overseer; Dr. J. S. Parker, Lecturer; H. C. McMullen, Steward; Sim Perry,

Assistant Steward; Wm. Graham, Chaplain; E. Carleton, Secretary; T. J. McMullen, G. K.; Mrs. S. C. Allen, Ceres; Mrs. McMullen, Pomona; Mrs. M. E. Hardy, Flora; Mrs. C. C. Stamper, L. A. S.

The County Grange elected as principal officers in the year 1876, S. B. Gilbert, Worthy Master; George Todd, Secretary. In the year 1877, Dr. J. B. Bailey was elected Worthy Master; S. B. Gilbert, Overseer; T. J. Reynolds, Secretary. Election of officers for 1878: Dr. J. B. Bailey, Worthy Master; Thos. Keith, Overseer; and H. Cooper, Secretary. The year 1882, Dr. J. B. Bailey was elected Worthy Master; Wm. Price, Overseer; and Mrs. Joe Bailey, Secretary. Jno. F. Dearing served from 1884 to 1890 as Worthy Master; A. M. Monroe, as Overseer, and W. C. Thornton, Secretary for the same time. M. W. Stamper was elected Worthy Master in the year 1890; A. M. Monroe, Overseer; and J. W. Thrash, Secretary; and these continued in office up to and including the present year of 1894.

It will be seen from the above named officers, ladies and gentlemen, that some of the best citizens of the county have given their time and attention to this order, and many of them, with others whose names are not recorded, have faithfully labored to elevate the order and better the condition of the working classes of the county.

The names of the Granges that have been organized in Newton county, are as follows: Bethel, Pinkney, Mt. Hebron, Centreville, New Ireland, Oakland, Spring Hill, New Hope, Pine, Forest, Evergreen, Spencer, Poplar Springs, Cedar Creek, Tallahatta and Lake—total sixteen.

Newton, in Grange matters as well as fertilizers, has been the leader, and is called the banner county in this order. Her citizens have held responsible and respectable positions in the State Grange. Dr. J. B. Bailey has served on Executive Committee, as Lecturer, Overseer, and Master of the State Grange; Mrs. Joe Bailey, wife of Dr. Bailey, as Treasurer six years, and as Flora of the National Grange. John. F. Dearing, as one of the Executive Committee, and Lecturer two years; A. M. Monroe as Steward a long time, and as Secretary of the Darden Monumental Committee. The monument was erected at the A. & M. College in the year 1891, and is a lasting memorial to the memory of the lamented Grand Worthy Master of the State and National Grange—Capt. Put Darden.

THE GOOD RESULTS OF THE GRANGE.

The effect on society and the morals of the county, has been very marked. There are several reasons for this, and prominently among them is the Grange, and the admission of women to the order. The refining influence of woman is ever potent in any circle of society into which she enters. To know that she is expected to be present always incites to a greater degree of morality, as it is known that no deviation from this rule will be tolerated where she is expected to appear and participate. It is not only so where the sexes are associated together in the transaction of the business of the order, but her gentle, kind and moral influence prevails, and dominates the same society when met outside the order. The Grange and the female contingent in it has no doubt largely encouraged the temperance movement and given strength in that direction which has proved of great benefit to temperance workers.

The educational interest has particularly received substantial benefit from the order. It not only advocates schools in all parts of the country, but is a school within itself; to educate, not only the young, whose minds are bright and susceptible of good impressions, but it has enabled the old men of the country and the middle aged, who had no early advantages, by association and by active work, to learn and investigate many things of which they knew nothing before; to read for themselves and become more independent than they were before they became members of the order, It has encouraged education in a way that both men and women have learned to express themselves more freely and fluently and more intelligently, orally and through the press and in general conversation, than before. Its social relations are wonderful. Here in the Grange it is where men and women that differ widely upon politics and religious doctrines may come together and call each other brother and sister, and have a kind and loving feeling, that have been heretofore regarded as having no congeniality, as having no joint interests; they have been strangers, though being acquainted; they now feel a close tie that binds, and that is for the good of the whole country. It serves to obliterate all distinctions in society; to take all who are deserving and educate them up to a higher plane and to better acts and aims in life; to imitate the qualities of better and more intelligent men and women, and seek such relations that would add much to their standing in society, that would inspire to greater success in life, making better citizens, better husbands and wives, raising the standard of citizenship in the country.

The general interest and benefit for the farming classes have been great. The mass of farmers, before this organization was introduced, had no idea of any improved methods; no access to any kind of agricultural literature; nothing but what by careless observation (many times) had been handed down from father to son, and often a retrograde movement was made instead of an advance. The ever severe teacher, experience, and the often repeated failures of the farmer, had not taught him the knowledge so much required for his advancement in this direction.

A system of intelligent farming is now introduced, an interchange of opinion, a personal experience, a trial of various modes of doing the same work, are now canvassed and discussed, and the adoption of one most successful is the result. No man who wishes to learn and is inclined to do anything on his farm, can fail to improve his stock of agricultural knowledge if he will attend regularly upon the meetings of this order, and listen to those who, from practical experience, have succeeded, by pursuing certain methods known to the most intelligent farmers of the country. The use of fertilizers in an intelligent way claims as its authors the best farmers and Grangers of this country. To take a view of the figures of the relative production of the county for the ten years embraced between the years of 1880 and 1890 will show what an intelligent use of fertilizers will do under Grange farming and improved methods.

The product of cotton in Newton county for the year 1880, was: bales of cotton 6341, bushels of corn 261,207, estimated value of products sold and on hand in the county, $634,264. The product of the county for the year 1890 was 13,097 bales of cotton, 392,619 bushels of corn; estimated value of products sold and on hand, $919,330. If the crops of 1892 could be shown it would probably run to 15,000 bales of cotton, with a corresponding increase in all other products, and an estimated value of all sold and on hand would run largely over a million dollars. This is good proof of the advantages of fertilizers used by the farmers, most of whom belong to the Grange, and who have had the advantages of close intercourse with the best informed lecturers on these subjects, and small experimental stations at the grounds of the Patrons' Union, and the advantages of our A. and M. College, which yearly send a deputation of its faculty to talk to and inform our people upon the best methods of farming and applying fertilizers. Various speakers have honored the County Grange. Distinguished men from other States have come to our county to enlighten our people, of which more will be said in another place, all of which has been at the instance of the Granges of Newton county.

The State Grange met in December, 1889, in the College Hall, in the town of Newton, and was presided over by Dr. J. B. Bailey, Master of the State Grange. This meeting was one of interest to the order, and had some distinguished visitors as attendants. Judge H. F. Simrall repepresented his section of the State, and S. L. Wilson, State Lecturer, from Chickasaw county, and afterwards Master of the State Grange, was present. Quite a number of delegates from various portions of the State were present. It was the first meeting of this body after the death of Captain Put. Darden, Master of the State and National Grange, and the chair and stand were appropriately draped in mourning. Upon this occasion the writer was requested to make the address of welcome to the assemblage of delegates at this meeting of the State Grange, and upon being introduced said:

"*Ladies and Gentlemen and Delegates of Mississippi State Grange:*

"It is my pleasant duty to welcome you to our town, and in doing so we are not unmindful of the distinguished honor you have conferred upon us in selecting this point as a suitable place for the holding of your deliberations. Especially is this so when so many places in the State making more pretentions than we, and who might have entertained you better than we are able, have cordially invited you. Yet we hope as you have made this selection to make your stay both pleasant and profitable. I have never had the honor conferred upon me of being a member of your order, my lot in life having been thrown in a different channel. Yet I have observed the progress of your order from its earliest incipiency and have noted with peculiar certainty the steps of advancement made by it in the twenty years of its existence in our county. An organization having inscribed upon its banner, Religion, Temperance, Progress and Reform, I can bid Godspeed. Yea, I can do more than that. I feel that I can take each member by the hand, and say, my brother or my sister. I have observed the improvements of your order at your homes, around your firesides; in your social relations and friendly intercourse with your neighbors. I have seen the great improvement made in your farms, more system, order, better price, greater yield, more brought to market and crops more diversified than ever before.

"I have observed that you have taken the lead in education, have done more for your children and society at large. You have admitted your women to your order, which is a step in the right direction. When I come to eulogize or pass any encomiums upon women, I feel inadequate to the task. Suffice it to say, that woman is a prime factor connected with anything relating to us, and that her admission into your order is eminently right. She is always willing to lend her aid, which is one of the greatest incentives for man's accomplishing a higher destiny in life. I observe that you have not only been progressive but aggressive. You have looked to the interests of your order, which has benefitted the country at large. You have corrected abuses in legislation and asserted and enforced your rights in State and Federal relations.

"It is a well understood fact that no State is ever fully developed unless its lands are owned and tilled by the persons who live upon them, if engaged in agricultural pursuits. It is not my purpose to give you a dissertation upon agriculture, or dictate a course of farming, yet it is well understood that it is not the greatest number of acres under cultivation that always pays the best, but small areas well cultivated bring the best results to a country. I would like to impress upon you that I consider it your highest duty and one of the surest to success, that you cultivate the friendliest relations with all classes not engaged in agriculture. It is a great tribute to the producing class to say that they feed and clothe the world; and the greater the number who are dependent upon them for support, the greater will be the demand for their products, and consequent enhancement of value. Antagonize no interest. The professional men must exist, the citizen, the mechanic, the merchant, the architect, the sculptor, the painter, the manufacturer and the railroader. In fact every trade must live from your labor. Encourage large urban population and the increase of consumers if you wish the farm to thrive.

"In all the great events of life, whenever there is a necessity for a great man to carry out a certain great purpose, he has been found. In the dark days of the inquisition, when men's consciences were called in question; when not only their political, social and religious rights were proscribed; their social standing ostracized, their property confiscated, but their lives were taken in the most tortuous methods—in those days there arose a man that not only defied the Federative Diet at Worms, but defied the world and proclaimed a freedom of thought and a liberty of conscience that has spread itself to all the enlightened nations and of which we are to-day the favored beneficiaries.

"There was a time when our forefathers considered they were oppressed, when the mother country imposed upon the colonies. There was a time when brave men dared to oppose these wrongs, and formed a declaration of principles, declaring all men free and equal; in support of which they pledged themselves in solid compact to support it with 'their lives, their property and their sacred honor.' In this dark hour there was a man found who was willing and able to take control of the military forces, which he led to glorious victory, establishing a country "without a model and without a shadow;" a country from which the whole world is expected to be christianized, and of which we to-day are the prosperous people and favored recipients. When it became necessary that one man should rule the whole of Europe, Napoleon Bonaparte was found equal and willing to undertake the task. And as an example of his courage and military genius, when at the bridge at Lodi men who were veterans, who had made many a charge and who had accomplished many a daring feat, were commanded to cross the bridge. In vain did they essay to do it, and at last returned and said: "Sire, it is impossible." The laconic but characteristic reply was: "Follow your general." The bridge was crossed, the Austrians were conquered, and the world knows the result.

"For centuries the farming classes have considered

themselves oppressed. For ages have they been the dupes of monopolies, living in a country whose taxes they have paid without representation ; whose laws they obey and have no hand in making ; who bear the heat and the burden of the day, and only get the wages of those who come in at the eleventh hour ; who feed and clothe the world without being able to name the price of their production, or raise their wages. Will it be saying too much to assert that this and kindred organizations will be the agents to remedy all these things ? That if they progress at the ratio that they have in the last twenty years, that wonders will be performed ? Legislation will be changed ; laws that govern commerce will be altered ; much of the systems of finance and even political economy will be so amended as to fit themselves to the great wants of the masses, and not have dictated the unjust and unequal terms which are now foisted upon them. If this organization should bring this order out of chaos ; if it should prove the great remedial agent for the distribution of justice and equality ; if its working should reach a higher plane in the administration of the laws of the land, in giving to each the benefits to be derived from a prosperous and well-governed country, favor and uphold justice, strike down monopolies, anarchists and communism, with all their kindred evils, it would be a 'consummation most devoutly to be wished.' This order has the probability of a great future, if it can accomplish its end. In union there is strength ; in co-operation there is success. Well organized numbers will insure you achievements. Then come from the hill-tops and the vales ; come from the mountains and the plains. Let no sectional or political prejudice hinder your success.

"Come as the leaves come when the forest is rended ;
Come as the waves come when navies are stranded ;
Come as the autumnal leaves fall in the vale of Valambrosia ;"

and with a united purpose and trust in God the victory will be yours.

In the progress of these great events, a thorough union of all the planting classes will give them control of the government and the making of the laws, and the responsibility of governing the country. Under these circumstances the hand of justice and wisdom, tempered with mercy and an honest administration and enforcement of the laws, it would make our country the admiration and wonder of the world.

"What means these weeds of mourning that I see before me—this empty chair and other indications of grief? The mute response of every member of your order is that our leader is gone—our chief is not here. No more will we see his genial smile; no more will we hear his cheerful voice or listen to his words of wise counsel; no more will we feel the warm grasp of his hand, for all that is mortal of Capt. Darden is deposited in the grave.

"The next pertinent enquiry is, who will take his place? Who will be our leader? Who will be our chief? Grief-stricken hearts at this moment of great calamity will say his place cannot be filled.

"The preachers, when they write of the death of one of their fallen brethren, engaged in the work of the Lord, sometimes say that 'God destroys his best workman and carries on his work.' Why not this apply to your departed chief? His place will be filled. Those of you who were engaged in the last war, and that understand military tactics, will remember that when a brigade or regiment was ordered to charge a given point—when the command is given the troops go forward, and, coming near the place to be taken, the missiles of death fly thick and fast; the grape-shot and cannister cut great swaths out of the advancing columns, but the order 'close up' comes from the well known voice of the commander, and mechanically and involuntarily the breach is closed and the ' solid wall of human wood' rush on to victory, carnage and death. Any order having on its banner Progress and Reform, cannot afford to stop even though it has lost a valued leader.

"When the lamented Gen. Warren, one of the most distinguished military men, fell at Bunker Hill, in the prime of his manhood — yea, in his 'glorious youth' — it would appear that the brightest star in the great cause of freedom was blotted out and all hope of that day was lost. But the heroic valor of Israel Putnam won the day and crowned the American arms with success. The grateful remembrance of this great sacrifice Warren and his comrades in arms, caused an imposing monument to be raised to their memory. A superb obelisk of gray granite, whose lofty spire pierces the blue ether which, Mr. Webster said was a 'plain shaft, that there it stood and there it will stand forever.' This monument is a fitting reminder of the great deeds of those heroes. But the remembrance of those great men whose names are inscribed on that marble shaft, were enshrined in the hearts of the people of that, and the present day, and will be in the hearts of their countrymen for ages to come.

"So it is with your departed hero. A monument by his people will be erected; upon it will be inscribed the name of one whose memory will still linger like a sweet fragrance from a broken vase, to remind you of the sterling qualities of head and heart which he possessed, and the unselfish interest which he manifested for the working classes. We drop a tear with the bereaved and lament the death of one so highly gifted and so much needed; but humbly bow to God's will, and devoutly pray that his successor may be worthy of the position, and able to accept the responsibility that devolves upon him. Again I welcome and thrice welcome you to our town."

THE ALLIANCE.

The Alliance movement came years after the Grange, and it was very popular for a time, and quite a number of Alliances were organized in Newton county. It was thought that organizations so nearly alike, having for their aims the same ends, should unite in one grand brotherhood. Some overtures from the Alliance were made to the Grange, but no union was ever effected. It appears that the Alliance, from the beginning, had more of a political element in it than the Grange. The people of the country had plenty of political agitation outside their orders, and to inaugurate a policy to still further augment this feeling and possibly divide the interest manifested in the Grange, did not appear expedient. The two bodies did not unite and the Alliance has but little following in Newton county as far as organization is concerned. About thirty Alliances were organized, with a total membership of twelve hundred.

CHAPTER XXIV.

PATRONS' UNION—ITS BENEFITS AS AN EDUCATOR—IMPROVEMENT OF SOCIAL, LITERARY AND DOMESTIC RELATIONS.

The Patrons' Union is situated on the eastern boundary of Newton county, two miles north of the town of Lake, and forms one of the principal attractions for entertainment and education in the county. It was organized in the year 1883, and has held annual sessions since that time without missing a single one. The idea was conceived by the Grange element of the county and put in operation by them, and has been largely sustained by them and brought to its greatest usefulness by their patronage and energy. It was an experiment at first by a few persons feeling that something of this kind was needed to more closely unite the people and give them a place of resort that they might have a common cause and individual interests.

The first year they met under a rude bush arbor, almost in the woods, and formed an organization and elected officers. The first officers were: Dr. J. B. Bailey, president; A. C. Farmer, vice-president; J. S. Scott, secretary. The organization included the counties of Newton, Scott, Lauderdale, Neshoba, Jasper, Smith and Leake, and from time to time the adjoining counties and those from distant parts of the State. After the first and second years of meeting, it was seen

DR. J. B. BAILEY.

that the organization was a success, and the bush arbor gave place to a very comfortable and commodious pavilion, which, with its various attachments, will comfortably seat one thousand or more persons.

Mr. M. L. Hand, one of the directors, and among the first originators of the Patrons' Union, kindly furnishes the following information of the value of the property, number of houses, and other matters of interest:

"We have at the Patrons' Union 90 acres of land outside of the guards (a wire fence); forty acres in cultivation, six in an experimental ground in cotton and grasses, thirty acres inside the wire fence, fifty cottages, some of them two-stories; large three-story hotel, furnished, value $2233; pavilion, worth $200; exhibition hall, $150; refreshment stands, $100; the 120 acres of land, worth $1250; a circular speeding track on which to try stock brought for exhibition and prizes, with suitable stalls for their accommodation, all well watered."

Mr. Hand claims that this part of the State needs a normal school to train teachers, and that the Patrons' Union offers a suitable place for their accommodation, and hopes our worthy State Superintendent will aid in this good work. He also claims that the origin of the Patrons' Union was the suggestion of some good old women belonging to the Grange, in the year 1882.

Following this will be found valuable information, very kindly furnished by Dr. J. B. Bailey, the present presiding officer, and one who has presided over every meeting since its organization. He says:

"The Patrons' Union was organized in 1883, under the auspices of the Granges of Newton, Scott, Lauderdale, Neshoba, Jasper Smith, Leake and adjoining counties. Its objects—the promotion of fraternal unity and educational, agricultural and social advancement. It is a delegated body, composed of five members elected from each subordinate and county Grange. Its officers are elected annually, and consist of president, vice-president, secretary, treasurer, chaplain and seven directors, each of whom shall be a member of the Order of the Patrons of Husbandry in good standing. Its first officers were J. B. Bailey, President; A. C. Farmer, vice-president; J. S. Scott, secretary. The present officers are: J. B. Bailey, president; T. J. Hamilton, vice-president; Floyd Loper, secretary; M. J. Chandler, treasurer; Rev. Irvin Miller, chaplain. Directors, M. W. Stamper, C. B. Haddon, G. A. McIlhany, J. R. Pace, M. L. Hand, T. I. Doolittle and Thos. Faucett.

"The meetings are held in the latter part of July in each year. The exercises consist of the reports of committees on agriculture, horticulture, educational and kindred subjects, which embrace every topic of interest to the people of this State; also discussions of the subjects with addresses, speeches, orations, declamations, recitations, essays, dramatic entertainments, music of various kinds, and prize contests. Distinguished men who have visited and addressed the meetings are: Capt. Put Darden, Master of the State Grange and National Grange; Col. J. G. McArthur, Lecturer of the State Grange; Col. H. O. Dixon, Treasurer of the State Grange; R. P. Walker, Past Lecturer of the State Grange; Judge H. F. Simrall, of Warren county, present Lecturer of the State Grange; J. C. Bingham, of Ohio, Master of the National Grange; Mortimer Whitehead, of New Jersey, Lecturer of National Grange; Ben. C. Harrison, of Alabama, Master State Grange; Gov. J. M. Stone, Ex-Gov. Robt. Lowry, Senators J. Z. George, E. C. Walthall and A.

J. McLaurin; Congressmen Thos. R. Stockdale, Jno. M. Allen, C. E. Hooker, C. L. Anderson, J. H. Beeman, Ethel Barksdale. Others who have addressed these meetings on various subjects are: Gen. S. D. Lee, President A. & M. College; Prof. John A. Myers, A. & M. College; Prof. S. M. Tracey, Director of Experiment Station, A. &. M. College; Prof. Willborn, A. & M. College; Prof. R. W. Jones, President I. I. & C., Columbus; Prof. Tom McBeth, President Cooper's Normal College; Prof. Anderson, East Mississippi Female College; Prof. Dickey, Lexington College; Prof. A. M. McBryde, President Connehatta Institute; Capt. Joel P. Walker, Meridian; Col. R. C. Jones, Louisville; Capt. W. H. Hardy, Meridian; Col. G. M. C. Davis, Carthage; Stone Devours, Vossburg; Hon. W. D. Gibbs, Yazoo City; Hon. George Wilson, Lexington; W. W. Stone, State Auditor; Hon. Dabney Marshall, Vicksburg; Senator W. W. Heidleberg, of Jasper county; Col. J. L. Power, Jackson.

Some of the farmers who have spoken at the meetings of the Union are: J. L. Hardy, J. F. Dearing, D. T. Chapman, A. M. Monroe, Hamilton Cooper, W. H. Martin, M. W. Stamper, J. H. Bassett, W. H. Langford, David Vance, H. H. Vance, J. K. P. Shows, of Newton county; A. C. Farmer, W. L. Lyle, P. S. McCormick, Green Talbot, C. B. Haddon, G. C. Harper, of Scott county; W. W. Richardson, Wm. Price, R. T. Trapp, C. A. Lewis, of Neshoba county; and a great many others from these and other counties, whose names are not remembered.

"The ladies, also, have borne no small part in the entertainments of the meetings. Among those who have taken prominent parts, are: Misses Lizzie Butler, Eva and Ely D. Campbell, Eulah Moorman, Bessie Eastland, Jessie Kirkland, Tressie Talbot, of Scott;

Misses Lida Kiney, Jennie Bassett, and Mrs. M. C. Ingram, of Neshoba county; Mrs. C. C. Stamper, Mrs. Joe Bailey and Misses Rosa Scanlan, Carrie Beattie, Nannie Smythe, Mary Kelly, Bessie McCord, Ruby Logan, Bertha Amis, of Newton; Misses Rochelle Chisholm, Mabel Rives, Lillian Walker, Mittie McLemore, of Lauderdale, and Miss Lisba Ellis, of Leake.

"Prof. J. S. Scott was Secretary for ten years, and died December 23, 1893.

" The Patrons' Union now owns about 120 acres of land and the buildings number over fifty. The value of the whole is estimated at something more than $4000. There are over two hundred stockholders and the number gradually increases. The experiment station was established in 1889, includes about ten acres, and is under the direction of the director of the State Experimental Station, A. M. College.

"The annual attendance of the Union has varied-- from about 2000 to 6000. It is the intention to make the institution perpetual, and its benefits and advantages increase each year.

"The Teachers' Normal Institute, held on the grounds, and under the pavilion of the Patrons' Union, in June and July, 1893, was considered a great success. Prof. Wickliffe Rose, of Tennessee, was director, with Miss Minnie Holman, Miss Mary A. Callahan, J. G. Dupree, Dabney Lipscomb and J. C. Hardy instructors. The Institute was held four weeks; from the 17th of June to 7th of July, with a total enrollment of 260 teachers from the various parts of the State. The expense of this Institute is borne by the Peabody Fund, which is now applied to this State as well as other Southern States. This was considered a great success, and elicited much praise from the citizens of the county and those who attended. Prof. Rose closes his report to the State Superintendent of Education with the following remarks concerning this meeting of teachers:

"The physical environments, the untiring zeal and devoted self-sacrificing spirit of the teachers, united with the efforts of instructors to make the Summer Normal at Lake the most successful school of the kind which I have ever been connected with. As I now look back upon the work, it seems to me the greatest educational revival I have ever witnessed.

"The exercises of the Patrons' Union on the Sabbath by no means should be omitted, as great attention is paid to this feature of instruction at all the meetings of the Union. It is always made convenient to remain over on the grounds one Sabbath, and that day is given up to religious exercises. There are generally three appointments to preach, and sometimes four. There is usually a 9 o'clock service, then at 11 o'clock, then at 3 o'clock in the afternoon, and again at night. The ministers are selected from the various denominations, and as a general thing the best of order prevails, and good attention given to Sabbath services. Some of the most prominent men who have preached on these occasions are: Rev. John Hunter, Rev. J. A. Hackett, Rev. J. B. Gambrell, Rev. J. L. Cooper, Rev. C. G. Andrews, Rev. Dr. Bardwell, Rev. R. W. Sims, Rev. T. B. Hollman, Rev. A. F. Watkins, Rev. A. M. McBryde, Rev. Dr. Kerr, Rev. W. B. Leavell, Rev. John Chambers, Rev. W. C. Black, Rev. J. M. Kenton, Rev. Irvin Miller, Bishop Galloway, and quite a number of other preachers whose names are not now recollected.

LITERARY AND SOCIAL ADVANTAGES OF THE UNION.

"The meeting of this body usually occurs about the fourth week of July, and continues for about one week. The first days are generally of a business character, getting ready for the exercises, a programme of which has been published for several weeks and distributed through the country. These exercises are very much varied and are usually of a very interesting character. On second day, some one appointed as the principal speaker of the day will, after some business connected with the order, address the people upon some subject assigned him, or selected by himself, upon farming or finance, the condition of the country, or any topic upon which his fancy might rest, but pertinent to the occasion. Reports of the various committees will come in for an afternoon hearing, such things as were referred to their investigation a year previous to the present meeting. These reports may be upon various subjects directly bearing on the good of the country—on the production, with least cost and labor, of any given amount of corn, cotton, grasses, peas, potatoes, and all other farm products; also the use of various labor-saving implements, the introduction of mowers and reapers; the raising of fruit and the best kinds to produce. Talks from any farmer in the county as to the best way to plant, cultivate and gather a general crop in the county in which he lives; talks upon any question connected with the farm and stock-rising; any question that any man might wish to ask, would be answered by good authority; and not only that, but some might differ with the answer given, and a debate might grow out of this question, which would be freely participated in and would throw much additional light upon the subject. As these committees report, they are discussed, and if there are objectionable features, they are freely canvassed and sometimes the objectionable parts are expunged from the report. From day to day these exercises occupy important places in the meeting. Some brother will be called on to give his experience on certain modes of farming, and his speech may provoke another, and sometimes interesting debates are brought out by practical men on various methods and experiences, which prove beneficial to all who give attention. To some this kind of entertainment becomes dull, and then it is the President will call on some young lady, little boy, young man, or any one who might be prepared, that would declaim or recite prose or poetry, selected or original. In this way, interspersed with instrumental and vocal music, the morning will be spent, when an intermission of one or two hours are given for refreshment and rest.

"At the appointed time the meeting is again called to order and proceeds to general routine business as heretofore, until the afternoon is over. The night service is a very entertaining one. Music from the first, both vocal and instrumental, occupy a prominent part in the exercises. As soon as the management could spare the requisite amount of money, a brass band was employed, which was quite an additional attraction to the occasion.

At night the Pavilion is lit up; the piano, organ, violin, harp, guitar, as additions to the brass band, are called into requisition. The program for the evening is probably recitations by young ladies, original or selected compositions by young men, recitations by little girls and boys. In this way the night, until 11 to 12 o'clock, passes very rapidly, and the amusements and entertainments are over.

"The third day is passed much like the second, only that new subjects are discussed—new speakers each day on some important topic, new recitations by different persons, and so passes another day. As a general thing, political topics are not discussed. Sometimes, a man well posted on a political subject, or on the needs of the hour, would be called upon to enlighten the people. No speeches made by candidates seeking office in be half of themselves are allowed. It often occurs that charades form a pleasant entertainment, by some young school people, and amateur theatricals by the young ladies and gentlemen of the county and schools, form excellent entertainment for the nights.

"A contest for prize for the best declamation by young gentleman, or best recitation by young lady, or a question to be debated by two young gentlemen, judges being appointed to decide, often elicits great anxiety and good entertainment.

"One of the most striking and enjoyable entertainments of the week is the sociable, at which the President or some other gentleman, directs, and the young folks are introduced to each other, and allowed to promenade around the grounds and enjoy themselves in every way that is proper on these occasions, (no dancing being allowed). These things go on from day to day, and from night to night, through the whole week until Sunday occurs, which day is devoted to preaching and the worship of God—as has been described. The attendance of the people is usually very large on Sunday; very excellent sacred music, both vocal and instrumental, is dispensed, and thus passes the Sabbath day.

" A day is given to the exhibitors of all kinds of agricultural products, all kinds of garden producductions, fruits—both green and canned—anything in the culinary art, all kinds of quilts, patch-work, embroidery—all the work of men and the cunning and delicacy of the women's hands can be exhibited, and small prizes offered for the best specimens. Much good work by ladies is seen and much is learned by these exhibits. A day is appointed for the display of stock, premiums being offered for the best young stock, for the best display of grown and trained animals. These things have been a great incentive to many to improve their stock, and take better care of what they had. It has increased the number of good as well as fine stock in the county, until, instead of being a constant buyer of the horses and mules needed, her farmers can spare a large number each year to other counties needing them.

"The benefits accruing to the patrons of this Union, and persons visiting it, are very plain to be seen. When the intelligence of any community comes together, all striving to one great end, and to enlighten themselves, even those who have had no early educational advantages may, by mingling with those who have, bring about a great improvement. For men and women coming to a given point in the county, all using their best efforts to promote the welfare of each other, and all contributing something to make the occasion attractive, cannot fail to be a great source of information, not only to those who are accustomed to such things, but to the crude mass of people who are anxious to learn. The information and education gained here is large, and forms an important epoch in the lives of those who attend these meetings; as a social entertainment it is a great success.

People come from the country who feel free and easy —bring their own provisions out in tent or house, leaving the cares at home, for a time. They come to spend a pleasant week in the enjoyment of the society of friends and the free entertainments given by those who have agreed to take part in the programme of exercises. There is no doubt of the social and friends-making qualities of the Union; as to its literary improvements in the county and the adjoining counties, there is no doubt. No one will deny the great benefits accruing to the people as a teacher of the better things to be learned. Not only have men and women become wiser in the accumulation of knowledge in all the branches taught in the great object lessons and practical experience, but have come to see each other with more kindness, more love, more toleration of views and opinions differing from their own, to be more disposed to hear each side of the question, and to decide as the merits, more than for creed or dogmas.

One month after the meeting of the Patron's Union, a yearly camp-meeting convenes on the same grounds. The site was originally a location for camp grounds for the Methodist church, and after it was improved by the Union it was sold by the church to the Union people with the reserved rights of holding religious services at the term designated—that is, a yearly meeting. This forms a very convenient point for a camp-meeting—probably one of the best in the State. These meetings are very largely attended and some of the best talent in the State attend and preach to the people. Taking it all together, with a probable addition to the yearly Normal Institute for teachers, makes it one of the most attractive places in the State.

The Normal Institute again met at Patrons' Union in 1894, with a large corps of competent instructors and over 200 teachers. This is considered a great success for this place.

CHAPTER XXV.

VARIOUS BENEVOLENT AND SECRET ORDERS OF THE COUNTY.

The benevolent and secret orders of the county consist of seven Masonic Lodges, located at Newton, Decatur, New Ireland, Connehatta, Pinkney, Hickory and Calvert. These Lodges have between two and three hundred members. The time-honored order of Freemasonry is one of the oldest orders of its kind in the world. It has claimed some of the best men of all ages of its existence as its members. It has among the members that make up the order the very best citizens in the county. Newton has, in addition to the Blue Lodge, a Chapter, No. 110, also a Council, called Meridian Council. Decatur also has a Chapter.

The Masonic Order sends no one out looking up recruits to increase its membership. It stands upon its merits and respectability. If any one wishes to join they can make their wishes known to some member of the order, and after canvassing his character, if considered worthy, he is admitted. This order dispenses many charities and does much good; but it is done so silently that few except the beneficiaries are apprised of it. To a casual observer, it would appear that this highly respectable and benevolent order is not increasing in this county as in former years; but it is stronger in Mississippi than for many years, having 275 working Lodges and a membership of nearly nine thousand. It carries no insurance, as modern orders do, and many times the order that carried the insurance would be chosen when the party joining did not feel able to join both.

The Knights of Honor organized in the town of Newton in the year 1879, and at Decatur in the year 1880. The lodge at Newton has thirteen members, mostly belonging in the county. It pays a benefit of not more than $2000 to families of deceased members, and it costs an average of $4.50 per month, according to the age of the member. The order at this place, since it was established, has had four deaths, and has paid $8000 to the beneficiaries. The lodge at Decatur has had five deaths, and has paid to beneficiaries $10,000. The average of that lodge of monthly dues is $2.50.

The Knights of Pythias is also an order of the same kind. It was organized in the town of Newton in the year 1884, and has seventy-four members. The amount of insurance is greater in the Knights of Pythias than the Knights of Honor, being $3000. This lodge has lost four members, and has received for those who were entitled to it, $12,000. The amount paid per month by each member is from $2.50 to $4,00, according to the age of the member.

Hickory has a Lodge of Knights of Honor. The Lodge has fourteen members; average cost to each member per month is about $3.00; death claims paid at Hickory amount to $8,000. They also have a Lodge of Knights of Phythias of about thirty-five members.

While these Orders do not obligate themselves to pay " sick benefits," or to pay expenses for medical attention, nursing, etc., the brethren are always willing to render such assistance as special cases may require.

The amount that has been paid out to relatives of the deceased, in Newton county, is largely in excess of the amounts that have been paid in by the members. These Orders are not increasing as rapidly as they did when first organized. There is great competition in insurance as in other business, and the old regular insurance companies appear to be getting the larger share.

CHAPTER XXVI.

FREE SCHOOLS OF THE COUNTY—WHAT THEY HAVE DONE TO EDUCATE THE MASSES—HOW THEY ARE ATTENDED—NUMBER OF EDUCABLE CHILDREN IN THE COUNTY, WHITE AND BLACK.

The free schools of the county holds a place in the minds of the people, which is very prominent and justly so too; for much of the prosperity of the county or any country depends upon the manner in which the youth of the same is educated. Prior to the war there was nothing in our State in the way of free schools and but little in the South, usually confined to cities and to endowed schools; hence the country enjoyed none of these benefits. There were some colleges endowed by private friends or appropriations from the State, but nothing that was a general tax upon the people for the education of the masses. "Two years after the State of Mississippi was admitted into the Union," says Lowry & McCardle's History, "Congress had given thirty-six sections of land to, and in trust for the support of a University, and in 1833 all but half of one section was sold for $277,332.52, and this sum, with $8,400 received for rents, constituted the endowment. But no further steps were taken until 1841, when the Legislature met in joint convention to select a location for the College. The places voted for were Oxford, Mississippi City, Brandon, Kosciusko, Louisville, Middleton, Monroe, Missionary Station. Oxford was finally selected over Mississippi City by a majority of one. Oxford received fifty-eight, Mississippi City fifty-seven. The State continued to use the funds of the University which it held in trust. On a final settlement in 1857, the balance due the University was found to be $874,324.49. The State still uses the fund and the annual appropriations to the University is not a donation but payment of interest on the debt.

The Legislature of May 13th, 1871, established a University for the higher education of the colored youth of the State, and appropriated $10,000 per annum for ten years for its support. This University is in Claiborne county, near Rodney, being the old site of Oakland College, which was bought from the Presbyterian Synod. It was also given one-half Agricultural Land Scrip fund, the proceeds of the sale of 30,000 acres of land which the State secured from the United States under Act of 1862.

The Agricultural and Mechanical College, at Starkville, under the management of Gen'l S. D. Lee, was established by an Act of the Legislature in 1878. Its success from the first was apparent, and it has become one of the foremost institutions of the kind in the United States.

In the year 1883 co-education had been established at the University of Mississippi, and twenty-three young ladies matriculated. The following year, while the subject of a dormitory for them was under discussion, Gov. Lowry took a practical view of the matter, and urged the immediate establishment of a College for young women rather than risk the experiment of co-education at Oxford. Accordingly the College known as the Industrial Institute and College was established at Columbus.

" Over three hundred girls were enrolled at the opening session. It was the first State institution in America to be established for the training of women in the industrial arts, and time has demonstrated the wisdom of its establishment."

The State, aside from making very generous appropriations for the colored race at Alcorn University, has also established a State Normal school at Holly Springs, and for many years made an appropriation to Tougaloo University, a colored institution, in Madison county.

The year 1893 is the twenty-third year of the Free School system in our State and county. At first very little interest was taken in it. By some it was thought to be an intrusion upon the rights and privileges of the old-time teachers and styles of teaching, and there was but little interest taken in the schools.

The colored people, more than the whites, appreciating some education at no cost, evinced considerable interest in free schools. There was very little care taken in the selection and examination of teachers, and many were allowed to teach who were not competent. In this way a large amount of public money was wasted on incompetent teachers, both white and black. The average salaries of the white teachers for first few years of the public schools was about $50.00; it is now, male, $30.00; female, $28.35; and that of the colored teachers a little less, male—$21.10; and female, 17.10; with not enough regard to the latter as to their competency to teach.

Times have very much changed. The annual examination of teachers is a step largely in advance towards the right direction in procuring competent teachers, and still in some instances this system of thorough examination has been thwarted by incompetent teachers securing the aid of others in solving the questions propounded for their examination ; though it is now conceded by all that these examinations are right and most of the teachers are agreeing that a thorough test is the proper way. By this means a young teacher, as soon as he proposes to teach, begins to improve his talent and-education, knowing that there is no chance to get first-grade certificate unless the examination can be passed.

This severe test of scholarship, necessary to pass and procure first-grade papers, adds very much to the value of the county teacher ; and when they once stand this examination they continue their studies in order to meet the next, and by such application are surprised themselves to know what they can accomplish by study and investigation. The State is largely indebted to our present worthy State Superintendent of Education, J. R. Preston, for this improvement.

Some extracts from the Mississippi Public School Report, by Superintendent Preston, will doubtless be of interest to the admirers of the free-school system, showing the relative attendance of children in a number of States enumerated.

The following figures show the number of children in every one hundred of population on an average who go to school :

"In the United States an average of 13 to every 100 go to school. In Texas, in the year 1892, 14.7 ; Alabama, 1890, 12 ; in Georgia, 1891 and 1892, 12.2 ; Missouri, 1891 and 1892, 16.2 ; West Virginia, 1891 and 1892, 16.7 ; Indiana, 16.9 ; Kansas, 1891 and 1892, 16.7 ; Mississippi, whites and blacks, 1891 and 1892, 15.3 ; whites in Mississippi, 1891 and 1892, 17.75. This comparison shows that Mississippi, measured by the standard, is far above the average in the United States —more than 20 per cent. above—and she stands in fair contrast with Indiana, Kansas and Missouri, States in which public schools have been long established and highly developed."

The same report gives the average number of days the schools were maintained in the United States, in 1891 and 1892, 137 days, or six months and seventeen days. "In Massachusetts, 171 days; in New York, 185; Maryland, 185; Ohio, 165; Illinois, 155; Virginia, 118; Kansas, 127; Texas, 106; Mississippi, 102." The term of the county schools in this State, is 80 days, or four school months, taught consecutively or to suit communities, at intervals in the scholastic year. Where there are separate school districts the local population is taxed extra, and where a school may be maintained from seven to nine months. Also when the voters of any county express, through the boards of supervisors, that they wish a longer school than four months, by agreement they can have it. Our worthy State Superintendent urges very strongly for a greater length of time to be given to the free schools of the county. He thinks seven months by all means should be allowed the country children.

Newton county, as well as nearly all the counties of the State, is largely agricultural and many of the farmers of the county are compelled to use their children in making and gathering the crops. This would prevent many of them from patronizing the schools, at least for three months, and at the same time would have to pay a tax and get no benefit of it. Both sides of this question have many advocates and it is one which the voters will be called upon to decide at no very remote date.

As the tax payer is usually interested in the way the public revenues of the State are expended, it will not be uninteresting to give some figures from the valuable report already quoted:

"Total revenues of the State for public school purposes, $1,392,927; amount expended for public schools, $1,192,844; amount expended for State Institutions, $128,128; total amount expended by State for education, $1,321,072; amount expended by separate school districts, $238,008; total assessed valuation of the State of Mississippi, $185,398,984."

The same report claims "that there are 516,183 educable children in the State. Number enrolled in the State public schools, 334,923; number of public schools taught, 5,986; number of teachers employed, 7,497; number of separate school districts, 58.

A comparative view of several States is made in the Mississippi Report of the amount expended on the assessed value for educational purposes. "Mississippi expended in 1892-'93 for public schools, $192,844; for the University, at Oxford, $32,643; for the A. & M. College, at Starkville, $30,720; I. I. & C., at Columbus, for females, $23,325; Deaf & Dumb Institute, $17,750; Blind Institute, $8,161; Alcorn A. & M., at Rodney, for colored youths, $13,000; State Normal, at Holly Springs, for colored of both sexes, $2,500. The expenditures for all purposes amounted to $1,321,012, a sum which is equivalent to a levy of 7.1 mills on the total assessed valuation of all the property in the State. Arkansas spends 6.8, Texas 4.8, Massachusetts 4.4, New York, 4.5, Iowa 12.3, Illinois 14.4, Kansas 14.3, Nebraska 18.7. Mississippi leads among the Southern States and ranks eighth among the States of the Union in the amount expended for education in proportion to the valuation of property. And from the enrollment it appears that the people of Mississippi are patronizing the free schools in a greater degree than almost any State in the Union.

To further aid the teachers of the State and make them more efficient, the State Superintendent appoints a competent man to hold County Institutes, whose first duty it is to attend at Oxford a Normal Institute for teachers, where the best methods are taught, and by this means these best methods are carried to all the counties by men specially selected by the State Superintendent, and paid by the counties. The white and colored teachers are each allowed one week, which costs the county about $80.00. Normal Institutes are now being held for teachers, paid for by the money appropriated by the Peabody Committee. Four of these Normals were held in the State last year, two for the whites and two for the colored. The one at Oxford reached an attendance of 467. The one at Patrons' Union, at Lake, was attended by 260. The Normal at Holly Springs, for the colored youth, reached 90; the one at Tougaloo 75. These Institutes are great helps to those who have any ability, and who avail themselves of the opportunity to attend them.

With all the advantages now given to free schools, and the interest now taken by the patrons of the the schools, and the persistent efforts of our State Superintendent of Education to give the counties better informed and better educated teachers; all these things have a tendency to make the schools more interesting and profitable to those who attend them. It is now well understood that a teacher applying for a good place and to draw a salary from the county, must be able to teach and to stand the examinations.

The amount of education imparted to the youth of the county is remarkable. While there are no highly educated persons who go out from the public schools of the county, yet the rudimental branches of an education are learned, and the students in all parts of this county are prepared for higher schools, and more liberal education at the colleges of the country if they are able to bear the expenses of attending them. It is rarely the case that a youth in this county, ten years old, can be found who cannot read and write. This applies to the colored as well as white.

It is something remarkable about the colored folks, that they are more anxious to learn than the white people. They will travel greater distances under more difficulties and straightened circumstances to school, than any one of their more fortunate white neighbors. Some of them have made some progress; some have received liberal education. As a general thing, owing very much, no doubt, to the very poor training of their teachers, they have learned little. The children rarely go beyond the simple rudiments of reading, spelling, writing and ciphering a little. Some of them appear to have been injured by what little they have learned, while others are, to some extent, improving, and profiting by teaching in the county. The education received by the white children is of more solid and useful character, and thousands of persons in this county owe to the free school system of the State a debt of gratitude for providing the means of an education, which they would not have received without it.

The amount given to each child in the county for educational purposes, from five to twenty-one years, which is the school age in this State, in the years of 1892 and 1893, intended to reach $1.80 each, but the increase of scholastic population caused it to be reduced to $1.78 for each child for the four months, which is less than forty-five cents per month. From Mr. Preston's report it will be seen that the State had 516,183 educable children; 334,933 are enrolled; average attendance, 194,993. It is understood that the

State makes the allowance for all who are between the ages of five and twenty-one, whether they go to school or not. It will be seen that the whole number of educable children do not go to school, yet the appropriation is made as if they did; so there is more than $1.78 expended on each scholar, and by this fewer teachers are employed and get better wages than if all the educable children in the State were enrolled and attended school, and there were more teachers to pay. The following information, furnished by our worthy superintendent of education, Thos. J. Reynolds, will be found to contain valuable facts in regard to the free schools of Newton county:

"Number of white educable children, as taken from the assessor's roll for the year 1893, in Newton county, 3925; number of colored, 2438; making a total of 6369 children between the ages of five and twenty-one years. The children actually going to school, as taken from teachers' reports, 2931 white, and 1643 colored, making a difference in the county of the enrollment by the assessor and those who actually attend, 1786. This would look as if many were very careless, or that the schools were not situated so as to meet the wants of the county. In this, however, both conclusions would be somewhat erroneous. The school houses are so distributed in the county as to very well meet the wants of the people, and the people exercise a reasonable degree of prudence in sending their children to school. Yet there is such a long period allowed for the school age in this State, that the apparent discrepancy is explained."

The age of five years is a very early, and often an improper, one to start a child to school, and twenty-one is a very extended period to allow persons to attend the public schools.

HISTORY OF NEWTON COUNTY. 249

It is very frequently the case that parents live too far for the little children of five years to walk to school, and thus it is that class is often barred by inability to get there. It is often the case that many persons, before they arrive at the age of twenty-one, are employed in permanent business, or if they are females, they are often married, and in both instances they do not attend school, but are counted as educable children, and the State allowance is made on them.

NUMBER OF SCHOOLS, TEACHERS, AND COST.

There are 47 white male teachers in Newton county; there are 25 white female teachers; there are 22 male black teachers, and 8 female black teachers; one Indian school taught by a white man, making a total of 103, of all classes and sexes, who teach public schools in the county. There are five private schools in the county.

The amount of money paid for free schools in New- county for the year 1893, was $10,585.30. Of this amount, $195.40 was interest on the sixteenth section lands that are rented, or that have been sold, and the money is at interest. Number of frame school-houses in the county, 70; number of log houses, 18. Average salary of white teachers, $30 per month; average salary of colored teachers, $16.45 cents per month.

POLL TAX.

Superintendent Preston's report says: "Under the new Constitution the poll-tax was increased from one dollar to two. The amount received from polls for the scholastic year 1892 and '93, was $252,942, of which $5229 are reported as collected after the June report to the State Auditor, and consequently did not enter as a factor in the State distribution for the past scholastic year."

The poll-tax constitutes almost exactly 25 cent. of the State distribution. To this extent the voters of the State are required to pay equally in support of public schools. The total number of taxable polls in the State is 259,912. Only 126,471 paid the tax, leaving 51 in every 100 who pay nothing to the school fund.

An extract from report made to State Superintendent by T. J. Reynolds, superintendent of education of Newton county, will be found interesting. He says of the school fund:

"I have had but little experience under the old revenue system, but find we are about $2000 short, owing to the fact that the board of supervisors have failed as yet to make any levy.

"By practicing the strictest economy which is practicable under the law, without materially affecting the salaries of efficient teachers, I can keep the business moving with but little friction, and keep within the limits of the State distribution. The salaries of the county first-grade teachers will average about $30.00. I believe that a good majority of the people favor the levying of a county school tax sufficient to extend the public school term six months.

"There has been a decided improvement on the part of teachers in regard to their knowledge of text-books, owing mainly to the fact that this improvement was necessary to insure success in examinations.

"I have endeavored to carry into effect the suggestion of our State Superintendent, 'Hold an honest examination and make a license a test of merit.'

"It is also evident that much improvement has been made all along the line of conduct and management of country schools.

"We are making arrangements to procure a good teacher's library. I believe that much good will result from it and that the educational interests will be greatly promoted thereby.

"Our county institute for white teachers the past summer was merged into the Summer Normal at Lake, and while not exceeding 30 per cent. of our teachers were in attendance, yet the effect for good can scarce be estimated. I believe that the present system of institutes will prove to be much better than the old plan.

"The institute for colored teachers was held at Decatur and conducted by Prof. G. W. Turner, with good results.

"We have one separate school district at Newton, Hickory Institute, Newton Male and Female College, Connehatta Institute, Lawrence Institute and Union High School. All seem to be in good condition, having opened up with fair attendance.

"The operation of the present law, so far as districting is concerned, I think in the main, about as good as it is possible to have it, and seems to give very general satisfaction.

"With a few worthy exceptions, I cannot say much in favor of the country school-houses, and there seems to be but little interest manifested in the equipment of the same. When our people learn properly to appreciate the comfort and the educational interests of those bright little boys and girls who brave the winter storms in quest of knowledge, they will make greater preparation for their accommodation.

"I some communities I find it quite difficult to induce parents to provide their children with adopted books, but this obstinacy is fast passing away.

"The masses seem to appreciate the public school system and gladly embrace the opportunity of cheap education. Yet there are some chronic grumblers who object to it on various trifling pretexts and of course who would object to anything."

INDIAN SCHOOLS IN MISSISSIPPI.

The following letter from Mr. H. S. Halbert, published in Mississippi School Report, is not without interest to those wishing to know something of the advancement being made by the Choctaw Indians in our midst in the way of acquiring an education. There are, according to the census of 1890, 351 Indians in Newton county and the progress they are making will be better known after reading Mr. Halbert's letter, as follows:

"It may be well to state in the very beginning of this report, that the census of the Indians in some counties of Mississippi, for several causes, has always been imperfectly taken.

"In most of the counties there are more educable Choctaw children than the assessor's books show. This remark applies particularly to Newton county, in which are reported sixty children — thirty-six males and twenty-four females—an enumeration entirely too low. During the scholastic year 1892-'93 five Choctaw schools were taught in Mississippi — all taught by white teachers. The total number of children enrolled in these schools is 126—sixty nine males and fifty-seven females. Two schools, eighty days each, were taught in Leake county; seventy-eight educable children are reported in this county—fifty-six males, forty-two females. Twenty-nine males and nineteen females, total forty-eight, were enrolled and attended the two public schools. One school, eighty days, was taught in Kemper by Rev. W. W. Carmack; twenty-four educable children are reported in Kemper county.

Sixteen attended Mr. Carmack's school, eight males, eight females. One school was located in Scott and one in Nehoba, but neither were taught. In the latter county are reported 197 educable children. Two schools were taught by the writer, one of sixty days, in Newton county. Twenty-eight children attended the Newton county school, fifteen males and thirteen females. Of these eighteen, considering the peculiar circumstances of Indian life, attended the school with commendable punctuality. Eighty children, thirty-five males and forty-five females, are reported in Jasper county. Of these, seventeen males and thirteen females, total twenty, attended the public school which is located among the remant of the historic Okla-Hannali or Six Towns Indians. Of these, twenty were quite punctual in their attendance. The attendance of the remainder was quite irregular—some only coming two or three days.

"Their poverty is the great cause of much of the irregular attendance of their children; their parents frequently need their services at home in labor upon the farm and otherwise. During the winter months, inclement weather, the want of sufficient clothing, especially with those children who live at a distance, not infrequently causes an irregularity of attendance. But as their condition in life improves, and it is slowly improving, these hindrances will gradually disappear.

"In my own educational work among the Indians, I make use of both the English and Choctaw languages. Our Mississippi Choctaws are strongly attached to their native tongue, and there is no immediate prospect of its being supplanted by English. Even those most proficient have at last only a superficial knowledge of our language, and great numbers of the children have none at all. Experience soon proves that it adds much to the efficiency of teachers among these people to acquire at least a passable knowledge of their language. My plan is to ground these Choctaw children in the elementary English branches, and to so drill them in these studies that the instruction will be a practical benefit to them in their business relations with the white race, and in short will have the tendency to improve in every respect their condition in life. I drill them thoroughly in their reading and spelling lessons, translating for them the English into Choctaw, and requiring them to memorize the English words and their meaning.

"I have found it a good plan, and would suggest it to others to write a short story or narrative in simple English on the black-board with a parallel translation in Choctaw. I require them to copy off the English and read it over and over until the words and phraseology are thoroughly imbedded in their memories. This plan answers all the purposes of a practical lesson in English composition. In arithmetic they are required to discard the Choctaw names of the numerals and make use of the English alone, as our English names are so much shorter than the knowledge of the Choctaw. They soon realize that it is a great economy of speech to make use of the English names. Six times nine are fifty-four, a concise expression of seven syllables in English. A Choctaw boy or girl soon finds out that it is a greater saving of breath to make use of this short English expression, that to use the equivalent in his native tongue, "Hannali bat chakkali kat pokoli talapi akucha ushta," nineteen syllables.

"I think it would be well to permit all teachers of the Choctaws to have some latitude in the matter of text-books. My own experience is that the old "blue back" speller is better for them than Watson's. The latter is filled with a great number of words that a Choctaw never hears and will never use. Webster is free from this objection, and the teacher can better select from it common every-day words of which he can require them to memorize the spelling and the signification. Sometimes, at the request of their parents, during a very short period each day, I teach the Choctaw children reading and writing in their own language, making use of an elementary Choctaw book, entitled, "Chata holisso ai isht ia ammona." As the Choctaw alphabet is almost perfect, in a very short time they learn to read and write their own language with great facility.

"Upon the whole there has been a great improvement among our Choctaws in the last ten years. The great majority are anxious to secure the benefits of some education for their children. There is, however, one notable exception, Bogue Chitto Indians, of Neshoba, who are averse to having a school established in their midst. A potent argument by which these Indians are influenced by their old fogy Mingoes, is that the establishment of schools is only a preliminary to forced emigration to the West, that two generations ago schools had been established among the Choctaws, only to be followed by the treaty of Dancing Rabbit, and the subsequent emigration to the West, and a similar result will again follow if the Bogue Chittos should now accept the white man's offer of a public school. An absurd argument, it is true, yet it has its weight with the ignorant Tubbee element. Still, there is evidence that these prejudices are slowly dying out, and before long no doubt all our Indians, without a single exception, will favor the establishment of schools in their midst.

"The great majority of our Mississippi Choctaws seem to have no desire to go west to their own people. They are here to stay. Such being the case, they should be encouraged to patronize the few schools which the State has established for their benefit. We may, in conclusion, safely and truly say that our Choctaws are a law-abiding people. They are true patriots, intensely attached to our State, for on its very soil their traditions say, ages before the advent of the white man, the plastic hand of the Great Spirit fashioned the first Choctaw out of clay at the base of the sacred mound on Nanih Wai-ya Creek."

The early education in the county and the manner in which it was imparted, was very different from the plan now pursued by the teachers in this progressive age. Those old-time "old-field" school teachers did much good and imparted much knowledge to their pupils. Yet there was not enough of them, and their schools did not continue long enough. Before the introduction of the Free School system there were but very few advantages in educating the masses. Many of the early settlers, who were good, worthy men, had very little education. Many a good, responsible man of Newton county who succeded in building up the county, and whose sons made honorable Confederate soldiers, was entirely uneducated in books. The same old, uneducated men, if it occurred that they had to give their notes for anything which they had bought on time, when it became necessary to sign the note, they were unable to write their names but had to make his mark, thus: John *his* + *mark* Smith. Another man wrote the name, he made his mark, and a witness signed the note on the left to show that he saw John Smith make the cross-mark. These notes, signed by these farmers of the county, were not considered bad paper, but as a usual thing, were more promptly met than a note whose signature resembled that of a bank check. The paper was more negotiable upon the market than many other papers of the county. Many old men could only sign their names, which was practiced for business purposes, and their signatures resembled some of the scrawls attached to the Declaration of Independence, placed there by the old patriots of that period.

The State Convention of 1868 proposed this free-school system—more probably for the benefit of the colored population than the white, as it was a Republican body. It, however, became a part of our State law, finally engrafted upon our statute-books, and it now appears to be a permanent fixture, which our people are using to the great advancement of the education of the masses. It is rarely the case now that a white or colored youth cannot both read and write and cipher, and understand the rudiments of the English language. This is a wonderful advance in the direction of education of the masses over the old system, when there was only the small proceeds of the interest of the sixteenth sections given for free-school education. Wherever this money was coming in a township it was divided pro rata between the persons sending to school, and to some extent supplied the amount promised to the county teachers.

The free schools, the Sabbath Schools, the Grange and Patrons' Union, have all, combined, been grand factors in improving the education, not only of those of educable age, but many older persons have been largely benefitted in this way. That with the very low price of newspapers and the multiplication of books of all grades, sizes and quality, have wonderfully conspired to educate. When bad literature has been patronized and its use exclusive to that of good and useful books, has been indulged in, the parties using such vitiated and poisonous trash have been injured. That, however, is no argument against the education of the youth of the country. But it is wrong to circulate bad, vicious, obscene and sensational literature of any kind.

People who read such only learn to do wrong, and frequently attempt to imitate some hero of romantic fancy and extravagant fiction—some fabricated, sensational, impure book, written for money, and which catches the unwary and leads them into trouble, and often to destruction and death.

The free school system of this, and all the counties of the State, will continue to grow, and while it is very necessary to educate, and improve the system now practiced and make it more efficient, great care should be taken not to overdo the work, and to be reasonable in our demands upon the tax-payers.

The teachers of free schools should be remunerated with reasonable, not stinted salaries, but we should demand well-informed, competent teachers, who are able to stand the county examinations, without assistance, and obtain a fair average of the questions. By all means require good moral character, and sober men—and not forget as much religious training as can come into the school, as is reasonable under the circumstances, bearing well in mind that if the heart is not educated with the head that it probably would be better not to educate at all.

TEXT-BOOKS USED.

The books used in the public schools is a very important item connected with the education of the youth of the country. It is reasonable to conclude that a uniform system of school books should be adopted and taught in the State. This is not, however, the case. Each county is left to select for itself. Under this management a multitude of books, from all sections of the country, North and South, are placed in the hands of the youth of the country. If the State should, after well canvassing the matter, adopt a series of school books known to be the best that could be obtained, and have them taught for a term of years in all the public schools, teachers knowing that, would prepare themselves in these books and be more conversant with them, and teach with more ease than with books they have no knowledge of and that are only taught in few localities in the State. The History of the United States which should be used should be one free as far as possible from any sectional bias, giving truthfully whatever may have occurred at any time in the history of the States, without attempting to prejudice one section of the country against the other by giving garbled extracts and unkind and often exaggerated statements in reference to things that have occurred, and particularly in reference to the great civil war between the States.

A uniform system of school books would cheapen very much the price of such literature, as they are all too high. But if a publishing house had the exclusive sale to a State, they could well afford to sell for less than to isolated counties. Then there would be a congeniality of feeling in the studies of one series of authors all over the State, as is the case in the study of our Sabbath School literature. The adoption of the text-books of any county is left with the Board of Education, who meet and examine the various books and prices offered to them and in their best judgment they select the text-books for a term of years to be used in the county. The books used in Newton county as per selection of our Board, are the following: Eggleston's History, Robinson's Arithmetic, Duval's State History, (Lowry & McCardle's State History and Civil Government is not adopted by Newton, but is used in sixty counties of this State), Steel's Physics, Harvey's Grammar, Swinton's Geography, Barnes' Geography, Steele's Physiology, Watson's Speller and Quackenboss' Composition. As a general thing, these are wise selections and as good as were offered to any board in the State.

CHAPTER XXVII.

RELIGIOUS DENOMINATIONS OF THE COUNTY—NUMBER OF CHURCHES AND THEIR RESPECTIVE MEMBERSHIP AND USEFULNESS IN THE COUNTY.

THE religious denominations and the various churches of this county, demand more than a passing notice in these pages. In fact, the greatest interest that can attach to any county is its religious element. Without it all other advancements pale into insignificance, and are worthless, and man has lived to no purpose unless this great, important and ever to be desired object is prominent in his life.

No matter how great may be the commerce of a nation, or the agricultural and mineral resources and wealth—no matter how wise its statesmen and superior its legislative leaders and executive heads—all! all! will be considered worthless without proper regard to the Bible. Everything can be better spared than compromise individual salvation. Nothing should be more strongly opposed than a National indifference of obedience to God and the practice of the precepts of His Holy Book.

RELIGIOUS DENOMINATIONS IN THE COUNTY.

There are six denominations of Christians, as they style themselves, in our county. The one having the largest membership is

THE MISSIONARY BAPTIST,

Whose work has been large and varied in this county. They are prominent in Sabbath School interests, and in the forefront of temperance reforms, and are zealous in foreign and home missionary work. They are a progressive and evangelical body of people who are earnestly at work for the good of souls and prosperity of the country. They have been led for the last fifty-two years in this county by Rev. N. L. Clarke, who still lives and works with all the strength of an old man for the prosperity of his church and the good of souls. He is also editor of the *Mississippi Baptist*, published at Newton.

This denomination has twenty-five churches, eleven ministers and a membership of 1776, in the county of Newton. The churches in the county belong to the Mount Pisga Association, which is now in the fifty-seventh year of its existence and embraces the following counties and parts of counties: Newton, Scott, Leake, Smith, Jasper, Lauderdale and Neshoba.

PRIMITIVE BAPTIST CHURCH.

The Primitive Baptists (or Hard Shells, as they are sometimes called) are not so numerous. They do not join in the Sabbath School work, nor are they in favor of home or foreign missions. They, as a general thing, are good men, and a highly respectable body and have some good preachers, and have the honor of numbering in their church some of the most worthy and honest citizens that have ever been in our county. They have five churches, six ministers, and a membership of 119 in Newton county, and belonging to the Bethany Association, now in its fiftieth year of existence. Their principal leaders of years ago in

BAPTIST CHURCH, AT DECATUR.

this county, have been the Revs. Pennington and McGee. They have several younger preachers, whose names are mentioned in the proper place.

M. E. CHURCH SOUTH.

The Methodist Episcopal Church South has never, in the settlement of the county, had such membership and influence as the Missionary Baptist. The work of this body in this county before the war was very small. The Congregational church was very strong, led as it was by Rev. J. F. N. Huddleston and his coworkers, and their influence brought many to that church. The Baptist churches were strong. The Protestant Methodist church also had a strong following. But the work of the M. E. Church in Newton county before the war, was remarkably light, though the church, immediately after the war, commenced to make greater demonstrations towards christian advancement than ever before.

The organization of the Wesleyan Methodist church is probably one of the best known to the world, considering the length of time since it was formed. Its progress has been wonderful in the 100 years of its existence; it is a church that proposes to supply the people of all countries with preaching. They require money if they can get it, but if not they give the gospel free and supplement the salary of the preachers by some other means. It may be that they do not get what they ought to have, yet it is the best the church can do for them, and the same people who would refuse to pay the preacher are supplied again by the Conference. As the country is being educated and enlightened, this idea of not paying the preacher is fast giving way, and as a general thing the Methodist preacher in our county gets his salary, is treated well by his friends and brethren, and is entertained on the best the country affords; they are usually zealous and progressive men who are willing to work for their calling, to the glory of God, and no doubt they are doing a good work in the county. They are always found on the moral side of every question; they are a power for temperance and Sunday schools; are fully up to the necessity of higher education; are noted for their missionary spirit both at home and abroad. Doubtless the Methodist preacher is a coming man in the affairs of morality and religion in the land. This body has nine churches, four traveling preachers and two local ministers; has a membership of 1,000 belonging to the Mississippi Conference. The early itinerant preachers in Newton county were, C. R. Strickland and H. J. Harris; W. G. Bartlett was a local preacher, living at Chunkey, and the Rev. McCurdy was a local preacher living near Decatur; James Carstaphen was also a local preacher of good ability.

CONGREGATIONAL CHURCH.

The Congregational church, which once had a large following of respectable people and a corps of good preachers, is now reduced to small numbers; quite a number of the members went to the M. E. Church South; the main doctrines of faith and practice being so nearly alike that quite little compromise would be made and that mostly in church government, so the members of this church could conscientiously become members of the one that had greater numbers and influence. They have four churches, four ministers and a membership of 210. They were ably represented in years gone by by Rev. J. F. N. Huddleston, Henry Jones and some other local ministers; they now have

Revs. J. C. Portis, J. M. Belew, T. H. Perry and Rev. R. M. Gilbert.

THE PROTESTANT CHURCH,

Also has small following in the county ; was once a a mighty body in the State of Mississippi, but owing to a large part of that church being associated with the Northern States, most of the Southern members and ministers went to the M. E. Church South. They, like the Congregational church, differ very little in doctrine, can easily make the change to the M. E. Church without much compromise. They have no churches, no ministers, with a membership very small. In former days they were led by such men as Rev. P. H. Napier, who was the president of the Conference for a time in the State, and after the war joined the Methodist Mississippi Conference ; C. F. Gillespie, who came to the Methodists ; Spencer Bankston, who remained with them ; J. E. Taylor, also came to the Methodist Mississippi Conference; Elisha Lott, a noted preacher on the style of Lorenzo Dow, a prominent man of Madison county, and a man of wealth, came often to this county and assisted in conducting the great camp meeting on Tilasha, in the eastern part of the county, where great crowds, in the early settlement of the county, congregated to hear the word.

THE OLD SCHOOL PRESBYTERIANS.

This body of Christians are among the most respectable church people of our country. They have not large numbers, but have usually been preached to by able ministers. This church is, and has been ever, famous for the education of its ministers. No doubt that in a country like ours, they have lost ground by requiring too severe a test of educational ability to allow a man to preach. Most of the other churches are willing when a man has any ability, to allow him limited license, and if he show any disposition to teach and preach and is willing to study and prepare himself, to grant him liberty to exercise his gift, especially so if a man have great piety and by Godly example so conduct himself as to be above reproach and use his talent for the church and salvation of souls. The Old School Presbyterians are more exacting. They require a more thorough education, so that a man may be able to write a learned exegesis that will bear the close scrutiny of a Biblical scholar and theologian. It is all very well to be an educated minister, but while this church is so exacting of the qualifications of ministers, the cause of the church may suffer. The people may be hungry for the word and other denominations come in and reap the harvest that is ripe. Hence it may be very just to say that this old and highly respectable body of Christians are too exacting on those who feel themselves called to preach. They have three churches, one minister, and a membership of 114 in this county.

This church was very early organized in this county, probably as early as 1842, by Rev. Dr. J. N. Waddel and Rev. Dr. Jno. H. Gray, Presbyterian divines. The former taught a school at Montrose, Jasper county. This organization was at Mount Moriah, southwest from the town of Newton, where there is still a flourishing church. Dr. Waddell continued to preach to that church until 1848; he was called to the State University to fill a Professor's chair. He was succeeded in turn by the Revs. Adams, King, McRae, Bell, Lee, McInnis, Emmerson, West, Bingham, Mosley, Coit, Kerr and Barr. Rev. Mr. Smythe also for a number of years preached to the churches in Newton county.

THE CUMBERLAND PRESBYTERIAN CHURCH.

This church is weak, more particularly so on account of not having sufficient force of preachers in the field. If all the churches would provide for the dispensation and preaching of the Gospel as the Methodist and Baptist do, and arrange it so that their ministers would go and preach to everybody and in all neighborhoods, their members would be largely increased.

The Cumberland church generally forms a very respectable portion of our community, who are generally sincere and pious. These ministers, though not having such severe test of educational qualifications required of them, are usually of from fair to good education and of respectable standard in community. They are with all the reformers of the country and are considered of a purely Evangelical church worthy of patronage. They have three churches, no ministers and a membership of about 100. If this church had any organization in the county or any regular preaching before the war, it is not known to the writer.

About fifteen years ago the Rev. Mr. Bailey, father of Dr. J. B. Bailey, commenced to preach, probably under a brush arbor, at Midway, near the house of Mr. Ashmore, who was a member of that church, and after preaching with marked success, succeeded in establishing a church, and a very good house was built at Midway, five miles north of Newton, which church has served as a place of worship for Presbyterians and Baptists. Mr. Bailey was succeeded by Revs. Milling and Ashmore, and occasionally Rev. McBryde.

CHRISTIAN CHURCH.

The Christian Church (or Campbellites, as some persons call them) have an organization and one church in Newton county. The church is at Hickory. They have no regular supply of minister. Their work of preaching is done by evangelists—men who come to the county and preach for several weeks. They are men well equipped for the work, and get a large attendance. There were large crowds who went to hear the Rev. John A. Stevens, at Morgan Springs, in this county, last summer, who is a man who appears to attract the people. Quite a number joined him, some from other churches and some who had not before been members. The intention of this order seems to be to get a good position in this county, and they are not lacking in zeal and ability. In some respects they resemble the Baptists; that is, they immerse candidates for membership in the church. But many of the cardinal and important doctrines of faith and practice differ so widely that there is no affinity or brotherly harmony between them. They have one church at Hickory, and about thirty members in the county; no minister.

HOLINESS PEOPLE.

There are some Holiness people in the county. This sect have no regular churches in which to worship, in this county. They usually come in to some remote part of the county and preach for a series of days, gathering into their order, usually, such members from other denominations as may be dissatisfied with their church or brethren, or who may be unstable in the faith of their own doctrines. These people have some very good preachers—men who appear to be devoted to God and His work, who profess to be holy. If they would establish a regular branch of their church and have more organization, with rules and regulations governing them, they might do more good. No one objects to a man's holiness of life and heart. More of it is needed in all the church membership. It is the essentials of a living church to have a membership which is converted, consecrated, holy, and devoted to the service of God. Yet there should be consistency always. There should be thorough organization, and a body of men equipped with the ability to preach and teach by precept and example.

COLORED CHURCH MEMBERSHIP.

The colored church membership of this county is large. They like to be called members of the church.

Dr. J. B. Gambrell, in giving a public lecture before a large assemblage of people in Boston, Mass., said, after saying many things in praise of the negroes, and in speaking of the advancement they had made, of the property they had gained, and the respectability they had attained, in close proximity with the white man, "that they lived closer to the Jourdan than to the Decalogue." This might apply very well to members of all colors and denominations; that we sometimes have more of the former than the spirit of godliness. The colored people deserve great credit for being as good and as religiously inclined as they are. They have many temptations, and many times do yield—so do white people.

The negro has great reverence for the church, and admiration of God's people, and respect for those disposed to serve God. The white people should set them the very best example, and give them every help in their power to improve in a religious way. The greatest number of colored church members in any of the churches in this county is the Mission Baptist who have seven ministers.

Fifteen churches, and a membership of 1,000 belong to the Third New Hope Missionary Baptist Association, which is now in its fourteenth year of existence. Abram Donald was the first colored Baptist preacher to preach in this county after the freedom of the slaves.

The next in order belong to

THE METHODIST EPISCOPAL CHURCH, NORTH.

It appears that our Northern brethren have so far been able to capture most of the colored people of the Methodist persuasion in this county. No doubt it results from the political relations which at first existed between the sections just after the war when most of the negroes voted with the Republican party, so it was that there existed here in the South a Northern and Southern Methodist church, and the negro in his church relations very naturally went with his political ally. The colored Methodists in Newton county have six local and one traveling minister; four churches, and a membership belonging to the Northern Mississippi Conference of 466; an estimated church property of about $2,500.

OLD SCHOOL COLORED PRESBYTERIANS.

There a few colored people who belong to the Old School Presbyterian congregation, and who are allowed to hold membership with the white church. They are, however, now trying to get a house of worship and minister of their own, and it is to be hoped that the white people of the community and county will assist them in this undertaking. Their house of worship will be near the Presbyterian Mount Moriah church, southwest of the town.

INDIAN CHURCHES.

The Choctaw Indians have two churches in the county, one near the town of Connehatta, which is a Missionary Baptist church, with probably thirty to forty members, that have a regular supply of an Indian preacher named Ben. Williamson, who has been preaching about five years, who learned to read after he was grown, and was licensed by the Baptist church of the Mount Pisgah Association. He is a man of uncommon ability for his chance ; appears to have large piety, preaches with great freedom and even eloquence; seems to be consecrated to the work of the ministry, and it is hoped he will do good for his people.

There is another church on or near Talasha Creek, in the eastern part of the county, with probably not so many members, preached to by Isham, a young Indian raised near Hickory. He does not possess the talent of Ben. Williamson, but appears to be a man of good moral character and in earnest in the work of the ministry.

Old Jack is the first Choctaw of Newton county that attempted to preach, and although old and apparently weak-minded, he set a good example, and did the best he could, and deserves to be rewarded and protected in his old and infirm age.

CHAPTER XXVIII.

SABBATH SCHOOLS—NUMBER IN THE COUNTY—TEACHERS AND SCHOLARS—INTEREST THAT APPEARS TO BE TAKEN IN SCHOOLS IN THIS COUNTY.

The Sabbath Schools appear to be doing a great work for the young people of the country. There is no part of Christian and systematic study of the Bible making more rapid strides than the Sunday School, all over the United States. Our State and county, though not being up with some others, have good records and are to be commended for their enterprise in this direction.

Each church in the county, except the Primitive Baptist, are heartily engaged in pushing forward this work among the children. In years gone by it was not so, and particularly so in the country churches; but now all appear to be earnestly endeavoring to do much in this way.

The Sabbath School has its peculiar fascinations for the young, and there is a growing spirit among the older people of the church to qualify themselves for teachers. Much depends upon the way a class is taught, as to what knowledge the pupils may derive from the Bible and its doctrines. There is a great co-operative effort among all Protestant branches of the church to formulate plans, prepare suitable literature, circulate books, cheapen the publication of religious tracts and the scriptures, so as with very small cost all these late advantages may be in the possession of every school in the land.

Much talent and large expense has been given to the publication of suitable literature, and employment of competent men and women, who are able to entertain and instruct in the various methods of making the Sabbath Schools both interesting and profitable.

One of the great and attractive agencies in the Sabbath Schools, is the improvement in music, and the concert of singing by the teachers and children, large and small, such songs as are attractive in time and sentiment, to suit the ages and conditions of the youths and children of the schools. Long ago the same music was used for the Sabbath School as the church. The style of the music was only suitable to more mature minds; the sentiment also of the same kind. But different opinions now prevail and the new methods appear to me the more acceptable.

The services were conducted usually much in the same way as the ordinary church meeting, observing the same conventionalities as used in the routine of church worship. All this was good at the time and much improved those who attended. Now things assume a very different phase. The systematic order of the day school much pervades the teachings and instructions now given in the Sunday Schools. Music, both of time and sentiment, is now composed to suit the more juvenile taste. Books of Sunday School music are used for the benefit of the schools. Many more persons are interested as teachers of the schools that were not in years gone by. It is a position that many business and professional men consider an honor to have. They become highly interested in this great work and make excellent teachers. Many ladies, both married and single, enlist in the work and many of them prove to be among the most efficient in the schools.

The great international movement to prepare uniform lessons to be studied by millions of Sunday-school children each Sabbath in the year, is a wonderful improvement. These lessons are gotten up on certain portions of the Scriptures, and there are sufficient helps in the notes connected with the Quarterlies to explain the most difficult passages without infringing upon the peculiar doctrines of any denomination. These international lessons apply to any school, but are more particularly applicable to schools where the children would be supposed to advocate different beliefs as to doctrine. Each denomination of Protestant Christians in the land may take the same lessons and may prepare notes on the subject to suit their peculiar tenets in relation to religious doctrines. This is where schools are denominational. The international literature and certain other societies who send out these Sabbath-school helps, make no comment on doctrinal matters. The principal thing in all Sabbath-schools is to teach Godliness, and to get all young people interested in the understanding of the truth.

The Sabbath-school at no time should claim as a prerogative the right over the church, but should always consider itself as subsidiary and auxiliary to it; to teach and advise morality, to direct the children in the right way, to encourage early piety, to get them interested in the study of of the Bible and to investigate for themselves; to urge upon them the necessity of prayer and the great importance of conversion; to store the youthful mind with knowledge of God; to warn against the great danger of sin and the necessity of a change of heart. The schools that have other ends in view and only use them as a pastime and social

Sabbath morning reunion of teachers and scholars are doing great injustice to those who attend them; the teacher who fails to impress upon the mind of his class the great cardinal principles of religion and the necessity of the observance of the commands of the Bible, and to love and fear God, and to shun evil, has failed of his mission.

The Sunday-schools in Newton county are well attended, having some of the best men and women engaged in the work. As a general thing it is well supported, having plenty of literature and good and attentive teachers. Most of the schools in the county continue all the year. Quite an interesting feature of the Sabbath-schools of the county is the annual meeting of all the schools in the county at some given place during the summer in a "County Convention." There is the place where general information is given as to the work going on in the county and State. All the schools are expected to send delegates to this convention, showing their numbers and the state of prosperity which they are in; to give a general statistical statement and all the particulars of advancement and evidences of the good work in their schools. It is here that various subjects are discused; interesting and important papers are read; speeches made on any topic connected with the progress of the schools. Here it is that many of the young people are invited to address the meeting, deliver committed composition, or write and read what may be pertinent to the Sabbath School interest.

It is always expected that the orator of the day will deliver a general address for the good of schools, and any new ideas on the Sabbath School system, and other moral and religious snbjects. Many impromptu suggestions are made by various friends who feel inclined to talk. Many important conferences and discussions are held, in which all who wish are allowed to take part, in short speeches, thereby bringing out much that will interest and improve the school. One of the attractive features is the music, vocal and instrumental, by various persons who have gone prepared to sing on this occasion. Aside from the interesting program is a sumptuous dinner spread on a common table, where all are welcome, and a general good feeling prevails. People from various parts of the county attend these conventions, and also of all denominations, and go home with better impressions and general good feeling for the Sunday School.

It is probable that there was not an organized Sabbath School in the county of Newton before the war. There may have been some little catechism and bible lessons taught, but no well defined Sabbath Schools. A great step forward in this direction has been made, and the county now has about thirty white schools. The number of teachers is put down at about 250. There are about 2000 white Sunday School scholars who go to the Sunday Schools in the county. Probably one half of these will represent the Baptist denomination, and the other half the other other denominations in the county. About 800 belong to the colored schools.

Whenever a church can establish a school of its own children, it should be established, as then more freedom is expressed in reference to doctrine and more attention given towards keeping it up. But when they cannot, which is frequently so in the country, a union school is always expedient and useful. These schools should be encouraged by all denominations until all the young, and as many old people as possible, shall be brought into them.

The colored people love the Sunday Schools, and will travel miles to attend them. There is no doubt but they give more attention to them than their more fortunate white neighbors. The colored Baptists of Newton county have the county organized, and hold yearly county conventions. They report at last year's meeting, fourteen schools, from the counties of Newton, Smith, Jasper, Scott and Neshoba; about 600 scholars, of which Newton has 300, and sixteen teachers. The Methodists have less; they, however, make very good reports from the four churches, which are reported as follows: Sunday schools, 7; teachers, 54; scholars, 394.

CHAPTER XXIX.

Law and Order in Newton County—The White Caps—What is Thought of Them.

Newton county, as a law-abiding, peaceable and orderly one, cannot be excelled in the State. With two-thirds white population and nine-tenths, if not more, of the people engaged in agricultural pursuits, go very largely towards making it a county where the behavior of the people far excel most of its neighbors.

There being no spirituous liquors sold publically, and but very little clandestinely, is one of the most important items towards good order and peace among the people, as it is seldom a difficulty occurs except some of the parties are under the influence of liquor. When it is taken into consideration that there are seventy-two churches in the county, about 5,000 church members, about forty-five sabbath-schools, 3,800 persons who weekly attend them, and about eighty day schools where 4,574 children and youth go to school, then it may be seen where the morals eminate from, and the causes which produce them.

The people also, of Newton county, as a general thing, are a proud, high-minded people, with a disposition to improve.

It is something worthy of observation that thousands of men go to the markets of the county, carry their products of all kinds made upon the farms in payment of their debts, and exchange them for goods and cash, and very seldom it is ever seen, a drunken man in town, or on the roads. Very little profane swearing, comparatively speaking, among the young men of the county, as where liquor is sold and used by them. A gathering of even one or two thousand may take place, as is often the case, at pic-nics or schools, or Sabbath-school gatherings, or a Grange gathering, or Patron's Union, and not a drunken or disorderly man will be seen.

The women of the county mingle freely with these gatherings, without any fear of being disturbed or insulted. Good order and good humor prevail, and all have a pleasant time. This is all traceable to the absence of liquor. The people are being so educated as to do without it. They do not need it and have no place for it. They know better now; they know it to be a great enemy to them and their sons, and they will not receive it again.

There is no better place to judge of the sobriety and good order of any county, than in the business of the circuit court. When liquor was sold in all parts of the county, the criminal docket was always crowded. Disorder prevailed in all parts of the county, and much expense and litigation were always on hand, and many grave punishments inflicted by the officers of the law. At the last spring term of the circuit court in Newton county, in a population of over sixteen thousand, only four true bills were found by the grand jury, and those of a trivial nature.

The whites and negroes agree remarkably well. It is rarely the case that there is a difficulty between them. There is no disposition on the part of the negro for social equality. He knows his place, and he conducts himself well, and the white people respect him. The white people largely educate the negroes, assist them to build all their churches, and when they are unfortunate and have their houses burned, or otherwise in ill-luck, their white neighbors assist them and treat them kindly.

The negro is not cheated out of his wages in Newton county. He is given a fair price for his work and is expected to give reasonable labor in return and then he is settled with. If he have a farm of his own, his white neighbors will treat him kindly if he behave himself and use only his own things. In this way the white and colored people get on well and there is very little trouble with the colored man appropriating anything to his own use that does not belong to him.

Many parts of the State have heretofore been troubled with a class known as "white caps," and this county has not been altogether an exception. But at present there appears to be but little or none of it left in the county. Some very good people may, in an evil moment, have been drawn into participating with this lawless order and some others might have wished it success, but it is not so now. People all over the country find that such lawless proceedings are wrong and will not be tolerated by law or accepted by good citizens. The result is the order of "white caps" appears to be in the things of the past, with a hope that it will not be revived again. With a few exceptions, as before stated, the "white cap" order has had but little recognition in Newton county. No arrests were ever made and but little trouble was experienced in the county in reference to it. The general behavior of the people of the county will compare well with the best in the State. No man need have any fears of going anywhere in this county on any business he may have, and the officers can execute any warrant they may have at any time without fear of being molested.

There is very little disposition to try to engage illicitly in the sale or manufacture of liquors. Very few stills have ever been found in the county. There appears to be a feeling against it, and the temperance cause has so many friends that there is little probability of any violations of law becoming flagrant.

CHAPTER XXX.

LANDS OF NEWTON COUNTY—LANDS IN CULTIVATION AND THEIR VALUE—NUMBER OF ACRES ORIGINALLY IN THE COUNTY—NUMBER OF ACRES OF PUBLIC LAND NOW SUBJECT TO ENTRY IN THE COUNTY—TREES, GRASSES, ETC.—LARGE CREEKS AND STREAMS—VARIOUS PRODUCTIONS—FRUITS, BERRIES, ETC.

THE importance of any county is always, if an agricultural county, as to the value of its lands, their durability and freedom from overflow, the amount of natural drainage and not of too rolling and broken a surface. Newton county, at no time making pretentions of being one of the rich counties, yet it has some very fine lands, has many natural advantages with timber and water, climate, and a diversity of soil, with never failing seasons, and one of the healthiest portions of the State. With all these combined, and the intelligent, sober and industrious population, would make it one of the most desirable counties in the State. With excellent facilities for marketing the crop, having 26 miles of railroad, with towns situated near the central part of the county that are considered among the best in the State as cotton markets and where goods from large stores are sold at as cheap prices as any towns in the State at retail.

According to the census of 1890 Newton county had 90,868 acres of improved land, and the assessment as given to the assessor of the county in the year 1890, averaged $6.11 per acre, which would make $555,203.48 as the value of the improved lands in the county. The number of acres of land originally in the connty was 368,640; of this amount only 6,080 acres was left unentered and as public land of the county; this was, as per report for the fiscal year ending June 30, 1893. The grant to the railroad was 34,240 acres, leaving the balance entered by the citizens of Newton county and some others outside of this State. Newton county has much of what would be termed oak and hickory ridge land. This land usually lies on branches and small creeks, and sometimes occupies high, broken and hilly country, with some table and valley land and some bottom land. Most of the timber on these ridge lands is undergrowth and some younger trees, though of considerable size.

When the county was settled in 1833, this land was covered with grass and large trees scattered thinly over the surface. Most of this original grass now gone. After the land was trodden down by the hoofs of the cattle and horses introduced, after the settlement and a general traveling over the county, these original grasses gave way, as the Texas grasses do after the sod is broken. After many years of burning and feeding of stock on the grass there came up an undergrowth. On these ridges grew very large oaks, hickory, chestnut, black gum, short-leaf pine, and a few others. Now all this land that is uncleared is covered with thick undergrowth of most of the growths named above. There is quite an amount of long-leaf pine timber in many parts of the county, some of it very large, making the best of lumber. Quite an amount of this fine timber has been used up by the steam mills, and yet there are large areas on which good milling timber is left.

The creeks originally had much swamp timber, such as white oak, beech, water oak, sweet gum, black gum, ash, elm, some walnut, hickory, magnolia and some others, and occasionally a large short-straw pine. There was no undergrowth in the swamps except cane, and that was in great abundance; this has given way and a small undergrowth, mostly of the same character of the large trees, has come up and forms valuable timber. In many places a multitude of vines of various kinds have come up in the places where cane grew, and in this event the swamps are very thick.

Some parts of the county have fine bodies of prairie land, an undergrowth on the timbered portion of these lands and makes them very difficult to clear and put into a state of cultivation. The shell prairies, heretofore bare of timber, are now producing haw, crab-apple, and some other growths, which cause them to be harder to clear. The sloughs which were too wet to produce timber, have filled up and are producing some of the best young oak, ash and hickory; of the latter is made the hoop-pole, spokes, etc.; the timbers that grow in these rich prairie sloughs are of the best the county affords. There is now very little open land; except where the lands are cleared very heavy undergrowth hides all the view, and prevents much fine grass from growing where it once grew.

As soon as a sandy land field is abandoned it comes up in a growth of short-leaf pine, whether they originally grew there or not. When a long leaf forest is denuded of its growth of large pines, used for mill purposes, a growth of oak and hickory springs up immediately. The long-leaf pine forest is never reproduced. Timber, except in the long-leaf district, is far more plentiful than when the county was settled.

This county has some very fine grasses that grow well without cultivation. The Bermuda, which is not a native, but was introduced a little over fifty years ago, grows well, produces good hay, is a fine grazing grass, but wants good soil, and is hard to get rid of if a person should wish to cultivate the ground it grows on. The carpet grass, as it is called, is a native of our country; grows well on bottom land, and also on medium upland. It is excellent for stock—quite as much so as Bermuda—will come as early, grow as late, and when the farmer wishes to change it is very easily gotten rid of. This grass, being indigenous, comes up on land after it gets a little worn; is excellent to prevent land from washing and to cover any embankment, and in all respects is more valuable than Bermuda. The Lespidesa, or Japanese Clover, grows in most parts of the county. This is a very small leaf clover, having very little root. It takes hold almost anywhere without cultivation, and forms very good grazing for stock. When it is on good land and not grazed too closely, it makes good hay. To make it a success as a hay crop, the land should be well prepared, the seed distributed as evenly as possible and pastured but little. It will then come to perfection in short time, and can be cut with mower. It cures very quickly in the sun, and makes a good and wholesome food for stock. This clover was supposed to have been brought from South Carolina during the war by the cavalry horses. It was brought to Charleston, S. C., probably seventy-five years ago. It is not a hardy plant; will stand very little cold; easily killed in the spring, and easily checked by drought. It is not a safe grass to depend on for general grazing purposes.

The Crab grass is in all the fields after cultivation.

The farmers rather it would not flourish as well as it does. It makes a fine summer grazing for all kinds of stock, including hogs. It makes a good hay if mowed in time and baled. It grows with great rapidity, and when well set and rooted in a field is difficult to get rid of. There is a water grass, which grows on all low, swampy land, which is excellent for grazing when tender, and makes good hay if cut at the right time and cured properly. The old time sedge grass is universal in our county; grows to some extent on woodland, but not to any perfection. It is in its best state to allow it to come up on land lying out and but recently cultivated. It is fine summer pasture and good milk producer. It is seldom used for hay.

There are a great number of noxious weeds indigenous to our soil, that come up in all soils when the ground is manured. These are the Jamestown, the night shade, the ground cherry, the Polk, prickly and smooth carless, and many others that are smaller. The Johnson grass is something new in our county. It was discovered probably in Alabama. It is doubtless a species of the sorghum; is a very heavy, rough grass; makes fine hay if mowed young. It comes early and grows very rapidly. If allowed to spread on land, it will take complete possession—nothing can be cultivated with it. It has very heavy roots that have joints something like the cane. It is not so hard to get rid of as was once supposed. If it is not plowed up and cultivated to some extent, it will die out in a few years. It appears to need cultivation. The hay is not so valuable a feed as the Bermuda grass.

The cocoa, or nut grass, is much to be feared, as it is considered one of the worst enemies to all kinds of crops when it is once well set. It is in many parts of the State west of us. It is in some gardens in Newton county. It is probably brought in the roots of fruit trees or clinging to strawberry plants. The root is a small black nut having bitter taste and pungent smell. The top resembles very much the chufa. It is to be dreaded as a plague. Every tree, plant or flower bulb sent to us, should be well examined before putting them out. When once well set with cocoa, or nut grass, requires the family to remove from the place to get rid of it.

CREEKS AND STREAMS OF THE COUNTY.

Newton county has no very large streams, nothing more than what would be called creeks, except Chunkey, a small river rising in the northern part of the county, near the town of Union, and running southeast and forming a junction with Ocotibbaha, in Clarke county, just above Enterprise, forming the Chickasahay river. Chunkey is the largest stream in the county and has some fine lands and timber of the quality of swamp growth heretofore mentioned. Tallahatta, another stream in the eastern part of the county; Talasha is also in the eastern part of the county; Pottoxchitto, Tallahala, Cedar Creek and Warrior, in the south and western part; Tuscalameta, a large creek in the western part, running north to Pearl river. Tarlow, Bogue Philemma in the southern part; Turkey creek in the central part; Connehatta and Sipsey in the northeastern part. Many of these streams have fine timber of the swamp variety. The lands of most of them are of strong character, but often overflow and much ditching is required. Many of these streams require long bridges which are built at the expense of the county.

PRODUCTIONS OF THE COUNTY.

Newton county produces corn, cotton, oats, wheat,

rye, tobacco, rice, sweet and Irish potatoes, goobers, cow peas, sorghum cane, large Louisiana cane; all these products may be grown abundantly and profitably with proper care and cultivation. Fruits grow well in this county. Peaches, when well cared for, come to great perfection; grapes and apples of certain varieties grow well; plums of almost all kinds do well here; pears sometimes do well, but as a general thing do not thrive; most of the trees now being grown, blight and die early. The latitude in which we are situated invites late frosts, after most of our peach and some other fruit trees have bloomed, and in the months of March and April they are often killed. If the peach orchards bear one good crop in three years, the owners are fortunate. All kinds of small berries do well in this county.

The strawberry, with proper care and cultivation, is a success. Raspberries come to great perfection. The wild and cultivated blackberry do well here. The large cherries do not succeed well. This county is well adapted to the growth of all kinds of vegetables; properly planted, and fertilized, they come to great perfection. Along this line of railroad vegetables and fruits might be grown for market with hreat profit to the producer if it could be disposed of properly in markets needing our products.

Newton county has received very large shipments of fruit trees almost every year for the last twenty. Thousands of dollars have been spent in this way. Something strange that there is no better results in the raising of better fruits, and more of them. Much depends upon the care taken of fruit trees, the careful cul ivation and intelligent fertilizing. Sometimes a man buying a lot of trees tries to do too much for them, and may over-fertilize them, or he may not put the proper kind around them. He may allow a deadly enemy, the worms, to destroy them. He may allow all kinds of stock to run at large in his orchard, and they destroy his trees. He may plant all kinds of grain crops in his orchard, which is very destructive to his fruit trees. He may be ignorant of the way to trim and cultivate. Sometimes trees are cultivated too close and deep; all these things should be carefully studied and enquiries made of the best authorities on those subjects.

It requires careful study and intelligent labor to succeed in making good fruit. Much depends upon the kind of soil in which trees are set, the drainage they get and the kind of trees selected. Buyers may be the victims of some unscrupulous dealer, who does not care as to the kind of trees sold.

If a farmer and fruit grower would succeed, he should be sure in the first place to get good selections, suitable to his section, and from a place as congenial with his own as possible. He should study well the kind of soil adapted to such fruit. He should then enrich his trees with just such material as they need. Work them properly and never plant a crop on the orchard ground, that would be detrimental to their life and growth. A grain crop upon the orchard should always be avoided; plant cotton and sow cow pea among the trees, and do not cultivate too close. Do not have the orchard too large. Have it small enough that every tree can have attention in turn, so that the worms will do no harm.

If Newton county could get sale at remunerative prices for the fruits and vegetables that could be grown contiguous to the railroad through the county, it would more than equal the cotton crop. If it could so be arranged that buyers from a distance, who needed our fruits and vegetables, would send some one to our section and buy what we could make, it would offer a market for our products, and in this way we would be remunerated. When such perishable stuff as fruits and vegetables are shipped, all advantages may be taken, and no benefit accrue to the producer. Exorbitant charges, great waste, and often dishonest dealing, will cut off the profits of all such crops. No good will ever come of fruit and vegetable growing until a general concert of action is had among the growers, and such action taken as will secure the return of the value of the products shipped.

PRODUCTION, AS SHOWN BY CENSUS OF 1890.

From the census of 1890 will be shown what Newton county produced, as returned by the farmers of the county. This will show the crop of 1889, as the estimate was made in the summer of 1890, before the crop was matured: Bushels of corn, 392,619; bushels of oats, 47,990; bushels of rye, 45; bushels of wheat, 13; proceeds of rice, $1900; proceeds of tobacco, $1762; number of bales of cotton, 13,097; number of farms, 2496; acres of improved land, 90,868; value of land, improved and unimproved, including fences and buildings, $1,427,870; value of farm implements and machinery, $73,330; estimated value of farm products, $919,390.

A comparison between the census of 1880 and 1890 is very striking. No one can look at the figures, as shown by each, and not be fully convinced that Newton county is largely on the increase in everything pertaining to prosperity and material development of its resources. In 1880, the products of the county were: Bales of cotton, 6341; bushels of corn, 261,207; bushels of oats, 58,336; bushels of rye, 82;

bushels of wheat, 653 ; gallons of molasses ; 30,356 ; tobacco, 8526 pounds ; rice, 29,673 pounds ; sweet potatoes, 64,601 bushels; estimated value of all farm products sold, consumed or on hand, $634,264 ; cost of building and repairing fences, $36,278; value of all farming implements and machinery, $58,253 ; value of farms, including fences and buildings, $868,866 ; unimproved lands, 61,045 acres ; number of farms, 1493.

A comparison will show about 25 to 50 per cent. on everything except tobacco, wheat and oats. Cotton is over double. Everything that is supposed profitable or that enters into the productions of the county for profit, will be shown has largely increased. The population, all classes, in 1880, was 13,436 ; in 1890, 16,624; showing less than 25 per cent. increase in population ; and the increase of the various productions of the most prominent classes, running from 25 to 100 per cent.

There are several reasons given for this large increase of substantial wealth and productions, with not a corresponding growth of population. First, it is the large increase in the use of fertilizers ; second, the improvement in farming by a more intelligent use of farm implements and better methods being used, which were obtained by a freer intercourse of the farmers among themselves at various Grange meetings—county and State—and a general discussion of improvements yearly for the last ten, at Patrons' Union ; also, the increased reading of agricultural journals Summing it all up, it may well be called a more intelligent and practical use of all the means in the reach of the farmer to increase his crops on less acreage. There are still some who do not agree, or at least do not act with the progressive portion of the agricultural world—who are not pressing every, advantage and freely adopting every new method that proves itself to be a success.

CHAPTER XXXI.

AGRICULTURAL PRODUCTS SHIPPED ON OUR RAIL-
ROADS IN NEWTON COUNTY — AMOUNT OF LUMBER
AND TIMBER SHIPPED ON THE RAILROAD IN NEW-
TN COUNTY—OTHER INDUSTRIES AND RESOURCES TO
BE DEVELOPED — PROFITABLE TIMBERS AND HOW
USED—NUMBER OF GINS, MILLS, PLANERS, ETC.

There is no doubting the utility and advantages of the railroads of our county. The old methods of transportation have all given way to newer means of railroad travel and an accommodation in getting over the country, and in turn, in receiving whatever may be necessary for the farm and in the family. The highest production of cotton any one year since the settlement of the county, will probably run to 15,000 bales. Considerable portion of this went to other towns in the State, and not shipped on the railroads in our county. Yet there is more cotton coming from other counties to the railroad towns in this county than goes away from this county to other towns. The best shipment of cotton any one year, going from the depots in the county, are given by their respective agents as follows: From Newton, 1888-'89, 11,203 bales; From Lawrence, about 250; from Hickory, 6,500; from Chunkey, about 250; showing an aggregate of 18,103, and will brobably go to 20,000 in 1894. This is a good showing for the county. It must be taken into consideration the large amount of other things brought to the road in this county; for a number of years large amounts of lumber, both rough and dressed, have been shipped not only from the mills situated immediately along the line of the road, but those on both sides of the road and a considerable distance in the interior. The white oak for staves, both long, pipe and barrel, have been brought in large quantities; spoke timber, of oak, has also been largely brought to the railroad. Hickory for spokes and felloes, has also afforded large exporting material. Hoop-poles, of which our county has a great abundance, has for years been brought to those railroad markets. Cross-ties, since the establishing of our towns, have from year to year been furnished to supply the road in the county and also wherever else they were needed. Live stock, in the way of cattle and sheep, are sent from our county on the road. To these are added hides, wool, furs, butter, eggs, chickens, geese, turkeys and ducks. The towns of Newton are among the best in the State for country produce. All these things aggregate an amount both large and surprising.

There is at Newton a spoke lathe, owned by Mr. Z. T. Doolittle. P. E. Blelack, in 1893, erected a hub lathe and furnished the Progress Manufacturing Company, at Meridian, a large supply of hubs. The town of Hickory has a hoop manufactory, and the town of Chunkey has a barrel factory, at which are made the best and most substantial cypress molasses barrels, made of the cypress off Chunkey river and hooped with the best kind of hickory. These barrels command ready sale at home and there is more demand from other places than can be supplied.

There are about fifty cotton gins in Newton county, most of them having feeders and condensers attached. None of them, as yet, have the Mounger attachment, which does all the work of ginning and packing and unloading by machinery. The most of these gins are run by steam, a few by water; probably not more than one or two in the county run by horse-power.

There are probably twenty steam saw-mills; several planing mills with dry kiln's attached to them. The greater part of this lumber is shipped to other States, though much of it is being used in the county for building purposes, fencing and bridge building.

The sweet gum that is now found to be valuable in our own and foreign countries; the young hickory that has come up in the rich alluvial prairie slough lands, offers the very best material for buggies and wagons of superior manufacture. The elm, growing among this rich young growth of hickory, is the best of its kind anywhere to be found. The young ash is very superior. There is a vast amount of beech of excellent quality, of good size and good heart, which, if it could be used, would prove very remunerative. It might be shipped to Virginia, North and South Carolina, Kentucky and Tennessee, for making tobacco boxes. There is a considerable amount of magnolia, which might be used in making furniture. The large swamp poplar is being brought to our road and shipped both northwest and to foreign countries. There is a great quantity of dog-wood which might be made useful in the construction of the best Texas saddle trees. Tupelo gum is in great abundance for the construction of bowls, trays or any wooden ware into which they may be turned.

In the northeastern part of the county there are some lands that have large deposits of iron ore. These lands are on the headwaters of Chunkey, and there is no doubt of this mineral deposit. To what extent it is valuable hhs never been tested. The large amount of iron in various parts of the country, and where furnaces are already erected, would preclude the necessity of the ore in Newton county being, any time soon called into requisition, though the time may come when it will be valuable.

PROFITABLE TIMBER OF THE COUNTY.

There are yet profitable timbers in the county that will sooner or later all be brought into requisition. The timber near the road has, to some extent, been used, though far from all being exhausted. There still remains much off from the road to be used. This is the long-strawed pine, for milling purposes; the white-oak, for staves, still in the swamps not yet penetrated; the post-oak, for hubs, enough in reach of the A. & V. road to serve for years the most extensive factory in the United States.

CHAPTER XXXII.

NEWTON AS A STOCK-RAISING COUNTY—KINDS OF STOCK—NUMBER OF YOUNG HORSES AND MULES IN THE COUNTY.

Newton as a stock-raising county will probably class high with any in the State, particularly that kind of stock of the must useful character. The county cannot boast of any fine race stock of horses, nor does it need any, as the breeding of that kind of horses has a very demoralizing tendency on any community in which it is practiced. It encourages gambling and all kinds of dissipation and immorality, and what can be more damaging to a community than an enterprise that would increase sin and immoral practices, and worldly indulgences, and obtaining money by the most doubtful and improper means? Men who breed thorough blooded horses for the turf are not the best models for the youth of the country.

The kind of stock bred in our county is the good work and saddle horses and the best of mules. Also some of the best of cattle have been brought into our county in recent years, such as Jersey, Holstein, Gurnsey and Durham, which crossed upon our common stock, make excellent milk cows. At the close of the war there was not a good stallion or jack in the county, and a Jersey cow was not known only as they were read of. About twenty years ago, Dr. G. E. Longmire, a physician and practical man, saw the necessity of good mules, and introduced a very fine jack into the county. There are many of these mules yet in the county, all showing the blood of the sire. About that time Mr. W. H. Martin, of Decatur, placed his fine horse before the people, but not with the success which he deserved. About twelve ago Mr. J. V. Knight brought one of the finest jacks that has ever been in the county, and placed him on his stock farm, seven miles southwest from Newton. Mr. Isham H. Brown, about the same time, placed a fine jack on his farm in the eastern part of the county, and the products of these two fine animals may now be counted by the hundreds, of fine, large, well formed, quick growth young mules that have filled our county. Mr. G. L. Doolittle, about this time, or a little later, introduced his fine horse on his farm, three miles north of Newton, and his colts are probably the best in the county. Dr. G. H. McNeill, a physician at Newton, and farmer and stock raiser, brought to Newton as fine a thoroughbred stallion as has been in the county, and his colts show some of the best saddle stock that has ever been in the county. He also, at the same time, had a jack, which did valuable service. These have been followed in rapid succession by different men in the county—McMullen, Holliday, Wedgeworth and others—until, at the present writing, there are at least ten fine stallions and as many jacks in Newton county.

The product of these animals may be seen at the various places of gatherings of the people in the county, and particularly at the Patrons' Union, where yearly there are premiums offered for the best stock of all qualities produced in our county. Mr. W. B. Richardson has recently brought to the town of Newton a fine stallion, "George Gordon," probably the most thoroughbred animal that has ever been in the county. He also has some fine mares and colts that will compare well with any ever seen in this county. This policy of stock-raising has caused Newton county, which has been a buyer of fine mules and other stock, to be able to supply each year to other counties as many as five hundred young horses and mules. The laws of this State to encourage the raising of stock, make the colt responsible, and in this way parties are always more sure of their money and more pains are taken, and more good stock raised.

The farmer of years ago did not appreciate that he could raise his mules and horses in this country, even where farmers were wealthy, had large slave property and abundant pastures, but pursued a more expensive policy of buying what he needed on his farm and paying for it with cotton. The Tennessee and Kentucky stock-raisers, taking advantage of this, made good use of it by shipping all the spare young stock that they could raise to the Southern cotton States, and the failure on the part of Southern planters to do their duty, was largely the gain of the stock-raisers farther north. A very conservative estimate of the number of young horses and mules foaled each year in the county of Newton, would be at least 500. As a general thing these mule colts are fine size and quality. The best and largest jacks are bred to the county mares and produce a stock of mules both of fine working and riding qualities and of good size. The horse colts are of good breeds, from fair to fine, and make good riding and work stock.

To show the increase of this particular industry, a comparative review of the live stock and some others, as shown by the census of 1880 and 1890, will not be uninteresting: Number of horses as shown in the year 1880, 2049; mules and asses, 749; working oxen,

1623; milch cows, 3630; other cattle, 6762; number of hogs, 19,376; sheep, 4838; wool grown, 10,756; butter, 117,420. The year 1890: Horses, 2666; mules, 1372; asses, 22; working oxen, 2387; milch cows, 4873; other cattle, 8405; hogs, 24,624; sheep, 7855; pounds of wool, 15,836; butter, not given in report. The smallest increase is that of the horses; yet that is accounted for from the fact that people saw the great need of work stock and turned their attention to the raising of fine mules, which the comparative statement of census shows to be nearly double in ten years.

The value in 1880 of a good four-year old mule, county raised, from 16 to 17 hands high, was from $125 to $175; now, in 1894, a good mule of that description may be bought easily for $100 cash, demand poor at that. Horses are lower now in this county than at any period since the war. Large numbers of Texas horses were brought here years ago. With few exceptions they were of very little account to the farmer. Their wild nature and bad qualities, made them very troublesome to work, and when once broken they were nearly exhausted by having to use such force to subdue them. This influx of stock, with the raising of all kinds in the county, and a large introduction of horses from the West, sold at auction, all combine to make stock lower than ever known before.

Quite a spirit of improvement is noted in the introduction of better cattle. About the same time, that better horses and mules were introduced in the county, better cattle were brought, particularly milk stock. The first full-blood Jerseys brought to the county were introduced by Hoye, Barber, Gallaspy, Johnson, Harris, Rathral, Chapman and Richardson. Mr. Richardson, at Newton, probably has the purest Jersey stock of any one in the county. They have never been allowed to run at large, but have been pastured, and are the purest strain in the county.

It is found that the introduction of the Jersey cattle into our county is a wonderful improvement, particularly in milk stock. A grade Jersey, that is, a half Jersey heifer from registered bull and good common cow, is one of the best milk cows for our country. They are very hardy, more so than full-bred. The milking qualities are nearly as good as full-blood, and the butter making qualities is far superior to the old common stock of the country. One good grade Jersey cow is worth two, or sometimes three, common cows for butter purposes.

The people of Newton county have prided themselves on their cattle and young stock. The Patrons' Union has for years offered premiums on good stock. The owners also of jacks and stallions have offered premiums on best colt shown at stated periods, sired by their respective animals. All these things, together with the great advantage of having young, handsome and able horses and mules, home-raised — that would serve for any purpose, has greatly increased the spread of good stock in the county.

Not so much can be said of sheep and hogs, though by comparative estimate of the census of 1880 and '90, there is a large increase of both, and nearly fifty per cent. on the growth of wool; yet there is not such increase as should be. This county offers many advantages for sheep-raising. The great trouble is in the fact that there are so many dogs, that the sheep cannot live in the range; some law of protection should be made to remedy this great destruction The sheep may, by full indemnity from this great destroyer, be made to pay as well, if not better, than any other stock now in the county. Hogs should be raised to fully supply all the pork and bacon to be used in the county. Trouble by theft no longer exists, as the severe penalty for such offences, and the improvement in the morals of those heretofore guilty of such crimes, have remedied the evil. There are some very fine breeds of hogs in this county. The Berkshire is a good breed; so is the Poland-China, and Essex mixed, considered the largest hog, and one of the most valuable now in the hands of the farmer. Great efforts should be made to acclimate and breed these hogs up to their full measure. There is no longer a range for hogs in our county. The farmer must depend upon what is grown in the fields to raise and fatten his pork. This can easily be done by properly preparing and planting crops for hogs. A very great drawback in the raising of hogs is the diseases with which they are attacked. All hog-raising counties have to contend against the same trouble. Much depends upon what a hog is fed as to the health of the animal.

Food for hogs, as for persons, should be varied; they should be fed on such things as will not only produce fat, but health and quick growth. A man should not be discouraged if he lose some of his hogs every year by disease; he should look well to the sanitary conditions, as to where they sleep, to a change of pasture and food, also give some remedies to act upon the liver and general system; endeavor to study up something with which to cure his hogs, if they get sick, the same as he would other animas in same condition.

POULTRY RAISING.

Newton county is one of the foremost in the State in poultry raising. The fowl mostly raised is the chicken; these are not the improved breeds that are mostly brought to market, but the old-time mixed colors and styles that appear to belong to this climate and latitude. The improved breeds, such as Brahma, Plymouth Rock, Wyandotte and others, do well for a time, and the young ones thrive and get ther growth very quick; yet they appear to be far more subject to disease, which usually proves fatal; they are usually taken with these diseases when in their best appearance. These diseases in poultry should be met and treated heroically, with a full determination to cure and stamp them out if possible. There is no doubt of fine breeds being far superior in size and quick growth; if the disease can be kept off they would prove a valuable addition to the acclimated fowls of the county.

The town of Newton probably receives as many chickens, turkeys, geese, ducks and guineas, as any railroad town in the State; these are largely from Newton county. The geese are used for feathers; they are abundant in the county, and materially assist the farmer in keeping the grass down in his cotton; it being claimed that ten geese are equal to one good hoe-hand in keeping the grass subdued in young cotton. Geese are rarely eaten by country people; they are shipped in large quantities to the cities and used there for the flesh and oil.

The same may be said as to the receipts of eggs at the towns of Newton county, only in a far greater proportion, as it is supposed that there is more profit in selling the eggs than the chicks. The amounts received and shipped from Newton county is almost incredible, and in the year aggregate a large sum of money; the firm of Rew & McClinton shipped from Newton a car-load of eggs to New Orleans in the spring of 1894. There were 200 cases, containing 30 dozen each, which was 6,000 dozen eggs; these eggs were gathered in the town of Newton in a very short time, as they cannot keep them at that season long. The average price of eggs is from ten to twelve cents for the year, and that is very good considering the price of everything else.

CHAPTER XXXIII.

Taxes of the County—Amount of Taxable Land—Personal Property—Price of Improved and Unimproved Land.

The importance of all countries is, to some extent, to be judged by the amount of tax they pay, as back of this tax lies the substantial wealth of the citizen. The more tax a man pays the more he has of the wealth of this world, and where it is given in as it should be, is a true index to his possessions. A comparative statement of the United States census and the county assessment will not be uninteresting to those who would be inquisitive as to the amount of wealth the citizens of Newton county have. The census of 1890 gives value of land, including fences and buildings, $1,427,870; value of live stock, $507,560. County assessment for the year 1893 gives the value of lands, fences and building, $1,083,774; personal property, $655,666. There is not so much discrepancy in these estimates as one would suppose. When men give in their property to the enumerator of the census, he is in no way particular about the price, as there is no tax to pay, and the matter may often be left to the enumerator to price it as he wishes, and as persons of same neighborhood price their property. When in is to be valued by the county assessor, it is a matter of more material concern, and one upon which a tax has to be levied. As a usual thing, the smallest price that can be placed upon property, and which the assessor and owner can agree upon, is the value placed. Exorbitant valuations should not be placed upon property, but a man should not claim as his prerogative to place his property lower than reasonable conservative valuation. Possibly a good rule to be governed by in this matter would be that a man would give in his property at just what he would take in cash for it, provided he wanted to sell it.

The amount of taxes collected in the county on the assessed valuation of property for 1893 was $17,742.57. Rate of tax is nine mills. The county is out of debt, with money in treasury. The average of improved lands in the county of Newton for the year 1890, shows $6.11 per acre. This being an average, as a matter of course, some of the lands of the county would run to a much higher, and some much lower, price than this. There are some select places, well improved, that the owners attach a high value to. There are many good places in the county of large bodies of land, which are valuable, and yet they would not bring their value, owing to the size of the tracts and poor improvements. The wild, uncultivated lands are also variously estimated ; some of them bring good prices, while others only nominal value. The railroad, which has large tracts of land in the county and are constantly selling, usually offer and sell their lands with one-fourth cash payment, from $2.50 to $3.00 per acre, giving three years, with interest at eight per cent. from date, on three-fourths of the land. It is not expected that the railroad lands should represent the best class of uncultivated lands in the county, and yet there are some lands in the hands of private individuals that could be bought for less than the price of the railroad lands. There is great fluctuation in the price of land, and there is rarely a panic of any kind when money matters become stringent, but the price of land is affected by it.

There is no doubt but the lands of this county are cheap and that they offer good investment for the permanent settler. The many advantages connected with our county should induce persons wishing homes to buy the lands of this county. It is no small thing to own a home, a part of this "eminent domain," and to claim citizenship in a county like Newton. Let the young farmer select a piece of land, not too large, go to work and erect a comfortable house, and put a reasonable portion of it under cultivation; commence to improve in a way to be a permanent settler, and in a few years the place will offer attractions which will make it desirable. Let the young men of Newton settle and improve Newton county lands. Distance may "lend enchantment to the view," but it is too often the case that "a rolling stone gathers no moss."

CHAPTER XXXIV.

SPIRIT OF IMPROVEMENT IN THE COUNTY—QUALITY OF DWELLING HOUSES, FARMS AND FENCES NOW BEING BUILT—EFFORTS TO PASS THE STOCK LAW.

IN all parts of the county may be seen substantial and more permanent improvements. In the early settlement the new comers put up such houses as could be conveniently constructed without much help from others. The small log-cabin was the one most usually built to suit the pressing needs of a small family. This house was usually 14x16 or 16x18, sometimes 18x20 feet, of round pine poles, with the bark taken off; one door, one window on the right or left of the chimney, which was made of sticks and dirt, with large fire-place. House covered with split boards, three to four feet long. These houses had no rafters but ridge-poles, and the boards laid on the poles and weighted with other poles; this was on account of having no nails, as they were scarce and high. The floor was often of puncheons. The spaces between the logs, called cracks, were ceiled with boards split, sometimes drawn but usually rough. In this house very frequently was done the cooking, this one room serving for bed-room, dining-room and kitchen. This style gave way to larger rooms, then double rooms with hall between, rafters with gable ends, plank floor with commodious lofts overhead where much household goods were stored, and sometimes formed good sleeping apartments when visitors came to see the family. Kitchens were constructed quite a distance from the dwelling; a smoke-house was put up and other improvements as the county advanced.

The early cabins were enclosed, if enclosed at all, by a rail fence and steps over the fence, not usually a gate. Out-houses consisted of small log crib and stables, with a good lot made of large rail-fence ten rails high, staked and ridered, with bars instead of a gate as an entrance to the lot. Very little attention was given to the sheltering of stock, except the work-horses; all others were expected to take the weather. A small field was cleared with no attention given to saving land by circling or hill-side ditching. Little attention paid to taking care of the premises. Very little care in the cultivation of vegetables and fruits.

The spontaneous productions of a new country were largely drawn on for supplies; afrer the fitst field was well worn another was cleared up and the first turned out to grow up in a second growth of timber. After a time, and by the better class of farmers, better log houses went up; these houses required much work and large help to raise them; they were of heavy hewn logs — sometimes two-story — with shed room, covered with shingles and having brick chimneys; these were considered fine houses. After the advent of the steam saw-mill came many improvements in the county, and yet when a man had a good log house he did not often change it even if he were able.

The log house in the country continued to be the style, with few exceptions, until after the war. It was sometimes the case that a large planter and slave owner would build a fine frame house and paint it white; the house would usually be very large, well built and expensive. It was the admiration of the county. It is now very different; most of the houses that white people put up are frame, with brick chimneys, and often brick pillars; the kitchen is now put under the same roof with the dwelling, with more modern conveniences. In most instances these houses are painted, having glass windows and other adornments of form and finish, more closely resembling the city houses. This is a very commendable spirit and should be encouraged, and whenever a man can build him a comfortable house, in the style of the times, he should do so.

There is a corresponding advance in preparing for stock by the construction of a barn for holding feed, for sheltering stock, and wagons and buggies. Much of the fencing is now done with wire and plank; this is by far the best fence, and if constructed of good material will last much longer than rail fence.

STOCK LAW.

Much has been said in reference to the stock law; that is a law to provide that all stock in the county be enclosed under fence and to allow the fields to be unfenced. Much has been said and written on this subject, and many of the States have the stock law. This county has had it submitted to the voters on two occasions and it has been defeated.

While it will not be the province of this history to advocate or condemn this law, it would be legitimate and right to speak of the benefits accruing from such a course, and also the inconvenience and hardship it will work to others. It is well known that fencing is very expensive; that large amounts of labor and money are expended yearly for that purpose; and with all the work and expense, there is much of the fencing in the county very badly kept up; and where a test is made, it is seen that there are very few lawful fences in the county. The census of 1880 estimated that the cost of building and repairing fences for the year 1879 amounted to $36,278, which amount was nearly equal to $3.00 for each inhabitant of the county. This will give the reader an idea of what the yearly labor is on fences in this county. It will not be expected that all this fencing would be done away with if the stock-law were established, for the stock would have to be pastured and good fences kept around them, but it probably would do away with two-thirds of it. To be compelled to fence stock would be to reduce their numbers. In that event, in proportion to the reduction of the number of stock would be the increase in size and usefulness, as far as the cows are concerned; also hogs. It means that we are to have better stock of all kinds; that will be better attended to, always on hand when wanted, not troubling the growing crop, and have not free access to the fields.

After the crops are gathered stock do cultivated lands nearly as much harm as the crop that has grown on them. The hungry stock in the winter denude the fields of everything that is expected to go back to the soil, tramp the land when wet, bury the grass and seed deep in the soil, and cause many washes that would not otherwise occur if stock were not allowed to go on the fields. The older States that have tried the stock law, all favor it, and would not, if they could, have the old law in force. The enclosure of the stock by the older States, means more meat, much more milk and butter, better horses, better crops, and less anxiety and trouble with the stock. Even the great State of Texas, more than five times larger than Mississippi, and having the best grazing lands of any State in the

Union, has long since had the stock law. Persons complain that it would work hardships on the poor man, who has no land, and that he would have to dispose of his stock and be entirely without the comforts and benefits which they bring him. This is answered by the no-fence man that the poor man who has no land is usually a tenant, and that tenant can always be accommodated to pasture land by assisting the landlord to fix pasture fences, and share the benefits of his grass. Take the expense and labor into consideration; take the difference in the quality of stock, their better grade and greater weight, being always ready at the command of the owner, there is much to commend the no-fence law. The improvement to the uncleared land is another reason why stock should be kept up. If the new lands in the woods are allowed to remain with undisturbed growth for a series of years, the accumulation and shade on the ground will much improve the soil.

As the country grows older it is expected the people will see the necessity of making all the needed improvements, and will adapt them to suit the demands and emergencies. There having been two unsuccessful efforts to pass the stock-law, when presented to the people again it may result in a similar vote. Yet the time will come when the necessity of passing it will be presented, and then they will act promptly upon it.

CHAPTER XXXV.

BY CO-OPERATIVE EFFORT WHAT MAY BE DONE IN NEWTON COUNTY—EMIGRATION VS. IMMIGRATION.

THAT the county of Newton offers many advantages to permanent settlers, there is no doubt—not only for persons who have been born in the county, but those seeking a home from other States. There is nothing like co-operation among the citizens of any city, town or county, to make all its advantages and resources available. There is nothing more necessary for men living in any county, to be content with their homes; to feel satisfied to stay there and to make permanent and substantial improvements, and feel that they are settled for life; whenever these things are assured, men will go to work to make themselves comfortable and put such improvements on their places, that every year they become more and more enhanced in value; become more and more desirable to the owner and attractive to those who visit our county with a view to settling in it.

Newton county possesses many attractive features for settlement. In the first place, it is considered to have good health, which is one of the blessings of life. The census of 1890 places Newton county as having the greatest number of persons to the family, it being 5.80, except two counties in the State, which are Covington, 5.90, and Lawrence, 5.91. This, of itself, shows the hygienic condition of its population, that they enjoy a greater immunity from disease than in almost any other part of the State.

The marriage licenses issued in the last five years average 150 each year. It has run as high as 170 in one year. This shows a disposition of the young people of the county to marry at home, as in most instances both parties live in, and remain in the county.

Newton county has fine water and in great abundance in springs and creeks, and the most excellent wells; also timber for building and wood. A soil that in many parts is rich or highly productive. Its poor lands, and those that have been worn down, are susceptible of very great improvement, which enables the farmer to continue his old lands under cultivation and to improve from year to year, and in a series of crops each will be seen to be an improvement on the former. These farms are yearly being improved by being fertilized and drained, and thereby become more valuable. Land hunters, instead of going to distant States and places where lands are high, will seek the ones which are so attractive and made valuable by care and attention. There is no doubt but this county is capable of producing a great variety of crops. If the farmer is not suited with the crop most common to be cultivated, he can plant a variety of others known to be remunerative.

There is no doubt but we have a well governed and law abiding people. The school and church privileges are good; Sabbath School interests predominate in the county; no liquors sold in its borders. To be able to bring up a family which has not been the victims of the open saloons, nor subjected to the demoralizing influences of such persons who frequent them, and to be privileged to raise up boys who have not seen every day the vice of the race course and gambling table, is certainly a consideration of great value. Our county is free from these, and all the advantages enumerated are great incentives to live in such society.

The innovations of polite society are sufficiently felt in our midst as to give us good manners, and to teach us good breeding, and a sufficiency of refinement to pass if we were thrown into circles demanding such change of deportment. Of high grades of society and sticklers for etiquette we do not have much to boast, and as little to crave. It is well understood that if our youth, when they leave home, are moral and educated, and if they propose to change citizenship, that they will readily adapt themselves to the more refining influences of better society.

That we have good railroads and good railroad towns, where the farmers may buy and sell to the best advantage, there is no doubt. The towns of Newton county offer some of the best advantages of any in the State. What we need is, by all means to hold on to our good citizens who have been born and raised in our county; to offer special inducements to good working, self-sustaining people to come into our county to live; to commence a systematic and substantial improvement in everything connected with our county, morally, religiously, and by a thorough enforcement of our laws; of a strict observance of the Sabbath, an encouragement of the spirit of temperance, as now practiced, with an effort to improve it; a general move n the way of improving the appearance of every residence and farm in the county; to study how to keep the soil on the hillside; to rotate crops, and cultivate so as to improve and not impoverish the fields; to fertilize liberally and intelligently; lessening the acres planted and increasing the crops; carefully drain every low piece of ground; terrace every level and slope so as to retain and not lose what is reserved on the land.

Improve the stock of all kinds by liberal feed and good shelter—having finer stock and making them better. Let every planter make it his motto—if it can possibly be avoided—to learn to do without rather than go in debt. Avoid extravagance, even if the money is plentiful.

Let the merchants so conduct their business that large credit sales will be avoided. Not take great risks, or let their accounts run too long without settlement. Make small profits and be sure of the money; do not employ too much force to conduct business. Give close attention to all details of a mercantile establishment. Buy for the cash if possible, and save the discounts. Do not despise the day of small things, and do not try to make all the money in one year. Give close attention, practice economy in everything, and success will follow. Let it be understood that the farmer, merchant, lawyer, doctor, school teacher and preacher, are all necessary to make up a good community. Let each feel that he is to some extent dependent on the other. Each has a separate work in society, and all should harmonize and co-operate, so as to let the work of one be felt and benefitted by the other. By constant effort in this direction our county is sure to improve. In a short time rapid strides in the direction of an increase of population will be seen. The price of lands will appreciate when they become scarce in market, and that will be effected by greater population. Then it is that the owner becomes alive to their value. Then it is that he will persevere in his efforts to still further improve and beautify his home. There will be great demand for land in Newton county, because it is pleasant, healthy, convenient to market, good climate, with never a failure in the crops; always rain and sunshine, with four months of mild winter and eight months of delightful weather; a rainfall of from 56 to 60 inches in twelve months; a mean temperature of 65 to 70°, and the extreme of heat 100°, and of cold at 15°.

Taking all things into consideration, we may congratulate ourselves that we have a county of which we ought to be proud--one making rapid strides to the front, doing much for the elevation of its citizens and the morals of society. Our taxes are only $9.00 on the thousand dollars, which is less than most of the counties of the State. If we do our duty we will continue to prosper, and we may expect to secure some of the best citizens of other counties and States to settle and make permanent homes with us. We have no reason to be discouraged if we will work together. Any want of co-operation on our part, any disposition on the part of citizens not to perform their duty, and not to encourage union and good feeling, and a failure to perform such duties as have been enumerated, would not only do much to discourage those who have full confidence in the ultimate success and advancement of Newton county, but will discourage those who grow up from year to year, and who are seeking an opportunity to invest money in homes and business. Also would discourage any immigration to our county; would serve only to operate in the direction for evil to the material prosperity of our county.

It is a grievous thing to know that so many of the citizens of Newton county, who were born and raised here, and have been in this county many years, are seeking homes in distant lands. They go where the lands are high in some instances, where crops are uncertain, and have great lack of rains. Many sell out in this county, take small prices for their lands and go to a new country, and when they reach their new homes they have not enough money to make investments; they are consequently renters; they pay enough rent on each acre of land they cultivate every year, to buy good lands in this county. They have many inconveniences in the way of no timber, great scarcity of water, and much more rigorous climate. When a poor man goes to one of these States he is more likely to remain poor. If he have money to start with, it is probable he will stand a better chance of making more. Our doors are open to all who come with a view to improve the county and be self-sustaining; who will cultivate the soil or go into any other business by which they can add to the material wealth of the county or give employment to others. Yet we would rather allow our lands to grow up wild and have no immigration, than have such a class as would be offensive to our citizenship and of such character as would add nothing in the way of morality or law-abiding persons — such as know nothing of our laws and care less for our prosperity.

Newton county has probably 17,000 to 18,000 population; if it could by judicious management and proper encouragement, induce other persons to come to our county and increase its numbers to 35,000 or to 40,000, everything would assume a new phase. More enterprise, more wealth, more and various industries would spring up all over the county. The fine timbers and hard woods now needing development would be a profitable investment to those handling them. The land would be taken up; the old lands would be greatly improved; new lands would be much enhanced in value, and everything that now lags would act with new life. We would have more produced, better churches, better schools, better school-houses ; our towns would double their size in population and business ; our railroads would be improved; our taxes— though much smaller than many counties—would still be less ; a more dense population always tends to greater aggregation of capital and more expensive investments ; and under such circumstances our county would become a manufacturing as well as agricultural people. Banks would spring up in our towns, and many things to enliven business and encourage a still further increase of population, which means larger wealth and more importance of our county in the State.

CHAPTER XXXVI.

Professional Men of the County.

The professional men of Newton county will come in these pages for something more than if they were men who devote themselves to the ordinary pursuits of life. It is expected when a man assumes the position of a professional, that if he is not, he should be, learned above his fellows. Consequently, he should prepare himself, first, by better education, and then by continuous study, and particularly those branches pertaining to his profession, so as to meet the exigencies or any emergencies into which he may be thrown. There is a grave responsibility resting upon a man assuming the duties devolving upon him in the line of his profession. If he is a lawyer, he is expected to understand the laws of his State, and a general knowledge of jurisprudence. He should be able at once to advise a client as to what course to pursue if his services are called into requisition. The lawyer is a very useful man, and when one is needed there is no way to get along without him.

The laws are intended to be just; the lawyer is expected to know what the law is and claim it for his client. The law is intended to right those who are wronged, and yet sometimes a man thinks he is right and is very often mistaken; when the light and justice of law and equity are thrown into the scales against him, he has no case before the court. Again, a man may fail to get justice even in the midst of the most enlightened community and the ablest judges and profound lawyers. Upon what hypothesis should these facts be based, that men with good causes fail to get justice and those with bad causes come out the winners in law, when all is supposed to be founded on justice and equal rights to all?

There are often failures in juries to do their duty; then failure in the witnesses to testify truthfully; then sometimes legal technicalities which, to the uneducated, are a perversion of justice; and lastly, the eloquent and argumentative appeals of able and sometimes unscrupulous attorneys that hold the destinies of their clients in their grasp. Hence the great responsibility resting on the lawyer. The lawyers are the men who make the laws of the country, hold the most important offices in the government, control politics, govern and form all legislation, direct most of the large corporations of the country, and dictate a policy by which the country and people are controlled; all will then agree that they are important factors in any country.

The physician has also a very delicate and responsible position in society. He should be a man of good common sense, well read and entirely sober, to be a suitable man to practice physic. He should be well acquainted with all the theories of medicine and practice, the effects of various drugs upon the whole system, to be able to diagnose a case, and act with promptness and decision. Yet many very useful doctors are not always very learned men; and on the contrary, many learned men, theoretically, are not skilled practitioners. Much depends upon a man's good, common sense, and the knowledge of what is the matter with his patients, and a careful and conscientious regard for human life. The lawyer's responsibility to his client often involves his monied interests. The doctor's responsibility to his patient often involves his life. Both are great, but the doctor's is the greater.

The minister of the gospel is another very important professional, and upon him devolves a great and important work. The assumption of clerical duties and preaching of the word of God and teaching and warning the people, should be entered into with the greatest solicitude. The most important thing connected with the preacher is to know or feel that he is divinely called to preach. This should first be satisfactorily settled in any preacher's mind, and then his life should fully conform to all the requirements of his holy office. God does not judge a man by his excellency of speech, enticing words and eloquent language; but upon his faithful discharge of duty, standing as a true sentinel on the walls of Zion, and giving the alarm when the enemy approaches. Should he not do this, and the city is taken, the blood of the people shall be required at his hands. The two professions heretofore mentioned, one responsible for money, one responsible for life, while a third is responsible for a man's soul—surely of all the responsibilities, this last is the greatest.

The teachers occupy a very high and exalted and responsible position and one that requires much ability to fill. The teacher who only works for the salary promised, surely has missed his calling. When they only wait through the weary hours of a four month's free school to get $100.00 they are poorly equipped in mind or principle to teach school. No teacher ought to wish a certificate above what he knows he is not able to understand. Whenever they are interested in the teaching of children whose parents expect them to know much more than the pupils, every exertion should be made to impress the child with the importance of learning and to be fully able to teach the books in the hands of the scholars. A teacher should well understand the text-books that are taught in the grade he is teaching. Pride and a conscientious discharge of duty should always be the cardinal points to be observed by teachers. They have the grave responsibility of training the children and the parents suppose they are competent. They should not abuse this trust. They should be proud of the position they occupy, and when they have discharged their duty they should have their reward, not only in dollars and cents, but in the gratitude of the public whom they serve.

The lawyers now in Newton county are Thos. Keith, T. B. McCune, both of Decatur, men who have long been engaged in the practice; Mr. Keith is a graduate from the law school at the State University, at Oxford. Mr. J. M. Gage, of Hickory, is the only member of the bar in that town; is a sober man, having considerable experience in the legal profession. S. B. Ross and J. R. Byrd are young attorneys at Newton. E. C. McCord and J. G. Benson are young lawyers of Connehatta. All these men are devoted to their profession, and are doing as well as the limited litigation of the county will permit.

RESIDENT PHYSICIANS OF THE COUNTY.

Dr. J. B. Bailey, Conehatta; Dr. J. M. Cleavland, Union; Dr. A. W. Grissett, Newton county; Dr. W. A. L. Lewis, Union; Dr. C. W. Carraway, Hickory; Dr. F. B. Nimmocks, Lawrence; Dr. L. F. Cotten, Lake; Dr. G. G. Everett, Newton; Dr. J. C. McElroy, Newton; Dr. F. G. Semmes, Hickory; Dr. A. H. Pucket,

Newton; Dr. E. B. Partin, Decatur; Dr. E. B. Pool, Lake; Dr. W. N. Davis, Battlefield; Dr. G. H. McNeil, Newton; Dr. J. J. Harralson, Conehatta; Dr. F. O. Horne, Union; Dr. H. B. Ross, Newton; Dr. S. B. Hinton, Decatur; Dr. O. L. Bailey, Lake; Dr. Wm. S. Norris, Stamper; Dr. Clarence Gilman, Hickory; Dr. H. D. Leverett, Hickory; Dr. Spivy, Chunkey; Dr. John W. Ferrall, resident dentist at Newton; and Dr. J. P. Harris, resident dentist at Hickory.

SOME OF THE OLD DOCTORS OF THE COUNTY.

Dr. Josiah Watkins, who came to the county about 1850, was a man who ought to be remembered. He was a Virginian by birth (and very proud of his State)—and also proud of his profession—a man of strong mind and felt that he was master of his profession. He would neither ask counsel nor did he desire consultation in a case to which he was called; felt what he did not know was not known to the profession. He was devoted to his patients, a man of great energy and sobriety, and made quite a fortune practicing medicine. He died in 1873.

Dr. M. M. Keith, of Decatur, was a man who was thoroughly equipped for his profession; was also a a Virginian by birth; had a good collegiate training, was considered a fine physician; a man who had his convictions and who had the courage to stand up for them. He was sometimes engaged in politics; represented the county of Newton from 1856 to 1861; was also a member of the secession convention of 1861. Dr. Keith died in 1883.

Dr. J. C. McElroy is a physician that has probably done more practice than any other doctor that ever lived in the county. He commenced in Decatur, after his return from the Mexican war, to which he went from Tennessee, his native State, and continued until 1862, when he took a company into the service of the Confederate States. He was Captain of Company D, 39th Mississippi Regiment. He also served Newton county in the Legislature from 1861 to 1866. He has been practicing medicine in the town of Newton and vicinity for more than twenty-five years. The doctor, though a small man, has been able to undergo great hardship—having always practiced on horseback. He is considered a fine physician, and has the confidence and practice of some of the best people of the county. He is still to be seen going his regular rounds of practice or closely engaged on his farm. He has many friends and has done much for the poor of the county.

Dr. S. G. Loughridge, an old physician now residing at Garlandsville, was once a resident of Newton county. He long since moved to Jasper county, where he made quite a fortune, much of it by the practice of medicine.

Dr. J. S. Parker, who died last year, 1893, deserves more than a passing notice among the older physicians of the county. He was born poor and raised hard and without education, and until he was a man of family had no idea of practicing medicine. During the war he was thrown into hospital service and had the care of some patients and soon learned to administer medicine. He applied himself and soon became a good doctor, and at one time did as much practice as any physician in the county. He was called to several cases of yellow fever in the epidemic of 1878, which he faithfully, and in most instances, successfully treated. There was no man who ever practiced medicine in the county who did more for the poor, both white and colored. He visited the sick with the least assurance of ever getting any pay for it, and much of his labor was entirely lost. Dr. Parker was greatly respected. He was a conspicuous Granger and took lively interest in politics. Although he did much free practice, he realized a considerable sum from his profession.

Dr. Wm. A. L. Lewis is probably the oldest practicing physician in the county. He came to Union in the year 1837, and has been associated with all the changes incident to the prosperity and adversity of the county since. Dr. Lewis went into the Confederate service with the 36th Mississippi regiment, and was the assistant surgeon most of the time, often acting for the brigade. He was detached awhile as surgeon of Con. Ray's sharpshooters, and while thus engaged, was wounded. He was at Franklin and remained there with the wounded. Though now quite old, he retains his good health and cheerful disposition and still has a fine fund of humorous narratives with which to entertain his old friends when he meets them.

CHAPTER XXXVII.

Various Towns of Newton County.

The town of Decatur was settled in the year 1836, and named in honor of Commodore Stephen Decatur, of the United States navy.

The act of the Legislature authorizing the county commissioners to buy, or receive by gift, eight acres of land for a county site, as near as practicable, in the center of the county, was passed on February 25, 1836. The land is said to have been donated by Mr. Isaac Hollingsworth, and is about three and one-half miles from the geographical center of the county. Some time in the same year a public sale of town lots was made, and the lots for the court-house and jail agreed upon. The first court-house, a small log house, was placed on the lot upon which the postoffice now stands, south of the present court-house and east of Gaines' blacksmith shop. It is supposed that James Ellis built the first court-house. Samuel Hurd is said to be the man who built the first jail. The second court-house is said to have been built by Willis R. Norman. It was situated where the present court-house now stands. It is not known who built the second jail.

This second court-house was burned by General Sherman's army, February, 1864, and the third court-house was built by Montgomery Carleton about the year 1867. The third jail was built by Thomas Wells.

HISTORY OF NEWTON COUNTY. 329

The third court-house was very peculiarly constructed. The court was held on the ground floor, the other rooms being on the second floor. This house was burned September, 1876, supposed by accident.

A fourth court-house was built of brick in the year 1877, costing the county about $7000. This building is a strong and substantial one, with court room and two ante-rooms in the rear of judge's stand on the second floor, and four commodious and comfortable rooms on the ground floor for the officers and grand jury. The court-house is furnished with a good iron safe, and in the fall of 1893 the board of supervisors had constructed of brick a vault on the outside of the court-house, immediately adjoining the chancery clerk's office. This fire-proof brick vault is for the better preservation of the county records. There is an excellent small jail, a frame house with iron cages for the safe-keeping of prisoners. The jail is comfortable and safe.

There has never been but one legal hanging in Newton county, and that was Sam Suttles, a desperate negro, who murdered his wife, and was tried, and hanged by Sheriff G. M. Gallaspy.

Decatur was never noted for fine buildings, either store-houses, churches or dwellings. There was no church in the town until 1851, about twelve years after it was settled. Then the Baptist church, a plain, frame building, without paint or ceiling. In the year 1888 a new church took the place of the old one—a very much improved structure in size and finish. The first Methodist church, which was built after 1855, was burned by Sherman; it was a plain frame house, about as the first Baptist church.

The Methodists now have a nice church at Decatur,

well built and neatly finished, of goodly size and appearance.

No school-house of any good size had ever been built until 1886, when a good two-story frame building, sufficiently large to accommodate the town was erected.

Until about 1865 the people of Decatur paid very little attention to schools. Then it was that a spirit of improvement in that direction set in, and fine teachers were paid good salaries to take charge of the schools. The prominent teachers of those times were Prof. Marshall and his wife; after that, Robt. Bell, a Presbyterian minister. Probably the most competent and accomplished teacher ever employed at Decatur was J. J. Perry, who was afterwards Maj. Perry, and after his return from the war, was sheriff and lawyer.

The prominent merchants of Decatur: Johnston & Johnston, Hurd, Dansby, Drinkwater, Nimocks & Loper, Steinheart—the latter probably the only Jew ever to sell goods in the town of Decatur); George Armstrong, Montgomery Carleton, Barrett, Russell & Hoye, W. H. Gallaspy.

Some the most prominent men of the town were: J. H. Wells, W. S. Nimocks, E. S. Loper, Sam'l Hurd, J. C. McElroy, Dr. Keith, Montgomery Carleton, E. Scanlan, J. A. Ware, Isham Dansby, J. J. Perry, J. F. N. Huddleston, T. B. McCunn, M. J. L. Hoye, Thomas Keith, A. McAlpin and E. Carleton.

Decatur, for many years after its settlement, was a great place of resort for people from all parts the county. From its early settlement up to about 1879 or 1880, it was noted for the liquor drank, and in that that town had been more fights and murders than any other place in the county.

There were nine men killed by their fellow-citizens from its early settlement to 1858 or '59. The names

HISTORY OF NEWTON COUNTY.

of these men killed and the party killing will be found in chapter six of this History.

It is very pleasant to note the great change in the town of Decatur. It is now one of the quietest places anywhere to be found, and is a good point for business. Russell & Hoye, since the war, have carried on an extensive drygoods and general merchandise business with great success. There are now five places of business in the town, two good churches, one Sunday school, a good school-house, good court-house and jail, a good hotel and some neat private residences.

Decatur will no doubt retain the court-house for many years to come. There are some excellent people living in and around the town. It is surrounded by good farming lands, and has good people and thrifty farmers living on them. It has a good steam gin and and tan-yard, and some of the best Jersey cattle breed in the county.

UNION.

The town of Union was probably settled as early as 1833 or 1834 and it was the place where the courts were held. The original site was about half mile from the present village. There the first courts of the county of Neshoba were held in a black-jack log cabin with dirt floor. Jail in same proportion. The town is very centrally located for the county site when the two counties were together.

Union is situated directly on the stage line running from Montgomery, Ala., to Jackson, Miss. There was a large amount of travel on the stage before the railroad passed through the country. There was also much mail matter received and distributed from that point. Dr. Lewis, of Union, says the first court held in the above named house was presided over by Judge

Thos. S. Sterling, with John Watts, Esq., district attorney. The courts were held here until after the division of the county in 1836; then the county site of Neshoba county was removed to Philadelphia and the Newton county court-house established at Decatur.

Union had no very fine houses. Sherman's army passed through and burned much of the town; since that time some better houses have gone up. The stores are small but sufficient for the business. There are some comfortable dwellings in the place. The town and surrounding country have always claimed some of the best citizens of the county.

This is a good place for business and has some distinction as a place of educational advantages. A high school was established and maintained for years by Rev. J. C. Portis, assisted by an able corps of teachers. The school is now under the management of other persons.

Union has two frame churches—a Methodist church, which is new and attractive; the Baptist church not so good. The school buildings are good and amply sufficient to accommodate a large number of pupils. Two Sabbath Schools are kept up at the place; a good steam mill for grinding and ginning.

The merchants are: Viverett, Lewis, Cleavland and Portis. Among the early settlers of the town, Quimby, (merchant and a man of means), James J. Monroe, George Boyd, Mrs. Lewis and family and Mrs. Lane, afterwards Thompson, Daniel, Hunter, Lewis, Viverett Portis, Cleavland, Ragan, Park.

The neighborhood of Union is one of the best in the county, having good level lands of durable nature, good water and a very healthy and desirable place.

PINKNEY.

The name of Pinkney dates as far back in the history

HISTORY OF NEWTON COUNTY.   333

of Newton county as any other name in it. It is not known from what the town derived its name; the probabilities are it was settled as early as 1837—probably earlier—and was a place of some importance and trade. Lane and Boyd, merchants at that place, are reported to have had a stock of goods of $10,000, who issued a fractional currency called "shin plasters," and were correspondents with the Decatur bank, and when the bank failed it naturally carried the firm with it. Where these people got their goods is not known, probably from Vicksburg, or New Orleans, or Mobile—all hauled in wagons over terrible roads.

This place has had from time to time, some business. About twenty years ago Mr. S. D. Daniel commenced a general meschandise business and sold a large amount of goods and made some money. The place has a good mill-seat that has from time served a good purpose and been a means of convenience and profit. The name of Pinkney has given way to Stamper, at which place there is a store kept by Mr. Boulton, also a postoffice with daily communication with the railroad. The water-power is owned by Mr. Stamper, who has a turbine wheel which does fine work. This mill grinds, and is a great convenience to the people and profitable to the owner. It also furnishes a good place for "trouting." The families living about there are: Stampers, Bolton, Ferrall, Hansford, Freeman, Collins, Mapp, Russell and Norris.

TOWN OF NEWTON.

This is the oldest railroad town in the county. In the year 1855 J. N. Shofner had a country store about one mile south-east of where the depot now stands. No business was done at Newton until 1860. John R. Johnson, of Decatur, established a retail grocery; W.

A. Payne had a retail grocery, and family grocers Brame & Morgan, built a business house; Hyde & Sharman had livery stable; Johnson kept hotel; Roger W. Doolittle owned the land on which the town was situated, and sold to parties moving to the place as early as spring of 1860. The town was named for Newton Doolittle, now living near this place.

In September of 1860, the first train of cars reached the town of Newton, and from that time until the first of June, 1861, was the terminus of the railroad. The stage line ran from Enterprise to Newton by way of Garlandsville, and a great many persons were conveyed through the country, taking the cars at Newton to go west.

These were exciting times, and a large number of distinguished people came to Newten to take the train. The year 1860 was a very dry year; not enough corn was made to do the country. It was the first time the people had ever seen corn shipped in sacks to this county. McGrath, a Northern man, built a good storehouse on the lot now occupied by W. B. Richardson, in 1861, and did considerable business, but after the war had gone on for some time he went to the Yankees, as his sympathies were with them.

Newton was now a suitable place for military purposes. Being in a good country, conveniently situated for the gathering the tax in kind, a commissary department was established at this place, probably in 1863. Large houses were built. Mac. Jamison had charge of this department, and afterwards it was taken charge of by J. J. Ludloe, assisted by Capt. E. Scanlan. This was also a healthy place and suitable for hospital, and one was established in the first part of the year 1863. Drs. Bozeman and Blunt were the first to take charge of the hospital; then Dr. Hurndon; and

NEW METHODIST CHURCH AT NEWTON.

HISTORY OF NEWTON COUNTY. 337

after that by Dr. Carter, assisted by Coffman and Morrison. Dr. A. H. Pucket was for a time connected with the hospital at this place. This hospital and commissary required a number of houses to be built, and Willis R. Norman was awarded the contract for their erection. There were seven large houses built for hospital purposes and whatever were necessary for commissary stores. The number of soldiers supposed to have been treated here were about 1000. About 100 died.

These confederate soldiers are buried about three-fourths of a mile from the depot in a private burial ground of the Doolittle family, and when they were buried they had a wooden board with the name and command on it. These have all decayed, and there is not a vestige of anything to mark the last resting place of these Confederate soldiers. There is no other burial ground of Confederate soldiers in the county. Would it not be right that the citizens of Newton county erect a monument to the memory of these brave men, and that the citizens of the town of Newton make it their yearly duty to give some attention to the graves of the Confederate dead? The United States government established at Vicksburg a national cemetery for the burial of the Federal soldiers. They searched this county for soldiers who had been killed, and their remains were carried to that city and interred. It is said that the cemetery at Vicksburg contains the remains of 16,000 Federal soldiers, more than any living population the city has ever had. They mostly fell around Vicksburg, but many were carried there from other places. This cemetery is one of great beauty, and is a fitting tribute by the nation to her fallen sons. We should recollect that we owe a debt of gratitude to those who fell on the Southern side, and the Federal government will not provide for them. Whatever is done will be done by private hands, yet we can do something and it should be no longer delayed.

On the 24th day of April, 1863, Grierson's raid of cavalry and artillery came through the town of Newton. They destroyed McGrath's store-house and some goods, the store-house of Mr. Hamilton, and probably one commisary house or hospital. They burned the depot, and also destroyed some military stores which were loaded on the cars on the side-track. They did not destroy any private residences, or any private property.

Immediately after the war, in the year 1865, some little business was done. J. R. Johnson sold liquor and general merchandise. Marine Watkins, and E. & A. J. Brown, and W. S. Nimocks had some goods and and did some business during that fall; some other business was done, but not to amount to much.

In the year 1866 some capital came to the town, and more business was done in a larger way than had been done the year before. The next year, 1867, Watts & Nimocks, J. N. Shofner, J. G. Moore & Co. were added to the merchants at Newton. In the year 1868 but little more business was added to the town. In August, 1869, the firm of Richardson & Co. came to the place. This firm consisted of W. B. Richardson, T. F. Pettus, and Maj. Stevens, of Brandon. They had large capital, put in a heavy stock of goods, and bought cotton very liberally. The business status of the town was now established. From that time it continued to grow. From less than 2,000 bales of cotton in 1867 it rose to something over 11,000 in the years 1888 and 1889. The trade of the town has continued to increase and is now one of the best towns on the A. & V. railroad.

Newton, originally very poorly built, most of the

houses being rudely constructed, and added to from time to time as necessity required. All the original buildings had become very much dilapidated, were closely crowed together on one street. The town had been fortunate in escaping any fire of any consequence, up to the 29th of May, 1883, when a large part of it burned, supposed to be the work of an incendiary. This was one of the most terrible conflagrations that ever swept over a small town. The fire occured about 4 o'clock in the morning, and in about two hours it was a pile of smoking ruins. So swift was the fire, so terrible the heat from the old wooden material, and the surprise by which the people were taken, that but very little little was saved. The principal sufferers were W. A. Dunagin & Co., Mack Watkins & Co., J. C. Barber & Co., A. E. Williams, T. M. Scanlan, R. W. Doolittle, H. S. Buckley, W. B. Richardson, T. C. Viverett, Geo. Davidson, Estate of M. J. L. Hoye, Mississippi Baptist, Mrs. Armistead, and Misses Watts & Brown. All these houses and their contents, and also the post-office, were swept away in a few moments. The books of all the concerns were in safes, and were saved. The aggregate loss was from $65,000 to $75,000, with probably about half or little over insured. T. C. Viverett had no insurance; R. W. Doolittle had none; estate of M. J. L. Hoye lost one house, with no insurance. Scanlan & Dunagin had very large losses without the corresponding amount of insurance. The storehouses left were Buncum & Leverett, Rew & McClinton, G. C. Oliver, Mrs. M. J. L. Hoye, Bingham & Parker.

After the smoke of the great fire had blown away, quite a feeling of despondency at the losses of the town was clearly visible. Then came the insurance adjusters, who represented some of the best companies in the country, and who acted in a spirit of fairness towards the losers in the fire. Terms were agreed upon, and very soon all the arrangements were made to pay most of the losses.

The town council, at a very opportune time, passed an ordinance defining a limit in which none but fire-proof brick or iron houses should be erected. This was a very proper step, which resulted very favorable to the building up of the town in a better class of houses. Very soon persons came from a distance who well understood the business of brick work. Mr. Hugh Wilson, a good business man from Meridian, came and at once went to work about the first of July, after the fire, and by hard work and close attention, by the first of September had the first two hundred thousand brick ready for the brick-layers. A force of about twenty men were put to work under the able contractors of wood and brick work, Miller, Dabbs & Taylor. The two latter made as good time as any on the wall, and by the first day of October, one month after starting the wall, two new brick houses stood complete for T. C. Viverette. Then followed in quick succession W. B. Richardson's elegant brick store, 50x110 feet; next Geo. Davidson's; next, two others for T. C. Viverette, on the east side of the main street; next, the drug store and millinery store built by W. B. Richardson; next one by P. E. Blelack joining and between Viverette and Davidson, on the lot occupied by T. M. Scanlan; next, Bingham & Parker, on the south end of the old commissary building, more recently the Clark, Dansby & Co., house. This house of Bingham and Parker is a splendid brick structure of two double stores of 25x100 each, fronting W. B. Richardson. All these houses have plastered walls, work done by J. J. Kane, of Meridian. The work overhead on the inside of these houses is of

HISTORY OF NEWTON COUNTY. 341

beaded ceiling, oiled and varnished. Cris. Miller, of Meridian, master mechanic, assisted by competent men from a distance and the home workmen, did excellent work in finishing up the stores. All this work was done by the same contractors except the P. E. Blelack house, which was done by C. H. Doolittle, and Bingham & Parker's by Wedgeworth.

In six months from the time dirt was broken for the making of the brick, every house was up and ready for being occupied. Now Newton has more handsome brick store houses than frame ones that were destroyed by fire—houses that invite capital and are an advertisement to the town. By energy and a timely use of money, the merchants did their part. By the magic touch of the labor and skill of Wilson, Miller, Dabbs, Kane and Taylor, a pile of smoking ruins have risen Phœnix-like from the ashes, and to day stands a monument to their well directed efforts of industry, knowledge and perserverance.

Newton, after the war, as almost every other town in the State, was cursed with the sale of liquor. It was thought that no town could do business successfully without the sale of liquor. A great amount of it was sold and much disorder prevailed; much cost to the county and greatly increased the circuit court business. For about twenty years after the war liquor was sold at Newton. By proper legislation, and the moral sentiment prevailing, and the necessity of cutting off the sale of liquor, on account of schools, was finally accomplished, and so we have it that it is unlawful to sell liquor in any quantity in the town of Newton and most parts of the county. Business since that time, much to the surprise of some, and to the gratification of the temperance element, has increased, and the town, since the liquor trade was abolished, is a more prosperous and far more respectable place than it ever was before. The callabose has almost gone into disuse. Very few arrests are now made, and of the thousands of people who come to town, it is rarely that the place is disturbed, and very seldom an oath is heard on the streets. Ladies are free to go at any time in any part of the town without disturbance, and are also employed at the postoffice and in business houses and have never been insulted or annoyed. All this is what the temperance movement has done for the town and county.

The rising generation is being brought up not to know what a general use of whisky is. To say that no liquor was used and none sold in the town of Newton, would probably not be stating the subject fairly or truthfully. There is no doubt but sometimes liquors are brought to this town and sold and used under disguised names, and at great risk; yet it is so minimized as to be of little importance compared to what it originally was. This feeling of reform is fast taking hold of persons who were, although good citizens, good business men, and not addicted to the use of liquor, but who thought no business could prosper in any town without it.

The town of Newton has twelve business houses, a postoffice doing large business, three churches, three livery stables, two newspapers, barber shop, and two hotels. W. B. Richardson does a very large business, larger than any other house in town, and buys nearly one-half the cotton brought to the place. Without Mr. Richardson, Newton would be a great loser, and unless his place was taken by another such man, the business of the town would greatly decrease. He is prudent, conservative, sober and diligent in business; is very kind to his customers, at the same time looking well after his own interests. He is always in the cotton market, and is well supplied with goods; has large credit business, and has made a large amount of money.

Bingham & Parker is a strong firm, well situated and well equipped with ample means. They are sober, discreet, looking well after their own interests; have only been here a few years.

T. C. Viveret & Co. is a firm very recently commenced business; have good name and credit and all the money they need; are sober and industrious, and are among the best citizens of the town.

R. W. McClinton, who succeeded Jno. T. O'Ferrall, is a firm doing large cash business, who have ample means, are industrious and sober and have been very successful.

W. A. Dunagin, manager of W. A. Dunagin & Co., is a progressive business man; is sober and alive to all the interests of his firm. Previous to the fire he had made money and was a great sufferer by the event; but he is not discouraged, and is doing a good cash business.

Newton Mercantile Co., a new limited association of some very good men in the country and some good men in town, who have combined in a stock company and employed T. M. Scanlan, a man of energy and sobriety, to conduct it. They have an excellent stand, good brick building, and are prepared to do a large business.

The firm of W. A. Williams, succeeding to the firm of A. E. Williams, is well situated in new brick store, and is conducted by M. Williams, one of the most experienced merchants in town.

Baucum & Leverett, situated on the east side of the main street, are doing fine cash business. They are young men who have built up a fine trade from small commencement, and are among the prosperous merchants of the place and are making money.

Chambliss & Jourdan, a new firm from Enterprise, where they have long enjoyed a prosperous business, are men of means and good capacity. The business is conducted by Mr. Chambliss, who is a sober, discreet man, and whose prospects are good. They are situated in one of the brick stores built by Bingham & Parker.

Mrs. M. J. L. Hoye, who succeeded her husband, late in business here, has large capital, and has associated in her house her three grown sons. The business is conducted by Mr. I. M. Hoye, who has been with the house since 1876. This house has been very fortunate since it was established at Newton. For the first twelve years, with M. J. L. Hoye as general manager, though not living here, and with I. M. Hoye, F. B. Loper and the writer, employed in the house, made sixty thousand dollars.

The drug store owned by H. C. Price, a young man from Crystal Springs, has only been in operation a short time; he bought out McWatkins & Co. Mr. Price is a moral, sober, energetic man, well understands his business, and has one of the neatest drug stores in the State, and will no doubt make money.

Mrs. Ella Armistead has a good millinery establishment and has been very successful in pleasing her customers, has a host of friends and has made money.

In the same place is a fancy grocery business conducted by E. P. Armistead, which appears to be doing a prosperous business.

Misses Watts & Brown keep a good millinery store, and have one of the best locations and neatest brick stores in town. They also keep up general dress making and are well prepared to serve customers, and appear to be doing well.

Rew & McClinton have a family grocery store, conducted by J. R. Kelly, which attracts good trade and is doing well.

Racket Store, by J. M. Patterson, is something new at Newton—there never having been one before. This store has only been in operation a few months and may succeed well.

H. C. Majure, postmaster, who is accommodating and polite, is assisted by J. C. Bell, who is a jeweler, and does general repair work in his line.

The *Mississippi Baptist* is published in Newton by L. S. Tilghman, and edited by Rev. N. L. Clarke. Mr. Clarke is a good writer, a very zealous minister, remarkable ability and great energy, and though quite old is always at his post as pastor, citizen and editor, always doing something to further the cause of morality and religion. S. B. Ross, one of the owners of this paper, also a contributor to its columns, has large experience in newspaper business, is an experienced typo, besides being a good writer of miscellaneous articles. He is also a lawyer and agent for monied syndicates.

J. R. Byrd is a young lawyer who has had advantages of the Lebanon Law School. He is industrious and appears to be making money.

Dr. J. C. McElroy is one of the oldest physicians in the county; has been engaged in his profession in this county about forty years, is a good doctor and receives a good share of the practice of the town and vicinity.

Dr. A. H. Puckett is a well-read physician, born in Tennessee, but has been associated with the county and town of Newton about thirty years, and receives a share of the practice incident to the town and county.

Dr. H. G. McNeill is a young man of great energy, a native Mississippian, who has fitted himself well for the practice of medicine. He is a graduate of the Medical College at New Orleans and after years of practice took a post-graduate course in New York City, so as to still further prepare himself. He does a large practice in the town and surrounding country.

Dr. G. G. Everrett, long associated among the practicing physicians of Newton, is now an invalid, unable to do any work professionally.

Dr. H. B. Ross, a young physician who has but recently come to Newton to practice, is a young man having educational advantages, is a graduate from Atlanta, Ga., Medical College. He is devoted to his profession, and has those personal qualities that cannot fail to win him friends and business.

There are three churches in the town of Newton. The Baptist church has Rev. N. L. Clarke, as pastor. Mr. Clarke has been the pastor here since the organization of the church about twenty-five years ago; is well known and universally respected for good works and unremitting toil for the cause of the church and salvation of souls.

Rev. J. M. Morse is a fine looking young man, belonging to the Mississippi Conference; is with this church for the fourth year. He is very acceptable to his people; is a good pastor and preacher, a good citizen and reliable under all circumstances.

Rev. T. D. Barr, a young man representing the Presbyterian church, has had good opportunities; is an able preacher, a very zealous advocate of his Master; is very acceptable to the people and his charge at this place. He has done more to advance and permanently establish the cause of his church than any preacher the Presbyterians have ever had here.

The town has three good preachers of whom the people may be justly proud.

HISTORY OF NEWTON COUNTY. 347

 Go here or go there, go near or go far,
 You'll not find such men as Clarke, Morse and Barr.

 The municipal officers of Newton are: Capt. T. F. Pettus, mayor, and S. M. McElroy, marshal. Capt. Pettus came to Newton in 1872 as one of the firm of Richardson & Co., and conducted the large business for about fifteen years. He then sold his interest to W. B. Richardson and was appointed as Consul to Ningpo, China, by Mr. Cleveland. He remained abroad about four years and returned and lived at his home at Newton, and in January, 1894, he was elected mayor. Capt. Pettus is a good business man, a practical book-keeper and well informed on all subjects. He is related to ex-Gov. Pettus, of Mississippi, and Gen. Pettus, of Alabama. S. M. McElroy, the marshal of the town, is a young man raised at the town of Newton, son of Dr. J. C. McElroy, is a sober and steady officer.

 J. J. Armistead, as mayor, and J. P. McMahan, as marshal, years ago, were probably the most efficient officers this town ever had, and would have been capable of administering a city government anywhere in the State. They were the officers when the town was disorderly through the sale of liquor and they did good work in preserving the peace and order of the place.

 T. H. Selby, book-keeper for W. B. Richardson, is as well known to the people who come to this place as any man in it. By his efficiency and steady habits, and faithfulness to his employer, he has been able to retain his place in the same house about twenty-five years. E. E. Powe, in the same house, is also a sober, steady man, and appears to be a fixture in the business. J. S. Sones, also, is a good business man and well retains his place. E. H. Selby, assistant book-keeper, is a worthy young man, well deserving the confidence of his employer. T. J. Jackson is a coming man behind the counter; is sober, industrious and deserves a good place.

Dr. J. T. Watts, the agent for the A. & V. Railroad, came to Newton in 1862, and has held the place since, without ever making a change. He is the oldest agent on the road, and by faithful and efficient service has been able to hold the Express and Railroad office since he came here. His long stay at our place is indicative of good behavior; close, sober attention to business will succeed.

I. M. Hoye, the book-keeper of the business of M. J. L. Hoye & Co., and their successors—over a period of eighteen years, including his management of the business at present, and being administrator of his brother's estate, which is the largest that has been in the courts since the war, shows, like other two mentioned, that a close and faithful attention to business for employees is always a sure road to success. Mr. Hoye has saved quite a snug sum of money by his hard work and economy.

Mr. J. M. Williams, the efficient book-keeper of Mrs. M. J. L. Hoye, has been with the firm since the death of Mr. Hoye. Mr. Williams is one of our best citizens, and from one of the best families of the county, and by his ability and close attention to business is holding a good place. Messrs. Eugene Kelly and Walter Love, with W. A. Dunagin, are both sober, steady young men, giving good attention to business; so is Earnest Ross, with H. C. Prince. Mr. Rogers, with Rew & McClinton, is a man competent, attentive and sober. W. J. Reynolds, with the Hoye house, is a young man that may be trusted, is sober and moral. Miss Fannie Sansing, a very deserving and competent

MALE AND FEMALE COLLEGE AT NEWTON.

young lady in the house of Baucum & Leverett, well understands the duty of clerk, and proves herself worthy and profitable to her employers. Victor Scanlan, who is employed in the Mercantile Company, is a young man born and raised in the town of Newton; he is talented, sober and reliable. Mrs. Mag. Blakely, with Mrs. Armistead, is a very competent and deserving woman. J. W. Guthrie has been alternately merchant, mayor and superintendent of education of Newton county, is now keeping hotel. Judge J. D. Tolson, for some time employed in mercantile pursuits, has always been an acceptable and reliable citizen.

Mr. Hand, with Chambliss & Jourdan, is a new man in our midst, but is always at his post. Tom. Bingham is always there, for he was brought up that way. Sam. Parker, our competent and clever telegraph operator, is well thought of. Sansing and Doolittle are the cotton weighers and are successful in their line. Wilson & Doolittle are our livery men—and know how to accommodate the traveling public. I. W. Walker is also another man in this line, and is as clever a fellow as ever drew a line over a pair of horses, for Judge Mayers says so.

Newton has a good school building, costing $3,000, with three rooms below, with large hall overhead, which serves a room for school purposes, and also any other occasion when it is necessary to accommodate large crowds.

The teachers at Newton have been: Hamiter and West, King, Emmerson, Miss Fielder, Miss Byrd, Miss Ward, Woodbridge, Campbell, Jayne, Miss Watts, Brown, Ward, Mrs. Blelack, Spratt, Foster, Fant. Miss Leggett, Miss Minor, Miss Armistead, Miss Ross, Miss Robinson.

Newton has two good hotels, two grist mills, and

two gins, the latter ginning about 500 bales of cotton each season, a barber-shop, spoke lathe. The receipts of cotton will run to between 11,000 and 12,000 as the maximum shipment, with the best facilities for handling, weighing and storing of any town on the road. It will not be considered egotistical or stating it untruthfully to say that Newton is the best county town on the A. & V. road—receiving more cotton and produce, and selling more goods than any other town in the county.

There has never been but one white man killed in the town—that was G. W. Cheek, in 1870. Two Indians were killed outside the corporation, and probably some negro man. This is a good showing for a town having liquor for sale twenty-five out of thirty-four years of its existence.

LAWRENCE.

The town of Lawrence is one of the most suitable places for a town in the county. A fine country surrounds it, fine water and a beautiful level situation. It was laid out and owned by R. E. Wilson, who had large mill interests near the place. It was settled in 1866. It has never had a large trade. Messrs. Andrew Jones, J. A. McCain, R. E. Wilson, Daniel McFarland, and William Dennis were among its first settlers. Then came Mr. E. T. Beattie, who became a prominent citizen of the place, as depot agent, merchant and postmaster. J. Z. Jones and W. H. Sisson were also merchants. Mr. Sisson died of yellow fever at Lawrence; contracted it, no doubt, from opening clothing brought from infected cities. Mr. Jones still remains as one of the principal merchants and farmers. Yellow fever had quite a hold on the citizens of Lawrence in the epidemic of 1878; about nineteen cases and several deaths occurred. Yet most of the citizens left the place.

Lawrence has two churches—the Presbyterian, with L. D. Barr pastor, and the Methodist, with Rev. Mr. Witt, pastor. The Methodist church is new and stylish; it was completed in 1893.

J. Z. Jones and Threefoot Bros. have stores at Lawrence; so has Hunnicut & Bunyard, a new firm from Alabama. A steam saw mill and steam gin and grist mill are also in the place. Dr. F. B. Nimocks, a successful and well qualified physician, enjoys the confidence and practice of that commuity. J. A. McCain, a large land owner and farmer, has one of the finest peach and apple and pear orchards at Lawrence any where to be found. Mr. McCain has the most excellent variety of fruits, with the best method of treating trees to insure crops and prevent destruction from worms, with the most improved methods of shipping fruit to insure safe delivery, of any one in the county. Mr. E. D. Beatie is also a good fruit man, having a larger orchard of pears, fine apples and strawberries, and more grapes than any other one man in the county.

HICKORY.

The town of Hickory was settled in 1860. The land was owned by A. E. Gray and wife, who sold out the lots, and donated the necessary right-of-way for railroad purposes.

The town is situated, as is stated, where General Jackson camped with his army on his march from New Orleans to Nashville, after the great battle of the 8th of January of that year at New Orleans. That is possible and very probable, as it is well known that the army referred to crossed Pottoxchitto creek just south of Hickory, and the bridge was constructed a short distance below where the bridge on the public road now stands. It is further stated that a portion of the old timbers of the original bridge are still in the creek. Hence it is possible that the army camped on the site of the present town. The military road runs through the place.

The town was named Hickory in honor of "Old Hickory," General Jackson, whose name is a household word as one of the greatest men of his day. Judge Gray named the place.

The railroad was completed to Hickory in 1860, but regular trains did not run to that place until after the road was completed through, in June of 1861. It was necessary to transport troops through the State, and the road was completed sooner than it would have been.

A. E. Gray was appointed as the first railroad agent in 1861 and held the place until 1866. He was also appointed after that time, probate judge of Newton county, was also sheriff of Newton by appointment, was justice of the peace for beat No. 5 in this county, in some of the most troublesome times this county has ever had. Judge Gray has been quite a conspicuous figure in the county and town of Hickory, and is now the Honorable Mayor of the place, and in his old age, without any interest personally in schools, is working hard for educational interests and separate school district in his town. He was the first merchant at the place and has resided there thirty-six years.

The town is beautifully situated, the ground being perfectly level and is drained to the creek by ditches. The stores and railroad surround a public square with ample room for all business purposes. The roads from all parts of the county are good to the town.

There were a few men who did business there before the war: Gray, Heidle, Edwards and Jim Bell. But business did not commence to be done on any very large scale until several years after the war. Then Gray & Ward, Barber & Thompson, Ogletree & Brown, W. N. Raines, Lem Nelson, saddle shops and retail grocery; Pennington & Bros., Harper & Bro., Norman & Co., retail grocery; Cook & Johnson. First drug store was Osburn & Grissette, Wm. Hyde also had a drug store. For many years the largest and most important business was done by I. I. Barber and his brothers, who were associated with him from time to time. He first introduced fertilizers in the county, had large saw mills in different parts of the county in operation, had large farming interests, bought and sold stock, bought most of the cotton that came to that place, and did one of the most extensive trades of any man in Newton county. W. N. Raines also did large business for a time and kept the post-office in his store and had a large number of friends and customers who patronized him.

The town of Hickory, like that of Newton and Decatur, was for a long time cursed with the sale of liquor, with a large amount of disorder and much loss of life, as the result. It is said that twenty-two men were killed after the war in Hickory, and no doubt every one on account of whisky; most of them were Indians. It cannot be said to be an intemperate town now; on the contrary, it is one of the most civil and orderly places in the county. It has been visited by one or two destructive fires which burned most of the original store-houses, and it has now some large, handsome and convenient places of business. It also has quite a number of new style dwelling houses that show taste in construction. It is a real pleasure to go to Hickory

356   HISTORY OF NEWTON COUNTY.

and meet its sober, law-abiding and hospitable citizens. The town is seven miles west of the Lauderdale county line, and from the many good roads running to it, and the enterprise and capital of its merchants, will always command good trade. Its convenience to different parts of the territory adjoining, will always claim for it one of the best business points in the county. The town has about 500 inhabitants with a good class of merchants, with capital enough to do the business of the place.

There are three churches in Hickory. The Methodist church is one of the finest in the county, very conspicuously and centrally located, and has been supplied for the last four years by Rev. J. M. Morse, the same that supplies the church at Newton. The Baptists have a comfortable church, very well situated, but not so new and commanding in appearance as the Methodist church. They are supplied by Rev. Mr. Hall. The Christian church at Hickory is the only one of that denomination in the county; it is small but sufficiently large for the present demands of its members. This church has no regular supply, but is preached to by various ministers of this faith who come from time to time in the county.

Hickory has at present the following places of business: Walton, Gillaspy & Russell, is a substantial firm consisting of three young men who were principally brought up in Newton county, who have been trained to business; they have ample capital and are doing a large and profitable business. The first two named parties live in the town; the latter, S. D. Russell, lives in Jasper county and is a successful planter and merchant; J. L. Wells, who succeeded to Wells & Hailey, is a young man who was brought up in Newton county, and who did successful business in the county before going to the railroad. Buckley Bros. is another firm who are well known in the county, and who are active young men in business. G. W. Rayner, who was a Newton county farmer, has for some years been engaged in business at Hickory, is a well known man in his town and county. J. C. Barber & Co., a well known firm, have, one way and another, with some of the Barber family been engaged in business at Hickory for the last twenty-five years; J. C. Barber is a son of I. I. Barber, is sober and steady, and brought up to close business life. Nelson & Hopkins is a respectable firm who have long been in business, and have good reputation as business men. McDonald Bros., who have until recently been very prominent in the business interests of Hickory, are intelligent and well qualified for mercantile pursuits; they are now out of business but still remain at Hickory. Pierce & Everett are men who came from the farm to town. They are safe, conservative men, who do small business; they are reliable and trustworthy. W. A. Russell, a young man who was brought up in the town, of a well-known and prominent family in the county, has succeeded his father, Frank Russell, in business, is well situated in one of the nicest stores in the town. Basket & Massengale, a new firm who are well situated in the town, are doing a small, neat business. J. A. E. Dowling, one of the oldest druggists in the place, assisted by his good wife, appears to be doing a nice business. Caddenhead & Jordan are young men recently moved to Hickory, who are doing a good business; have probably the best and largest stock of drugs ever brought to Hickory. They are active and reliable men. Mrs. Nelson has millinery, is very conveniently situated, and the ladies of the county may be well supplied with goods in her line. Miss Bettie Rew, also in the same line, is a well experienced lady and keeps good stock and is securing a liberal share of the patronage. Mr. Will Hopkins, a well known Newton county man, has confectionery and fancy groceries, where customers may be well supplied. Mr. Frank Johnson, a well known citizen, has a blacksmith and wood shop, where all kinds of work in his line can be done. Mr. Stevenson has steam gin and grist mill; also has attached an industry in the way of barrel-hoop manufactory, that if properly worked may prove of great benefit to the county. F. H. Hannah has steam saw mill and planer immediately in the town, where a large amount of lumber is sawed. J. H. Wells has a good livery stable, where the traveling public may be accommodated. Depot is kept by R. H. Melton, who is also express agent and telegraph operator; he is a sober and reliable man.

Hickory has three physicians; Dr. Semmes is considered a fine physician and is well patronized. Dr. Carraway is also considered a skillful physician, and has the patronage and confidence of the people.

Dr. Gilmore, a young man raised in the town of Hickory, son of a very popular doctor, late of that place, has just received his diploma, and will, no doubt, command the the patronage and respect of his and his father's old friends.

Dr. J. P. Harris is a resident dentist, is a Newton county boy, who has worked his way up, and deserves the patronage of the people.

J. M. Gage is the only lawyer at Hickory, is a man well known to the people of the county, and gets a good share of the practice connected with this part of the county.

Hickory is surrounded by fine bodies of swamp and upland timber, large amounts of which are brought to that place for shipment.

HICKORY INSTITUTE, AT HICKORY.

Hickory has a good school; the citizens have built a house well suited to accommodate the wants of the community. This school is called Hickory Institute, and has been presided over by some useful and practical teachers. Prof. J. C. Hardy, now principal of the Jackson graded school, was once a teacher at Hickory. Prof. W. E. Thames, one of Newton county's best young men and most useful teachers, for a term of years conducted as principal the Hickory Institute. Prof. L. M. Cox has had the school for the last term.

The people have decided at Hickory to make this school a separate school district, and have voted a ten mills tax on the property of the town for its support.

CHUNKEY.

The town of Chunkey was settled in year 1861. Preparations were made, and probably some houses put up before the railroad was finished through to Meridian. John Dyess and John Warren are said to have been the first men to sell goods at the town. After the railroad was built, John I. Cook was the first station agent; he was succeeded by Levi Jones, after the war, who was agent of the railroad and merchant for many years. Dr. Hughes was also a merchant at the place after the war. The land on which the town is built was owned by Ben. Murphy, W. J. Bartlett and Levi Jones.

The old settlers were Murphy, Dyess, Warren, Bartlett, Clark, Hughes, Mayberry, and the Misses Kid, who were educated and accomplished ladies, who have long been residents of the town and still live there.

Chunkey has always been famous as a good milling town, as there is fine timber near the place; has a mill at the place, or near it, and is shipping large amounts of lumber. It also has a barrel factory, operated and owned by Mr. Collier, who makes a good molasses barrel out of fine cypress, and gets ready sale for them. There is also a turpentine orchard and distillery, owned and operated by McDonald & Co. This is the first and only one that has ever been put up in the county, and there is no doubt but this one and others might be operated to the advantage of the owners.

There has never been a large amount of cotton shipped from Chunkey, nor has it ever been considered a place of any great importance, yet there are lands joining the place, and the lumber and turpentine interests that might make it a place of much more importance if the energy and capital were invested to develop it.

Present business houses are: Jno. F. Mays, McDonald & Co., George Armstrong, Mrs. Z. Belew, Frank Buckley and Mr. Collier. Mr. Lee Murphy is station agent; Dr. Spivey, a sprightly young doctor, is the physician for the town and surrounding country.

Citizens are: Jones, Buckley, Clark, Murphy, Kid, McDonald, Mays, Belew, Collier, Spivey, Hughes. Some others live near who are prominent citizens in the county, as Castles, Dyess, Armstrong, Pennington, Graham, Jones.

The town of Chunkey has two churches—Methodist and Baptist. It has always been considered a quiet and usually a sober town. There is a school near the town which is operated on the plan of the free schools of the county.

On the 13th of May, 1861, John Warren and a man named Mayberry engaged in a fight which resulted in the death of both. Warren was a merchant and Mayberry was probably a merchant and citizen of the town. These two men are all that have been known to be killed in the town.

TOWN OF CONNEHATTA.

The town, originally called Centerville, is situated in the northwestern part of the county, about eleven miles north of Lake. It was settled in the year 1867, by J. L. B. Carver, and had small business until 1869. The land on which the town is situated, formerly belonged to Ben Bright who sold it to J. J. and Thos. Thornton. Thornton, Easterling & Co., did large business here from 1869 to 1880. Thornton & Co. continued until October, 1883, when the entire business portion of the town was burned except one house. Liquor was sold in the town from 1867 or 1868, until 1872, by Hurst, Clark and Snipes.

B. F. McGowan opened business in 1872 and continued until 1880, when J. M. Haralson became associated with him. This business was sold to Joe Baum & Co., in 1883, and soon after closed up. R. B. Pace commenced business in 1872, continued three or four years, when the building and stock were burned, and the business discontinued. Mr. R. B. Pace opened business here again in 1884, and continued until 1890. Centerville Co-operative Association began business here in 1877. This was called the Grange store; capital advanced by the Grangers and a manager selected to conduct it. W. L. Kelly was the first manager; in 1880 he was succeeded by A. F. Loper; in 1886 A. J. Small succeeded Loper; in 1890 Small was succeeded by Floyd Loper. The business was discontinued in 1892 after being operated fifteen years.

Frank Smith commenced doing business about 1881; his house and stock were burned in the fire of 1883. He rebuilt in 1884, and in a short time sold to Newt. McMullen, who in the year 1886 sold to Capt. Thos. Faucet, who in 1892 sold to E. L. Faucet.

W. F. Petty commenced business in 1884 and continued only a short time.

Capt. Thomas Faucet commenced business of general merchandise in the year 1886 and continued until 1891.

Loper & Pace opened general merchandise business in the year 1886. In the year 1890 Loper died and the business was continued by J. R. Pace & Co.

Kelley & Co. had mercantile interests in the town in 1883 to 1885.

J. S. Brown did small business in 1890; was succeeded by T. P. Williams, who did business only a short time.

S. Sanders did business about two years in the town of Conehatta.

J. W. Day & Bro. commenced to sell goods here about 1891. J. W. Day bought the interest of his brother and is still in business.

Floyd & Loper commenced business in the year 1892, was burned out in November, 1893, and reopened in 1894.

The town of Conehatta has been very unfortunate in reference to fires. Most of the town was consumed in 1883, and then after building up to some extent, was burned again in 1893. There are very few business houses left in the place, and consequently less being done in this way than for years. This inland town has ever been famous for its schools. Conehatta Institute was established in 1877, with Prof. F. M. Mosley as principal; he was succeeded by Prof. G. Hand; he by Prof. Wheat; and he by Rev. A. M. McBryde, J. S. Scott and Prof. L. L. Denson, The school continued under the supervision of McBryde and Scott for several years, prospering until it had 212 pupils. This was the pioneer high school and first chartered school iu the county. The school at Conehatta has done much to educate the youth of the county, and as a place of good society and clever people, cannot be excelled in the county. In the year 1888, the town having reached over 200 inhabitants, was incorporated; J. F. Williams was first Mayor. Resident citizens are and have been: Dr. J. B. Bailey, Dr. Thornton, J. M. Haralson, C. W. Day, Rev. A. M. McBryde, J. F. Williams, T. I. Graham, A. J. Small, W. L. Kelly, Geo. D. Pace, Thomas Faucet, Dr. J. J. Haralson, J. W. O'Brien, A. F. Loper, J. A. Pace, Mrs. O. C. Jackson, T. M. Thornton, T. P. Williams, C. E. McCord, J. P. Clark, J. L. Frazier, J. S. Scott, T. O. McDonald, Floyd Loper, L. L. Denson, W. H. Lack, W. B. Thornton, F. E. McKee, Sol. Saunders, J. C. Wilson, D. Smith, T. W. F. Petty, Frank Smith, W. F. Petty, B. F. McGowan.

CHAPTER XXXVIII.

The Various County Officers who have held Office since the Settlement of the County—State Senators whose Districts Embraced Newton County, and the Immediate Representatives of the County, from 1837 to 1894—Judges and Chancellors who have held the Circuit and Chancery Courts of Newton—Sketches of these Distinguished Men by Prominent Persons of the State.

It will be endeavored to name all the officers of the county from its organization, and in doing this some omissions may occur, as there are no records to be examined, and all that can be relied upon is the recollection of these men by those who have lived in the county. In some instances a proper succession may not be followed, yet it is hoped the readers of these pages will recollect that when the records of a county are burned, there is no other reliable data, and if errors occur it is because the facts cannot be reached by memory.

The first probate judges, Judges Hudson, Furgerson and Shelton, are named as the first to hold these offices, though it is not known who held the office first, or in what succession they came. Then Judge Abner Haralson; after that Judge Hamilton Cooper held the office for eight years. Judge William Graham succeeded him and was judge for twelve years. Judge

HISTORY OF NEWTON COUNTY. 367

Thames was elected to the office in in 1866, and served about one year, or a little over, and was removed by the military authorities. A. E. Gray was then appointed and served a short time, and I. L. Bolton was appointed to fill his place. After the adoption of the new Constitution and election of Governor Alcorn and his induction into office in March, 1870, chancellors were appointed to hold the courts formerly held by the judges of probate, and whose jurisdiction was greatly enlarged. The names of the chancellors will appear with the judicial officers in another place.

SHERIFFS.

Hullum Redwine is said to have been the first sheriff, probably two terms; Bailey Johnson three terms; John Williamson three or four terms; J. H. Wells three terms. The last three died in office. Mike Ware was elected to fill out Wells' term. Edmunds, elected in 1864, resigned. J. J. Perry was appointed and was sheriff about three years. Cox was then appointed; then Gray; then Dr. Longmire; then Dr. Howard, and J. P. Dansby succeeded him and was sheriff about two years until Capt. Gallaspy was elected in 1872 and served eight years, and was succeeded by G. B. Harper, who served twelve years, and who is said to be the only man ever beaten for the office, those holding the office either dying in office or refusing to stand for a re-election. H. O. Horne succeeded Harper in 1892.

TREASURERS.

H. O. Kelly is reported as being the first treasurer of the county, succeeded by Wm. Graham, Patterson, Todd, W. H. Jones, A. McAlpin, A. F. Clarke, M. W. Stamper, J. C. Portis, F. B. Loper and Wm. B. Lewis.

HISTORY OF NEWTON COUNTY.

CHANCERY CLERKS.

George Armstrong, said to be the first chancery or probate clerk, R. P. Jones probably the second; J. P. Dansby was then clerk of both probate and circuit courts; James A. Ware was then elected in 1854 or 1855 and served until 1865; was elected again in 1866 as circuit clerk and served until removed by military authority. Thos. Keith was elected probate clerk in 1866 and was removed by military authority in 1868. C. S. Swann was appointed sometime in the year 1868, and was clerk until 1872, when Eugene Carleton was elected and served sixteen years, and was succeeded by F. N. McMullen who took the office January, 1888, and is the present clerk.

CIRCUIT CLERKS.

James Armstrong is said to have been the first circuit clerk; was succeeded by James J. Monroe, R. P. Jones served in both offices; so did J. P. Dansby and J. A. Ware. Thos. Dearing served by appointment a short time. T. M. Scanlan was elected in 1872; Jones and Hunter both succeeded Scanlan and both died in office. S. M. Adams was elected in 1867 and is the clerk at this writing.

SURVEYORS.

Booker is reported as the first surveyor of Newton county; Sid Castles longer than any other man; Job Taylor, E. D. Beattie, Sy Harris, Fred M. Lewis, J. M. Kelly; the last named is surveyor at this time.

CORONERS.

There are very few persons who are reported to have filled this place, some likely to have been left out;

HISTORY OF NEWTON COUNTY.

David Bradley, W. H. Martin and T. J. Coker, who is now acting in that office.

ASSESSORS.

George Armstrong is reported as an early assessor and collector of taxes of Newton county. He was probably not the first assessor. The names of Wm. Thames and Wm. Graham are both reported as being early assessors; James Castles is also mentioned. James Sims, John C. Williamson, Young Waul, J. P. Hardy, James Sessums, A. Mott, J. C. Portis, J. B. McAlpin, S. M. Adams, J. J. Phillips, J. B. Boberts and J. M. C. Bullard. These do not come in every instance as they succeeded each other, but most of the assessors are named.

SENATORS AND REPRESENTATIVES FROM 1837 TO 1894.

Year	Senators.	Representatives.
1837	Oliver C. Dease.	
1838-'39	Oliver C. Dease	James Ellis.
1840-'41	John C. Thomas	James Ellis.
1842-'43	John C. Thomas	W. B. Dozier.
1844-'46	Simeon R. Adams	J. M. Loper.
1848-'50	W. P. Carter	Wm. Thames.
1852	Shields L. Hussey	Wm. Thames.
1854	James J. Monroe	Wm. Thames.
1856, '57, '58	C. G. Miller	M. M. Keith.
1859, '60, '61	Wm. Thames	M. M. Keith.
1861-'62	Wm. Thames	J. C. McElroy.
1865	Robert Leachman	J. C. McElroy.
1866	J. W. Brooks	J. C. McElroy.
1870-'71	J. T. Hardy	I. L. Bolton.
1872-'73	Jno. Watts	I. L. Bolton.
1874	T. B. Graham	Wm. Thames.
1875	T. B. Graham	No Representative 1875
1876	T. B. Graham	Isaac L. Pennington.
1877	H. C. McCabe	Isaac L. Pennington.
1878-'80	Asa R. Carter	Martin W. Stamper.
1882	Thos. Keith	D. T. Chapman.

1884.............Thos. Keith................... { I. L. Bolton.
                                                  J. H. Regan.
1886............R. P. Austin................... { D. T. Chapman.
                                                  W. L. Robberts.
1888............R. P. Austin .... { J. H. Regan.
                                                 J. R. Pace.
1890............A. M. Byrd................... { J. H. Regan.
                                                 W. L. Robberts.
1891, '92, '93....A. M. Byrd.................. { A. E. Graham.
                                                 R. H. Taylor.
1894............A. M. Byrd.......... .... { A. E. Graham.
                                                 Thos. Keith.

CHAPTER XXXIX.

JUDGES, CHANCELLORS AND DISTRICT ATTORNEYS OF NEWTON COUNTY.

JUDGE THOS. S. STERLING.

JUDGE THOS. S. STERLING was the first circuit judge who held the courts in the counties embraced in the Choctaw Purchase of 1830. Newton county was one of them, but was a portion of Neshoba from 1833 to 1836.

Judge Sterling was born in one of the Northern States, and had liberal education. He was a graduate of one of the prominent colleges of that section. He came early to Wayne county, and married Miss Falconer, sister of General Thos. P. Falconer, a man of prominence and a lawyer of ability.

Judge Sterling was noted for his amiability of disposition and kind consideration for every one. He was popular with the people, as was shown by his election, before his promotion to the bench, as a senator from the counties of Wayne and Jones, in the years 1830 and 1831. He did not live to a very great age, and was not in any public office after he came off the bench. He was judge probably two terms.

JUDGE HENRY MOUNGER.

The following is a sketch of Judge Mounger, by

Hon. A. G. Mayers, Judge of the 8th Judicial District of Mississippi:

"HON. HENRY MOUNGER was a native of the State of Georgia. He was a nephew of Governor Jack Clark. He was educated at Athens, Ga., and among his classmates were John A. Campbell, late of Mobile; Hugh H. Harralson, of Ga., and George R. Clayton, of Columbus, Miss.

He came to Mississippi and located as a lawyer at Paulding, soon after the organization of the county of Jasper, and formed a partnership with Gen. John Watts (afterwards Judge of this District); he soon came to the front as one of the leading lawyers in East Mississippi, and was engaged in every case of importance in his district. He was a very impressive speaker, and his high character for truth, honesty and fair dealing, had a wonderful effect upon the juries. He was quite successful as a criminal lawyer, and his services as such were in great demand in his district.

He was elected judge of the circuit court of his district, and presided with dignity, ability and impartiality. Having been soundly converted, he was licensed as a local preacher in the Methodist Episcopal Church, and he opened his courts with prayer.

He married Miss Celia Millsaps, a daughter of Judge Uriah Millsaps, of Jasper county. Their children who survived them are: Rev. E. H. Mounger, D. D., W. H. Mounger, Esq., Mrs. Ranson J. Jones, Uriah Mounger and Elijah Mounger, Celia Jones, and Susan Cook and Elizabeth Reed.

In 1847 he formed a law partnership with the writer, which continued until his death, in July, 1851.

It is but the simple truth to say that Judge Mounger was no ordinary man. He was a noble specimen of the Christian gentleman; in every relation of life he exhibited those traits of character which elevate and adorn mankind; he was charitable and liberal to the full extent of his means; he was ardent in his friendships and generous to his foes; he sought peace with all men, but possessed a moral and physical courage that was equal to all occasions. His last illness continued ten days; he was fully aware of his condition, gave directions as to his affairs, and bade his family farewell; he was not afraid to die, for he knew in whom he put his trust. His remains were followed to the grave by the largest funeral procession that was ever seen in Paulding.

JUDGE A. B. DAWSON.

Hon. A. B. Dawson was elected Judge of the 4th Judicial District, which embraced the county of Newton, and served a term of four years and was succeeded by Hon. John Watts. It has been found difficult to obtain any data in reference to Judge Dawson. The supposition is that he was a Georgian and came early to this State and was elected after being here for several years, as Judge for one term. He afterwards resumed the practice of law and died in a few years.

JUDGE JOHN WATTS.

Hon. John Watts, whose portrait occupies the frontispiece in this book, was so nearly and closely, and for such a long time associated with the people of Newton county, as to deserve more than a passing notice.

Judge Watts was born in Chesterfield District, South Carolina, May 26, 1805. His father, a prominent and influential citizen, came early to Wayne county, and his family was a very conspicuous one in the same county. There were but few facilities for educating young men in that new country; however, the best that could be provided was given to this rising young man. After leaving school, which he did at a very early age, quite a preference was shown him by his fellow-citizens, and they first elected him to the office of justice of the peace, then captain of a militia company; he then acted as deputy sheriff; was then elected circuit clerk, and during the term he was clerk studied law and was admitted to practice in the supreme court of the State in the year 1831. He then opened a law office in the town of Winchester. Within a few years he became a candidate for district attorney and was elected by the people for eleven years. He was elected in that and other districts in which he lived, judge of the circuit court for twenty-two years, and but for the conduct of the military in the reconstruction of the State, would have remained until the end of his term. His last public service was in the State Senate in the troublous times of Radical rule, where he did good work for his people.

It will be seen that for thirty-seven years he was a servant of the people, elected by the suffrages of the people. These were places of honor and great responsibility. In all these years he served the people of Newton county—as this was at all times in his district. He was the district attorney who assisted in the first court ever held in this county, even before the county was divided from Neshoba, and continuously so as attorney and judge, with the exception of four years, up to 1868. He was also Brigadier-General of State militia at one time, and made a fine commanding officer.

Judge Watts, as has been intimated, did not have the educational training that he would have liked and appreciated, but he used well what he did have, and filled every position to which he aspired in political life with honor to himself and justice to his constituents. He had the honor of presiding over the bar at the State capital, when he considered it the best in the South. He was always elected by the people, showing that they approved his course. For more than thirty years he was in office, and was never defeated but twice.

Judge Watts felt proud of any position that his fellow-citizens conferred upon him. No pains were spared to do his duty. He was a pattern of young men for sobriety and diligence in official duties, feeling that the performance of these duties was his highest obligation and reward. Judge Watts had great pride of character, was a fine looking man, of commanding size and appearance, and always presided on the bench with a dignity befitting his honorable position. He was a conscientious man, who tried to do his duty, and the people who placed him in the high position set the seal of their approval on his conduct by keeping him in office. He loved to mingle with his old friends, irrespective of party. It was well known that he was an "old-line Whig," and for the greater part of his official life he was on the weak side of politics. Yet such were his magnetic qualities among the yeomanry of the country as to win them to his support, and by his consistent course of justice and care for their cause as to keep them with him.

Judge Watts was a Methodist preacher for about thirty years, and amidst all his hard work and active duties of his profession, found time to devote much good work to his church. He was kind and sympathetic, a loving father and husband, a good neighbor, and great peace-maker among those who had difficulties. He lived to the ripe age of seventy years, and died at Newton, May, 1875, surrounded by his children and friends, and was very greatly mourned.

JUDGE JONATHAN TARBELL.

JONATHAN TARBELL was appointed judge of this district by Gov. Alcorn, in 1870, and succeeded Judge Watts, who was removed. Gen. Tarbell was a Northern man from Oswego, New York; was a lawyer of some ability, and was afterwards appointed as one of the supreme court judges of the State. He was not the judge in this district for more than two years, probably not that. He came South as a political adventurer, and after the State resumed her position under Democratic administration, he removed to Washington City, and died there several years since.

JUDGE R. E. LEACHMAN.

The following sketch is by Capt. J. W. Fewell:

ROBERT LEACHMAN was born in Virginia in 1806. His parents removed to Kentucky when he was very young, and in the latter State he was reared and educated. Having received a fair education, he attended Transylvania University Law School, where he was graduated in that profession. In his early manhood he removed to Greene county, Alabama, where he practiced law for many years. Some years before the commencement of the war between the States, he removed to Lauderdale county, Mississippi, where he continued the practice of law until he was appointed United States District Attorney, in 1866. He had been a Whig in politics all his life, and when the war ended he became a Republican. He was a member of the State Senate just after the close of the war. Having served for some time as U. S. District Attorney, he was, in 1868, appointed by General Gillam, Military Governor, judge of the circuit court for the district embracing Newton county. Upon the reconstruction of the State and the election of Governor Alcorn, Judge Leachman was, upon the practically unanimous request of the bar of the district, re-appointed, and he held that office until 1876, when he was succeeded by Judge James S. Hamm, the first appointee under Democratic rule. Judge Leachman continued to reside in Meridian for several years after leaving the bench and until his family was broken up by the death of his wife and the death or marriage of his children. He then removed to Anniston, Alabama, where he lived with his daughter, Mrs. Douglass, up to the date of his death, in 1891. His first wife was a Miss Rencher, a sister of Dr. C. R. Rencher, of Enterprise; his last, a Miss Brooke, of Greene county, Alabama.

Judge Leachman was a man of dignity and firmness on the bench, and his judicial course gave general satisfaction to the people and bar. He was never charged or suspected of any corruption in office, and bore himself throughout the corrupt and trying times of his judgeship with admitted fairness and integrity.

JUDGE A. G. MAYERS.

The following sketch is contributed by a friend who has been long and intimately acquainted with Judge Mayers:

Judge ALONZO G. MAYERS, of 8th Judicial district, is one of the few remaining land-marks of East Mississippi. A native of Wayne county, born in 1821, he had only such educational advantages as could be obtained at that early day in the schools of his immediate vicinity. That distinguished orator and statesman—

Edward Everett — declared that the boy or girl who could read correctly, spell well, write a legible hand, and understand the three first rules in arithmetic, had the foundation, and could thereafter educate himself or herself, without the aid of schools. This truth is illustrated in the life of Judge Mayers; his father died, leaving a widow and several children, he the eldest. His first employment was that of clerk in general stores in the towns of Quitman and Garlandsville; his idle time was spent in study and miscellaneous reading. Before he reached his nineteenth year, he was esteemed a fair scholar and a well informed young man.

Seeing no employment that promised better results, he adopted for a short time school teaching, but it is said by those who knew of his career as a "school master," that any boy who asked to be shown how to work a difficult sum, generally received a severe reprimand and was sent back to his seat with the information that "boys to learn to cypher, should work their sums without assistance."

While as a boy, pursuing such vocations as afforded a support, his mind was fixed on the law; in the meantime he acquired a vast store of information; he had read history, poetry and fiction; his literary taste was most excellent and refined. Among the poets, Byron and Moore were his favorites, and often, when with one or two chosen friends, he would repeat some of the most beautiful stanzas from these honored authors.

He read law at the village of Garlandsville, with the late Judge John Watts, and was licensed at a term of the circuirt court of his native county before he attained his majority.

He located at Raleigh, in Smith county, in 1844, to practice his profession, and was regarded as one of the rising young men of the State. He was a candidate in 1845 for district attorney; he was a pronounced Whig and the judicial district largely democratic; he entered the canvass with limited means, but attractive in person, marked energy, ready and full of exquisite humor, he received a cordial and generous support. In one of the counties of his district, after being from home several weeks, night overtook him at the house of an old gentleman who had a good following in his neighborhood; was close-fisted, but scrupulously honest. The young lawyer had not a penny in his purse, but after supper he exerted himself to be agreeable--he wanted not only the influence of his host, but no charge for his night's lodging—he made a splendid impression, and before bed-time was informed that he would *sweep the beat.* Next morning, when the servant announced that the stranger's horse was ready, with one foot in the stirrup, he grasped the old gentleman's hand and said, " Good bye, Uncle Johuny; it's no use to ask my bill, for I know you don't keep tavern." He was defeated for district attorney by his Democratic opponent by two votes.

While practicing at Raleigh, an elderly lady, of large wealth for that country, Mrs. P., became involved in a lawsuit about a negro. She appeared at court, and went to the office of Mr. Mayers and said, " Mr. Mayers, I am in trouble and I want you to tell me what to do." He said, "Give me ten dollars, and I will do so." She carefully counted out ten dollars in silver and handed him, and inquired, " Now what shall I do? "Employ a lawyer, madam."

Some years after his candidacy for district attorney, he was nominated by the Whig party of his Congressional district against the late Hon. A. G. Brown, for Congress. Governor Brown wrote him proposing a list of appointments for joint discussion. Mayers replied "That he understood that Brown had made all his arrangements to be returned to Congress, and that Mrs. Brown confidently expected to spend the coming winter in Washington, and that he could not find it in his heart to disappoint her, and, therefore, he would decline the contest and pursue his profession."

In 1847 he removed to Paulding, and formed a partnership with the late Judge Henry L. Mounger, and the law firm of Mounger & Mayers continued until Judge Mounger's death in 1851. In 1848 he married Miss Elizabeth C. King, of Rankin county, who, with their two children, died in 1852. The same year he removed to Brandon, where he has since continuously lived. In 1856, he married Miss Nannie L. McLaurin, of Covington county. Four children were born to them, all grown, married, and living away from their native county. While practicing his profession at Brandon, he frequently contributed articles to the Brandon *Republican*, and at one time became a half owner of the paper, and was its editor for several years. An ardent and uncompromising Whig, a pungent and graceful writer, he not only enjoyed an enviable reputation as an editor, but added largely to the interest and circulation of the paper. He forged his way to the front, not only as an intelligent and safe leader of his party, but as a newspaper writer, so much so, that he was offered a large salary to edit the Vicksburg *Whig*. This flattering offer he declined, but it is fair to say, that it cost him a great effort, for the newspaper business possessed an attraction and charm for him that was difficult to withstand.

Thoroughly grounded in the text-books, well up in the adjudications of our own and other State and Federal courts, Mr. Mayers was a successful practitioner. A good pleader, ready, and full of resources, he was seldom caught at a disadvantage. Governor Robert Lowry read law with him, and on being licensed, the law firm of Mayers & Lowry was formed, and continued for over sixteen years, and did a large and lucrative practice. They are devoted and life-long friends, and of them it may be truly said, they were as

"Distinct as the billows, yet one as the sea."

The firm was dissolved by the elevation of Mr. Mayers to the circuit court bench of the eighth judicial district, in 1876, appointed by Gov. Stone. He was re-appointed by Gov. Lowry in 1882, and again in 1888, and again appointed by Gov. Stone in 1894. At the expiration of his present term he will have presided continuously on the circuit bench of his district, for twenty-two years, an honor that has fallen to the lot of few men, if any, since the organization of the State government.

His administration for eighteen years has been wise and conservative. The criminal laws have been strictly enforced and good morals promoted.

As a judge he is fair-minded, and uniformly courteous to the bar. With a keen sense of the ridiculous, and a fund of humor, he occasionally breaks the monotony of the court-room at the expense of judicial dignity. While on his way, some years ago to hold court, and just before reaching Smith county court-house, he passed a tall, gaunt fellow riding a small, poor, weak-looking scrub of a pony. Glancing at the animal, which was very much like, but less in size, than Yallow Blossom's horse, "Bullet," in the Georgia Scenes, he remarked that the law preventing cruelty to animals should be enforced. Pending business in court, just before the dinner hour, a loud long hollo was heard. The judge ordered the man brought into court. He was the owner of the poor horse. Are you the man that hollod?" "Yes, jedge." "Why did you hollo?" "Jedge, I thought court had adjourned," but it had not. "Why, sir, did you hollo?" "Well, jedge, I just give a keen hollor, and bantered any man on the ground for a hoss swap." "Did you want to trade the horse you were riding this morning?" "Yes, jedge, that's the very critter." "You are excused, sir."

Judge Mayers was born four years after the admission of Mississippi as a State in the Federal Union. His recollection of prominent men and events in the State are perhaps more accurate than almost any man now within its limits. His native county was prolific in honors won by her citizens, and not only their history, but that of others who contributed largely to the civilization of the State, is remembered by him. It has been one one of the pleasures of his judicial career that he has held courts in all the counties in which he has lived and practiced law. On one occasion, while holding Jasper county court, for some misdemeanor, he ordered a man to jail for twenty-four hours. In a few minutes a neighbor of the unfortunate person in prison walked up to the judge's stand, and in rather a loud whisper, said: "Judge, you should not have sent that man to jail; he is a distant kinsman of yours." His honor replied, in a much louder whisper: "If a man can't send his kinsfolk to jail who can he send?"

By a change of venue, the noted case of Col. Jones S. Hamilton, charged with the killing of Roderick D. Gambrell, was carried to Rankin county. The trial lasted forty-six judicial days. Judge Mayers presided, and demonstrated not only his ability as a jurist, but exhibited a most commendable degree of patience.

With a superior knowledge of human nature, sincere and ardent in his friendships, genial and generous, possessing breadth and discrimination, and devoted to his church, he always receives a hearty and sincere welcome from those who have the pleasure of his acquaintance. He is still active, his mind clear, with an almost unerring memory. He has a beautiful home at Brandon—a carefully selected library of choice books. The yard is shaded by imposing forest trees, and the woodlawn extensive and picturesque. Always fond of poetry and music, the judge, "in days of yore," drew a delightful and sweet bow, and now when entertaining friends at his hospitable home, he occasionally brings out the fiddle and the bow and dispenses the sweetest of music. Scotch and Irish airs, interspersed with dancing tunes of "long ago"—"Logie O'Buchan," "Rory O'More," "Coming Over the Borders," "Comin' thro' the Rye," "Wearing of the Green," "Come Haste to the Wedding," "Forka Deer," etc.

Judge Mayers has been a prominent figure in East Mississippi for half a century, and this writer indulges the hope that the Great Master will smooth his pathway for the remainder of his journey.

CHANCELLORS OF NEWTON COUNTY.

CHANCELLOR CHRISTIAN.

Judge CHRISTIAN was appointed chancellor of the district in which Newton county is embraced, and served acceptably to the people of the county and district. He was considered an able chancellor and upright man, and his removal was regretted by the people of the district.

CHANCELLOR DENNIS.

JUDGE DENNIS was appointed to fill the vacancy caused by the removal of Judge Christian, and served only a short time—probably held one or two courts in Newton county. After that the appointments by Governor Stone were made, and Hon. T. B. Graham was appointed, the first under Democratic rule in the State.

CHANCELLOR GRAHAM.

Hon. Thomas Keith contributes the following sketch of Judge Thos. B. Graham, chancellor ;

The subject of this sketch, Hon. Thos. B. Graham, is a native of the State of Alabama, and was moved by his parents to this State in his early youth, about the year 1864, and was reared to manhood in the adjoining county of Scott. He received a collegiate education, having graduated with distinction at the University of North Carolina. Soon after leaving college he chose the law as his profession, and after thorough preparation, entered upon a lucrative practice in the county of Scott and the adjacent counties. He was for a number of years the law partner of the late A. B. Smith.

A patriot, he was active in raising the first company of volunteers in the cause of the Southern Confederacy that enlisted from Scott county ; was elected captain of the company, from which position he rose to that of colonel, and at the surrender of the Confederate forces he was in command of the 20th Mississippi Regiment.

He was a member of the State Senate from the district composed of the counties of Scott, Jasper and Newton at the time of Governor Ames' impeachment, a position in which he wielded great influence, particularly in all legislation pertaining to finance, he being perhaps the best posted man in the State as to the financial condition of the State.

Governor John M. Stone, recognizing his eminent fitness for the office of chancellor, during his first term as Governor appointed him chancellor of the district, which office he has held continuously to this date, and is now universally recognized throughout the entire State as one of the best chancellors who has ever presided in the State.

In politics, Chancellor Graham is a Democrat of the true type, and is well posted on all political questions, both State and national. He is yet in the prime of life, and well qualified to fill any position to which he may be called.

His postoffice address is now Forest, Scott county, Miss.

CHANCELLOR EVANS.

Sketch by Col. J. J. Shannon:

The writer first met Judge Evans in Paulding, at the April term, 1848, of Jasper circuit court. He resided then at Marion, Lauderdale county, and though a young man, was recognized as one of the prominent lawyers of the district. Newton was then in the Fourth Judicial District and extended from Noxubee county to the seacoast. From that time to the suspension of legal business by the war in 1861, he was employed in most of the important civil and criminal cases in the district, and was conceded to be at the head of the bar. As a circuit court lawyer, he had no superior in the State. He was a skillful pleader, prompt to grasp the strong points on his side of the case, and quick to take advantage of any mistake by opposing counsel. Besides, he was a forcible, able and logical speaker, and a most successful advocate before a jury. During the many years that he practiced law in Newton, there was no lawyer who attended better known to the people of the county, and none who stood higher in their estimation.

He was a native of New York, but came to Mississippi while quite a young man. He was ever true to the fortunes of his adopted State, and no native of the South espoused our cause in the great struggle for independence with more zeal and fidelity than Judge Evans.

At the close of the war he resumed the practice of his profession and was employed in the most important cases in the district, until his appointment by Gov. Lowry as Chancellor, on the 12th of May, 1883. He was re-appointed by Gov. Lowry, May 12th, 1887, and by Gov. Stone in May, 1891, and resigned in March, 1891.

His retirement from office was regretted by almost the entire bar of the district, and he was regarded, during the time he held the office, as one of the best, if not the best, Chancellor in the State. He performed every duty of the office with the most scrupulous care and fidelity. He insisted on a strict accounting from administrators, guardians and trustees, and in that way many estates were saved by his vigilance for the benefit of minors.

His integrity and strict impartiality were conceded by all, and his retirement from the bench was a loss to the State and to the people of the district.

CHANCELLOR HOUSTON.

WILLIAM T. HOUSTON was born in Newburn, Ala., May 4th, 1849. He is son of S. M. Houston, and his mother was Miss Mary E. Herndon. He was educated in Alabama, and studied law at Washington University, St. Louis, Mo. He began the practice of law at Okolona, in the fall of 1872. Was elected Senator in 1885, from the 10th District of Mississippi, composed of the counties of Chickasaw and Pontotoc.

On the 27th of May, 1874, he was married to Miss Mary Fooshee, who came to Mississippi from North Carolina, in 1857. He removed to Aberdeen in 1887, and to Meridian in 1889, where he succeeded to the practice of Judge Thos. H. Woods. He was appointed Chancellor for the district of which Newton is one of the counties, April 4th, 1892. Judge Houston's home is at Meridian, Miss.

DISTRICT ATTORNEYS OF NEWTON COUNTY.

ATTORNEY WOOD.

HON. GEORGE WOOD, who was for a number of years district attorney in the district in which Newton county was embraced, was a native of the State of Connecticut, but many years ago came South and was fully identified with the people of Mississippi. He was considered a good lawyer and a faithful State's attorney and served probably from 1847 to 1858 and was succeeded by Richard Cooper. After the war he was appointed, by Gov. Stone, Chancellor for the Meridian district, which position he held until his death and was succeeded by Hon. S. Evans.

RICHARD COOPER.

Contributed by Capt. W. H. Hardy:

RICHARD COOPER was elected district attorney in the 4th Judicial District, which embraced the county of Newton, in 1858, and was re-elected in 1862, thus filling that responsible position for a period of eight years.

He was born in Savannah, Georgia, the 26th day of March, 1818, and when nineteen years old came to this State, and settled at Brandon, in Rankin county. In 1838 he taught school in that county and read law at night by the light of pine-knot fires, and the following year moved to the Republic of Texas and settled in Montgomery county, where on the 26th day of September of that year, he was admitted to the bar by the district court of the 4th Judicial District.

He had previously, before going to Texas, been united in marriage with Miss Margaret V. Garvin, of Nashville, Tenn. Becoming dissatisfied in Texas he returned to Mississippi and entered upon the practice of his profession. At the time of his election, 1858, he resided at Raleigh, Smith county, but removed the next year to Brandon, where he lived till his death, which occurred on the 4th of January, 1874.

Mr. Cooper was small in stature, but handsome in form and feature; black hair, dark brown or hazel eyes, a bright, benignant face, and possessed of a most amiable and cheerful disposition, he was universally admired. As an evidence of his personal popularity, he was elected district attorney in a strong Democratic district, although he was an ardent Whig.

He was a good lawyer and a model prosecuting attorney for the State. He was a graceful and fluent speaker with a splendid voice. On the hustings he was second to no man of his time unless perhaps to Mr. Prentiss.

He was Grand Master of Masons in 1859; Bell and Everett elector in 1860, in which he made the most brilliant canvass of the State, known since the days of Davis, Prentiss and Foote. In 1868 he represented

Rankin county in the Constitutional Convention which reconstructed the State.

He was a man of great personal magnetism and was loved by all who knew him, and he was known far and near as "Dick Cooper." He was intensely social, leading, as that quality often does, to conviviality. Alas! that was the weak place in his armor, and the fatal shaft penetrated it, and like that other great genius, whose career, though so brief, illumined the history of our State with its genius and oratory, Prentiss, his constitution was undermined and gave way, and he died, as before stated, lamented throughout the State and was buried at Brandon with Masonic honors.

He was for several years conscious of his approaching end, and had made peace with his Maker, and died as becomes a Christian. Peace to his memory!

THOMAS H. WOODS.

Sketch contributed by Capt John W. Fewell:

THOMAS H. WOODS, who long held the office of district attorney for the district embracing Newton county, was born in Kentucky in 1836. He removed with his father's family to Mississippi in 1847. He was educated in the common schools of the country and at Williams College, Massachusetts. He was admitted to the bar at De Kalb, Kemper county, in 1859. He was elected to the Secession Convention of 1861, and was the youngest member of that historical body. When Mississippi seceded, Mr. Woods volunteered and entered the Confederate States service. He became a captain in the famous 13th Mississippi Regiment, of Barksdale's—afterwards Humphreys'—Brigade of the Army of Northern Virginia. Returning home with the handful of survivors of his regiment when the war had ended, Capt. Woods at once resumed the practice of his profession. Although his experience was limited, his talents and capacity were immediately recognized and he was elected, in 1865 to the responsible position of district attorney. To that place he was re-elected in 1866. He was removed from the office by the military government in 1869, and resumed his private practice successfully. But, on the restoration of the civil authority, he was again elected district attorney in 1871, and again re-elected in 1875. He was elected to the Legislature in 1881, and served very conspicuously in that body in 1882-'83.

In the meantime, he had built up a large and lucrative practice, to which he devoted close attention, until he was appointed, in 1889, to the office of Judge of the Supreme Court, and he became chief justice of that great tribunal, to fill an unexpired term. In 1891 he was reappointed, and for a full term of nine years; he is still on that bench. It will thus be seen that Judge Woods' career has been a most honorable and successful one.

As a soldier, as a private citizen, as an official, Thomas H. Woods has always done his duty. One can find no words more really eulogistic than these. Of great talents, of unquestioned integrity, of the most winning manners and captivating address, of great powers as an orator, a forceful writer and a learned lawyer, Judge Woods has been and is entitled to the high distinction to which he has attained. His opinions as a judge are pointed, clear and cogent, and his reputation as a sound and learned expounder of the law is spreading to other States of the Union.

In the prime of a splendid manhood, Mississippi may well expect new achievements by her son, upon whose brow she has already placed a laurel wreath in recognition of his past services. The name of Thomas H. Woods is written in a conspicuous place in the roll of Mississippi's great men.

ATTORNEY SIMON JONES.

Simon Jones was appointed district attorney by Gov. Jas. L. Alcorn in 1870, and continued until 1872, when Hon. Thos. H. Woods succeeded him, being elected by the people. Mr. Jones was a native of Marion county, Miss., was not a man who was acceptable to the people, and they were pleased to be rid of him.

ATTORNEY A. Y. HARPER.

The following sketch of Col. A. Y. Harper, who was district attorney for the district embracing Newton county, is furnished by a friend who was closely associated with Col. Harper in most of his official life:

COL. A. Y. HARPER was born in Sumpter county, Ala., about 1835 or 1836; when about fourteen or fifteen years old he removed with his parents to Scott county, Mississippi, and pursued his studies in the common schools of the county until he was prepared for college, and then entered the State University, at Oxford. At the beginning of his college life he took a high stand in his class, and graduated with the first honor. After leaving college he commenced the study of law and was admitted to the bar a short time before the late civil war. He formed a copartnership with the late Hon. Richard Cooper, at Brandon, Miss., and pursued his profession until the breaking out of hostilities between the States, immediately after which he raised a company, was elected captain, and united with the companies in forming the 6th Mississippi Regiment. At the battle of Shiloh, the field officers being all wounded, he assumed command of the regiment and handled it with great skill and bravery. He was afterwards elected Lieutenant-Colonel of the regiment, and continued with it until he was elected Supreme Court Reporter, when he resigned.

After the war he located at Forest, Miss., was elected district atttorney, and served the State in that capacity for several years with distinguished ability. After declining a re-election he removed from Scott county to Okolona, Miss., and continued the practice of law. From Okolona he removed to Birmingham, Ala., and there pursued the practice of the law until he was appointed to a position in the Department of the Interior under Mr. Cleveland's second administration, and which position he now holds. He is a lawyer of marked ability.

HON. S. H. TERRAL.

The following sketch is contributed by Col. J. J. Shannon:

JUDGE TERRAL, who served three years as district attorney in Newton county, from 1876 to 1879, is a native of Jasper county. He was the son of Rev. Jas. S. Terral, one of the pioneers of that county, and one of its most prominent and esteemed citizens. He was educated at the University of Mississippi, and read law at Quitman in the office of his brother, the heroic and lamented Col. Jas. S. Terral, who was killed at the head of his regiment in the battle of Corinth. He was admitted to the bar in 1859, but the war coming on in 1861, he organized a company in Clarke county and was mustered into the 37th Mississippi regiment, and was afterwards elected major, in which capacity he served until the close of the war. Among the many gallant sons of Mississippi who perilled their lives in defence of the "lost cause," there was none whose bravery and devotion to the South surpassed that of Major Terral.

At the close of the war he returned to Quitman and resumed the practice of law. He soon occupied a prominent position at the bar, and in November, 1871, was elected district attorney, which office he held for eight years. In 1876 the judicial districts were changed and he was assigned to the 8th district, which included Newton county. He was an able and vigorous prosecuting attorney, and during the time he held the office he had no superior in the State.

In May, 1892, he was appointed circuit judge of the seventh district, which position he has held continuously since that time. Besides his legal attainments, which are of the highest order, his well known integrity, his patience, impartiality and uniform courtesy to the bar, have made him popular wherever he is known.

He still resides at Quitman, where he was admitted to the bar in 1859, and is universally esteemed and admired by the people of that county. Though twenty years in office as district attorney and judge, he is still in the prime of life and we trust has still before him many years of usefulness and honor.

HON. GREEN B. HUDDLESTON.

GREEN B. HUDDLESTON was born in the State of Georgia in the year 1846, and removed with his father, J. F. N. Huddleston, to Decatur, in Newton county, in the year 1856. He attended the schools at the place of his residence, and at a very early age, after the war commenced, went to the army. In one of the battles in which he was engaged, he received a wound which resulted in the loss of one of his legs. He returned home, and after the war went to school at Cooper Institute, at Daleville, a short term, and returned to Decatur and taught school and studied law alternately. He was admitted to the practice in 1867 or 1868, and removed to Philadelphia, Neshoba county, and married the daughter of Dr. Eliab Fox. He afterwards removed to Forest, in Scott county, and was elected representative in 1873 and did good service for the county. He was elected in 1875 as district attorney for the 8th judicial district, and continued in that position for twelve years, having very little opposition. Mr. Huddleston is a fine lawyer, and from the beginning showed brilliancy in his profession. He may well be considered the ablest lawyer the county has ever furnished. He is amiable in disposition, genial in his intercourse with men, a devoted friend and pleasant companion; he is a forcible speaker, and always comes to the front in any body of men in which he is thrown, either legal or political. He is living at Meridian, and is receiving a good practice.

R. S. M'LAURIN.

The following sketch is contributed by S. H. Kirkland, Esq.:

R. S. McLaurin was born March 14, 1855, near Trenton, in Smith county, Mississippi, and was reared on a farm, attending the common schools of the country until 1876, when he entered Roanoke College, Virginia, remaining for one session. He returned home and entered immediately upon the study of law in the office of his brother, Senator A. J. McLaurin, in Brandon, Mississippi, and was admitted to the bar at the April term, 1878, of the circuit court of Smith county, at Raleigh, Mississippi. He at once entered upon a lucrative practice, and attained high rank as a lawyer.

He remained at Raleigh until April, 1882, when he moved to Brandon and formed a copartnership with his distinguished brother, which continued until January, 1888. He was elected district attorney for the 8th district of Mississippi over three able and formidable competitors at the November election, 1881, and filled the office so ably and acceptably to the people that he was re-elected for the next term without opposition. He has, by his skill and conscientious devotion to duty, retained the confidence of his constituents; his genial and generous nature has made him the idol of a large circle of friends. He married Miss Annie Jack, of Brandon, Mississippi, December 24, 1890.

CHAPTER XL.

SKETCHES OF THE MORAL AND RELIGIOUS STATE OF THE PEOPLE—CHURCH HISTORY OF NEWTON COUNTY AND THE MOST PROMINENT PEOPLE WHO HAVE BEEN CONNECTED WITH IT SINCE ITS ORGANIZATION. BY REV. N. L. CLARKE.

THE opening up of a new country to Christian civilization, and its attendant blessings, has ever been an interesting event in human progress; and has been observed with interest while going on, and its history read with pleasure in after days. Such scenes of interest have transpired in all the States of our heaven-honored country; and wonderfully in our own beloved State. Few of the States of America, if any, have presented a fairer opening to the home seeker than Mississippi. Blessed with a delightful climate, a fruitful soil, an abundant supply of wood, timber for all purposes, and water without stint; reaching to the gulf on the south, near to, and in part embracing the Tombigbee river on the east, and lined by the great Father of Waters on the west, it was favorable, not only for agriculture and easily procuring a living, but also for convenient transportation and trade with surrounding States; just such a country as the honest, industrious and law-abiding citizen would wish to make his home in; especially in the more elevated parts of the State, in which our own county is situated.

ELDER N. L. CLARKE.

HISTORY OF NEWTON COUNTY.

Newton county is a part of the territory of the State obtained from the Choctaw Indians by the United States in the treaty of Dancing Rabbit, in the year 1830, and is pleasantly situated on the upper waters of the Chickasahay and Tuskalameter rivers.

The desirable character of the country led to its early settlement by white people; a few as early as the year 1833. This early beginning was soon added to, so that by 1835 quite a population was scattered over the county. This citizenship, at the first, was chiefly from the southern and older parts of the State, and southwestern Alabama; though as the country came more into notice, valuable additions were made from Georgia and other eastern States.

Among the early settlers we may name the Blakeleys, Clearmans, Gilberts, Fergusons, Sims, McFarlands, Hollands, Wests, Saffolds, Prices, Thompsons, Grahams, Johnstons, Thames, Lopers, Millers, Paris, Ellis, Redwines, Wauls, Paces, Herberts, Jones, Cookseys, Merchants and Boyds, with many others who had homes in the county—valuable citizens, men of energy and of fine property, who gave their aid in establishing order, and in putting the machinery of law in motion. Among this early citizenship were found firm and active friends to education, so that schools were encouraged from the early settlement of the country. There were also devoted, pious Christians, and of the various religious orders that have been common in this State. The country was pleasant and productive, and while fields were being opened for support, and houses erected for family comfort, the great interest of religion also received attention. We regret that we now know so little of the men who first labored in these interests in our beloved county. But they, with their labors and the generation for whose good they toiled, now belong to the past. Now and then, it is true, we see monumental remains of their labors, and pick up scraps of history that throw light upon their times, their character and their work. Those plain but faithful men did pioneer work, laying the foundation upon which others have continued to build. Raised up with the privileges of the gospel, citizens moving into the county felt a great lack without it; hence encouraged ministers of their acquaintance to visit and preach for them; first in their own houses in various parts of the county. Soon, however, buildings were erected for public convenience. These buildings, humble it is true, answered the double purpose of church and school-house. These primitive buildings though, soon gave place to more commodious, and these to still better, so that at this date the buildings in the county for purposes of worship and education, reflect great credit on the citizenship of the county for piety, energy, intelligence and numbers. So far as is known the gospel was first preached in Newton county as early as 1834, or at furthest in 1835, by Rev. John McCormick, and at the residence of Mr. Wm. Blakeley, who, in 1833, moved into the county and made his home in the now Hickory community. This early beginning in gospel work in the county, was kept up and increased by various ministers, some resident in the county and some from other counties.

Among the early settlers in the county, there were ministers of the gospel, Rev. Mr. Redwine, Episcopal-Methodist, resided for a time near Decatur, and preached to the people. Of his history, labors and success we know but little. Wade H. Holland, near Mount Vernon, in the south part of the county; Cader Price, near New Ireland, and James Merchant, near Decatur, were early settlers, and Baptist ministers;

and though they remained in the county but for a short time, yet they labored faithfully in the cause of Christ, and did much to prepare the way for future success. These were incipient stages in a great work in a new field. Yet it was a beginning, the fruit of which was not allowed to perish.

PROTESTANT METHODISTS.

The field so early entered by the Rev. Mr. McCormick, was diligently cultivated by himself and others, both ministers and lay members, so that they were working in an organized form as early as the year 1836, and building up Protestant-Methodism, of which order Mr. McCormick was a laborious and successful minister. Likely their first church was organized at this date, 1836. Soon other ministers of the same order came to their help. Of these we name Elisha Lott, Spencer H. Bankston, Phillip Napier, Chas. F. Gillespie, James E. Taylor, — Gilbert, and likely others of less note. These were able and energetic men, men of influence in building up their denomination, and winning souls to Christ. With them were able and efficient lay members, with their devoted wives, who gave themselves to the work. Among these we may name as foremost, the Blakeleys, Jones, Gilberts, Clearmans, Johnstons, Lopers and Houstons. At what point they first constituted we have now no way of knowing. This we know, however, that as early as 1845 they had several churches that were active and energetic in work — as Johnston's camp ground, Blue Springs, and Bethel. These were in the eastern and southeastern part of the county. In after time, they had a place of worship four miles west of Decatur, known as Lilly Dale. These interests grew, and from the date, 1846 to 1855, increased in members and influence, so that at the last date they had in the county four churches, and membership reaching three hundred and fifty. About this time, however, we mark the beginning of a declension in their interests. Several causes led to this. Several of their ministers grew old and died, or quit the field; others, leading men, connected themselves with other religious orders, so that at this time but one small church exists in the county, with one minister, the Rev. Wm. Gilbert. These people were pioneers in Christian work, in morals and education; and did much to aid in the development of a new and interesting country. We may add to the list of ministers already named: A. Y. Davis, W. W. Garrison, Hillery Bounds, Dan'l Bankston and Wm. Reaves. Davis moved to the northwest, Bounds to Texas, and Bankston was lost in the war.

EPISCOPAL METHODIST.

In the early history of our county we find among the population valuable citizens identified in faith and practice with the Episcopal Methodists, and members of that order, both ministers and laymen. The fact of Mr. Redwine's early residence in the Decatur community, has already been named; just when he came, how long he remained, the extent of his labors and the results, I have no means of knowing. This we know, that while in the county he preached to the people, held camp-meetings, and labored for the good of the people. While this was so, near the centre of the county, John and Edward Waul, Episcopal Methodists, and valuable citizens, located in the south-east part of the county, secured ministerial aid, and constituted the Spring Hill church. It is most likely that the ministers aiding in this early work were Joel and James

Carstaphen, and also likely Rev. Mr. Shockley, who at a very early time had charge of a circuit embracing Newton county. This church, so early organized, yet lives and labors in the cause. I have no way of knowing in what year the itineratizing work was begun by the M. E. Church in Newton. So early, however, as 1841, the Rev. Mr. Shockley, then a citizen of Neshoba county, had charge of a circuit embracing Newton and Jasper counties. Mr. Shockley was a man of fine personal appearance, vigorous minded and a ready and forcible speaker. He died at Paulding, Miss., while on his work -- likely in the year 1843 — leaving his work to other hands; nor do I know to whose hands.

A gap here occurs in the history of the work of the M. E. Church that I have no facts with which to fill up. There existed churches in different parts of the county from its early settlement, as Spring Hill, Decatur, White Plains, and quite early at Chunkey. About the year 1848, the Rev. Mr. McCurdy, a Methothist Episcopal minister, moved from Alabama and settled north-west of Decatur, and gave attention to the interests of his people. Mr. McCurdy was a farmer, of vigorous mind, and in speaking rather strong than eloquent. Likely in the year 1850, the Rev. Mr. Bartlet moved to the south-east part of the county, and located at the place since known as Chunkey station, a pious, devoted man, and an earnest preacher. These men, though most of the time only local preachers, yet exerted an influence for good, and helped the cause they loved. In the year 1848, the Rev. Mr. McGruder had charge of the work in Newton county, and was aided by Mr. Taylor, of Hillsboro. During no year since then have the churches been destitute of pastoral oversight, and almost every year has witnessed an advance in the cause, either in increase of membership, a widening of their influence, or the improvement of their houses of worship in comfort, or in appearance and value.

I give here the names of the ministers that have had charge of this interesting work as far as I can get them: Redwine, very shortly after the county was possessed by white people, Shockley, McGruder, McCurdy, Bartlet, Vance, Smith, Deskins, Wedgeworth, Daniel McDonald, Murdoc McDonald, Fikes, Hays, Cox, Meadow, Carmack, Renfroe, Hinds, Boyles, McDonald, Chatfield, Cotton, West, Peebles, Downer, Rivers, Parker, Morse, Williams, Armstrong, Bancroft and Royner; a gifted, able minister, raised up in our own county. It is well known that there were others that were connected with the itinerating work in the county, but I have not been able to obtain their names. These were orderly and pious men, of various force of character and grades of eloquence, but all devoted to the interest of the work committed to their charge. Under their labors the interests of Methodism has had a steady advance in the county. These laborious pastors have been connected with the labors and yearly aid of the Presiding Elders, of which order of ministers I find the following names: Nicholas, Green M. Rodgers, B. B. Whittington, J. M. Pew, H. H. Montgomery, Wm. Price, H. J. Harris, Williams, Gann, Learie, Little, McDonald and R. J. Jones, Sr. These are all the names of Presiding Elders I have been able to obtain. Under the labors of these able and efficient ministers, both pastors and elders, aided by able and influential private members, men and women, Episcopal Methodism has advanced in the county, and increased in numbers and influence. They now report in the county ten churches aggregating three parsonages, a membership of 1,000—113 joining in 1893—610 persons in Sunday-school last year, and church property amounting to $11,075.

A fair exhibit of the strength of Episcopal Methodism in the county, and the means by which this state of progress has been brought about, would lead me to make honorable mention of many pious and devoted lay members, both men and women, who have labored in this work. But in a notice so brief but few of these can be mentioned. Prominent among these I name the Watts', Lopers, Everetts, Browns and Selbys, of Newton; Wauls', of Spring Hill; Barnets, Rainers, Johnstons and Wauls', of Hickory; Clarke and others at Chunkey; Barretts and Graham and Johnston and Addys, of Decatur; Hortons, at Conehatta; Chandler and others, at Lawrence; Wells', at Union. These, with many others that might be named, have labored with untiring zeal for the building up of the cause they loved. Some have grown old in the work, and have died and passed to their reward, leaving their work in younger hands; but their works remain, enduring monuments of their energy and zeal. These have been great and good men and women, who have left their impress on society, and whose labors have served to advance morality, piety and intelligence in our beloved county. The readers of this sketch, no doubt, will call to mind many others who might with equal propriety be named, and feel that the writer may aim to discriminate for one against another. By no means; all cannot be named, and in selecting, many of great worth may be left out, the names not occurring to the mind of the writer.

PRESBYTERIANS.

At an early day in the settlement of East Mississippi, Presbyterians formed a very respectable part of the population; and some of these were in Newton county—men of means, character and influence; Adams, Patterson and Dansby, at Decatur and vicinity; Willises and Vances, near Erin; McFarlands, Thompsons, Evans' and McRaes, in the south and southwest. These were valuable citizens, and soon had preaching for themselves and families, more or less convenient. Likely the Rev. John H. Gray was the first minister of this order that preached in the county. At a very early period he moved to Mississippi from Alabama, and located in Jasper county, established preaching, founded a school, and gave to the locality the name Montrose. Mr. Gray was a man of fine ability, finished education, and in the prime of life. Associated with him was Prof. J. N. Waddell, a young man, an able educator, and minister of the gospel. These able men preached in the country as they had opportunity. Soon they established a preaching place in the lower part of Newton county—established a church, to which they gave the name Mount Moriah. This body still lives and works, and has prospered. The original founders have grown old or died, and the work has passed into younger hands, active and intelligent men who labor to build up the cause of Christ.

For a time the Presbyterians had no other organization in the county. Some years after, though, they constituted at Erin, and further on after at Lawrence, and more recently at Newton. It would be pleasant to the writer and gratifying to the reader if I could give the names of the ministers that have had charge of this work in the county through the years past to this time. This I cannot do, but come as near the facts as possible. In the years 1849-'50, Mr. Adams, who succeeded Mr. Waddell, was preaching in this part of the county, and had his home at Montrose. Mr. Adams was from the North, and had labored in Greene county, Alabama, before coming to Mississippi. Mr. McDonald was in the country before this, but just the place of his labors I am not able to state. Mr. Money for a time traveled through the county, likely as an evangelist. I remember McRae, King, Bell, Moseley, Emmerson, Smythe, Bingham, Coit, West, Kerr and D. L. Barr, who is the present efficient pastor of the Presbyterian churches in Newton county, with the exception, it may be, of Erin. The membership of these churches are respectable, pious and attentive, and churches in a growing and prosperous condition. This brings us to the present time, with the following showing as to the status of Presbyterianism in Newton county: Four churches, with houses of worship, one parsonage, one resident minister and a membership of 114. Much might be said of the intelligence, ability and zeal of the ministers who have labored in this work through such a course of years, and their faithful co-workers, but space does not permit. Good and great men they were.

PRIMITIVE BAPTISTS.

In contemplating the moral and religious condition of Newton county it is necessary to make mention of the Primitive Baptists. The existence of this church in Newton county is the outgrowth of the division that took place in the Mount Pisgah Association in 1843. The division grew out of a difference of opinion on the subject of Missions, Home and Foreign, and Christian benevolence in general; those opposing missions withdrawing, some as churches, some as individuals. Those churches formed a separate denomination, bearing the name Primitive Baptists; of which order there are several churches, making altogether a creditable membership with resident pastors who preach to their people. These ministers, as well as they can be remembered, are, McGee, Ferguson, Ishe, Stamper, Hollingsworth, Dunnegin and Smith, as also some liberated gifts. These Baptists have in the county six churches, with a membership of 170 persons. Their churches are composed of orderly, valuable citizens, trustworthy and law-abiding; and, though opposed to missions, as understood and practiced by other orders of Christians, yet are attentive to sustain worship in their own congregations, and by their own pastors; maintaining strict discipline among their own membership, and are earnest advocates for spiritual Christianity and reliability of character.

REGULAR BAPTISTS.

Regular Baptists were found among the very first settlers of Newton county, respectable in numbers and character. Of these we may name the Prices, the Paces and Smiths in the west; the Phelps, the Waltons, the Millers and Paris in the northwest; the Thames, Thomas and Johnstons in the northeast; the Harrises, the McGees, the Fergusons and Everetts in the southeast; Wests, Hollands, Nichols, Simmons and Merchants, near the center and southern parts of the county. These were citizens of character, farmers who gave aid to society and strengthened the moral bearing of the population as it increased.

Among these were some ministers. Elder Cader Price for a time lived near New Ireland, a man of piety and much usefulness, and likely the first Baptist minister that preached in the county. Wade H. Holland, also a preacher, a man of energy and much force as an exhorter, lived for years in the southern part of the county, and preached and baptized. James Merchant, a licensed Baptist preacher, at an early period, moved from Simpson county and lived for a time a mile and a half south of Decatur, and for a time preached in the surrounding country. These ministers, co-operating with the private membership in the county, and aided by ministers from other counties, succeeded in planting the Baptist cause in the county at an early period after the country was possessed by the whites. It is understood that the first Baptist church constituted in Newton county, was in the date 1836, near the place known as New Ireland, and was called Ebenezer, is yet living and at work, and worshipping at Beech Springs, Neshoba county, under the pastoral care of Elder H. Bruce.

The same year, the records show that the second Baptist church was constituted, and in the Beulah community, and bore the name Enon. In the year 1848, in January, this church moved its place of worship to Decatur, and its name was changed to suit its locality. In connection with this change of name and locality, the writer of this sketch became a member of said church, and also pastor; which pastorate he has held continuously to the present time. This beginning of Baptist work in the county gave encouragement, and soon other constitutions took place, namely, Bethel and Mount Vernon in the south, and Pleasant Hill in the west. Efficient in this work were the resident ministers already named, but these were aided by experienced ministers from other counties.

Elder John P. Martin did much to bring about the organization of Bethel church. Stephen Berry, of

Scott county, aided Price at Ebenezer. Elder S. Jones, of Neshoba county, aided Price at Enon, possibly Rigsby, of Lauderdale. Holland was alone in the constitution of Mount Vernon. Other churches were soon constituted: Rocky Creek in 1842; Mount Pleasant near the same date; Princkney, in 1847; and so, year by year did the cause advance in the county, and new interests were planted, even up to the present time, so that at this date we number in the county twenty-five churches, containing a membership of 1776.

This result has been brought about by the labors of ministers resident in the country, or those who lived adjacent in other counties, and extended their labors to this. These ministers have been aided by a noble host of deacons and private members, men and women, pious and devoted, many of whom have passed to their reward, while others live to labor still. Noble spirits! It would be very pleasant indeed for the writer, here to pay a tribute to the memory of the great and good men with whom he labored in days past in Newton and surrounding counties, who now rest from their labors. Among those ministers who have resided in other counties, but have helped in this, I name the following: J. P. Martin, of Smith county; W. P. Carter, Bryan I. Bigsby, Matthias Wolf, R. Y. Rasberry and J. L. Blanks, of Lauderdale; R. T. Gatewood, A. Goss, Stephen Berry and L. P. Murrell, of Scott. Of the latter, it may be well said, that few such men have lived in our country. Of fine personal appearance, great dignity of deportment, affable and easy manners, great candor of expression, with a mind of almost the first order, and to these adding unquestioned piety, and an earnest and honest devotion to the cause of the Redeemer, he possessed vast influence for good. Bro. Murrell's style of speaking was

HISTORY OF NEWTON COUNTY.   411

easy, a plain declaration of the facts he wished to communicate. His great theme was salvation by grace; Christ crucified; man a sinner; Christ a savior all sufficient; and the work of the Holy Spirit. Few men were clearer in describing the work of conversion; the travail of the soul from death to life; justification by faith, evidenced by good works, formed a part of every discourse. Brother Murrell was a sound and consistent Baptist, an untiring worker in the Kingdom of God. His ministry covered a period of nearly fifty years, during forty-five of which he was pastor of the Pleasant Hill church, near Conehatta; had entered upon his forty-sixth year as pastor before he died. He had entered far into his eighty-third year at the time of his death. Thus closing a long life of great usefulness. Long will he be remembered.

In addition to what has been stated, I mention A. Winsted, David Killen, J. M. Moore, G. W. Breland, O. F. Breland, and L. B. Fancher, all of Neshoba county, who have greatly aided by their labors, in building up the cause of Christ in our county. As, also, John Williams, S. King, J. L. Latimore and Jas. Thigpen, of Jasper county. We also give the names of ministers that have been citizens of the county, either raised up here, or have moved into the county : David Cooke, A. Phillips, Moses Thomas, N. L. Clarke, who moved into the county in the year 1847 ; W. F. Barrett, E. L. Carter, John and David Williamson, A. Clarke, Daniel Dove, H. Reece, A. Gressett, Lewis Jenkins, I. A. Hailey, J. W. Johnston, Henry Gill, A. J. Freeman, J. K. P. Shows, P. Vaughn, W. D. Maguirk, John C. Elerby, George Williamson, Z. K. Gilmore, H. B. Cooper, J. W. Arnold, T. I. Wells, H. O. White, W. P. Vaughn, J. E. Chapman, B. W. Dearing, H. Bruce, W. M. Yarbrough.

412   HISTORY OF NEWTON COUNTY.

These ministers were of diversified gifts, and ability in the gospel work, and recognized as elders in the churches. Some of them have laid by their armor and passed over the river; others have gone to other counties, while the remainder are citizens of the county, and workers in the cause of Christ. These ministers, and this creditable membership, embracing the old, the middle-aged, and the young, are friends to education, to piety and every good work, and are abiding true to the great cause. All the denominations have houses of worship, and preaching regularly, and are laboring that others may have the same blessed privileges. The writer of these sketches has been conversant with gospel work in this county since 1841, and views with interest the progress of every work that has tended to benefit and elevate our beloved county in intelligence, morals, temperance and Christianity. The great fight for the cause of temperance engaged in by the united force of all religious denominations in the country, and the victory gained, should excite to the liveliest emotions of gratitude to God. May the blessings of God long rest upon our beloved county.

CONGREGATIONAL METHODISTS.

This order of Christians was founded and organized for religious worship in the State of Georgia, between fifty and sixty years since. The leading minister in the movement was the Rev. J. F. N. Huddleston. Some years after, several citizens of this order, with their families, moved to Mississippi and settled in Newton county; also Mr. Huddleston, their pastor. These persons were organized for religious worship in the year 1857, six miles north of Decatur, in Newton county. The constituent members were Wm. Mapp, W. A. McCune, A. J. Smith, J. A. Mapp, Susan McCune, Mrs. Mapp, also J. F. N. Huddleston, pastor. The organizing Presbytery were Revs. H. T. Jones, B. M. Huddleston and J. F. N. Huddleston. The church received the name Mount Zion. This was an active, zealous body. Mr. Huddleston was a man of fine mind, an able and fearless speaker, bold and fearless, and in the prime of life; with a commanding personal appearance, and warmed by an ardent zeal, he took well with the masses. Backed in his labors by an active membership, the doctrine he advocated was received by many, so that soon there were several churches of the Congregational faith in this county and adjacent counties. Also ministers were raised up in this and other counties. Some of these ministers have died and others have left the county. I may make honorable mention of Capt. John Maxey, a soldier, a christian and minister. This order of Methodists now claim to have in the county four churches—Mount Zion, Mount Hebron, Blue Springs and Pleasant Valley, with a total membership of 200; three ordained ministers, John C. Portis, J. M. Belew and Thomas H. Rivers; also one licentiate and one exhorter. They consider their prospects for the future encouraging.

CUMBERLAND PRESBYTERIANS.

This order of Christians have lived and worshiped in other parts of our State from its earliest settlement. About twenty-five years since, or more, they began to preach in Newton county—first about Union and New Ireland, and with such success that several churches were formed. Ministers active in this work were Nicholson, Bailey, Boydston, Cooper, Ashmore, McBride and Millen. In recent years their cause has seemed to decline, so that now they have in the county one church and two resident ministers. They have been an active and zealous people.

DISCIPLES.

Located at Hickory, Mississippi, there has existed for the last eight or ten years a church of Disciples, numbering in all about thirty-six persons. These are followers in faith of Alexander Campbell; have no resident ministry, but are visited from time to time by active and able ministers from a distance. Prominent among these people I may name Gage, Hanna-Gray, and their families; also Mrs. Pinkston. They are zealous, active and progressive.

COLORED PEOPLE.

Up to the close of the war between the States the black population had membership with their owners, each according to his choice. After they were made free, however, they thought it best to go to themselves, thus forming churches of their own color; first in the stronger communities, and then in the weaker, so that almost all the colored people in the county now have church privileges within their reach. In many of the churches before the war there were public speakers and exhorters. These soon became ministers to their own people, and were ordained; and others, impressed to that work, entered the ministry. And such was the number of these, that these churches of colored people have pastors of their own color. Many of these have but little education; while others, by close application, have acquired a fair knowledge of the Scriptures and of church organization, management and discipline. These churches are self-sustaining, or do not call on the whites for help, unless to aid in building houses of worship. The colored people in Newton county holding to the faith and practice of the Regular Baptists, or otherwise called Missionary Baptists, have in the county fifteen churches, having a membership of 1000 persons. I would be glad to give the number and names of the resident ministers, but have no way of coming at the facts. These churches are engaged in mission work, and are friends of education and Sunday Schools.

JOINERITE BAPTISTS.

Of this order of people there is one church in the county, having a creditable membership, and two resident ministers in the county, viz: Rev. Joseph Keene and Rev. Joseph Rhodes. These people agree in opinion with the Rev. Wm. Joiner, who some years since withdrew from the Mt. Olive Primitive Baptist church, in Kemper county, differing from it on several points. The seceding members were organized into a church, with Mr. Joiner as their pastor. Having formed themselves into a separate organization, they labored to propagate their doctrine and practice. Several churches in various parts of the county have been organized, and several ministers ordained. Only the one exists in this county.

The colored M. E. Church North, have a membership of 466, have four churches, six local and one traveling preacher; have seven Sunday-schools, fifty-four teachers and 394 scholars, with an estimated church property valued at $2,500.

The Baptists have something over 300 scholars in the Sunday-school, and hold regularly a Sunday-school convention; representing from Newton and adjoining country, an attendance of 600.

CHAPTER XLI.

MISCELLANEOUS EVENTS OF THE COUNTY, FROM ITS EARLY SETTLEMENT — KILLING OF A NEGRO BY A YOUNG LADY — LOST CHILDREN — MURDER OF A YOUNG LADY BY A NEGRO — KILLING OF A YOUNG LADY BY A RACE-HORSE AT DECATUR — ACCIDENTAL KILLING OF A MAN FOR A BEAR — CHASING THE WOLVES OUT OF THE COUNTY — ACCOUNT OF THE KILLING OF A BEAR — BUILDING PUBLIC BRIDGES — OLD-TIME HORSE-RACE — OLD-TIME MUSTER-GROUND AND DRILL — CIRCUIT COURT IN THE LONG AGO — CUTTING NEW ROADS TO THE COUNTY SITE — JUSTICE COURTS OF THE OLD PERIOD — VERY NEAR APPROACH TO A RIOT AT DECATUR.

Some things of an interesting and tragic nature will happen in every county, and have occurred in this county, that will probably be of interest to the readers of this history. These incidents are given as they occurred, without any exaggeration, from persons who were in the county and are now living.

To give anything untrue or even of romantic tendency, merely to attract attention, would be far from the intention of the writer, and while these things may sometimes be considered exaggeration, they are substantially correct as received from testimony that is considered in every way reliable.

KILLING OF A NEGRO MAN BY YOUNG LADY.

In the year 1862, near the town of Newton, on what is known as the McAlpin place, three miles east of town, a most remarkable event occurred. Mr. Jas. Walker lived on a place in the country, and had only three white persons in his family -- himself, his wife and daughter. Mr. Walker was old, so was his wife; his daughter, Miss Susan, about twenty years old. Mr. Walker had gone from home and only the wife and daughter were left. The young lady looked from the dwelling toward the gate, and saw a man with a sack over his head, coming; as the man approached the house he met Mrs. Walker in the yard and with a part of a rail he felled her to the ground. The man then started for the house-door, where Miss Susan was; she saw the terrible situation, and with uncommon presence of mind--and particularly for a young woman-- reached for a gun which was loaded and probably in the gun-rack over the door, and just as the man came on the door-steps she fired at close range, killing him instantly; he fell in the door-way. He proved to be a negro man, a slave belonging to one of the neighbors. Her self-possession and heroism doubly saved the life of her mother and a wretched fate to herself. She was warmly applauded by the people of the county, and received quite a number of fire-arms to protect herself in the future.

It is not understood how long Miss Walker had known the use of the gun, but it is evident that she had had some practice with it, and it was very fortunate that she did know and acted in self-defense, and saved her life and that of her mother. Miss Walker is at present living at Morton, Scott county, in the family of Mr. Pettus.

A LOST CHILD.

In the early settlement of the county, when neighbors were far apart and the population small, a child in the neighborhood west of Decatur was lost. It occurred in this way, as related by an old settler:

Mrs. E. S. Loper went to a neighbor's house in the afternoon. She took with her two white children and a little negro child. She was spending the time pleasantly in the house of her friend, and the children went out to play. When she was ready to go home she called the children. The white children came, but the black child did not. After repeated calls and diligent search she went home, supposing the child had gone before her. To her great surprise, when she reached home the child was not there. The news was at once spread abroad over the country and friends came in force to assist the family in finding the child. Torchlights were used, for it was by this time dark, and people from different parts of the county joined in the search, and all in vain. For days the child was hunted, all to no avail. Mr. Loper, being a very kind and sympathetic man, felt such deep interest in the little one that was lost he offered $1000 in gold for the child returned alive. Nothing was heard from it again. The reader will at once ask what became of it, as no trace of the remains was ever seen. It might have been carried off by a bear, for there were some in the county at that time. It is more probable that a thief and robber may have seized the child while he was a little way off from the white children, and stifled its cries to prevent its giving the alarm, and have taken it entirely out of the country. The only visible signs of its departure from the house was its tracks going down the hill from where the children had been playing.

A LOST WHITE CHILD.

Another instance of a lost child occurred in Newton county in the year 1858 or 1859. It was the little boy of J. W. Flanagan. Mr. Flanagan and wife went to church on Sunday morning, about three and one-half miles away, leaving the child and some other members of the family at home. The little boy went out of the yard, and from thence to the woods alone, and when the parents returned from church no trace of the child could be found. Neighbors came and made a fruitless search on the evening and night of the first day. It was renewed on the next day, and in the afternoon of the second day the child was found, after being more than twenty-four hours lost alone in the woods. When found the little boy was seated on the ground or log, and appeared very much unconcerned about his safety.

Children are said usually to be shy and even wild when found attempting to make further their escape after they have been some time lost. It is a terrible feeling to look for a lost child; the certainty of their death can be borne with much more composure. The thought of an innocent little boy or girl of five or six years old being alone in the woods, with fears that it has fallen a prey to some wild beast or savage Indian, or has fallen over some precipice or into some stream, or may have been bitten by some poisonous reptile; or they are suffering from great tnirst or hunger. These things are terribly harrowing to all sympathizing persons, and particularly to the fond parents of the lost child.

MURDER OF A YOUNG LADY.

A young lady named Miss Brittain, was foully murdered by Tony Anderson, a black fiend and supposed accomplice, about 1887 or '78, in the southern part of this county, not far from Garlandsville. The wretch who killed her was caught and promptly hanged. The suspected party who assisted in the tragedy escaped.

YOUNG LADY KILLED BY A RACE HORSE AT DECATUR.

One of the saddest events that has ever happened in the county, was the killing of Miss Teas at Decatur in the year 1838 or '39. The Teas Bros., Albert and Jourdan, who have previously been spoken of in these pages, were prominent men in the early settlement of the county. They were merchants and stockholders in the bank and a family of some prominence. Horseback riding was the most usual way that ladies took outdoor recreation, and race horses were plentiful about Decatur at that time. It is said that Miss Teas objected, so probably did her mother, to riding the horse, for it was one of the race horses of the place, belonging to Mr. George Williamson, but it was considered gentle and her brother insisted that she should do so.

Her ride appears to have been pleasant and would have ended so, if the parties had not unfortunately gone to the race-track, as they were then called. These race-tracks were very near the town of Decatur, the starting point being near where the Methodist parsonage now stands. The animal ridden by Miss Teas thought when he reached the starting point that he ought to run a race although ridden by a lady. The lady was unable to hold the horse and was thrown, and either her foot remained in the stirrup, or her clothing caught on the pommel of the saddle, and in this condition she was dragged and her body terribly bruised and mangled. She lived only a short time

HISTORY OF NEWTON COUNTY. 421

after she was taken home. It was a terrible shock to her brothers and her aged mother.

ACCIDENTAL KILLING OF A MAN FOR A BEAR.

The killing of Mr. Lusk by his nephew, is a very thrilling thing as related by an old settler. Lewis Lusk and his nephew went bear hunting in Connehatta swamp. The cane was very thick and the uncle wore an overcoat made of material very much resembling a bear. The young man saw his uncle, supposed it was a bear, and through an opening in the thick cane he fired, shooting his uncle through the heart. The young man, though a rough backwoodsman, was so overcome with grief, that after telling what he had done, did not speak for three or four days. The mental agony was so great as almost to derange the man and he never did get fully over the sad event.

CHASING THE WOLVES OUT OF NEWTON COUNTY.

Bears and panthers were both found in the county, though not so plentiful as smaller game. The wolves were numerous and did much damage to sheep. Men in the county took it upon themselves to hunt them down and drive them from the county. Some did it for the fine sport it offered, while others did it for the purpose of ridding the county of the destructive pests.

Large packs of hounds trained for wolves and deer were taken to the woods. Hunters from different neighborhoods would meet at a given point and if a trail was not struck from 9 to 10 o'clock, a deer would be killed to feed the dogs and give fresh venison steak to the hunters. At night they would camp in the woods in the neighborhood of where they expected the game, build a big fire, cook and eat their supplies, tell their various and humorous stories, both new and old, and plan for to-morrow. They used their saddles for a pillow, a saddle-blanket for a covering and in this way pass the night, and after very early breakfast and sometimes "something a little stronger," and in that way be bright and fresh for the morning's work and sport.

The second day would be probably more successful, and after many adventures, many hard races, many hair-breath escapes by rapid riding and falling into unknown holes in the ground and in passing under stooping trees and through thick brushes, into quagmires and through reed-brakes, the day would be passed. Many would be killed and many chased away. By repeated hunts of this kind and by the liberal rewards offered by the county, they were finally destroyed.

KILLING A BEAR.

Bears are much harder to kill than panthers or wolves. No animal of our forest is as tough as a bear. A bear story is related by a reliable old settler. He says Coot Sellars went bear hunting one evening on Tuscalameta Creek and shot a grown bear with a large bore rifle. He had a fair shot and was well satisfied that the ball struck where he had aimed it. The old hunters knew if the rifle fired clear that it struck very near where it was aimed, as they had steady nerves and were good marksmen. Sellars' bear went off as if nothing had happened to him. The hunter felt sure he had wounded him badly, and went in search of bear dogs that he knew his neighbor had. Some time in the forenoon of the next day the dogs took the trail of the bear; they came up with him and chased him sev-

HISTORY OF NEWTON COUNTY. 423

eral miles, and he finally stopped to fight the dogs. The hunters came up; he refused to run further, but was full of fight, and it required several well directed shots to kill him. The large ball that he had been shot with the evening before had gone through his liver, and if he had not been further pursued and killed, would probably have gotten over the wound.

BUILDING PUBLIC BRIDGES.

When it was necessary to build in the early settlement of the county, men who understood the work would go long distances, and neighbors would board them while they did the work. This was a slow but sure way of getting a bridge, as all the timbers had to be gotten out of the woods. The sills were all hewn, the flooring was made of heavy split puncheons, and the balusters were made of poles. Yet the work was strong and substantial, and served good purpose in allowing planters to go to market and to the courthouse. The roads, in many places, were almost impassable in winter. It was impossible to causeway all the wet places, owing to there being so few hands in the county, and when the roads did get bad in the winter they remained so until summer.

OLD TIME HOUSE RAISING.

When a man was able to build a good log house, it required quite a number of hands to assist in raising it. The house was constructed of large logs, hewn on the inside after raising. At an occasion like this, hands were so scarce that they would come for more than a dozen miles away to assist in the work. When the crowd assembled there was usually a director of the building, and men worked cheerfully and did a good, neat job. When meal time came there was plenty to eat and there was also plenty to drink, and everybody was in the best of moods. Sometimes, in connection with this work or a "spring log-rolling," which was quite a place of resort to test a man's strength and endurance, was the old-time quilting by the women, and at night an old-fashioned dance on rough floor, yet all in pioneer country style, and well enjoyed by the crowd. The music was a poor fiddle in the hands of old-time darkies or country white men. In this way much good work was done with as much sport and genuine amusement in its way as was ever enjoyed by country people. It might be a party of the older men went fire-hunting for deer; this was done by having what was called a fire-pan, constructed of light hoop-iron, forming a basket, in which a pine torch was kindled; this pan had a long handle, say six feet long, carried on the shoulder of the hunter, the light being in the rear instead of in front of the hunter. When the light shines in the rear of the hunter he can see the eyes of his game and even the wildest animals are not disposed to run from this light. In this way the eyes of the deer can be shined, and the hunter, knowing them from other animals, gets at close range and able to shoot with his pan of fire on his shoulder at his game. Sometimes inexperienced hunters would kill a colt, as their eyes very much resemble a deer's.

AN OLD-TIME MILITIA MUSTER.

At stated periods of the year, the State militia of each county expected to have a mustering, and go through a regular drill according to the military tactics of the State. All males between the ages of eighteen and forty-five years were subject to militia duty. This meeting of citizens for military purposes was a very important matter, and if it had been kept up until 1861, the Southern people would have known much more of the duties of the soldier than they did. But it had been abandoned; for nearly fifteen years there had not been a military procession formed in the county, and everything connected with the evolutions, of the manual of arms and drilling of a company of men, was new and difficult.

Each county had its quota of regulars and several counties would form a battalion or regiment and on certain occasions would meet and be drilled by a Major or Colonel and be reviewed by the Brigadier General of State militia. These preferments of high office in the militia, brought no money, yet it displayed many a man's ability to command troops and made him a conspicuous figure in the political world, and was an occasion of great enjoyment by the country people. The regular meeting of the county militia was always a scene of much mirth, and often many things occurred in the commands given by a new captain or lieutenant in bringing in the raw and awkward material of young country lads and even the older and inexperienced men composing this body. A sense of the ridiculous would sometimes occur in these commands given by the officer. An example is taken from an occurrence which actually happened, as related by one of the company, will serve to illustrate. This did not occur in Newton county, but in an adjoining county, and doubtless many probably as glaring and ludicrous as the one narrated, did happen in Newton county. A young lieutenant—about six feet four—with very large feet and of most uncomely proportions, with a voice like a bass drum and awkwardness of a backwoodsman, was in command on the occasion stated. He was as defective in grammar and elegance of speech, as he was of good looks and military dignity. He formed his company into single file and brought them to right dress, and his command, if he had known his tactics, would have been, "Two ranks, form company; right face; forward, march." He was entirely unable to give the command that would bring about this evolution and he called out to a subordinate officer that he thought more competent than he, "Ben, thus double 'em."

These things were laughable then; they are amusing and interesting to think of now. Yet many a drill officer who has made a good commander, found many difficulties at first in learning and impressing the military movements on the soldiers.

AFTER THE MUSTER.

The greatest excitement prevailed after the muster was over. After having been under severe duty for several hours, feeling the restraints of a soldier and becoming weary of constant military movements and fatigued by uncommon movements, they are at last dismissed and feel the freedom of a common citizen. These annual musters usually occurred at or near a town where there was plenty of something to drink—better, as the most of them thought on that day, than their spring water. After they had imbibed pretty freely, as a natural sequence many fights occurred. As a general rule they were of the old style, "strike a ring and nobody touch" until one or the other cried out "take him off." This kind of fighting in this our enlightened day and much refinement and education, would be considered a disgrace to civilization. The order of the day is now to carry a "small gun" about a man's person and at the least provocation to use it, and that to badly wound or kill. Which is the better?

HISTORY OF NEWTON COUNTY.

Which is the more manly? Which brings the less remorse of conscience and trouble?

The old-time way was the best; it was the safest. Many a man of the old-time has had a hand-to-hand fight with his neighbor and friend—was "whipped," or got the best of it, and neither was disgraced. Sometimes "discretion has been the better part of valor," and he "lives to fight another day."

When a bullet is put through a man's head or body he meets an untimely end, and the man who did it, may or may not suffer the penalty of the law, but will always regret it.

CIRCUIT COURTS OF NEWTON COUNTY IN EARLY DAYS.

The circuit courts of the county, which met twice in a year, as they do now, were great places of resort, and formed very important meetings of the people. Many men, as they are now, were called to the court-house on business for the week, such as the jurymen, witnesses, etc. A large number went for the recreation and excitement attendant upon such occasions; many more went to get "something to drink," as it was always very plentiful on those occasions. In those days there were very few public gatherings in the county; no Granges or pic-nics to call the people together, and at the circuit-courts, came many lawyers from a distance, and in those days some of these lawyers made excellent speeches on all the political topics of the day. This last, of itself, was a great attraction to the people. One of the most noted and gifted speakers of this period was Richard Cooper, who was district attorney, and who found it a pleasure to regale and instruct the people who attended the courts.

Cooper was not the only one, but many in those days did the same thing. Quite a number of prominent lawyers came to Decatur circuit courts from different parts of the country—from Kemper, Neshoba, Scott, Scott, Lauderdale, and particularly Jasper county, where was a large and learned body of attorneys, who received lucrative practice in Newton county·

The circuit court week at Decatur, was often the occasion of much discord, large amount of drinking and fighting, and often the offending parties being brought before his honor to be reprimanded, jailed or fined. Large preparations were made by the hotel-keepers, the general merchandise dealers, and particularly the saloon-keepers to have plenty to drink.

This intemperate use of liquor was kept up until about fifteen years ago it was removed from that part of the county. Now Decatur, during court week, is one of the most civil places in the State. The citizens come and go without the use of liquor, or any disturbance to the court.

In the early times men who came on business staid all the week; all who came without business, and who were intemperate, usually staid most of the week. In the early settlement of the county there were few hotel accommodations, and when the weather was pleasant men who remained built fires out on the public highways and thus spent the night. They would "stake" their horses or turn them loose, and sometimes cruelly keep them tied up for an unreasonable time. After court adjourned all restraints were thrown off, much disorder and many fights indulged in. Liquor was sold by the pint, quart or drink. To make it cheaper than by the drink, men would join and buy a gallon and take it to some convenient place, and drink freely and most of the crowd who remained on the ground would be drunk.

A DRINKING JUDGE.

Some of the early judges of the State drank; possibly they are not all exempt now. An amusing circumstance is related by an old pioneer of this county —how a presiding judge of the circuit court of the county of Newton loved his dram. It occurred, says the old man, at one of the courts held at De catur, that a judge who had exchanged circuits with the judge who belonged on this circuit, had imbibed pretty freely the night before, and next morning was "mity dry." Some one told him there was whisky to be had but nothing to get it in. His honor was not to be disappointed, and told the man to take the wash-bowl (that he had just used to bathe his face and hands), and bring some in it. When the man came back with the gallon of "relief" in the bowl, there was no glass to drink out of. His honor—again equal to the emergency — stooped his head to the wash-bowl and drank like a horse. Thus bracing himself up and sharing it with others, he was prepared for his breakfast and the duties of the day.

These courts usually lasted through the whole week and not only were great sources of profit to merchants and liquor dealers, but everything that was raised in the county, in the way of fine stock, was usually displayed and traded and sold; all kinds of huxters of county-raised fruit, parched goobers and even the ginger-cake man, with barrel of potato beer. All had some hand in supplying those who had come to the court-house.

PUBLIC ROADS THAT WERE IN THE COUNTY IN ITS EARLY SETTLEMENT.

There were but few roads in the county when it was first organized. The great military road from New Orleans to Nashville, Tenn., cut by General Jackson's army in the year 1815, ran through the eastern part of Newton county. It was 75 to 100 feet wide, and ran very near on an air-line from the objective points. All the large streams were bridged in a substantial manner. This road was for a long time a great thoroughfare through the county; went directly to Columbus, Miss., where the land office for some time was situated. On this road, about four miles north of Hickory, was situated a trading post called "Jusong's Stand." It was not in any way connected with the Government, but was kept by a private individual named Jusong, who was said to be a very disreputable character.

At this place liquor was kept and trading was done with the Indians, and travelers were entertained who passed through the country. It is said by some, that persons stopping at this place were robbed and murdered for their money and thrown into a large lake near the place. Of this, however, the information is only traditional and cannot be taken as altogether true, yet it is more than probable.

There was a stage road running though the northern end of the county. This road ran from Montgomery, Alabama, to Jackson, Mississippi, and was much traveled by persons making this route. There was another road, from Winchester, Mississippi, passing through the southwestern part of the county, going to Jackson. It will be remembered that Wayne county, in which Winchester was situated, was one of the original fourteen counties that organized the State government, in the year 1817, and had its existence as a county as early as 1809. This county had direct connection with the capital of the State, and this road through Newton county was used in that way.

CUTTING ROADS TO THE COURT-HOUSE.

After the organization of Newton county, in 1836, it it became necessary to cut roads to the court-house through the most central and thickly settled portions of the county. In those days it took most of the able-bodied men of that portion of the county to do it.

A circumstance, as related by an old settler, in reference to the road from Decatur south to the Jasper county line, which is nearly twenty miles, shows the spirit and style of the times.

The cutting of new roads by large crowds in those days, like log-rolling, house-raising and fire hunting, all formed fine sport as well as hard work, and were entered into with a great spirit of enjoyment. It is said that a party of hands commenced at Decatur and worked south, and another party commenced at the southern boundary of the county and worked north, and the meeting point was at Pottoxchitto creek, three miles north of Newton. Most men in those days were good hunters. Some guns were with the crowd; some deer were killed. Camp-fires at night enlivened the scene; good, neighborly feeling pervaded the minds of the road-cutters, and they are now nearing the end of their work. It is now understood that when the work is completed, and the workers from each end meet, that a barrel of whisky is to be in readiness, but not to be "tapped" until the work is completed. When all the work is done and accepted, the barrel is to be opened free to all.

The old-time men, who have witnessed such a meeting, are the only ones that can describe such a scene. The young reader can better imagine than can be described what occurred after the barrel was opened. It was good luck that nobody was killed, and the recollections of that event formed subjects for comment and amusing conversation for years afterwards.

The recollections of those days have gone down from father to son, and what glimpses of it after fifty-eight years that may appear to the writer, from some one who has heard his father tell of it, may be of interest to the reader.

CONTINUED RECOLLECTIONS OF OLD TIMES.

The muster ground, the old-time circuit court, the log rolling and road cutting of early days brought the people together as probably nothing else would. It was here they met and tried their strength, tested their metal and endurance, their courage and their ability to direct, fitness to rule, etc.; to distinguish themselves in every thing presented to test manhood, or inspire confidence.

After these new roads and new bridges, came the "old-field" country school-teacher. In connection with and in close proximity to, was the local preacher. After him came the traveling and called preacher; with them came the organization of the churches, and the old-time camp-meeting. These latter places were great places religiously and sometimes were places of much disorder and violation of law by wicked men. But the men of God still continued to work. The Methodists, with their traveling ministers and camp-meetings; the Baptists with their regular supply and missionary spirit, all combined under general associations; the Presbyterians stationed in certain strongholds, all combined to permeate this county, until they now have all the religious advantages a country could wish; and following and going hand in hand, all the school privileges that the State is able, and that is munificent and promises to be better still. Sometimes the preaching was from very unlearned men, whose dress and general appearance indicated that they were poor in this world's goods, with no ability or disposition to conform to the fashions. They were often like Moses in one respect, "slow of speech" and high-sounding words or beauty of language, but they were faithful and sincere and were the humble instruments in bringing many to repentance.

JUSTICE COURTS.

The backwoods justice of the peace has in all ages of the evolutions of civilization, been a great source of amusement to most of the critical world. These courts are sometimes the cause of great merriment and occasionally things occur that savor so strongly of the ridiculous that their actions, though sincere, are a mere travesty of justice. Yet often the forms of law as coming from these rural officers, may have appeared very rough, and the language of the unlearned magistrate might have been inappropriate and even uncouth. Often, though, these rough men had good judgment and high sense of honor, and their decisions would stand the tests of higher and more learned courts of the country.

One of these primitive and unlearned justices of the peace in Newton county, says an old friend of his, "was an honest, straight, correct, conscientious man, but had not read as much law as Wm. L. Sharkey."·

One of the old justice's neighbors found a runaway negro straggling around and concluded he ought to be at work for some one, took up the negro and carried him to Squire ——. Says he, "Squire, I have found this negro strolling about doing nothing. I believe he belongs to some one. I took the responsibility of taking him up without a warrant from you; did I do right or not?"

The squire put on a solemn look, studied awhile and said, "I am not certain that you did right, being a common citizen. If it had been I, clothed with the authority of the law as I am, I could have arrested him and no one could have complained."

In another instance, a man caught a runaway negro and carried him to a "Judge of Probate" of Newton county, and asked what should be done with him? The old judge, assuming the usual degree of dignity of such men on such occasions, said he would consult the law on the subject. He did so, but looked in a part of the code relating to stray stock, and concluded he had no right to stray the negro, as he was not a horse, mule, or any other animal that were mentioned under the head of estrays.

Ky. Murphy, an impulsive man, sitting on the jury at Decatur, saw a deer chased by the dogs, run very near the court-house, and exclaimed in language more dramatic than classic: " Great ——, Judge, yonder goes a deer." The sheriff, it is said, headed off the deer and killed it."

NEAR APPROACH TO A RIOT.

Sometimes a very near approach to a narrow escape from death strikes the party connected with, or participating in the event, with a great deal of solemnity. There are times when the good advice of a few cool-headed and sober men will prevent a terrible conflict that might have cost the lives of many valuable citizens. Such a calamity was once averted by the timely interference of some of the prudent white men which otherwise might have resulted in the killing of a hundred negroes, and some white men.

It was at Decatur, at the fall term of the circuit court, held by Judge Tarbell, a Yankee appointee from the State of New York, who was a tolerably fair man, but could only see one way, and that was the way his politics, of the Radical order, directed him. George C. McKee, who was a Republican candidate for Congress, and Jim Lynch, a Philadelphia negro preacher, who had drifted down South for political preferment, and who was a candidate for Secretary of State—and, by the way, he was elected—these men had an appointment to speak in Newton county, at the court-house. The county was probably as well organized by the Radicals for political purposes as a county well could be. Harvey, the white carpet-bagger and negro schoolteacher, who married a negro woman in this county and then deserted her, had been the means of the thorough political drilling and organization, and who was capable of doing the work assigned him by his political allies higher in power than he, was the leader of the negroes on the day referred to. The negroes went to Decatur that day from all parts of the county, armed with their guns; and were insolent and sometimes abusive. They fired off their guns on the public road, and sometimes obstructed the passway by assembling themselves in it, and it was with difficulty that parties passed to the court-house on some of the roads. Just before the the time to speak Harvey formed his regiment of negroes near where the Methodist church at Decatur now stands.

He was mounted on a good animal belonging to one of the negroes, and after he formed his line, rode up and down as a colonel of regiment would do, reviewing and giving orders to his troops. He wore a uniform befitting the occasion.

These negroes marched up in the direction of the court-house. McKee and Lynch were soon to commence to speak. The white Democrats, seeing the trouble that might ensue, went to those speakers and told them that if any trouble occurred that day on their account, if a riot should be brought about by these unlawful proceedings of armed negroes marching to a public political meeting, that they would be held responsible; if there was any killing done, they would be the first to become victims. With this understanding, Harvey, with his regiment of armed men, were halted about seventy-yards from the court-house door, when they laid down their guns and proceeded to hear the speeches. The white people took the precaution to take position between the guns and speakers. McKee made his speech first. He said nothing that would in any way be insulting to the white Democrats. His speech was his announcement of his candidacy, and quite a number of amusing anecdotes that got almost everybody to laughing, and for a time any anticipated trouble was lost sight of. After McKee, Lynch commenced his speech, which was well said under the circumstances. He appeared to have been an old-line Whig, and what he said was much in advocacy of the old-time Whig party, and was spoken in such a spirit as not to be offensive to any one. He spoke from the court-house door, just the position of the present court-house. There was no fence around the house at that time. From a window over where Lynch spoke it is said said some one spat tobacco upon his face. He did not resent it in anger, but made some very humble retort from a passage in the Scriptures. When he was getting pretty nearly through, a very impudent negro, Dick O'Neal, who at another time had cursed a respectable citizen of the county at the point of a double-barreled shot-gun when our people were too much afraid of the Federal authorities to resent it. This Dick O'Neal got into some dispute with R. P. Gary, a white Democrat, which led to high words, the negroes listening and waiting for a chance to use their guns. At this juncture of excitement some negro cried out, "To your guns." At once a break was made by the negroes, and quite a number started for their guns. Just at this moment, Lynch seeing the trouble and probable fatal results to himself and many others, shouted at the top of his voice, and with such emphasis that all could hear him: "Men, come back here." He was in time; the negroes stopped and returned. They could not have reached their guns. There were over a thousand men in Decatur. A proposition was made to take the negroes' guns and use them against them, but wiser counsel prevailed, and it was not done. The negroes returned, the speech was finished, and no one was killed or hurt. If one pistol or gun had been fired; if one white man had been shot, probably no county in the State could have excelled Newton in point of numbers killed at a political riot. So near and yet not to happen; and, fortunately for the good name of the county, no one has ever been killed for his political opinions.

RACE COURSE.

The old-time race-tracks, as they were then called, were great places of resort and much wickedness and great immorality. These tracks were generally located at or near some town in the county where a level place could be had, of about 1,000 yards long. The tracks were laid off in a straight line, running parallel with each other about twenty feet apart and about four feet wide. They were cleared of all timber and roots, and made smooth and packed hard to form a good and safe place for running.

These tracks were free to all who would keep them in good repair, and when a race was made between different parties the horses were kept and trained for several weeks before the race. During that time the news of the approaching race would be known all over the county and large crowds would assemble to witness the sport. There was no law then — as now — against betting on a horse-race, and much of it was done.

The day appointed came, and the parties to the race came to time and the race was run or forfeit paid by the man backing down. The stakes, that was the money bet on the race, were deposited in the hands of disinterested parties, and two judges on each side were chosen to determine the result of the race on a fair basis. Spectators would go, and large crowds would assemble and station themselves at different parts of the track to get a good view of the racing. Some would go to the head of the track, where the horses were started; some would take their places along the line of the track, but the largest part of the crowd would be at the place where the horses came out of the track. The riders would usually be men of light weight, or youths who were experienced and fearless riders. Each side had a good hickory switch, and if occasion required — which it usually did — used it vigorously on his horse. Two judges were stationed at each end of the track; the ones at the starting point were to determine which horse had the start of the other; the one getting the start had the distance subtracted from the distance he would be from his opponent at the end of the track. If a horse got twenty feet the start of his opponent and came out thirty feet ahead, he was declared the winner; if he came out only twenty feet ahead he was declared beaten. Everything was supposed to be done fairly, and yet there often occurred difficulties and the money was not given up.

There was great excitement just before the race; all eyes were on the horses; when the word would be given, "clear the track, the riders are up," everybody looked in one direction; the horses would be turned by their trainers once or twice, and the last time they would be led down the track and turned loose and told to "go," which they understood; they were then off at their best speed. These places were noted for excitement and many who did not own the horses would bet, and in this way large amounts of money would change hands. After the first trace other races by other parties, on their ponies and saddle-horses, would take place. The distance would be shortened to about three hundred yards for smaller stock, and much amusement and much small betting was indulged in.

These were places of great demoralization and many harmful things came from them. The young men were taught all the wicked practices of gambling and immoral transactions, and the older men would do things surrounded by these occurrences that they would not otherwise indulge in. It might be safely said that three-fourths of the men who attended horse-races and shooting matches, would bet on them if they had the money. After the race would follow the usual dissipation consequent upon such occasions. Great harm, and no good to society or the country, was the result of these races. The people of the present day in this county may congratulate themselves that they are not cursed with horse-racing as in the days of our fathers.

FOURTH OF JULY BARBECUE.

We all know the import of the 4th day of July. On that day, in the year 1876, our independence was declared, and the great struggle that went on for the consummation of that much desired object was accomplished. After the revolutionary war was over, this 4th of July was considered by all the States a national holiday, to commemorate in the minds of all the generations that followed that period of great peril, and a just appreciation of what was accomplished. In no way was this done more strikingly than when the memorable 4th came on, to have a grand barbecue and invite all the people in the surrounding country. The citizens living in a certain neighborhood would agree among themselves to furnish the provisions for the occasion. A subscription was taken up and each man who felt inclined would furnish his share. This entertainment usually consisted of fresh barbecued meats and bread, and sometimes some vegetables. These subscriptions would call for from forty to seventy-five carcasses of small animals, such as mutton, pork, kid, and some beef, and a sufficient amount of cooked bread to go with the fresh meat.

In order to prepare this meat nicely, a long pit, from 40 to 100 feet, according to the necessity, was dug about four feet wide and two feet deep. Several hours before the cooking commenced a fire of green wood was put in the pit and reduced to coals, and two sharpened green oak sticks that would reach across the pit, were run through the carcass of each small animal or each quarter of beef and laid over the pit to cook. A seasoning of salt, pepper and vinegar was made and applied as it cooked, with a mop; in this way, as the meat cooked, it was well seasoned. Possibly no way of cooking meat is preferable to the barbecue. This meat, on the long green sticks, would be turned alternately from side to side until it was done.

After the dinner was cooked it was placed upon a common table constructed of plank, without cloths, and a general invitation to come to the table. The ladies, who were always present in force, were served first by gallant young men, who usually brought the choice parts to them.

While dinner was being prepared a general entertainment was going on at a rude platform or rostrum in an adjoining grove. A suitable man had been selected to read the Declaration of Independence, also a good speaker had been invited to orate upon this occasion and this topic, and the oration on this day was considered a regular "spread eagle," as it spoke of "revolutionary valor." If after the first speech dinner was not ready, some other gentleman, who could speak well extemporaneously, would be called upon to entertain the crowd until the meats were done.

A great number of men who came to the public barbecue were ill-bred, and after getting on the ground became partially drunk, were impatiently waiting for the word, "gentlemen, help yourselves." When the word was given, with knife in hand to carve the mutton, pork and beef, often would be heard in the mad rush to dinner a cry of some one imitating the bleat of a sheep or noise of a cow, and many things said and done that disgusted well-fed and well-bred people. There were always a few in a large crowd that would behave badly, and show strongly their animal traits of character which predominated. Yet all was free, and the badly behaved man who had no self-respect or patriotic pride, who came for a free dinner, filled themselves and returned to the "grocery" to further imbibe if anybody would "treat them."

There was no aristocracy at one of these patriotic celebrations, but alike the best and wealthiest and worst and poorest, attended them. Ladies were always protected from insults, and, taking them altogether, they were very amusing and interesting events. Everybody that wished heard a good, well prepared and well delivered speech on the liberty of our free republic, got a good meal without cost and had the liberty of getting drunk after dinner.

The wildest scenes sometimes prevailed in the afternoon of the 4th. Free fights were the order of the day. A barbecue at a town without whisky, would be like "Hamlet without the Prince." Many has been the man that dates the day of a bit nose, a gouged eye, a bruised face and otherwise mutilated body, from the 4th of July, 18—, when he and his neighbor indulged too freely and then fell out and had all this unnecessary fighting.

Many persons in the South have lost interest in the 4th day of July. This should not be. Southern valor, Southern blood and treasure were as conspicuously employed and as lavishly used, and more than in the Northern section in achieving this independence. Therefore it belongs to the Southern people by conquest and inheritance as well as any other section. Let not the failure of the "Lost Cause" to the South, abate our zeal for the welfare and remembrance of our original Magna Charter, which granted our rights and our liberties.

Not only did our people have grand barbecues on Fourth of July occasions, but at times, when great political contests were at stake, such as gubernatorial and presidentlal elections, the Democrats would have a barbecue and the Whigs would assist. The Whigs would have one and the Democrats would assist. Each political party would attend the other's feast, partake of his bounty and be soundly abused politically ; all was taken in the best of spirits. If the Whig candidate came first the Democrats would say, just wait until our man comes ; and both parties would come to hear, and sometimes it was a joint discussion, and then both parties would join in the dinner, equally interested and enjoy the severe raspings given the respective speakers, and each other's politics. In this way did Prentiss and McNutt, Brown and Matthews, Quitman, Foote, McRae, Davis, Guion, Freeman, McWillie, Singleton, and McClung, and the Yergers, and all the prominent men in politics of those days, in this State, make some of the happiest efforts of their lives. Everything is very much changed now. When the present generation meets it is with much good order.

Many are the entertainments and picnics attended with the best of order, well-cooked provisions, and in great abundance, placed on a common table. A variety of entertainments for the young as well as the old ; the school children are now always made prominent, and do not come as an unknown quantity.

The present manner in which we get up our public entertainments lacks something of the convivial spirit, the strong and often dramatic style of the olden time ; yet the present is more orderly, more conducive to good society, and more in accordance with the age. Let us not forget the old-time barbecue, and the old Fourth of July.

SHOOTING MATCH.

This was another kind of sport much in practice by

the early settlers of the county. It was not so much indulged in and not so numerously attended, and not with the demoralizing results as the horse-races. These matches were usually attended by the best rifle-shots of the county. Shot-guns were also used in these matches in competition with the rifle; most usually the stake put up to be shot for was a beef. Some man in the neighborhood would furnish the animal and a price would be set upon it, and parties wishing to shoot would pay a stated amount for a chance to shoot. These "chances" would be priced at a given amount and each chance allowed a shot. One quarter of the beef would be put up and the chances taken and paid for and the shooting commenced. The nearest shot to the cross would take the choice piece. The next nearest would get second choice, and in that way the first quarter would be disposed of. Then a second quarter would be put up, and then a third and fourth, and after the meat was all taken the hide would be "shot off."

If a man shot with rifle he had choice to have rest or to shoot off-hand. If he had a rest the distance would be increased; if he shot off-hand he would get nearer the target. If a man shot with shot-gun or musket he would select the smallest shot he could find, and would be placed a certain distance with an off-hand shot. Each man had his target, and after the shooting judges would decide as to which were the best shots and nearest the centre of the cross on the target. This kind of sport developed some remarkable marksmanship, and the Southern men were the best shots, and were more familiar with fire-arms than any soldiers in the late war, and much of their proficiency was from the custom of shooting-matches, and the free use of the gun at home and in a game country. Yet these things had a very demoralizing tendency; much intemperance and idleness followed those shooting-matches and led many men to bet money on their ability to "drive the cross" with target rifle either off-hand or with rest.

The days of such amusements are gone from our country, and as many other vices have found lodgment in the great cities, where congenial devotees indulge this sport with many of the other sinful amusements so much practiced.

CHAPTER XLII.

WEATHER NOTES — THE YELLOW FEVER EPIDEMIC OF 1878 — GRAPHIC DESCRIPTION OF THE SCOURGE AT LAKE.

The great freshet in 1833 was considered the largest ever known before or since that time. The coldest weather supposed to have been in the county, was in the winter of 1833 or 1834, notably the "cold Saturday;" that was a familiar word with all the old citizens of the county many years ago. There was also, in February, 1852, a severe cold spell, probably equal to the first one alluded to; it lasted all the month; creeks were frozen over, and on small ponds of water the ice was so thick as to bear up horse and rider. In the early part of the year 1885 the thermometer fell to zero in this county. The warmest weather ever recalled in this county was in the year 1854; also 1860 and 1861 were very warm and dry. The year 1855, taking winter and summer, was probably the dryest ever known in this county. It was the first year that the magnetic telegraph had gone through the State, and certain credulous persons ascribed the drouth to the presence of the wires conducting this subtle fluid called electricity.

The year 1839 was famous for being a good cotton year; so were the years of 1855, 1860 and 1861. Corn was very scarce in 1861, there being but little made the previous year, 1860. The year 1852 had a very cold spring and very dry summer, and the cane in the swamps went to seed and then died. Never have the swamps had as good cane since. In the year 1857, the 13th of April, there was a snow that covered the ground one inch deep. This was a fine corn year. One of the most severe killing frosts that destroyed most of the growing crops of corn and cotton was on the 16th of April, 1848. In the year 1870, November 12th, was a severe snow, considered very early for this climate. The leaves on the trees were not killed, which caused the snow to adhere to the leaves, and much timber was broken down. In the year 1868 was probably as heavy snow as ever fell in this county, measuring eight to ten inches.

In the years 1882 and 1883 were the great cyclones in this State. They came from the southwest, and passed with great fury, doing much damage, through this county. The year 1882 was when the court-house at Monticello, in Lawrence county, was blown away, and papers from the clerk's office were scattered all over the country, some having been found from that office more than a hundred miles away. The severest storm ever known in our State was supposed to have been in 1883, when the town of Beauregard was destroyed. The great falling of meteors, called the "falling of the stars," occurred in 1833. So filled was the whole of the atmosphere with electricity, that it is said the manes and tails of the horses were so charged with it that they felt as if they were frozen.

In the year 1866, the 28th day of May, occurred a wind and rain storm of great severity. The storm was at least one hundred miles wide; did not blow with the severity of a cyclone, but continued a long time, with heavy rain. The result was that more timber was blown down than ever was known. Two years afterwards there was more sickness than had ever been experienced in the county.

YELLOW FEVER PANIC OF 1878.

This dreadful scourge, which visited the Southern States, at least the Gulf States and some others, was one of great severity, and caused much suffering and loss of life. The sea-coast cities had so long been accustomed to visitations of yellow fever that they had become familiar with it, and could not bear the idea of a strict quarantine, so as to prevent its introduction from ports which are more or less infected with it the year round. Some supposed that the city of New Orleans was never free from it, and some claimed that it was indigenous to our coast country. After the railroads penetrated the interior, it was found that the fever could be brought by various means into the country, and when it got a start it became epidemic in healthy parts of the State. After the great scourge of 1878 very vigorous measures were passed to prevent the introduction of fever in our midst; nor have we had a general epidemic since. The fever has only prevailed in isolated portions of the country, where it was accidentally admitted, no doubt, by carelessness of quarantine officials.

Jacksonville, Florida, has, since 1878, been visited with the scourge with great loss of life. In the year 1893, by the carelessness of quarantine officials, the fever was admitted into Brunswick, Ga., and continued for several months, destroying a large number of lives and generally prostrating commerce.

In the year 1878, the fever appeared very early in New Orleans, probably as early as June or July, and as the fall season approached, came more and more to the interior. Vicksburg became terribly infested with it and there was no stoppage of the railroads. Fifty cases per day were reported at Vicksburg with no prospect of its stoppage. About the 1st of September it reached Lake; on the 11th day of that month the citizens left the town of Newton. Several days before this a number of cases had occurred at Lawrence and vicinity. About this time a general quarantine was declared, stopping all trains, all mails and all travel in the county which would cause the spread of disease.

All communication was cut off except by telegraph. The people on the railroad towns were panic-stricken. Never had there been such consternation and fear of approaching disease. The sufferings of the towns in the State were terrible to read of and contemplate. Thousands of persons in this State died, and many more thousands had the disease and recovered. Immediately after the epidemic, Col. J. L. Power, Grand Secretary of Masons, and Grand Treasurer of Odd Fellows, published a pamphlet report, giving many graphic and pathetic details of the great affliction. Our neighboring town of Lake is put down as having a population of 350; total cases of yellow fever, 330; total number of deaths, 80. Several citizens of Lake had removed to Newton county. Dr. F. E. Daniel, who had been assigned to duty at Lake by the Howard Association, at Jackson, made the following report:

"One physician and four nurses arrived from Vicksburg; more needed. We want mattresses and blankets, also a druggist, and a cook for the soup house. Every household is broken up; not a family has escaped the fever.

"After the storm many new graves sunk and emitted extremely offensive odors, which attracted the buzzards. Of course it was remedied, but seems to have strongly impressed the prevailing fever, which heretofore, although malignant in many cases, was amenable to treatment. It is now unmanageable, and treatment heretofore successful beyond the average results, appears to make no impression whatever. Many cases have black vomit in the first stage (during the fever) and sometimes in a few houses after being attacked.

"The wind was from the north after the storm, and the grave-yard is north and near the town; an excellent family, seven in number, living nearest the graveyard, were all attacked at once, and most violently. They are, Mrs. Hugh McFarland, whose husband died recently, her three children (two now dying), her sister, Miss Fannie Sanders, her mother and father, Mr. and Mrs. P. Sanders. Dr. Gresham, of Forest, is in the same house, now convalescent. Among the recent cases, in addition to those above mentioned, are Capt. W. M. Thornton, President of the Citizens' Aid Association; he is doing well. His wife is convalescent; also Col. D. S. Holmes and wife; their son is very sick. The last deaths are Miss Lula Lowery, Col. Yarborough, Mayor of Lake, and his wife. Several of the Lowery children are now down. You can form no idea of the suffering and distress here; the houses are generally small, and several patients in the same room frequently. Many die who could be cured under more favorable circumstances. Frequently the shock of seeing a child or husband, or brother die, and be carried out, instantly prostrates the patient previously doing well. This fever was extinguished here at one time, but the people, deceived by the appearance of safety, opened up the infected houses and aired the bedding. and the next day we had some twenty new cases. Meridian has been and is still supplying us with everything.

"The facts with regard the gasses arising from the

graves and the airing of the infected bedding, are significant and important, and emphasize the necessity of the utmost caution and most stringent measures to prevent the spread of the deadly plague."

"The county continued in a state of quarantine until about the first of November—after a white frost and all danger of the fever was over. No county can be too particular in preventing the spread of an infectious disease; strict quarantine against infected districts will do the work, though it may stop all business for a time. After the return of the people to their homes on the railroad, business was resumed, and by the first of the year 1879, there was no appearance of the distress save in those stricken towns that the fever visited.

ROBBING TREASURER PORTIS.

One of the most important officers in the county is its treasurer; who is expected to be a man of great honesty and to have good business qualities.

In the long succession of years Newton county has never lost anything by her elected treasurers. If any deficit occurred it has been made up by the bondsmen. The robbing of Capt. J. C. Portis, treasurer of Newton county, has always been a mystery, and the people of the county naturally feel some anxiety to know how it occurred. The circumstances as stated by the ex-treasurer himself are given, and thus it will be fairly placed before the people. Capt. Portis is a Congregational-Methodist minister, was an active soldier in the late war; belonging to Company B., 8th Mississippi Infantry. The company to which he belonged had many hard conflicts; was with Gen'l Bragg in his famous Kentucky and Tennessee campaign; was in the battles of Mumfordsville and Perryville, and

Stone River; on the 20th of September, 1863, was at the battle of Chickamauga, which is considered one of the most desperate battles of the late war; where a greater per cent. were killed than in any engagement between the States; he was at Missionary Ridge, Lookout Mountain—styled the "battle above the clouds"; and Capt. Portis says the "most sublime conflict recorded in the history of modern warfare." He was in the opening of the Georgia campaign in 1864, and on the 14th of May of that year, in a charge on the enemy's battery, was wounded in the right arm, which necessitated amputation at the shoulder-joint. In this condition he returned home, and in 1871 was elected county assessor, and served one term; was then elected county treasurer in 1875, and served four terms.

Capt. Portis says, on the evening of November, 1882, while on his return from Decatur, where he had been on business connected with his office, and when within one and one-half miles of his home at Union, that he was attacked by two masked highwaymen, taken from his horse and robbed of $1380. No definite clue was ever obtained as to who committed the dastardly act. Capt. Portis and his bondsmen, who compose some of the best men in the county (twenty-six in number), promptly paid the full amount of the deficit to the county treasury. While some censured Capt. Portis, he still continued to hold the office for fourteen months, and until the close of the term. Capt. Portis, at the solicitation of friends, ran for the office again, but was defeated by Capt. F. B. Loper. The amount paid by Capt. Portis' bondsmen was secured to them by him, which required nearly all his real and personal property. This deficiency to the bondsmen has nearly all been paid—only about $200 behind. Capt. Portis expresses great gratitude to his friends, who so cheerfully responded to his relief. His own words are: "A more noble set of men never signed an official bond."

The robbing of Treasurer Portis was thoroughly investigated before the grand jury of this county, but no proof could ever be brought before that body that satisfied them of the identity of the parties committing the act.

RECOLLECTIONS OF TWO OLD AND HONORED CITIZENS.

The following correspondence from two of the oldest citizens in the county will not be without interest in this history; one from Judge Hamilton Cooper, who died July 8, 1894, in his eightieth year, and was among the last letters ever written by him. Judge Cooper, up to his death, possessed great mental vigor and was the means of adding much to this volume of early recollections in this county that probably no other man could have given. The Judge, in this last communication is in some error, as his statements do not altogether agree with the printed records of the State. The names of the men who organized the county are taken from the printed acts of the Legislature, and they are, Wm. Donalson, Michael Thomas and Francis Jones. The latter name is probably incorrect and Judge Cooper may be right, as he writes that it was Freeman Jones, and the probabilities are that the prints have it wrong and that it should be Freeman in place of Francis Jones, as the former is a well known name in the early settlement of the county. He is also mistaken as to the organization of the county, as the act was passed February 25, 1835, and the county was organized after that date. Judge Cooper writes:

KEENAN, MISS., May 24, 1894.

A. J. Brown, Esq, Newton, Miss:

DEAR SIR—I have been to see W. J. Jones, and we

have had a long talk in regard to some things that pertain to the early history of Newton county. We are of the opinion that Judge Hudson was judge of probate when Newton was a part of Neshoba county. The circuit court that was held at Union was held as a court for Neshoba. The first court for Newton was held at Pinkney. The courts were organized in 1835. The commissioners were, Dempsey Smith, Roland Williams and Freeman Jones (not W. J. Jones' brother, but old Freeman).

"James Ellis built the first court-house, in Decatur. The first "grocery" was two forks put in the ground, a pole placed on them and poles from the ground to the ridge-pole and covered with four-foot pine boards, and one barrel of whisky put in it. The counter was constructed of forks driven in the ground, poles put on them, and a few four-foot boards on the poles.

Henry Thomas put up the first store. James Ellis' house served as the first tavern. The first grist mill was built by Joshua Maxwell, on Chunkey Creek, not far from where Thomas Wells now lives; the second one, Tilasha, north of the road leading from Decatur to Old Marion (in Lauderdale county), by Robert P. Jones and Freeman Jones. After Hudson, old man Furgerson was judge of probate, then Robert Parish, then Abner Haralson, then Geo. W. Shelton, then Hamilton Cooper, then Wm. Graham, then Wm. Thames (who were elected); afterwards I. L. Bolton and A. E. Gray, by appointment. Tavern charges were so high for some time after the settling of Decatur that many persons would carry provisions with them to the courts and camp. You can get the date of the organization of the first Grange from M. J. Chandler, as "Pine Forest" was the first, and their minutes will show the date. The first Masonic Lodge in the county was at Decatur, Evergreen, No. 77, organized in 1846; Decatur Chapter, No. 31, was organized in 1850; and there was a Council at Decatur until 1861.

Your friend and obedient servant,

HAMILTON COOPER.

The communication which follows, from Dr. William Lewis, now living at Union, will also show a man of advanced years, but well possessed of his mental faculties and good memory, as is shown by his recalling events with much vividness as early as 1837. His seeing the first court-house at Decatur does not settle the point that court was never held at Pinkney, as it is probable that court was held in Newton county before the court-house at Decatur was built.

Dr. Wm. Lewis writes under date May 5th, 1894:

Mr. A. J. Brown, Newton, Miss.:

I came to Newton county in 1837. My mother bought Mr. Walton's place, just two feet over the Neshoba and Newton lines to the residence. Mr. Walton, to give us possession, moved into the old Neshoba court-house, a few feet away. This old court-house was of blackjack logs. Timber was scarce; the house had a floor of mixed straw and mortar about one foot thick and which was very hard and firm.

There was scarcely any farms; cattle everywhere, on wet places, cane brakes with broad stretches of only large trees of hard wood variety, with occasionally a large, short-strawed pine. There was no thick undergrowth, no long, young short-leaf pine; could see a deer at some places, half a mile.

Mr. George Boyd was a grocery keeper; Jas. J. Monroe a clerk. Boyd moved to Pinckney, opened up a large store of general merchandise with capital of about $10,000. The style of the firm was Boyd & Lane.

In the back of their store they had a "shin plaster" bank based upon Decatur bank. Every five dollars of their "shin plaster" was taken up by the Decatur bank. In 1839, Decatur bank broke, which carried Lane & Boyd under. To give an idea of the recklessness of such business: I was in old Pinkney, the boys were playing marbles and betting on same. My luck was in and towards evening I was the possessor of a Decatur $5.00 bill. I went to Lane & Boyd and purchased a few articles tendering my $5.00. Mr. Boyd took it, and as he was busy asked me to go back and look in some barrels and get my change.

Union then was half mile east of the present little village; only one man ever killed there, S. D. Daniels. The first court-house I saw in Decatur was a log house; also the first jail house I saw there was a hewed log house, ceiled inside and grated windows—in those times considered very safe.

CHAPTER XLIII.

Sketches of Persons whose Portraits Appear in this Volume: Rev. N. L. Clarke, Dr. J. B. Bailey, A. B. Amis, Esq., R. H. Henry, Esq., and Mr. A. W. Whatley.

REV. NATHAN L. CLARKE,

WHOSE portrait appears on page 401, is now living at Newton, editing the *Mississippi Baptist*, a religious paper representing East Mississippi and supplying the wants of the Mt. Pisgah Association, the General Association, and the people generally.

Mr. Clarke is probably as well known to the citizens of Newton county as any man in it. There is scarcely a man or woman in the county who does not know him personally, or by reputation; and there are very few boys or girls in the county who have not heard him preach. All the people of the county do not know what a work he has performed since he came into the county; nor do all know what a useful man he has been. It is intended in this brief sketch to place before the readers of this book some of the work that has been done by Mr. Clarke, feeling that it is only an humble and inadequate tribute to a man whose name should be held in grateful remembrance and high esteem by every one in the county.

He was born in Burke county, N. C., 7th February, 1812, which makes him something over eighty-two years old. He left his native State and came to Sumpter county, Ala., in April, 1835, where he remained for three years, and in the year 1838, joined the Baptist church, and was baptized at Gainesville, Ala., on the 10th day of June of the same year. Having impressions that it was his duty to preach, he returned to North Carolina and devoted himself to the study of the languages. On the 11th of May, 1839, he was granted liberty to exercise his gifts as a preacher, and in November of the same year he was married to Miss Powell, of his own State. He left North Carolina and settled at DeKalb, Kemper county, Miss., in the early part of the year 1840, and spent the summer of that year at that place. The latter part of the year he moved to Neshoba county, and in the following year, 11th of April, 1841, was ordained Elder, and entered immediately into pastoral work in the counties of Kemper, Neshoba and Newton. In the fall of 1847, moved to Newton county and became member and pastor of Decatur church, January, 1848. January, 1849, took work in the Mt. Pisgah Association as missionary, still holding the pastorate of the church at Decatur, preaching for several years in the court-house before there was a church built at that place. For eight years before the war he took missionary work in connection with his pastoral work, giving from two to three weeks of his time, and riding at least 350 miles per month to do the work and preaching at least twenty times in the month and sometimes oftener. His missionary work carried him to Kemper, Leake, Scott, Smith, Neshoba, Simpson, Covington, Jasper, Jones and Lauderdale counties, besides the home work done in Newton county. During the war a portion of his time was taken up as missionary to the army wherever he could reach it. After the war from 1866, he was again engaged eight years in missionary work, much in the old fields of his labor in years before, doing the usual amount of riding and preaching.

After the war he served as one of his charges, the church at Sylvarena, in Smith county, about 50 miles from home, for eight years. Also the church at Sharon in Smith county, about the same distance as Sylvarena, five years. Still keeping up the work at Decatur and other charges to occupy his time for four Saturdays and Sabbaths in the month. Has been since 1850 continuously an officer in the Mt. Pisgah Association; for five years the clerk and the balance of the time the moderator of that body. He has been in every meeting of the Mt. Pisgah Association, taking active part since 1841, has never missed a meeting. He has presided over the General Association with probably two exceptions since its organization in 1855. He has preached in the county since 1842, which would be fifty-two years; has held the pastorate at Decatur since 1848, which would be forty-six years; has preached at the town of Newton since the organization of the church in 1869, which twenty-five years without a change. In all the time he has preached at Decatur he has missed less than half dozen times, and the same could be said of Newton, unless called away by duties at the Associations. In all these years he has never asked or taken a rest-week. He has baptized something over fifteen hundred persons, and assisted in the organizing of sixty churches within the bounds of this Association.

As a citizen, Mr. Clarke is classed among the best; his honor and integrity is never questioned; he is industrious and frugal; always providing to make home comfortable; his credit stands well; he is good for his debts; as a neighbor he is kind and accommodating;

in his relations with the world he is social, genial and cheerful; as a preacher he stands far above many of his associates; he has a liberal education, and has always devoted himself to study, and particularly the Bible. There is no place that Mr. Clarke feels so much his authority as in the pulpit; he is not rough, yet he is plain, and feels that when he stands up in the sanctuary of the Lord that it is his duty to speak the truth, and those who come to hear him must take his understanding of the scriptures. He is tender, loving, kind, and sympathizing, with no affectation or flattery, yet willing to treat all with deference and respect. As a presiding officer he knows his duty, and is not backward in the discharge of it. He is a dignified and competent official; willing to treat every one with respect; yet if a member, no matter who he is, gets out of order, his rulings are without favor or affection; he carries his point and sustains the dignity of his position.

Mr. Clarke has the confidence of his people, the high esteem of other churches, and his good works will follow him.

DR. J. B. BAILEY.

The name of Dr. J. B. Bailey, whose portrait may be seen on page 225, is a man of whom special mention should be made in the history of Newton county.

All men are expected to do their duty in any community in which they live; but that few do their whole duty is well kown. It is expected that most men will work for their own interest. It is very natural that they should; most men will work when they expect a reward for their services; yet few men, comparatively speaking, will devote a large portion of their time from their own labor that could be employed in the accumulation of wealth, for the public weal. Dr. Bailey, probably more than any other man in the county, has given his time, attention and abilty, to further the educational and industrial interests of the working classes in his section of the State. He has been the President of the Patrons' Union since its organization, and has never failed presiding over that body during its sitting — this being the twelfth year. To do the work preparatory to one of these meetings, and to give constant care and attention to all the details, is no small tax upon the time, tact and talent of any one.

Dr. Bailey is a fine presiding officer; dignified, courteous, and always on the alert, he is equal to every emergency. He is polite and genial without affectation, with a knowledge of human nature which will fit him for the arduous duties devolving upon him. He has great patience and exercises much ability in the management of the large bodies which have from year to year assembled at the Union.

If there is one trait more predominant than the many good ones which he possesses, it is that freedom from bias and unjust discrimination in the selection of persons to conduct the exercises of the Union. The poorest, meekest and humblest individual, if he have merit, is as sure to be noticed by Dr. Bailey as the most prominent and wealthy persons on the grounds. A disposition of self-sacrifice and to prefer others to himself, appear to be predominant characteristics. All these qualifications make him a man worthy of emulation. His good deeds, and works of kindness and love for others, will live after him.

Dr. Bailey was born in Shelby county, Alabama, in March, 1843, and came to Mississippi in 1869. He was raised a farmer boy, and was educated principally in common schools of the country, having but little opportunity of attending the higher schools. He enlisted in the Confederate army in 1861, and served four years as a private in Company I., 27th Mississippi Regiment of Infantry. At the close of the war, he was in school awhile, being one of the first to enter Cooper Institute. He afterwards taught school three years in this county, and then entered the Alabama Medical College, Mobile, from which college he received his degree of doctor of medicine. In 1859 he was married to Miss Joe Day, and from that union has five children—one son and four daughters. He joined the Grange in 1874; was Master of Centreville Grange several times; was Master of the County Grange two years in succession; was Master of the State Grange three years, succeeding the lamented Capt. Put. Darden; represented the State Grange in the National Grange meeting at Topeka, Kansas, Sacramento, Cal., and Atlanta, Ga.; was at the first organization of the Patrons' Union, gave it its name, and has been its presiding officer ever since its organization, having attended every meeting; been a trustee of the school at Connehatta since its establishment, and is now a trustee of the A. & M. College at Starkville. Dr. Bailey is regularly in the practice of his profession, and has the patronage and confidence of a large part of this county. He is a member of the Cumberland Presbyterian church.

A. B. AMIS, ESQ.

In selecting a person who is the best educated man that has ever gone from Newton county, it is appropriate that a page should be devoted to his portrait.

A. B. Amis, Esq., now practicing law at Meridian, was born in Scott county, but came with his parents to Newton county when he was quite an infant. Mr.

A. B. AMIS.

Amis, though having some means to assist in educating himself, found the sum inadequate to carry him through, and for a time was thrown upon his own resources in order to make money to complete his education.

He first commenced to go to school in the common schools of the country, and then attended for two terms of nine months each the Connehatta Institute. After that he went to the Chamberlain-Hunt Academy, at Port Gibson, where he attended school for eight months. October, 1885, he attended the Tulane University, at New Orleans, but only remained until January, of 1886. In October of 1886 he entered the University of Mississippi, at Oxford, where he remained successively until February, 1888, when he was compelled to quit and teach in order to obtain means to finish his studies. After teaching the greater part of the years of 1888 and 1889, he returned to the State University and entered the senior class. In June, 1890, he completed his course. In July, 1890, he was appointed tutor in Mediæval and Modern History at the University, which place he held for two years. In the meantime, he took a two years' course in law, and graduated in June, 1892, with second honor, with a general average of 98½ per cent. During his course at the University, for two years he was a member of the editorial staff of the *University Magizine*, published by the Literary Societies.

In June, 1892, he was a member of the faculty of teachers at the Patron's Union Teachers' Normal Institute, held at Lake Camp Ground. In January, 1893, he removed to Meridian and entered into the employ of Threefoot Bros. & Co., and Marks, Rothenburg & Co., as their salaried attorney. June 11th, 1893, he was married to Miss Mary S. Langford, of Connehatta.

January, 1894, he severed his relations as attorney with the above named firms and formed a law partnership with Floyd Y. Lewis, of Meridian, where they are now practicing their profession.

Mr. Amis is 27 years old; is a sober, energetic, self-made man, a profound thinker, a fine writer and a good speaker. He delivered a literary address at Newton at the close of Prof. Mabry's school, June, 1893, which did him great credit. Hon. T. C. Catchings, one of the brightest speakers in the State, and Senator A. J. McLaurin, had both favored the schools at Newton with addresses on commencement occasions and Mr. Amis' compared favorably with both of them. His address was not only clothed in elegant language, but it was reasonable and convincing, and delivered in such a way as to show that he was a profound thinker and graceful orator. Taking him in all the phases of his character, and his varied acquirements, this writer feels that no mistake was made in selecting him as the best scholar that has ever gone out from Newton county. Aside from his learning as a literary man and lawyer, his sober habits and attention to business, should recommend him to those needing his services. Newton county feels proud of Mr. Amis.

R. H. HENRY, EDITOR OF THE CLARION-LEDGER.

It will be seen by reference to Chapter 22, that the worthy gentleman above named was the first to publish a newspaper in Newton county. It is therefore fitting that he be the subject of a portrait, which will be found on page 197. The following excellent sketch of his honorable and useful career is from a recent issue of the *Times-Democrat :*

"R. H. Henry, editor, and one of the owners of the *Clarion-Ledger*, was born in Scott county, Miss., forty-

A. W. WHATLEY.

two years ago. He attended the Hillsboro Academy until the school was broken up by the war, then such schools as the country afforded. At the early age of sixteen he became a printer's apprentice and worked four years at the case, mastering the "art preservative" before laying down "stick and rule." This thorough training in a printing office has been of incalculable benefit to him, and to it he ascribes much of his success in life.

"When only twenty Mr. Henry established the *Ledger*, at Newton, Miss., where he published it for four years with decided success. He moved the paper to Brookhaven in 1875, and remained there eight years, where he did remarkably well, beside making a name as being one of the best and most successful newspaper men in the State. Tiring of the limited field afforded by Brookhaven, Mr. Henry, in 1883, decided, against the advice of his most intimate friends, to try his journalistic fortunes at the State capital, moving his paper to Jackson in January of that year, and christening it the *State Ledger*. The journal at once took rank with the best papers of the State, and became an instantaneous success.

In 1886 Mr. Henry was elected State Printer, and was re-elected in 1888 and 1890, defeating the last time the strongest combination possible to form in the State. In 1888 the *State Ledger* was consolidated with the *Clarion*, under the name of the *Clarion-Ledger*, with Mr. Henry as editor, under which title it is still published.

"Mr. Henry has attended five National Conventions, serving on some of the leading committees. He was made chairman of the committee appointed by the National Convention of 1884 to present complimentary resolutions to Tilden and Hendricks, and accompanied the committee on that mission. As editor and publisher Mr. Henry's success has been most remarkable.

"Commencing life with no means save his indomitable energy and confidence in himself to succeed, he has, step by step, by constant application and hard labor, worked his way up to the topmost round in Mississippi journalism, and is to-day the editor, manager and principal owner of one of the most influential papers in the State. Indeed, he has, by some of his press brethren, been styled "the Napoleon of the Mississippi press," and certainly no newspaper man of the State is more entitled to the appellation than he, for it is a well-known and recognized fact that Mr. Henry never made a failure in any of his newspaper enterprise. He is a bold, aggressive writer, being always ready and willing to express himself on any public question."

FARMER A. W. WHATLEY.

The subject of this sketch is Mr. A. W. Whatley, who was born in Newton county, November 7, 1864, and whose face appears on page 467. Mr. Whatley is considered the working man among those represented in this history; that is, he makes his living by manual labor. As much attention should attach to a man who works with his hands as those who work with their brain. It is just as necessary to have laboring men as it is to have professional men. The world could better do without the professional man than the man who tills the soil. A man who works in field or shop for his living, deserves as much respect as those who have professions.

Mr. Whatley had very little advantage of an education, but can read and write, and do ordinary business of farm and railroad (requiring an education). He is more or less required to make reports of his work and to keep his accounts with his hands. He has learned much in this way since he went into the railroad business. Mr. Whatley is six feet two inches high, and his average weight is two hundred pounds. He lived with his parents until he was twenty-one years old, and then went to work for himself on the farm and bought a good place south-west of Newton, of 160 acres of land. He says he does not owe a cent to anyone. After he had farmed for several years he hired himself as a common railroad hand to do work under a "section boss," and by his efficiency and steady habits secured in a short time the care of a section on the road, which place he now holds on the Mississippi Valley road, at a salary of $50.00 per month. He is renting his farm in Newton county, and is working on the road with a view to saving money by which he may be at no remote period independent. He early married Miss Richie, of this county, and by that union has four children. His first child, Glover, was so large and fine-looking that he was awarded a prize of $25.00 in gold at the Patrons' Union as the best specimen of a baby. Mr. Whatley's first wife died, and he has again married. He is a man of great strength and power of endurance. He can do all kinds of farm and railroad work, and is particularly good with the ax, and maul and wedge. In one day Mr. Whatley split one thousand rails; the timber was pine and "was cut." Mr. Whatley is of good, moral, sober habits; was never under the influence of liquor. He is an amiable, well-balanced citizen, and deserves a place among men who distinguished themselves in their sphere.

PORTRATIS IN THIS VOLUME.

In selecting persons whose faces appear in this work,

it has been the intention of the writer to get those who are well known and who are now or have been clearly identified with the county. This selection has been made from the various avocations in life—from the judge upon the bench and preacher in the pulpit, to the farmer who feels it an honor to till the soil and walk behind the plow-handles.

In making these selections careful attention has been given to the choice of such men as could be referred to as honorable citizens who have proved themselves worthy in the community in which they live, and to the people whom they serve, and who have been able to attain some success in the line of employment in which they have been engaged.

In every instance the selection is a sober, reliable man, who can be referred to as one who has done something for himself, and willing to do for others. These are all self-made men, never having been endowed with great patrimony; and while some may have had better educational advantages than others, their success in life and usefulness as citizens depends on their intrinsic worth and industry. It is not intended to refer to any one as a success in life unless his course is consistent with goodness. No matter how conspicuous a man may be, nor how much he may attain in life, he should be considered a pattern to the youth—"great only as he is good." It is not the amount of money that a man may acquire that should make him acceptable in life or remembered when he is dead, but a right acquirement of wealth and a proper use of it while he lives, would make him the benefactor and Christian patriot. All men should acquire something of this world's goods and should so use it as to be profitable to themselves, and when necesssary, dispense it for the benefit of others.

www.ingramcontent.com/pod-product-compliance
Lightning Source LLC
Chambersburg PA
CBHW021937240426
43668CB00036B/66